Happy Birth[illegible]

from Dad [illegible]

We love you [illegible] d

wish we could be there to

see you, maybe another

time, but our hearts are

sure full as we thought about

you all day. We have

alot of wonderful memories

of the last 53 years. So

even if we can't be there

our thought are as well

as our prayers.

THE PRESIDENTS OF THE CHURCH

THE PRESIDENTS OF THE CHURCH

Insights into Their Lives and Teachings

TRUMAN G. MADSEN

DESERET BOOK

SALT LAKE CITY, UTAH

ART CREDITS

Joseph Smith (p. xii) and *David O. McKay* (p. 238), unknown artist

Brigham Young (p. 20), Dan A. Weggeland

John Taylor (p. 56), A. Westwood

Wilford Woodruff (p. 86) and *Lorenzo Snow* (p. 116), Lewis A. Ramsey

Joseph F. Smith (p. 148), John W. Clawson

Heber J. Grant (p. 172) and *George Albert Smith* (p. 210), Lee Greene Richards

Joseph Fielding Smith (p. 272), Shauna Clinger

Harold B. Lee (p. 298) and *Ezra Taft Benson* (p. 354), Knud Edsberg

Spencer W. Kimball (p. 326) and *Gordon B. Hinckley* (p. 408), Judith Mehr

Howard W. Hunter (p. 380), William Whitaker

All art used courtesy of Museum of Church History and Art

Visit us at deseretbook.com

Library of Congress Cataloging-in-Publication Data

Madsen, Truman G.
Presidents of the church : insights into their lives and teachings / Truman G. Madsen.
p. cm.
Includes bibliographical references and index.
ISBN 1-59038-321-4 (hard : alk. paper)
1. Church of Jesus Christ of Latter-day Saints—Presidents—Biography.
I. Title.
BX8693.M328 2004
289.3'092'2—dc22

2004009754

Printed in the United States of America 18961
R. R. Donnelley and Sons, Crawfordsville, IN

10 9 8 7 6 5 4 3 2 1

CONTENTS

PREFACE

Someone has said history is biography. For me biography is most vivid and engaging when it is most intimate and concrete.

In this written version of my biographical lecture series, "The Presidents of the Church," I have sought to introduce the presidents in that way. The audio format enabled me to be conversational, intimate, preoccupied at each stage with the question, "What does all this have to do with me?" Something of that style remains in the book.

It is obvious that these chapters are only a slice, only a set of highlights, of what for each president should be a full-scale and comprehensive biography. The footnotes illustrate that a veritable feast of documents is available. Through them one may continue the conversation.

My hope is that these snapshot portraits will move readers to sink shafts deeper into the biographical mines, the better to regain and retain the jewels of a gleaming legacy.

One cannot miss in these life stories of men, and their truly remarkable wives, one powerful assurance: the future belongs to Christ. These leaders and their families endured some of the worst turbulence and trauma that the human soul can face. Having paid the sacrificial price of full discipleship, they emerged into life-transforming missions.

From such lives and teachings—and those who embrace them in common cause—all the human family may find new hope, new faith, and new love.

CHRONOLOGY

1801 Brigham Young is born in Whitingham, Vermont (June 1)
1805 Joseph Smith is born in Sharon, Vermont (Dec. 23)
1807 Wilford Woodruff is born in Farmington, Connecticut (Mar. 1)
1808 John Taylor is born in Milnthorpe, England (Nov. 1)
1814 Lorenzo Snow is born in Mantua, Ohio (Apr. 3)
1820 Joseph Smith receives the First Vision (spring)
1823 The Angel Moroni visits Joseph Smith (Sept. 21–22)
1829 Joseph Smith receives the Aaronic Priesthood and is baptized (May 15)
Joseph Smith receives the Melchizedek Priesthood (May or June)
1830 The Book of Mormon is published (Mar. 26)
The Church of Jesus Christ of Latter-day Saints is organized (April 6)
1835 Joseph Smith organizes the Quorum of the Twelve Apostles (Feb. 14); Brigham Young is included in the first quorum
1836 Joseph Smith dedicates the first temple in Kirtland, Ohio (Mar. 27)
1838 Joseph F. Smith is born in Far West, Missouri (Nov. 13)
Joseph Smith is imprisoned in Liberty Jail (Dec. 1)
John Taylor is ordained an apostle (Dec. 19)
1838–39 The Saints flee Missouri (winter)
1839 Wilford Woodruff is ordained an apostle (Apr. 26)
1842 Joseph Smith organizes the Nauvoo Female Relief Society (Mar. 17)
1844 Joseph Smith, with his brother Hyrum, martyred in Carthage, Illinois (June 27); John Taylor is present and receives multiple wounds
1846 The Saints begin their exodus from Nauvoo (Feb. 4)
1847 The first Saints enter the Salt Lake Valley (July 24)
Brigham Young is sustained as President of the Church (Dec. 27)
1849 Lorenzo Snow is ordained an apostle (Feb. 12)
1853 Brigham Young breaks ground for the Salt Lake Temple (Feb. 14)
1856 Heber J. Grant is born in Salt Lake City (Nov. 22)
1866 Joseph F. Smith is ordained an apostle (July 1)
1870 George Albert Smith is born in Salt Lake City (Apr. 4)
1873 David O. McKay is born in Huntsville, Utah (Sept. 8)

Chronology

1876 Joseph Fielding Smith is born in Salt Lake City (July 19)
1877 Brigham Young dies in Salt Lake City (Aug. 29)
1880 John Taylor is sustained as President of the Church (Oct. 10)
1882 Heber J. Grant is ordained an apostle (Oct. 16)
1886–87 Lorenzo Snow is imprisoned for plural marriage
1887 John Taylor dies in Kaysville, Utah (July 25)
1889 Wilford Woodruff is ordained President of the Church (Apr. 7)
1890 Wilford Woodruff issues the Manifesto discontinuing the practice of plural marriage (Sept. 24)
1893 Wilford Woodruff dedicates the Salt Lake Temple (Apr. 6)
1895 Spencer W. Kimball is born in Salt Lake City (Mar. 28)
1896 Utah becomes the forty-fifth state (Jan. 4)
1897 Church membership exceeds 250,000
1898 Wilford Woodruff dies in San Francisco, California (Sept. 2)
Lorenzo Snow is ordained President of the Church (Sept. 13)
1899 Harold B. Lee is born in Clifton, Idaho (Mar. 28)
Lorenzo Snow reemphasizes tithing (May 8)
Ezra Taft Benson is born in Whitney, Idaho (Aug. 4)
1901 Lorenzo Snow dies in Salt Lake City (Oct. 10)
Joseph F. Smith is ordained President of the Church (Oct. 17)
1903 George Albert Smith is ordained an apostle (Oct. 8)
1906 David O. McKay is ordained an apostle (Apr. 9)
1907 Howard W. Hunter is born in Boise, Idaho (Nov. 17)
1910 Joseph Fielding Smith is ordained an apostle (Apr. 7)
Gordon B. Hinckley is born in Salt Lake City (June 23)
1918 Joseph F. Smith receives the revelation on the redemption of the dead (D&C 138) (Oct. 3)
Joseph F. Smith dies in Salt Lake City (Nov. 19)
Heber J. Grant is ordained President of the Church (Nov. 23)
1919 Church membership exceeds 500,000
1935 The first stake outside of North America is organized, in Hawaii (June 30)
1936 Heber J. Grant introduces the Church welfare program (Apr. 7); Harold B. Lee is named director of that program (Apr. 18)
1941 Harold B. Lee is ordained an apostle (Apr. 10)
1943 Spencer W. Kimball is ordained an apostle (Oct. 7); Ezra Taft Benson is ordained an apostle the same day
1945 Heber J. Grant dies in Salt Lake City (May 14)
George Albert Smith is ordained President of the Church (May 21)
1947 Church membership exceeds 1,000,000

Chronology

1951 George Albert Smith dies in Salt Lake City (Apr. 4)
David O. McKay is sustained President of the Church (Apr. 9)

1953 Ezra Taft Benson is appointed U.S. secretary of agriculture (he serves until 1961)

1958 Gordon B. Hinckley is named an Assistant to the Twelve (Apr. 6)

1959 Howard W. Hunter is ordained an apostle (Oct. 15)

1961 Gordon B. Hinckley is ordained an apostle (Oct. 5)
Harold B. Lee directs the development of the Church correlation program

1962 The first Spanish-speaking stake is created, in Mexico City (Dec. 3)

1970 David O. McKay dies in Salt Lake City (Jan. 18)
Joseph Fielding Smith is ordained President of the Church (Jan. 23)

1972 Joseph Fielding Smith dies in Salt Lake City (July 2)
Harold B. Lee is ordained President of the Church (July 7)

1973 Harold B. Lee dies in Salt Lake City (Dec. 26)
Spencer W. Kimball is ordained President of the Church (Dec. 30)

1975 Spencer W. Kimball organizes the First Quorum of the Seventy (Oct. 3)

1978 Spencer W. Kimball receives the revelation on the priesthood (June 1)

1979 The 1000th stake is created, in Nauvoo, Illinois (Feb. 18)

1982 Church membership exceeds 5,000,000

1985 Spencer W. Kimball dies in Salt Lake City (Nov. 5)
Ezra Taft Benson is ordained President of the Church (Nov. 10)

1988 The Church completes 100 million endowments for the dead (August)
Ezra Taft Benson urges members to flood the earth with the Book of Mormon (Oct. 1)

1991 The 500,000th full-time missionary is called

1994 Ezra Taft Benson dies in Salt Lake City (May 30)
Howard W. Hunter is ordained President of the Church (June 5)
The 2000th stake is created, in Mexico City, Mexico

1995 Howard W. Hunter dies in Salt Lake City (Mar. 3)
Gordon B. Hinckley is ordained President of the Church (Mar. 12)

1996 Church membership outside the United States exceeds membership within the United States (Feb. 28)

1997 The 2500th stake is created, in Santiago, Chile (Nov. 22)
Church membership exceeds 10,000,000

2000 The Church prints the 100 millionth copy of the Book of Mormon (February)

2001 Gordon B. Hinckley dedicates the 100th temple, the Boston Temple (Oct. 1)

2004 Church membership exceeds 12,000,000

1

JOSEPH SMITH

Only two months before they were to die at Carthage, Hyrum Smith said of his brother Joseph: "There were prophets before, but Joseph has the spirit and power of all the prophets."[1] This chapter is an attempt to outline the meaning and vindication—in life and death—of Hyrum's comprehensive witness.

When the boy Joseph Smith came home from an interview with the angel Moroni at the Hill Cumorah, he confided to his gathered family that he had been warned that their lives would be at stake as the work of the Restoration continued to unfold. They must be careful, and they must not speak unwisely or without discernment about the Lord's work in the presence of their enemies.[2] There had already been attempts—we know of at least two—on the life of young Joseph. His was a family that was drawn together by such trials. And, as Joseph foresaw, at least in part, it was a family that provided the testimony and eventually their very lifeblood as witnesses of the greatest dispensation in the history of mankind.

At one point after the martyrdom, Wilford Woodruff

was asked by Mother Smith to give her a blessing. Her burdens were tremendous. She had earlier lost a son, Alvin, a fine and strapping and faithful oldest son who had intertwined his life with the promised Book of Mormon and the prophetic destiny of his younger brother. (After his death, when anyone mentioned the Book of Mormon in the Smith home, they broke into tears because in their minds it was inseparably connected to Brother Alvin.)[3] She had lost her husband prematurely. His life was shortened because of the depredations of Missouri. She had lost her youngest son, Don Carlos, in 1841, another gentle and faithful servant of God. She had lost two sons, Joseph and Hyrum, at Carthage on June 27, 1844. And now she had lost her son Samuel, only thirty-some days after his brothers' martyrdom. It is an understatement to say she was bereft. Wilford Woodruff, knowing he might not see her again in the flesh (for he was about to set out for yet another mission), blessed her, saying that her fallen sons were "the most noble spirits that ever graced humanity," and calling her the greatest mother in Israel.[4] So she is.

STEADFAST HYRUM

After some study and reflection, I have concluded that in the whole history of man—including secular history, great literature, and even our sacred history—there is no equal to the brotherhood and intrafamilial loyalty that existed between Joseph and Hyrum and their family. This is even more impressive because Hyrum was the older of the two.

In both the Old Testament and the Book of Mormon, it is often the firstborn, or at least an older brother, who veers away from the faith of the father and the mother. In the Book of Mormon, we have a book that culminates in near-universal fratricide—two huge civilizations destroyed, with one annihilated—because two older brothers rebel against a younger brother. The tradition of "eternal hatred" grows in their language and in their relentless warfare. They swear the destruction of those whom they claim robbed them of their authority, their power, their possessions. They would rather die than reconcile. That's the story of Laman and Lemuel in opposition to Nephi. But it is not the story of Hyrum and Joseph.

Moreover, not only was Hyrum the older brother, but he was five years older. When Joseph received the outpouring of heavenly gifts and such promises as "This generation shall have my word through you" (D&C 5:10), Hyrum might have said in his heart of hearts, "Why not me?" But he did not.

When others who were not of the family were called to their positions, many, as the Prophet said, "aspired unduly"[5] for power, the wrong kind of power. When they were chastened by revelation, warned that they exalted themselves and that they must beware of pride, they faded away. But Hyrum did not. He was always at Joseph's side; there was only one period of six months, according to an affidavit of Hyrum, when they were separated. Many of those who observed the two meeting one another remarked that their faces lit up when they first glimpsed each other.[6] The Prophet Joseph left on record this statement: that Hyrum exhibited the very meekness and humility of the Lord Jesus Christ.[7]

Hyrum Smith spoke with personal knowledge when he said in powerful testimony, as noted earlier, "There were prophets before, but Joseph has the spirit and power of all the prophets."[8] He would have to have made a lifetime study of ancient prophets and apostles to make such a statement. And my testimony is he did. He would have to know his brother, not just intimately but in all the sacred circumstances that brought him to the fore in this work. He would have to have shared Joseph's tremendous burdens and his tremendous enlightenment. He did.

And on the day when the Prophet Joseph first introduced baptism for the dead, he took his brother down to the river. By that point Oliver Cowdery had defected. After Joseph baptized Hyrum—we don't know for whom—he said, "Today I weld the link of priesthood that was broken by Oliver Cowdery, for in life we shall be one and in death we shall not be separated."[9] I wonder if John Taylor was present to hear that statement or learned of it later, for that is almost the exact phrase he used when he wrote what we call Section 135 to seal the testimony of the Doctrine and Covenants. In Doctrine and Covenants 124 a promise is given to Hyrum "that he may act in concert also with my servant Joseph" (v. 95). In concert! Little children who ran with the message that came from Carthage that awful day said, "Joseph and Hyrum *is* dead."[10] A grammatical error, but profoundly true—they were one.

THE SPIRIT OF THE PROPHETS

So Hyrum's testimony is a weighty one: Joseph was indeed possessed of the spirit and power of the ancient prophets. Acknowledging this helps us envision the vast and comprehensive contribution that came in this dispensation.

To sketch the spirit and power of the prophets, let us begin at the beginning and talk about Father Adam, father of a dispensation, the one, with Eve, from whom all of us can claim descent. Joseph Smith was also the father of a dispensation and father of those of this era—and that includes those who are our forebears who through our vicarious labor will count themselves as belonging to this dispensation.[11] The posterity of the

Prophet Joseph, both symbolically and literally, will expand like that of the common father of us all (see D&C 132:30–32).

There is also Enoch. For a time in the early part of this dispensation, the name *Enoch* was a pseudonym for Joseph Smith, a device used to protect him if a revelation fell into the wrong hands. We know little about the ancient Enoch; but it was Enoch, the seventh from Adam, who aspired not simply to teach, to change lives, to lift—but to purify an entire city, to build a Zion, which was indeed a geographic, an economic, a political, a social, an educational miniature of the very city of God. Not only did he aspire, but almost alone in the history of man he succeeded.

More than twenty revelations were given to the Prophet Joseph on the "hows" of establishing Zion. The early Saints did not, as a people, fully rise to it. Covetousness and sin and relapse led them away, and they were driven from the Zion the Lord had designated. But Joseph left on record a prayer, eloquent beyond my words, that someday, somehow the Saints would so prepare themselves that they would return, and in the designated place they would build a glorious temple and a glorious city preparatory to the day when Enoch's Zion would come down from above and be met with the earthly Zion, which would be raised from below (D&C 84:100). One source tells us that the Prophet taught that Enoch was "predisposed from his infancy . . . to every divine manifestation."[12] And so, I suggest to you, was Joseph Smith.

We turn to Noah. Lorenzo Snow once overheard the Prophet respond to the question, "Who are you?" with the reply, "Noah came before the flood. I have come before the fire."[13] Prophetic. Profound. The earth was indeed baptized with water in the days of Noah, and only eight souls were saved (1 Peter 3:20). The Prophet Joseph Smith sought to prepare us and our heirs for the day when the earth will be baptized by fire. Only those filled with the Spirit of the living God will be enhanced and purified by that fire, while others will be burned. It was the message of Noah that we repent, that we gather, and that we prepare. That was also the message of Joseph.

We turn to Abraham, Isaac, and Jacob, the great triumvirate, the great source of the house of Israel. All blessings that were promised to Abraham were promised anew upon the head of the Prophet Joseph Smith in our generation—but he was told that if he hoped to receive these blessings, he and his brethren must do the works of Abraham and honor him (D&C 132:31–32). And that included the willingness to give all, even that which they cherished most, if necessary, in building the kingdom of God.

The parallels between the ancient Joseph, son of Jacob, and his latter-day namesake could be multiplied on and on. Joseph, the favorite son; Joseph, envied by his brothers; Joseph, cast into the pit, indentured to Potiphar, a man of great power; Joseph, the great resistor of temptation; the one who rose to temporal prominence and became a ruler in Egypt and thus both the temporal and spiritual savior of his own family.

The Joseph of our day was betrayed by his brothers at times, not those who were his brothers in his family, but those who were his brothers in the gospel. Yet he did have an erratically struggling brother named William, with whom there was a terrible alienation for a time. But like his own father, Joseph gave priesthood blessings to all of his family, Hyrum being witness, and promised that even William, in due time, would rise to the full measure of his mission.[14] There is a sense in which the modern Joseph, as the Joseph of old, ultimately will be known as the spiritual and temporal savior of this dispensation.

There isn't time to magnify the parallels in the life and teachings of Joseph Smith and the preeminent prophet, Isaiah. But every theme that has to do with the last days—including the culminations of history, the healing and uniting of that which has been separated, the building up of the kingdom in preparation for the day when the lamb and the lion shall sit down together—that was in Isaiah (see Isaiah 11:6), was translated by the Prophet, and was present in whole chapters in the Book of Mormon. Joseph Smith, like Isaiah, envisioned temples. Isaiah is preeminently a temple prophet, and Joseph took a phrase that some insist applies only to the Old World and applied it to the new: The day shall come when "the mountain of the Lord's house shall be established in the top of the mountains" (Isaiah 2:2).

Joseph yearned to witness that day. He yearned to be the Joshua who crossed into the promised land. According to one prayer we have recorded, he yearned to say to the Lord what was said anciently: "If it should be . . . [the] will of God that I might live to behold that temple completed"—and in this case he was talking of Nauvoo—"I will say, Oh Lord, it is enough. Lord, let thy servant depart in peace."[15] But it was not to be. Even the Nauvoo Temple was built, as he himself said, with a trowel in one hand and a sword in the other, which is an idea that takes us back to the troubles experienced by Ezra and Nehemiah (see Ezra 4:4–5; Nehemiah 4:7–8),[16] and he died before it was completed.

What of Job? In one revelation the Prophet was told, "Thou are not yet as Job" (D&C 121:10). The word *yet* was itself prophetic. He wasn't then, at that point, as Job—his friends still stood by him, although there had been betrayers. But, like Job, Joseph Smith did suffer terribly in the loss of several of his children, in the loss of some aspects of his health, in the loss of his possessions (finally culminating in bankruptcy), and not least in the loss of his brother Alvin and his father. He and his brother Hyrum, in a period of imprisonment lasting six months, were on display, as Hyrum once wrote, like "elephants."[17] Their jailers even sometimes denied them the right to pray. And some of their enemies and even some of their friends said, in effect, "Why don't you curse God and die?" (see D&C 21:11–23). They did neither; they honored God, and they lived.

Joseph was a modern Moses, a man like unto Moses, so designated in the revelations (see D&C 28:2), and denied, as was Moses, entry into the promised land. He led the Saints through the wilderness: New York to Ohio to Missouri to Illinois. But not to the Great Basin. Joseph once said in a spirit of levity, "Moses was a stammering sort of a boy like me."[18] But Moses gave the law. Moses came down from Mount Sinai and found the people who had lapsed back into idolatry and laid upon them the Law, the Decalogue. That same law was given, along with a renewal of covenant, on the very day this Church as a small group entered the land known as Independence. The Prophet received a revelation pertaining to the keeping of the Sabbath, and in that same revelation the Lord recapitulated the Ten Commandments and then gave two additional ones: "Thou shalt offer a sacrifice unto the Lord thy God in righteousness, even that of a broken heart and a contrite spirit," and "Thou shalt thank the Lord thy God in all things" (D&C 59:7–8). Joseph was a Moses to this generation, and Joseph's truth-gems and doctrines and ordained practices will be handed down with like reverence and care by those who have come to know who he was and what he did.

As for the Psalmists—I will not dwell on them except to say that 2 Nephi 4 is for me as rich and mighty a song, as deep an expression of a soul of man, as I have ever read. The Prophet, of course, would say that he only translated it; but he also comprehended it and lived it.

We know of Elijah, that he could control the elements, and we find the same priesthood power manifest in incidents in our dispensation. We know Elijah was betrayed by Jezebel and had to run for his life (see 1 Kings 19:3). So did Joseph, in his own time. We know that Elijah became the master of the keys of sealing and that those keys were placed by Elijah upon the Prophet (see D&C 110:13–16). Those keys live in the Church to this day.

If we move to the New Testament we focus on three more: Peter, James, and John. I suggest to you that, like Peter, Joseph bore his testimony with knowledge: "Thou art the Christ" (Matthew 16:16). Like James he was a prophet of good works, and like John he was a prophet of godly love. The Doctrine and Covenants is permeated, through Joseph, with the spirit of those three, the three great high priests of the ancient church.

Joseph himself spoke a great deal about Paul and the similarities of their lives. On one occasion he spoke of walking hip deep in persecution and testified that he felt, like Paul, to rejoice in persecution (see D&C 127:2). Imagine the faith in Christ that enabled the Prophet to say, looking back, that "every wave of adversity . . . had only wafted [him] that much nearer to Deity."[19] That is enlightened faith.

THE ENGINE OF DESTRUCTION

I turn now to a personal narrative of a well-known story: I remind you that the shadow of the possibility of martyrdom went way back in the Prophet's life. It's true that he received a blessing from his father in the early 1830s in which Joseph Smith Sr. said in effect, "You will escape the sword of thine enemies, and you shall put the armies of your enemies to flight,"[20] and there are cases when that occurred. In Far West the attackers literally fled. But his father did not add, though he could have, "You will nevertheless face the fire of muskets."

In my home I have a little box of metal balls that those who play marbles would probably call "steelies." Our generation rarely understands that a musket did not fire like a repeating rifle with bullets. You had to tamp powder into the barrel and then tamp in the ball—one shot at a time. Those balls are almost a half-inch in diameter. The official account of the martyrdom of Joseph and Hyrum (see D&C 135) said that each of the two brothers "received" (that's a kind way to say it) four balls. (Generations later, however, when their caskets were opened it was determined that they received five apiece.) The Prophet's father, of course, wanted his sons to live long. Joseph himself gave a blessing to his brother Hyrum in which he speaks of blessings to come in his old age. Hyrum had to forgo that blessing in order to join his brother at Carthage.

I will not dwell on all the sources of opposition to Joseph. To this day we do not know them all or how they intertwine. I can tell you from reading documents and newspapers of the time, especially those published by enemies of the Church in Missouri and in the *Warsaw Signal* by the famous Thomas Sharp, that there was a gradual but very clear trend. It started with statements of opposition that were mild and even lawful. Opponents to the Church said, in effect, we must stand up against these people. But then the journalistic rhetoric becomes worse. There are pleas that somehow the law must be sidestepped to stop the career of the Prophet or his people. In the end these voices say, in essence, "Whether it is lawful or not, these Mormons must be exterminated." That the people at Carthage said, "If the law will not reach them, powder and ball must"[21] is an acknowledgment both that the law, distorted in its imposition, couldn't finally do away with the brothers, and that violence would.

The *Nauvoo Expositor* was "designed as an engine to bring

destruction," as William Clayton put it.[22] William Law had been part of the rescue effort when the Prophet was unjustly arrested in Dixon. He and others, some months before, had come forward and kissed the Prophet with a kiss of affection, denoting loyalty and love. Now three sets of brothers (including William Law and his brother) had become, sincerely or not, convinced that they would do the world and even God a service to wash their hands in the blood of Joseph Smith.[23] They held secret meetings. We don't know all the details. We do know that at some point, according to the story, some 150 to 200 people were willing to go forward, put their hands on a Bible, and swear that they would not rest until Joseph Smith was gone.[24]

There were threats from all quarters. One of the threats was that there wouldn't be a Smith left alive in Nauvoo within two weeks.[25]

Joseph and Hyrum saw the noose slowly tightening around them. They knew perfectly well, I believe, when the city council decided that this newspaper (the *Nauvoo Expositor*), which was in every way salacious, needed to be stopped, that it would cause the flurry that it did cause. But they made the decision to stop it, as we read from one source, because as the Prophet said "that God showed to him in an open vision in daylight that if he did not destroy that Printing press that it would cause the Blood of the Saints to flow in the streets and by this was that Evil destroyed."[26] He did not then go on to say, "But it may cost my blood." We know that they had previously used every means they could to contact both official and government leaders throughout the state and beyond. We know of petitions sent to Washington. We know even of a desperate letter from the Prophet to the Green Mountain Boys in Vermont—great patriots whom he had learned to love in boyhood. He thought maybe they could be touched with the truth that what was happening in Nauvoo was out-and-out religious persecution and prejudice.[27] He wrote to the president of the United States—nothing.[28] Arrangements were made to travel with two representatives of each jurisdiction in Nauvoo and beyond to tell the story and to answer the lies that were being told, with no real effect.

"NO MERCY HERE"

Then came the letter from the governor ordering that they come to Carthage—the entire city council and the Prophet with them. "There is no mercy—no mercy here," the Prophet said. "No," Hyrum agreed. "As sure as we fall into their hands we are dead men." But then the Prophet's face lit up and he said, "The way is open. It is clear to my mind what to do. All they want is Hyrum and myself; . . . they will not harm you in person or property, and not even a hair of your head. We will cross the river tonight, and go away to the West."[29] That was incredible to many of the Saints. And here is a case, again, where sometimes a man's worst enemies are those within his own household, as it were. From their point of view, real estate values would go down and further problems would arise. Some were so terrified of the threats of the mob that they threw their possessions in wagons and rode away. One journal entry records that the Prophet, in seeing some flee, said, quietly but perhaps with an edge, "Look at the cowards."[30] (That was a phrase used about him later on.)

Joseph and Hyrum went. They crossed the river. Our official annals record what happened next. A letter arrived from Emma. With it was a signed petition charging that Joseph and Hyrum were abandoning the flock—this after the Prophet had said publicly that he was willing, if necessary, to give his life. "When my enemies take away my rights," he had said, "I will bear it. But if they take away your rights I will fight for you."[31] He had even drawn his sword and put the world on notice that he meant what he said. Many delegations came to them. Apparently, if we can trust the record of Cyrus H. Wheelock (who was there), Joseph was impressed to say to his brother, "I will go back. You stay. You stay out of the hands of our enemies, and you get back to your wife."[32]

Neither the Prophet nor his brother had ever been present for the birth of any of their children. Mary Fielding Smith had given Hyrum his first glimpse of his son when he was in Liberty Jail. Knowing the sacrifices Hyrum had already made, the Prophet pleaded with Hyrum to leave him. At some point, according to Wheelock, Hyrum put his hands on the Prophet's shoulders and said (this coming from the man who was called sedate and serious, the man of principle, the great peacemaker): "Joseph, in the name of Israel's God I swear where you go, I will go and where you die, I will die."[33] The Prophet apparently did not want to accept that, but he read Hyrum's eyes. After a moment he made a light gesture and said, "Amen." And together they traveled back across the river.

A blessing had been given to Hyrum Smith early in his life in which he was told, in effect, that the time would come when, if he so chose, he would be a martyr for the cause of the Lord Jesus Christ. That day he made that choice. Yet he remained, in contrast to the Prophet, optimistic: "Let us go back and put our trust in God, and we shall not be harmed."[34] At one point Uncle John Smith asked the Prophet "if he thought he should again get out of the hands of his enemies"[35] as he had so often escaped before. Joseph replied, "My brother Hyrum thinks I shall."[36] Three times the Prophet pleaded with Hyrum to leave him. Three times Hyrum replied, "Joseph, I cannot leave you."[37] He was not saying, "I don't have the power." He was saying, "I have made a covenant and I will keep it." There was one more time on the road when, according to John Lowes Butler, Joseph stopped the group and insisted that they all return to Nauvoo and leave him and Hyrum to go on. Then he remonstrated with Hyrum again. Brother Butler records that the departing group rode back that entire distance, at least fourteen miles, with not one of them speaking a word. They felt in their hearts that that was the last they would ever see of the Prophet and Hyrum.[38]

THE SCENE IN CARTHAGE

The account of the scene in Carthage is familiar to you. At the Prophet's request, "A Poor Wayfaring Man of Grief" was sung in the tenor voice of John Taylor. He did not sing it with enthusiasm. The record shows all of them feeling dazed in the sultry, hot June humidity. They were depressed; their spirits were down. When Hyrum asked John to sing it again, John said, "I don't feel like singing." But he did it. The words are prophetic: "My friendship's utmost zeal to try, He asked if I for him would die. The flesh was weak; my blood ran chill, but my free spirit cried, 'I will!'"[39]

Their murder was clearly a conspiracy. Whether we can implicate anyone in a courtroom, starting with the governor and moving down, has already been demonstrated. We cannot. Not one person was convicted of any misdeed in the Carthage tragedy. All were exonerated. It seems to me Willard Richards's words were prophetic when he wrote a note in an effort to pacify what he knew would be the mood of the people. He said, in effect, "They were expecting that we will undertake reprisal. I tell them not."[40] In addition, the first thing Willard Richards did when they arrived back in Nauvoo, John Taylor groaning on the sled that they had improvised for him, was to say to the Saints, "Be at peace. Let the law settle this. And when it fails [he didn't say "if"], then leave it in the hands of God."[41] That's where it remains to this day. Many of those who came that day were no more profoundly involved than that they loved a brawl, some of them probably drunk, incited to riot, not knowing what they did.

It had been said to Willard Richards that he would escape someday from a veritable hailstorm of bullets without so much as a hole in his robe (D&C 135:2)[42]; and he, the largest target in the room—over three hundred pounds—escaped virtually untouched. He did have a bit of a nick on one ear. That room, when it was examined the next day, had thirty-six pockmarks where bullets had missed and gone into the walls.[43]

Joseph was the first man to meet the mob as they came up the stairs, and one of them received the best of Joseph's right fist and rolled back down the stairs. The Prophet did all he knew to do, including drawing a pistol that had been brought by Cyrus Wheelock. "I hate to use such things," Hyrum said. "So do I," said the Prophet, "but we may have to, to defend ourselves."[44] It is clear from the record that Hyrum went down without resistance, that he did not use the pistol, that he was wounded in his cheekbone near his nose and fell backwards exclaiming, "I am a dead man." The Prophet leaned down and said, "Oh! my poor, dear brother Hyrum."[45]

Then, and only then, did Joseph assert the right which he had spoken of in a letter written to Emma that day: they still had the right to defend themselves. Joseph's gun misfired at least twice. As guns protruded through the opening crack of the door, John Taylor used a hickory stick to push the guns upward so they would hit the ceiling instead of their intended target. "That's right, Brother Taylor," said the Prophet, "parry them off as well as you can."[46] (The strangest moment in the whole narrative to me is that as the 150 men surrounded the jail, somebody shouted "Surrender!" That seems to me to be an inappropriate thing to say.)

Finally, wounded terribly, John Taylor crawled under the bed. Willard Richards remained at his position behind the door. I've often supposed that if there had been only two men in that room, namely Joseph and Hyrum Smith, the story might be different, but there were two additional men the Prophet hoped could remain alive. What did he then do? According to Willard Richards, he quickly moved to the window.[47] It must have been clear in that split second that whether he leaped out the window or remained in the room where his assailants were shooting, his life would end either way. He was, as he moved toward the window, hit from behind. He then apparently pulled himself through that window and fell out.[48] When the attackers who were in the stairwell learned he had fallen, they ran downstairs and out to see. Other shots may have been fired at that point. Because of Joseph's simple act of going to the window, whether he intended it or not he saved two lives.

Then came the classic fulfillment of the proverb, "The wicked flee when no man pursueth" (Proverbs 28:1). Someone said, "The Mormons are coming,"[49] and the mob and many townspeople dispersed in every direction. When Samuel Smith arrived, having been shot at more than once himself, according to the account of his granddaughter, he found his two brothers dead—Joseph by the well, Hyrum upstairs.[50]

THE AFTERMATH

Now the aftermath, and my witness. Samuel had been part of the last meeting of the brothers, and according to his grandson, Joseph said to Samuel, "Because of your blessing," meaning a patriarchal blessing he had received, "you will not be killed. Your life will be prolonged a season." That season lasted just over a month beyond the martyrdom. "Here is a ring," Joseph said. "I want you to keep it, a keepsake of me."[51] That ring was handed down in the family. I stood one day in the upper room of the Carthage Jail and Patriarch J. Winter Smith, a grandson of Samuel, then almost ninety, took the ring from his pocket and bore his witness to me: "I know that my grandfather was a man of God. I know that he, with the Prophet Joseph and Hyrum, gave his life for the cause. I am honored to be here."

As soon as the word was out that the Prophet was dead, there were predictions that Mormonism was also dead. "Cut off the head," said they, "and the body dies. If the head is gone, the body is ours." One newspaper article concluded: "Thus ends Mormonism."[52]

But they did not understand. The blood of the prophets is the seed of the Church. The ancient Chrysostom died a martyr in his own time, with much less light than was given these dear brethren. He, it was said, deserved the martyr's crown because he did not seek it and did not fear it. Neither did Joseph and Hyrum.

As the Prophet was traveling to Carthage with Hyrum, the city council, and others, they came to a turn in the road and saw up to seventy men coming at full gallop, armed to the teeth. These were the troops sent by Governor Ford to insist that the Mormons surrender the state arms of the Nauvoo militia. Those with the Prophet were taken aback, fearing the worst. Joseph stopped the group and said, "Do not be alarmed, brethren, for they cannot do more to you than the enemies of truth did to the ancient Saints—they can only kill the body."[53] How much comfort would that be? But to them it was a comfort. And it turned out the men with him did not have to die. The Prophet then said, "I am going like a lamb to the slaughter"[54] (an Old Testament phrase from Isaiah 53:7) and then added, "I am not afraid to die."[55]

According to John Taylor, Joseph had earlier said to Emma, "If they don't hang me I don't care how they kill me." And I believe that was overheard or learned later by Willard Richards, which is why he said to Joseph in that last extremity, "I will be hung in your stead."[56] He meant it. No, they did not fear death. But certainly they did not seek it. I repeat, the Prophet wanted to be the Joshua of this dispensation and take the Saints across the river into the promised land. He was denied that privilege.

You know what has happened since. And it is only beginning. A professor of sociology and comparative religion at the University of Washington, Rodney Stark, has written, "We are seeing the rapid rise of the first new world faith since Islam appeared 1,400 years ago. . . . If one examines the pattern of Mormon growth over the past few decades, the rate is always greater than fifty percent per decade," and, "the more rapid growth is overseas, in Latin America and Asia especially." At present growth rates, Stark indicated, the Church would have more than two hundred million members one hundred years from now; it "will become a major world faith."[57]

Professor Stark was only saying what the Prophet himself had said, that this church would grow and nothing could stop it: "No unhallowed hand can stop the work from progressing."[58] We are flourishing. We will continue to flourish in righteousness. Truly, nothing can stop this work from progressing until it has reached every country, every clime, and sounded in every ear.[59]

The faithful brother Hyrum died as witness to every

crucial part of the Restoration. He knew the doctrine; he knew the organization; he knew the transmission of the keys of the priesthood; he knew the ordinances (including the highest ordinances of the temple); he knew the privileges and the promises, which he himself voiced often in patriarchal blessings, of this glorious dispensation; and he is a martyr as Joseph is a martyr. In due time the Lord himself will in fact be the one, the only one, who brings justice and judgment, including condemnation for those who went against the light and killed innocent men.

I close this chapter with words that seem to me—partly because of the context in which they were given and partly because we now have the perspective of 155 years—almost magical in their prediction. When, as the Prophet figuratively put it, he seemed while in jail to be in the deepest coal pit of Nova Scotia with the Rocky Mountains piled on top of him, he received these words from the Lord[60]: "The ends of the earth shall inquire after thy name, and fools shall have thee in derision" (and they still do; he's still called "Old" Joe—a man who never reached his thirty-ninth year!), " . . . and hell shall rage against thee . . ." (and so it did and so it has), " . . . While the pure in heart, and the wise, and the noble, and the virtuous, shall seek counsel, and authority, and blessings constantly from under thy hand. And thy people shall never be turned against thee by the testimony of traitors. . . . And but for a small moment and thy voice shall be more terrible in the midst of thine enemies than the fierce lion, because of thy righteousness; and thy God shall stand by thee forever and ever" (D&C 122:1–4).

2

BRIGHAM YOUNG

The Prophet Joseph Smith once said in an intimate conversation with Brigham Young, "Your name shall be known for good and evil."[1] We know that sentence from an earlier statement made by an angel to the Prophet Joseph. Strangely, I suspect the name Brigham Young is better known in the world today than that of Joseph Smith.

As a youth I attended family reunions held in the Lion House, which I learned was named after "The Lion of the Lord," who was Brigham Young. And from my grandfather I learned that as a boy he had lived just around the corner from the Lion House, where ZCMI later stood for so long. As a boy he heard daily the Lion House prayer bell, like a school bell, which meant, "Come in for family prayer." He would rush out of his house, across South Temple Street, crawl through a hole in the hedge, and arrive in the front parlor just as Brigham Young was about to pray. He told his family that even though he had been taught to keep his eyes closed during prayer, he sometimes could not resist opening his eyes as Brother Brigham prayed. Why? "I have lifted my head," he said, and, "turned and looked at the place where Brigham Young was praying, to see if the Lord was not there. It seemed to me that he talked to the Lord as one man would talk to another."[2]

On the day when Brigham Young first met Joseph Smith, Joseph was chopping wood. That very day they had prayer together, and Brigham had a spiritual outpouring and spoke in an unknown language. The Prophet later said of Brigham, "The time will come when Brigham Young will preside over this church."[3] He also said, and I paraphrase, "And he will be one of the greatest teachers of redemption through Christ who ever lived." So Brigham Young the Colonizer was also Brigham Young the Teacher.

BEGINNINGS

His beginnings were in Whitingham, Vermont. Today a monument marks his birthplace. He was born into a family of eleven children. He had four brothers, and all of them eventually joined him in the Church. Though he was there only until about his ninth year, Vermont had an impact on him that never really disappeared. Even today at the Vermont border is a sign saying, "Entering Vermont, the Last Stand of the Yankees." That's put there with pride. Vermont has in it, and in its history, strong people of fierce independence, and they belong to the Union out of sheer will. They are familiar with bitter cold winters. They milk cows in their shirtsleeves when the temperature is 30 degrees below zero; and they know about clearing timber; and they know about horse work and housework.

Brigham learned all of those in his boyhood. He moved with his family to New York, becoming skilled in maturity as a builder, a carpenter, a glazier, a painter, and a master of mantelpieces. His father, John Young, had served under George Washington in the Revolutionary Army. Vermonters were committed to the Revolution and the rights of the Constitution—then and now—in a very firm way. And I suspect that Brigham Young suffered all his life from knowing, on the one hand, the inherent principles of the Great American Dream and, at the same time, their abuse and violation in his own life and in the lives of his people.

Brigham Young's mother died when he was only fourteen years old. After that, when his father took another wife, who became his stepmother, Brigham found home less congenial and went to Auburn in New York, where he was again a furniture maker and painter. At this point in his life he had a remarkable experience that he did not understand until years later. It was on the night that the Prophet Joseph Smith went to the Hill Cumorah with his wife, Emma, and brought home the plates of what was to become known as the Book of Mormon. That night Brigham was wholly unaware there was anyone named Joseph Smith and unaware that it was the night of Rosh Hashanah, New Year's night in the Jewish world (which is an interesting coincidence). He was summoned from sleep by a woman who said, "Come out and look at the stars."

He walked outside and, with his neighbor Heber C. Kimball and others, saw a vision in the vaulted heavens. They saw an army coming through a channel of light, many soldiers abreast, dressed in uniforms that they later associated with the American army, and bearing muskets and swords. They could hear the sound, as it were, of their marching. And they had a sense of the concern and preparation for a great battle. This marching took place for more than an hour and exited in the west. They wondered at this, marveled at it, but learned only later that was the significant night when the beginning of the Restoration was marked by the return of the plates.[4]

"FIRE IN MY BONES"

His marriage took place when he was twenty-three, in 1824. They had a daughter, and then another daughter. And then a young man named Samuel Smith stopped in the area, a knapsack on his back in which he carried several copies of the newly published Book of Mormon. One came into the hands of Phineas Young, Brigham's brother, then shortly after into the hands of Brigham and also Heber C. Kimball. They read. They read carefully. Brigham by then had become a Methodist and had attended a number of religious revivals such as Joseph Smith experienced. Like Joseph Smith, he was not encouraged or inspired by the revivals, but was troubled and worried. When he received the Book of Mormon, he was careful and methodical; he said something like this: "I will continue to read and pray. I want to know if there is common sense in this Mormon movement."

In due time, he accepted the powerful testimony of a missionary and then accepted baptism. For a time immediately after that, he felt the same as his colleague and friend, Heber C. Kimball, had. "I wanted to thunder and roar out the Gospel to the nations," he said. "It burned in my bones like fire pent up. . . . Nothing would satisfy me but to cry abroad in the world, what the Lord was doing in the latter days."[5] He became a kind of traveling preacher. Then he had his encounter with the Prophet Joseph Smith, which made it clear that Joseph was not talking about a spiritual movement that involved only preaching. Joseph was talking about rebuilding the kingdom of God on the earth. That meant a whole society. That meant involvement in city building. That meant a temple at the center. That moved Brigham, and he offered himself and his services.

In 1834 he was present at a significant meeting in Kirtland held in a log cabin, which Wilford Woodruff described as so small that it could have held perhaps only twenty people. Many of those present later became prominent leaders and members of the Twelve. There Brigham began to comprehend the vast outlook of the Prophet Joseph Smith. On request, Brigham bore a five-minute testimony on what he saw as the future of the Church. Others did the same, providing the context for what the Prophet then said. He thanked them for their observations and feelings, and then testified: "You know no more concerning the destinies of this Church and kingdom than a babe upon its mother's lap. You don't comprehend it. . . . This church will fill North and South America. It will fill the world."[6] Brigham Young never forgot that vision and went to work.

ZION'S CAMP

Shortly thereafter Brigham Young received his education in leadership—the hard way. With his brothers and many others, he joined, at the Prophet's call (it wasn't a request, it was a call) what became known as "Zion's Camp." Brigham later called it the starting point of "my knowing how to lead Israel."[7] The hardship was real: they walked an average of thirty miles a day, a total of a thousand miles—about the same as the later trek from Winter Quarters to the Rocky Mountains—and then back. They went convinced that they could help the Saints in Missouri recover their homes and lands, and further convinced that they might have to fight in a war. Already could be seen the Prophet Joseph's sense of trust in Brigham when he said to him, "If I fall in battle in Missouri, I want you to bring my bones back, and deposit them in that sepulchre." The Prophet even said, according to Brigham, "I command you to do it in the name of the Lord."[8] Brigham promised.

Two episodes affected him profoundly. One was the time in the Zion's Camp march when, cold and hungry and barefoot and wet, some began to murmur. Not only that, but some also began to lapse into worldly patterns: profanity, little games, carping at each other. The Prophet Joseph called them together and said, in effect, "If we do not repent, if we do not behave like a camp of Israel, like men and women of God [by the way, there were many women along, and some children]—if we do not, some of us will die like sheep with the rot."[9] Not everybody repented, and many were suddenly stricken with deadly disease. Thirteen of the camp died. Others barely survived. Finally the Prophet called them all together again in the midst of that terrible sickness and said, "Now, if we unite in prayer and promise and covenant to go forward as the Lord Jesus Christ would have us do, this will be turned away."[10] It was. Brigham Young never forgot that.

The other experience is the sequel. Having come all the way back, amidst some jeers and some complaints—even from some of those who went—Brigham was asked by someone, "What have you gained by this journey?" And he replied, "Just what we went for."[11] It turned out that that's precisely what the Prophet himself said to Brigham Young and his brother, Joseph, as they later sat in his home in Kirtland: "Brethren, some of you are angry with me, because you did not fight in Missouri; but let me tell you, God did not want you to fight. He could not organize his kingdom with twelve men to open the Gospel door to the nations of the earth, and with seventy men under their direction to follow in their tracks, unless He took them from a body of men who had offered their lives, and who had made as great a sacrifice as did Abraham. Now the Lord has got His Twelve and His Seventy, and there will be other quorums of Seventies called, who will make the sacrifice, and those who have not made their sacrifices and their offerings now, will make them hereafter."[12]

Then he confided to them: "Brigham, you will be one of those apostles. Joseph [meaning Joseph Young], you will be one of the Seventy."[13] Brigham's own comment about his call to be an apostle is something like this: "I was mystified that I would be called. But I brought to the calling one thing. I brought grit, and I knew I would do my duty."[14] That's an understatement.

Concerning the call of his brother, Joseph Young, there were four generations of presidents of Seventy in the direct line from that Joseph: Joseph Young (son of the first Joseph), Seymour B. Young, Levi Edgar Young, and S. Dilworth Young. All of them were equipped to serve in filling roles that the Twelve could not.

On that occasion in Joseph's home, Brigham Young sang a duet with his brother, and it was while they were singing that that peculiar transparency came into the Prophet's face. Brigham said, "Those who were acquainted with him knew when the Spirit of revelation was upon him, for his countenance wore an expression peculiar to himself while under that influence."[15]

A LOYAL FRIEND AND LEADER

Brigham Young and Heber C. Kimball, who both had authority and the confidence and trust of the Prophet, witnessed the betrayals that led to the incarceration of the Prophet. I pause to say that the words of comfort given to him in Liberty Jail may also have felt like a bit of a stab. The Lord said to the Prophet in his anguish, "Thy friends do stand by thee, and they shall hail thee again with warm hearts and friendly hands" (D&C 121:9). Yes, but some of his friends, including William W. Phelps and Orson Hyde and others in high position, had sworn to documents in a way that would save their own lives at the cost of putting Joseph and Hyrum in prison. The Prophet would later say that of the original Twelve ordained at Kirtland, only two did not lift up the heel against him (see John 13:18; D&C 121:16)—Brigham Young and Heber C. Kimball.[16] Brigham's own comment about himself, spoken later, was, "Here is Brigham, have his knees ever faltered?"[17]

Several of those who apostatized came back, including Orson Hyde and William W. Phelps, but several of the original Twelve, under the wrench of the Abrahamic test, faded away and never returned to full activity.

While he was in Liberty Jail, the Prophet sent a message to Brigham that said, in essence, "You, Brigham, are the senior member of the Twelve. Now it devolves upon you to see that everyone who is in need of our entire flock is helped out of Missouri. Missouri will not hold us; we must leave."[18]

Ironically, because they had failed as a people to honor and live the law of consecration, it foundered, as it probably would today, on greed and covetousness and selfishness. It is ironic because, though they had failed to live the principle fully in Missouri, now they had to or they would not survive. Thus it was that Brigham Young initiated a covenant process wherein he directed all the needy Saints to pledge their time, their money, and their property and other holdings all to one purpose: to see that everyone—including the halt and the blind and the maimed and the widows and the orphans—was able to safely escape Missouri. He undertook that task with his colleague, Heber C. Kimball. Our people found themselves as exiles in a little community called Quincy, Illinois.

One footnote is that Heber C. Kimball made the last great legal effort to hasten the Prophet's release, but it failed. He then traveled to Liberty and was admitted down through the trapdoor and reported to the Prophet that their last hope was gone. Joseph and Heber then knelt and started to pray, but a guard interrupted them, shouting, "No prayer in here," pointing a gun.[19] So all they could do was sit and converse, with deep emotion.

Imagine the reunion when the exiles were given a welcome in Quincy and suddenly the Prophet Joseph Smith and his brother Hyrum came into town. A gathering was called; they sang a familiar hymn, "Glorious Things Are Sung in Zion"—a song sung by people who hardly had shirts left on their backs; and Joseph and Brigham embraced. In that setting Brigham Young was ordained, by the laying on of hands, to be the senior member of the Twelve and the president of that quorum. It wasn't a late idea in the Prophet's mind that Brigham Young would so inherit the keys. It occurred in Quincy, six years before the so-called "succession crisis," and there were many present to witness it.

DOCTRINES OF NAUVOO

Next came the task of turning a miasmic swamp into a beautiful city, Nauvoo (which is a Hebrew word meaning, literally, "a beautiful place"). I think it was at Brigham Young's initiative that it was later called "The City of Joseph."[20] Four new doctrines were introduced in that period—new to Brigham Young and new to the Saints. Brigham became a wholehearted advocate of all of them. Earlier, in Kirtland, Doctrine and Covenants 76, "The Vision" as we now call it, was introduced. It sheds a flood of light on the eventual outcome of our probation in this life and the degrees of glory in the life to come. But its reception, even in the Church, was hesitant and faltering, and some even left the Church over it. They could not give up the classic, traditional, heaven and hell dualism. Brigham Young found it a magnificent teaching, and, as a follow-up, learned in Nauvoo the first of the four doctrines we will mention: baptism for the dead.

Brigham was well aware, because he had attended the dedicatory services in Kirtland, that the Prophet had had a vision in which he had seen his brother Alvin and his own father in celestial glory and was taught, in effect, that we will be judged by the intents of the heart (D&C 137). It may be properly said that perhaps he was seeing a prophetic vision that hadn't yet come to full culmination. Then came the second part of that insight: We have access to ordinances that will open the way for such blessings. Every blessing and ordinance given to men and women in the flesh can, by proxy, be made available to those in the spirit world.

The reaction of the first group of Saints who heard this doctrine: they rushed down to the Mississippi River and started baptizing indiscriminately, men and women for each other, and so on. The Prophet had to say, in essence, "Wait, wait, this must be done in order; we must have a recorder," and so forth (see D&C 127:5–9).[21] Brigham Young became a convert to temple work, as we call it, and to the glories of vicarious service.

The second Nauvoo doctrine was not so well-received.

There was talk in Nauvoo, early on, of the principle of eternal marriage. That itself broke tradition and was difficult for many to understand. But then there began to be talk of a principle of plural families—misnamed, I believe, plural wives. Brigham heard of it and was troubled by it. Brigham said he would rather go to his grave than practice this principle.[22] He also said at one point, "Joseph, what if I cannot live it? What if this principle leads to my apostasy?"

And the Prophet replied, "Brigham, there are some of you who have come so far in dedication to the Lord Jesus Christ that you will never apostatize. Rather than that should happen the Lord would take you home." In Brigham's own journal he wrote, "I had that consolation."[23]

Elder S. Dilworth Young later recorded a traditional family story about Brigham's change of heart: One hot summer night Brigham's wife, Mary Ann Angell (the sister of Truman O. Angell, who became the architect of the Salt Lake Temple and also helped at Kirtland), was upstairs in the home that Brigham Young had built to replace the log cabin where they had earlier lived. Because of the heat, she pushed the bed over right under the open window to gain the benefit of whatever slight breeze there might be. She heard Joseph and Brigham walking together down the street and standing at the gate of the little fence that surrounded their property. They were talking about this principle.

Brigham said, "Joseph, are you sure that this is from God? Are you sure?"

And the Prophet replied, "I am. It has come directly from the Lord. We must live it."

Brigham started to protest, but the Prophet said, "Brother Brigham, the Lord will make it known to you. Good night."

Mary Ann heard the Prophet's footsteps as he walked down the road. She heard Brigham open the gate, walk in, come up on the stoop of the porch. And then she heard Brigham's voice. "Joseph," he called. "Wait." She heard Brigham go back out. "Joseph, the Lord has made it known to me. It is true. Good night."

"Good night."[24]

Before Brigham actually undertook the principle, he had many long conversations with Mary Ann. Then, in time, he entered into this principle of marriage as instructed by both the Prophet and the Spirit.

The third principle taught in Nauvoo was the temple endowment, or what was then called the fullness of the temple blessings. In Kirtland they had had the preparatory ordinances. But in Nauvoo Joseph began to share the full endowment with a select group, Brigham Young and his wife being among the first.

It was also to Brigham Young that the Prophet spoke most specifically about the sealing ordinances, and it was to him and Wilford Woodruff that Joseph gave the assignment to record and systematize and transmit the endowment to succeeding generations. Some years later, in the St. George Temple, using Wilford Woodruff's notes and Brigham Young's memory and inspiration, they did indeed systematize the endowment.[25]

In Nauvoo it became clear for the first time that one could be linked to his parents in an unbroken chain by sealing, the fourth doctrine we'll mention—more than simply being baptized for them, more than simply receiving other ordinances, one could be bound to parents forever. As soon as possible, Brigham was sealed to his own father, and then as far back as he could go.

TO GREAT BRITAIN FOR THE LORD

Next we consider the interlude of Brigham's incredible mission to Britain. Here was a great moment. How would it be to walk into the Church headquarters and say, "President, I would like to be the president of the British Mission, and I would like the Council of the Twelve to be my first twelve missionaries." That's approximately what happened. I think nine of the Twelve went on that mission to Great Britain, with Brigham Young among them. Their reminiscences detail how difficult it was for them to leave, how hard it was for the families, and how much opposition they faced. It's almost impossible to put in words. But they went in faith.

The Prophet had said to Brother Heber C. Kimball, "The work in England will be quick and powerful." He also said, "There is much of the blood of Israel in Britain."[26] After Heber's return, on hearing the reports of conversions of whole villages—men, women, and children who were of age—Joseph said that that "place was indeed 'holy ground,' that some of the ancient prophets had traveled in that region and dedicated the land, and that he, Heber, had reaped the benefit of their blessing."[27]

In the short six months of their missions, they often performed baptisms all day, one after another. More than six thousand people came into the Church. They published the Book of Mormon and began a periodical, *The Millennial Star,* that lasted a hundred-plus years. They passed out hundreds and thousands of tracts. The Church itself, which had been staggering and foundering in Kirtland, was now renovated. Instantly, almost, the new converts were filled with a spirit that told them they must go to Zion, even though the Brethren hadn't yet preached the idea of "gathering." These converts didn't even know what Zion was. But they went, and so began the migration.

If you are ever visiting in England you might want to stop in Chatburn—it's almost as enchanted and lovely and pristine as it was 150 years ago. Heber C. Kimball worked there for a time, and when he was about to return home to Nauvoo, he and Elder Joseph Fielding "walked to Chatburn and Downham for a last farewell. As soon as they were seen in Chatburn, the people left their work and flocked to the streets to greet them"—and the children simply followed him through the town. By the time he reached the end of the village, like the Pied Piper Heber was surrounded by children who were dancing and singing. He knelt down and embraced them, one by one, and then as he went on his way he had to stop three times to wash his eyes in the streambed from the profusion of tears he shed. He said, and Brigham Young later seconded it, that he felt like he was walking on sacred ground, and that the very hair of his head was being quickened by the Spirit of God, and that it filled him from head to toe.[28]

DEEPENING TROUBLES

Brigham Young likewise completed his mission and returned, bearing, as it were, his sheaves with him. When he arrived in Nauvoo he found serious troubles there. In some ways it looked like the Garden of Eden. He loved the spectacle of the house of the Lord, the temple not yet finished, but beautiful. He saw it one night in moonlight and was overwhelmed. But he was also aware that opposition was gathering and organizing and that the Prophet was apprehensive and needed his help.

Apprehensions were deep among the faithful Saints in that period—constant threats and accusations, constant gunfire, and warning letters coming from various authorities, especially from Missouri: "We are going to annihilate you." The press shows a transition: "Good riddance of bad rubbish if we drive them off."[29] But then later: "We must proceed lawfully to expunge them." Later still: "No, it doesn't matter whether we follow the law or not, they must be driven."

I've read the journal of a man who described sleeping on his musket every night as part of the Nauvoo Legion, ready for the call at any point—a call that usually came by the beating of a drum. The telling line in the journal said essentially, "I will only say that the anxiety about what might happen was worse than the actual event."

AN ATTORNEY'S CONVERSION

One of Brigham Young's later associates in Utah, Daniel H. Wells, was a squire in Nauvoo, or what we would call an attorney, knowing such rudiments of the law as one could get in those days. Though at the time he was not a member of the Church (he was baptized in 1846), he was an honorable man. He helped in providing or making available the land for much of the city of Nauvoo. He helped in legal skirmishes. He once said, looking back, that the finest lawyer he ever met was Joseph Smith.[30] Joseph Smith never studied law, but he had a lot of practical experience—Brigham Young once said Joseph had experienced forty-seven or forty-eight different trials.[31] And Brigham accompanied him in many. We now know there were many more.

Daniel H. Wells was present one day when the Prophet Joseph Smith was talking about salvation for the dead. Joseph said that God, even before the foundation of the world, had made provision for every case on both sides of the veil. He testified that through divine justice, as well as divine compassion, all the blessings of the gospel of Jesus Christ would be offered to all those who ever lived since the days of Adam.[32] Daniel Wells at that time didn't understand much about the temple, but he went home and said, "Where my father is and my mother, there is where I desire to be, and with my kindred."[33] Thus he began to open his heart to the gospel. He later became a counselor in the First Presidency, serving for twenty years with President Young.

THE PASSING OF THE KEYS

In the spring of 1844, Joseph met with the Twelve and gave them a final charge, emphasizing to them that they held the keys to the kingdom and could keep it going no matter what happened to him.[34] Of course, even though all of the Twelve hold the keys *in potentia,* only the president directs the use of those keys.

After the last-charge meeting, the Prophet kept only two of the Twelve at home: John Taylor and Willard Richards. John Taylor had the assignment of publishing the *Times and Seasons,* and Willard Richards was working day and night to bring the history of the Church up to date. All the others were sent away on one assignment or another, including Brigham Young.

He was in Peterborough, New Hampshire, when rumors began to circulate that Joseph and Hyrum Smith were dead. He did not believe it. But then came word in a letter that it was true. He walked from Peterborough to Boston, a distance of some seventy miles. Waiting for him was Wilford Woodruff, who had also received the news. They went to the home of a Latter-day Saint in Boston, went upstairs, closed the door of the bedroom, and sat down—and then for the first time gushed tears. When Vilate, one of Brigham Young's daughters, saw him in Salem, she said, "He looked as if everything that was dear to him on earth, had been taken away."[35]

In that setting Brigham Young asked the question, "Where are the keys of the priesthood?" And then he brought his hand down on his knee and said, "The keys . . . are right here."[36]

Brigham and Wilford returned to Nauvoo where, on August 8, 1844, Sidney Rigdon spoke to a gathering of the Church for nearly two hours. Sidney argued that he was the likely and entitled heir of the mantle of the Prophet Joseph Smith, that he was to function as the guardian of the Church. Then Brigham Young stood. Taking less than twenty minutes, he said, "The twelve are appointed by the finger of God . . . , an independent body who have the keys of the priesthood—the keys of the kingdom of God to deliver to all the world: this is true, so help me God. They stand next to Joseph, and are as the First Presidency of the Church. . . .

"You cannot fill the office of a prophet, seer and revelator: God must do this. . . . You must not appoint any man at our head; if you should, the Twelve must ordain him. . . . I again repeat, no man can stand at our head, except God reveals it from the heavens. . . . Does this church want it as God organized it? . . . I tell you, in the name of the Lord that no man can put another between the Twelve and the Prophet Joseph. Why? Because Joseph was their file leader, and he has committed into their hands the keys of the kingdom in this last dispensation, for all the world."[37]

He could have rallied many scriptures and many arguments, but he didn't. He simply bore witness.

This was the occasion when Brigham Young was "transfigured," appearing in a form and manner similar to that of

Joseph Smith. This is known in our annals as the "mantle experience." Some historians write the experience off as hallucinatory or as a legend that grew up later. But I have combed the sources and found at least a hundred journal entries or letters that were written in the very period. Brigham Young didn't look like the Prophet Joseph Smith. He was two to three inches shorter and heavier in the chest. He had a stocky build, and he certainly had a voice and a style of speaking that were different from Joseph's. And yet on that occasion there were many who suddenly felt they were hearing and seeing the Prophet Joseph Smith. Some people actually stood up and shouted, "It's Joseph!" Some children tugged on their mothers' skirts and said, "Mother, Mother, look!" Some who had been familiar with a slight whistle in the Prophet Joseph's speech caused by a lost tooth said they could detect even that in Brigham's presentation.[38] After Brigham spoke, the question was put to a vote. The vote was almost unanimous in the affirmative: "We sustain the Twelve, with Brigham Young at their head."[39]

As a postscript to the Nauvoo experience, we have on record a set of minutes of a family meeting held in 1846, where the Youngs and the Smiths met—including Mother Smith and many others. There Brigham Young taught in great depth about the powerful triple bond of blood, of sealing, and of kinship through the temple.[40] In that setting Mother Smith expressed her great love for Brigham Young and indicated that if her health permitted she would join the Saints in the westward move, provided she could be brought back to Nauvoo after her death and buried alongside her family. Remember what she had lost—her son Alvin, probably because of medical malpractice; her husband, who had grown prematurely old after the Missouri depredations; her son Don Carlos, who died of tuberculosis at age twenty-six; and then the triple blow of three sons in thirty-some days, Joseph, Hyrum, and Samuel. Her entire family, except for the daughters and William, ended up giving their lives in the cause of Christ. Her health did not, after all, permit her to go west, but she did receive her wish of being buried near her husband and sons.

LEAVING NAUVOO

Perhaps the exodus and colonization of the West can be understood through some short glimpses. The question can be asked, if you're detached and looking at our history, Why would Brigham Young encourage people in the middle of winter to leave their city? Why not wait until spring, when there is green grass and flowing water? George A. Smith, one of the early apostles, summed it up later when someone asked a related question in a different context: "Why did you people come out to this forsaken place?" And Elder Smith replied, "Why, we came willingly because we had to."[41]

That sums it up. Brigham Young was aware that the mob spirit was seething. The mobs waited for a while after the death of the Prophet to see what the Mormons would do. The Mormons did nothing. The mobs waited after that to see what a trial of those involved at Carthage might bring to light. But no one was convicted of anything in those trials. After that it all started over again: house burnings, rape, threats, taking over property.

So the Saints used their resources as best they could; they prepared with wagons as best they could; they planned carefully; and they hurried to use the one-million-dollar temple—a sacrifice if ever there was one—hurried day and night to use its privileges after a private, quiet dedication. Temple blessings were given to many, who for that spiritual reason were able to survive in the wilderness.

Brigham Young recorded one important day at the temple. (We understand that the gospel applies to the whole of life, that "wholeness" is holiness. Here is an illustration of that concept.) That morning, workers arrived in rough clothing, prepared to clean the temple, to make it sparkle. Then they changed into clean clothing and had a prayer meeting. Then they partook of the sacrament. Finally they were ready to begin the temple ordinances.

It took all day. In the evening, they went upstairs to the attic floor of the Nauvoo Temple and had a feast of cakes and raisins; then they brought in Captain Pitt's band, rolled back the carpet, and held a wonderful dance in the temple.[42] Brigham Young once spoke about the need to "get so much of the spirit of truth that you . . . can shout aloud with all your might to the praise of God. . . . Then you can dance, and glorify God."[43]

On this particular occasion, they danced until 2:00 A.M., past curfew. Finally Brigham Young stood and said, "Brothers and sisters, this has been a beautiful day. There really isn't time for you to go home and slumber and then come back and open the temple at an early hour. So the brethren will go into this room and the sisters will go into this other room, and you will sleep on the floor, and then we will reopen the temple at 6 o'clock."[44] And that's exactly what they did.

Then they had to flee. Brigham Young organized the Saints like the ancient camp of Israel, with companies of one hundred and captains of each company. He organized them according to the same principles he had seen the Prophet introduce in Zion's Camp. He instructed them to plant crops systematically, as they went along, for those who would come after. And he himself became the vanguard leader of the company.

It was a heartbreaking journey for many. At the cemetery in Florence, Nebraska, where Winter Quarters once was, is a sculpture with a handcart and a man and a woman standing before a small, open grave. That sculpture tells the story. On a nearby plaque are six hundred names of those who died at Winter Quarters, perhaps a third of them infants. The Saints lost children; they lost wives or husbands; some of them lost everything. But many of them made it out of Winter Quarters and started the westward migration.

"THIS IS THE RIGHT PLACE"

Brigham Young was quite ill when they arrived in the Salt Lake Valley. Others arrived before him: Orson Pratt, Wilford Woodruff, and Erastus Snow. A beautiful sculpture, the "This Is the Place" monument, shows what happened as they arrived—they lifted their hats into the air and cried "Hosannah!" Since they were in the vanguard, Brigham hadn't yet told them that they were in the right place, but they knew it in their hearts. Not long thereafter, Brigham did say it: "This is the right place."

Others who followed said, "I'd just as soon go another thousand miles as stop here. Couldn't we go on to California?" Perhaps to settle a controversy, President Young sent out scouts in every direction, telling them to go a hundred miles in their assigned direction and then return and tell the leaders what they already knew—that they were in the right place. Well, they went as assigned, and they returned and reported what Brigham knew they would.

Later Brigham said, "You that have not passed through

the trials, and persecutions, and drivings, with this people, from the beginning, but have only read of them, or heard some of them related, may think how awful they were to endure, and wonder that the Saints survived them at all. The thought of it makes your hearts sink within you, your brains reel, and your bodies tremble, and you are ready to exclaim, 'I could not have endured it.' I have been in the heat of it, and I never felt better in all my life; I never felt the peace and power of the Almighty more copiously poured upon me than in the keenest part of our trials. They appeared nothing to me."[45]

On his first day in the valley, Brigham Young stood up on a wagon, the only place that had any elevation on the parched ground, took off his hat, and made a kind of proclamation. His audience was 147 people, a thousand miles from any sort of civilization. His speech demonstrates the splendid audacity of Brigham Young. He said, "*Attention, the whole world!* . . . We are here to lay the foundation of a great work to be accomplished in these mountains in the midst of the desert. Right here the great city will be built. . . . There the Temple will be erected. . . . We will gather the Church here, we will bring the poor here from all nations. We will continue our operations, and fill these valleys full of Mormons from the Gulf of California on the south, to Hudson's Bay on the north."[46]

Those were pretty bold words, and they were recorded by a man who was there. And it happened. Brigham lived to establish four hundred colonies in the West—four hundred! When he first knocked on the door of the United States government and said, "Let us become a state," he conceived the state to be all of what we now call Utah, all of Nevada to the Sierra Nevada Mountains, all of Idaho to the Canadian border, all of

Arizona, a section of New Mexico, and two-thirds of California.

Do you think Brigham Young had vision? And to fulfill that vision, he saw to it that we made the beginnings of settlements in all of these places, even into Canada and Mexico. He was seeking to help fulfill the instructions of the Prophet Joseph: to "get up into the mountains, where the Devil cannot dig us out."[47]

By the way, his notion of city planning was derived from the Prophet's vision. The Prophet preferred establishing several small cities instead of one large one. Not only that, but the Prophet anticipated the very thing we have witnessed in the American culture—the coldness and the crime of big cities. Big cities have a reputation of not reaching out in neighborly warmth and hospitality. They have no horizon to look at. They have cement and steel and paved roads.

Contrast the garden spots of certain Mormon villages, which are an extension of Brigham Young's vision. And of course he laid out the city the way we know it now, with wide streets and a grid set up foursquare by the compass. I was once on a call-in radio program in Boston, Massachusetts, and it became clear that I was a Mormon. One woman phoned in and asked, "Wasn't Brigham Young the leader of a lot of the people who settled the West?"

"Yes."

"Well, didn't he plan the city known as Salt Lake City?"

"Yes."

Long pause. "Do you think we could get Brigham Young to come to Boston?" It's impossible to figure north and south in Boston. Not so with the cities laid out by Brigham Young.

After making his speech from the wagon upon entering the valley, Brigham Young took some of the Brethren and climbed the peak they later called Ensign Peak. There is still some controversy as to whether on that day they raised an American flag or a flag symbolic both of the state they planned to form and the Council of Fifty. The Council of Fifty, which the Prophet Joseph had organized, was a body designed to extend the power of constitutional government worldwide; it was also the action committee that helped a great deal with organizing and extending the exodus.

Whatever else they did on Ensign Peak, we know two things for sure: First, we know that Brigham Young later gave the temple blessings on that mountaintop to a man named Addison Pratt, who had been called from Nauvoo on a mission to the South Seas and served there for at least four years; when he arrived home there was no home, for the Saints had gone to the West. He went west, and Brigham said, "You shall be denied nothing," and gave him his temple blessings.[48] Second, we know that from that place the Brethren conceived again the symbolism of the gospel going to the world, as we sing in our hymn, "High on the mountaintop a banner is unfurled. Ye nations, now look up; it waves to all the world."[49]

One final comment about colonizing, summed up in three sentences Brigham Young said to a man named Helaman Pratt. President Young called Pratt in and said to him, "Brother Pratt, we are calling you to colonize in Mexico. You will be released when you die. God bless you."[50] Like so many, he had been mobbed out of two or three homes in the East and had begun to build an adobe house in the valley. But he obeyed and went, he stayed, and he died in Mexico. Out of that Nazareth of the Mexican colonies have come great Saints—leaders with the names of Romney and of Eyring and others like them. It was a soul-making colony.

When Brigham Young made such callings, the people

responded and few looked back. Once a man came to conference but wouldn't come into the building. He felt ashamed of his bare feet and his unkempt clothing. A friend came out after the meeting ended and said, "Why weren't you there? Brother Brigham said we need more ox teams to bring granite for the temple."

"Did he?" answered the man with the bare feet. "Well, I'll go," and he went with his team to Little Cottonwood Canyon.[51] Too poor to dress well enough to attend the meeting, but so rich in spirit that he would obey what was said there. That's the spirit of colonization.

When Harvard psychologist David McClelland visited Utah, I took him to the "This Is the Place" monument. We looked out over the valley and the beautiful homes and trees. I said, "You know why the Mormons came here to this valley?"

He said, "No."

And I said, "Well, according to George A. Smith we came here voluntarily because we had to."[52]

He smiled and said, "No, that's not the explanation. I'm a psychologist. I'm an expert on motivation. More than the desire for survival is here. I have been in places in the world where people have been surviving for four thousand years, and all they have built so far is a tent. Something more than that accounts for this civilization."

"THEY HAVE BEEN SHOT DOWN AS DOGS"

Some have not understood that the Saints in the Great Basin were seeking to establish an independent community, and they stayed independent as long as they could. All of life for them was surrounded by the restored gospel. It applied to government; it applied to the economy; it applied to home industry; and of course it applied to what we ordinarily associate with spiritual things. That independent spirit made us suspect to those in the East, and we had to demonstrate for many years that one can still be a loyal, dedicated American citizen and yet be, as it were, a nation within a nation.

As governor of the territory, Brigham Young faced some significant challenges. One had to do with the Native Americans who lived on the land. Most people are familiar with his famous statement, "It is much cheaper to feed the Indians than to fight them."[53] He actually said much more: "I am convinced it is cheaper to feed them than fight them. They have been shot down as dogs all over this country and the only man who has behaved in a Christian manner toward them was William Penn, and we are going to treat them as they are, children of God."[54] There were exceptions, and there were glitches, but Brigham Young, contrary to all expectation, was the major force in winning the confidence of the Indians. And through Jacob Hamblin, Brigham Young often helped them settle serious disputes among themselves. Governor Young's policies were wise enough and visionary enough that they led to Indian treaties that have lasted to this day.

Another of his challenges: I take you to a celebration that occurred in 1857 at the top of Big Cottonwood Canyon in a place known as Brighton. Brighton is the location of a magnificent, pristine bowl, as beautiful in its own way as the Alps. With wagons and many of their own cattle, the Saints went up the canyon to celebrate the 24th of July, the tenth anniversary of the Saints' arrival in the valley. At sunset on July 23, with American flags posted on peaks and on high pine trees, Brigham Young addressed the gathering, rejoicing that they had enjoyed comparative peace for ten years and "recounting the mercies of God to his people."[55] In the midst of the festivities, as in a movie, a lathered horse rode up bearing Porter Rockwell, who brought unhappy news to Brigham Young. The message: Johnston's Army was on the way west to put down the Mormons.

Brigham Young chose to let the Saints continue their celebration until nightfall, unburdened by the bad news. Shortly thereafter, Brigham Young called the Saints to a meeting on Temple Square. There he unloaded before the Saints, pouring out his heart. He stormed, he ranted, he raved. He said, "Over and over I have given houses I myself have built to unlawful acts. Now I have been among you to come out to a place nobody else wanted, and we have been peaceful citizens and now an army is coming west." Then he said at the end of the meeting, "Please come back this afternoon."[56]

In the afternoon, he stood up and, in effect, said, "Brothers and sisters, this morning Brigham Young addressed you. This afternoon, Brigham Young, the prophet of the Lord, will speak." In that speech he proposed what would be called the "scorched earth policy," and he asked for a vote. "Rather than submit, and rather than fight, will you burn your houses, will you bury the foundation of the temple, and will you go with me to another country, if necessary to Mexico? All in favor."[57] I don't know if anybody counted hands, but the great majority sustained their president.

Before destroying what they had built, however, they decided to try to stop the onward march of the army, which had 2,500 armed soldiers and 2,500 additional men helping with supplies. How do you stop such a march? You break their supply source and you stop their supply lines. Up at Fort Bridger, in Wyoming, the very people who had built the fort and struggled to live there asked for permission to burn their own homes and the fort. They left no supplies, no hay, nothing to eat, and moved west with all their livestock. Mother Nature helped with early snows. Eventually representatives of the army went to Salt Lake City carrying, in essence, a flag of truce. They met with Brigham Young and said, "Help us or we die."

Brigham Young agreed, with terms. You may come into our valley, he said, and then you must travel down such and such a street. You will then march south. You will not look to the right or the left or say obscene things about us or our women, and you will camp at a place we designate twenty miles to the south (present-day Camp Williams). Do that, and then we'll talk further. The army did as instructed, and the crisis was overcome. These events may have fulfilled, at least in part, what Brigham had seen in the night skies above New York.

Meanwhile, Thomas L. Kane, great friend to the Mormons, was able to convince President Buchanan that it was all a terrible mistake, and thus "Buchanan's folly" (or blunder)—as it is called in the annals—came to an end.

FIVE GREAT LEGACIES

Leonard Arrington, who wrote the classic *Brigham Young: American Moses,* observed in the epilogue,[58] "I can see five great legacies from Brigham Young." He said he, number one, created a unique ethnic society, a self-sufficient egalitarian commonwealth of Saints. That had been tried before in this country, but it had always failed. It did not fail under Brigham Young, and it hasn't failed yet. We are not yet a theocratic republic, but someday when He leads whose right it is to lead, namely a benevolent dictator named Jesus Christ, it will be a theocratic republic. It can be said truly that Brigham Young was thwarted in his vision and in his ability to have it established, and that we had to make compromises. But we did so with our eyes open, and we have continued to have the hope of an eventual fulfillment of a totally Christlike society. As a matter of fact, in his directions as to what should happen at his funeral Brigham indicated that if he died after we had returned to Jackson County, a future location of Zion, that's where he wanted to be buried.[59]

And he built all that he built from scratch. Of course, he would say, "I didn't do it, the Lord did," but he was the instrument.

Number two, he demonstrated the power of the covenant in cooperative ways—the covenant in Missouri, the covenant in Nauvoo. When the Saints left Nauvoo, they left a message in the temple for those who had to be temporarily left behind, a statement that said simply, "The Lord has beheld our sacrifice. Come after us." They promised they would help.[60] He introduced a powerful mechanism for migration called the Perpetual Emigration Fund, and it worked. Those people had to become, all of them, good Samaritans. They had to turn their cheek, they had to face the bitter wind, they had to walk the second thousand miles, and they had to see to it that even the blind and the maimed and the people with only one leg and the children and the aged could make it. And they did.

Third, said Arrington, he established the necessity of working out one's salvation. That includes making the earth a Garden of Eden. I once read a wonderful synopsis of a Brigham Young sermon where the author indicated that Brigham Young spoke about the Holy Trinity and how to get their crops in before spring. Others would say you cannot combine the spiritual and temporal that way. But Brigham combined them, as had Joseph before him, and he did it successfully. He stood up when the handcart crisis on the plains became clear and essentially said, "My sermon this morning is go and save the saints on the plains. Demonstrate your faith with your works."[61] It wasn't long before 250 teams were on their way.

There were four young men in the advance party, young men with courage and faith, and maybe a little desire for adventure. They went as requested, and they found a handcart company dug in, foundered, and literally without hope on the other side of an ice-filled river. The company was too weak and too emotionally debilitated even to attempt the river crossing. These four young men knew they had to cross the river and pick up each person individually and then cross the river again in water waist deep, and take the ice that hit them in the current, and then go back and back. They carried all of that handcart company across the river, so weakening themselves that their health was destroyed, and all died early in life. When Brigham Young heard of this act he wept and said, "They will be saved in the Celestial Kingdom of our God."[62] He preached that the temporal and the spiritual can combine.

Fourth, Arrington shows, he taught (as did Joseph Smith) that "if there is any truth anywhere in the world, it is part of Mormonism."[63] He even said once, "If there is truth in hell, then it is part of Mormonism."[64] He rejected, as we must, narrow sectarianism; he rejected the notion that we must withdraw from the world.[65] We must, instead, participate. He rejected the notion that the devil has a kingdom all his own that's appealing. On the contrary, he has nothing except distorted and twisted truth.

Fifth, Arrington said, is the legacy of Brigham's powerful

personality, which is still our heritage. We have spoken of that throughout this chapter.

I want to add three more legacies. First, he left us a temple legacy. We've already sketched the Nauvoo story. In addition, before his death he saw to it that four temples were undertaken in Utah. The first three—St. George, Manti, Logan—were all in operation before that great temple in Salt Lake, which was forty years building and which he did not live to see completed. He understood that there is a comprehensive plan of salvation, which is magnificently presented and combined in the covenant setting of the house of the Lord. He taught that the house of the Lord is full of divine glory and that every attribute and power we have as human beings can be enhanced and improved and glorified through temple service. This is the combination of things down-to-earth and sublimely spiritual.

It says in the New Testament, "Blessed are the meek: for they shall inherit . . ."—what? The beatific vision in the ethereal, mystical future? Is that what it says? No. It says, "Blessed are the meek: for they shall inherit the earth" (Matthew 5:5). Who wants this earth, unless it can be glorified as are those who inherit it? Brigham Young's teaching was that it will be. This is what I would call Divine Integration. The gospel of Christ is not an escapist religion. Brigham Young was a temple builder and he was constantly participating in the work. Great leadership came from that central temple, and look how the harvest is expanding in our generation. He may be responsible for a statement I've heard, which says that the day will come—perhaps in the Millennium—when you can go up in the tower of one temple and on the horizon in each direction see the tower of another.[66]

Second, he left a patriarchal legacy. He was, in fact, married to twenty remarkable women. He had children by sixteen of them. I have spoken of his family prayers. I have spoken of the spirit in his house. Acting as a guide, I once brought to the Lion House a woman from New England, cultured and refined, who had been taught, as had most of the world, that we had here a barbaric practice, a subversive and evil practice. Polygamy, along with slavery, was one of the twin relics, it was said, of barbarism. We walked through the Lion House and then the Beehive House and she said, "I know the difference between a brothel and a temple, and I will never say anything against Brigham Young again."

Susa Young Gates, one of his daughters, used to say that he taught all of his family to seek spiritual growth exactly as he had. Once she asked her father how she could gain a testimony. He said, "There is only one way, daughter, that you can get a testimony, and that is the way your mother got hers and the way I got mine. Go down on your knees in humble prayer, and God will answer your petition."[67] Brigham Young taught that the only ultimate kingdom of God is a family kingdom. The Church is simply an extended family. The Church is most close to what Jesus Christ wants of it when it is most like a family. It is not an instrument to replace the family. It is an instrument to glorify and extend and hallow the family. Brigham Young saw that clearly, and he lived it.

Brigham saw in a vision or a dream at Winter Quarters that our Father "organized" the human family before we came into mortality. But they "are all disorganized and in great confusion."[68] Our Father is intent on a family reunion, and ultimately all of us will have the opportunity of attending that reunion, if we will.

"THE GREATEST DISCOURSE I HAVE HEARD"

A final legacy of Brigham Young is his doctrinal legacy. Brigham Young lived thirty years in the Salt Lake Valley and preached almost every Sunday in the Tabernacle, with stenographers taking notes. All together, he gave eight hundred recorded sermons. If you could choose one, out of all those, what would be the most powerful, outstanding sermon? Wilford Woodruff gave his opinion. He wrote in his journal, "I went to the Tabernacle today. Brigham Young spoke on the text, 'And I, if I be lifted up from the earth, will draw all men unto me'" (John 12:32). Then said Wilford Woodruff, "I considered it, in some respects, the greatest discourse I have heard in this dispensation."[69]

What did Brigham Young say in that address? Three glimpses. First, he said that Jesus the Christ descended below all things, literally, according to the flesh, so that no case in human history, no person, no life, however tragic or sin-stained, would fall outside of his compassion or his power. He said, second, that the glorified nature of Jesus Christ is sanctifying for us, even when all we do is think of him. Brigham taught over and over that we should think of him, control our minds, and we will then be able to control our passions, and we will then let our spirits have ascendancy in our lives. If we do, we will inherit eternal life.[70] Therefore, for Brigham Young the tiniest details of one's life can be holy.

Third, he did away with the classical doctrine of original sin. He had learned that from the Prophet. What? Didn't Adam transgress? Yes, he did. But did he sin? Brigham Young taught a truth that's deep in the hidden past of Judaism that there was something divine in Adam and in Eve and that they didn't really do much falling. Knowingly and with insight, they partook of the forbidden fruit to make possible the experience of mortality. If you want to say that brought about terrible consequences and we suffer them, it is true. But if you want to say that we are guilty of some terrible original sin simply by being born, it is *not* true. The good news is that they, both of them, were enlightened, and we can inherit through their gift the fullness of redemption and a return to the very image of God.

As a matter of fact, Brigham Young taught that most of the falling of the human race really began with Cain. It was only after the rebellion of those who said, "I prefer to serve Master Mahan to serving the living God," that "men began from that time forth to be carnal, sensual, and devilish" (Moses 5:13). So Brigham Young taught that human nature can be righteous in nature, that the spirit is directly in tune with the power of God, and that the body, though it can be physically perverted, is not intrinsically evil. Therefore, Brigham Young believed that you cannot sin wholeheartedly. You still have the light and the candle of the Lord, even in your worst moments.[71]

Brigham Young taught that the power of the Atonement of Jesus Christ is a power arising from eternal principles and that these principles are binding throughout the eternities. He taught that time is a segment of eternity, that we are now in eternity. There have been earlier earth systems; there will be other earth systems after us, all with Father, Eldest Son, the necessary opposition, and redemption. He taught that the only way to become like our Heavenly Parents is to bring them into all of life, every level, every aspect. And he taught that evil is simply inverted good, or good made an evil use of.[72]

When Jedediah Grant was asked what he thought of Brigham Young, he had an interesting metaphor that when the world at large credits a man, they're very preoccupied with the handle or the sheath, looking for handles that are ornate, beautiful, refined, jeweled. On the other hand, "Brigham is . . . between a Roman cutlass and a beef butcher knife, the thing . . . that will save your life or carve your dinner every bit as well, though the handpiece is buck horn and the case a hogskin. . . . You, that judge men by the handle and sheath, how can I make you know a good *blade*?"[73] He was. He died saying, "Joseph, Joseph, Joseph!"[74] and Brigham's name, like Joseph's, will continue to be known for good and for evil.

3

JOHN TAYLOR

John Taylor, third President of the Church, was the only president not born in America. He was born in the rolling green hills of central England, near Westmoreland, the very place that William Wordsworth and other British poets have celebrated for its beauty and its pristine, spiritual overtones. He was born in 1808 to religiously zealous parents. Both belonged to the Church of England and brought him up with that sensitivity. In fact, when John was christened, his godmother and godfather said, in effect, that they wanted this boy to reject the corruptions of the world and become a true servant of God.[1]

He was surrounded by Anglicans. But he was troubled by what he called the "sterile rationalism" of the Anglican tradition. It was intellectual, but it seemed thin, and he found greater depth in the Methodist outlook, which was fervent and concerned with service and love. John Taylor had a great respect for the Wesley brothers, the founders of Methodism, throughout his life. It is interesting that the Prophet Joseph Smith was slightly more inclined to Methodism than to any other of the multiple sects in his home area; and so was Brigham Young.

In boyhood, young John had two experiences that spiritually "bent the twig." I've noticed, having studied Church history, how many times important men and women (important in the sense that they became leaders) had vital spiritual experiences, not just in their youth but in childhood. I know of three who had such experiences by the age of nine. John Taylor can be added to the list. He said that as a mere boy it was as if he could hear "sweet, soft, melodious, music," as if, he said, the very angels were singing.[2] He didn't know what to make of that. Later, but not much later, he saw in a vision an angel with a horn or trumpet, as if announcing a great message.[3] This he later felt was prescient of the new dispensation and its introduction by angelic administration, specifically by Moroni.

FROM SEEKING TO CONVERSION

In England, early in his teens, he had a fairly adequate education. Because he already had demonstrated skill with words, both in writing and in speaking, he was appointed as a kind of lay preacher to preach and exhort in the villages he traveled through. Even in that process he felt a certain lack in his understanding. He was, early on, searching for something. "You must yet go to America and preach the gospel," the Spirit told him.[4] Later, in Canada, he married the fair and comely Leonora Cannon. In Toronto he helped organize a group of people who could be called seekers. They were somewhat dissatisfied with their own religious traditions and were meeting to try to discover what genuine New Testament Christianity was like—and to see if there was any available faith that represented that outlook.

At the same time, the Lord was moving events in Kirtland, Ohio, where a man named Parley P. Pratt lived. A convert to the Church, Parley was very ill, as was his wife. She was so sick that some said she would not recover. In addition, she had struggled with the great disappointment of wanting children and not having them. Into that home came Heber C. Kimball, the man who may have been most like the Prophet Joseph Smith in prophetic outlook, in personality, and in spirit. He said, "Brother Parley, thy wife shall be healed from this hour, and shall bear a son. . . . Arise, therefore, and go forth in the ministry, nothing doubting. . . . Thou shalt go to Upper Canada, even to the city of Toronto, the capital, and there thou shalt find a people prepared for the gospel, and they shall receive thee, and thou shalt organize the Church among them, and it shall spread thence into the regions round about, and many shall be brought to a knowledge of the truth, and shall be filled with joy."[5]

Brother Parley responded to the call, went to Canada, and in a series of interesting circumstances met John Taylor. His first reception was ice cold. John Taylor felt Mormonism was emotionalism and a cock-and-bull story, as he said to his wife.[6] She replied, "He may be a man of God."[7] That didn't impress John, until she reported a couple of days later that Parley P. Pratt had administered to a blind woman and restored her eyesight. At first he didn't believe it. She said, "Well, you might come to the meeting tonight and see for yourself." He went, found the report to be true, and then started taking notes on Parley P. Pratt. He wrote down six consecutive sermons, scoured over them for three weeks, and then he and his wife presented themselves for baptism.[8]

Soon, in the spirit of gathering, they went to Kirtland. Many of the Saints in Kirtland were faltering. The

Kirtland Safety Society, the bank of the Saints, turned out to be unsafe, and people even in high places were blaming the Prophet Joseph. Among their number was Parley P. Pratt. One day John Taylor attended a meeting in the Kirtland Temple and heard Parley P. Pratt rail against the Prophet. Exhibiting the strength of his character, John Taylor—the recent convert, and not only that, but the recent convert of Parley P. Pratt—stood up and said, "Brother Parley, if the work was true six months ago, it is true today; if Joseph Smith was then a prophet, he is now a prophet."[9] Parley P. Pratt made his amends with the Prophet and resumed his role as one of our sterling missionaries and leaders. And in the providences of the Lord, within two years, John Taylor, the neophyte, demonstrated his worth, served in various assignments, including distant missions, and was called to the Quorum of the Twelve.

He had some premonition that this would happen but doubted it, suspecting that it was a prompting from the adversary.[10] Two common elements often show up in the important calls that come to our modern leaders, both men and women. One is that often they have had some impression or hint of the calling, but then attempt to put it aside. "No, it cannot be—I'm not prepared, I'm not worthy," and so forth. The other factor is that all have known buffeting from the regions of darkness.

John Taylor was called. Meanwhile, he continued his missionary labors for a total of eight years. He was called abroad to France, then to England. He also served for a time in the eastern states. He was separated from his wife for that duration, with very few visits home. During this time, he became known as the "champion of liberty." He was never one to avoid confrontation. He welcomed it, encouraged it; and he was a debater of the first rank. When faced with the terrible stories from other sects that circulated about the Mormons, he would appeal to them from the New Testament: Where are your apostles? Where are the spiritual gifts? Where are the faith evidences? Where is the process of laying on of hands for the gift of the Holy Ghost? Where is your authority?

Sooner or later most of his adversaries would return to defamation of character: Your church was started by this terrible man named Joseph Smith, who is an evil person. And John Taylor would reply from firsthand testimony: "I testify that I was acquainted with Joseph Smith for years. I have traveled with him; I have been with him in private and in public; I have associated with him in councils of all kinds; I have listened hundreds of times to his public teachings, and his advice to his friends and associates of a more private nature. I have been at his house and seen his deportment in his family. . . . I have seen him, then, under these various circumstances, and I testify before God, angels and men, that he was a good, honorable, virtuous man—that his doctrines were good, scriptural and wholesome—that his precepts were such as became a man of God—that his private and public character was unimpeachable—and that he lived and died as a man of God and a gentleman."[11] At the end of such encounters, someone, often more than one, typically came forward to request baptism.

"THE KINGDOM OF GOD OR NOTHING"

In his youth, as was common in England, John carried a snuff box of silver—a beautifully decorated snuff box. He also was among those who, typical in England, would go to grog shops, where alcoholic beverages were served. In the spirit of self-discipline he said to himself one day, in essence, "Who is in control of this, me or it? I will not be subject to snuff. I will not be subject to grog." In that same mode, he said, as a kind of constitution of his life, "I . . . will not be a slave." He meant that in all senses of the word *slavery*. He even said, in bold words, "I would not be a slave to God! I'd be His servant, friend, His son. I'd go at His behest; but would not be His slave. I'd rather be extinct than be a slave."[12] He championed self-control and free will and upheld the message of Christ that we are to leave behind us all forms of ungodliness.

Early on in his acquaintance with Joseph Smith, the Prophet counseled him, "Brother Taylor, never arise in the morning or retire at night without dedicating yourself unto God and asking his blessings upon you through the day or night, . . . and the Lord God will hear and answer your prayers; and don't let any circumstances prevent it."[13]

Another quotation from Joseph to him was this: "You have received the Holy Spirit. If you heed its teachings, the same will become within you a constant stream of revelation."[14]

Here are three other statements that reflect John Taylor's commitment:

"I prefer a faded coat to a faded reputation; and I do not propose to ask for accommodations that I am not prepared to meet."[15]

Another: "If a thing is done well, no one will ask how long it took to do it, but who did it."[16] He was a talented and trained woodcarver and turner, who had also grown up knowing the agrarian life, plowing and planting and harvesting.

And then he wrote in a poem the motto of his life, "The Kingdom of God or Nothing." Pictures of President Taylor once adorned many chapels, and that was the inscription accompanying the portraits.[17]

FULFILLED PROPHECY

John Taylor was one of those designated by prophecy to meet on a certain date in Far West, Missouri, at the place where the cornerstone had been laid for the building of a temple (see D&C 118:5). This dedication was to be performed, and he and others of the Twelve were to go to Britain on missions. Enemies said in public and in private that they would see to it that the prophecy would never be fulfilled. John Taylor and his companions resolved that it would. They traveled in the middle of the night when no one was around, went to the exact spot designated, performed the specified ordinations, sang a hymn, and then left for England. Thus, their enemies were foiled.[18]

I've heard some say that Mormons are strange people because they make a prediction and then go out and do it—and say it's a fulfilled prophecy. There are cases in which that applies perfectly. But the fact remains that there are hundreds of prophetic predictions in our literature that are beyond the power of any human being to fulfill. When they were or are fulfilled it is clear they are indeed prophecies inspired by God.

"HE WILL WRENCH YOUR VERY HEART STRINGS"

In three different talks, John Taylor quoted the Prophet as saying to the Twelve, "God will feel after you, and He will take hold of you and wrench your very heart strings, and if you cannot stand it you will not be fit for an inheritance in the Celestial Kingdom of God."[19]

In one of those declarations, the Prophet added that the Lord chose the very thing Abraham was the least willing to give up, namely his son. And "if God had known any other way whereby he could have touched Abraham's feelings more acutely and more keenly he would have done so. . . . But he had faith in God, and he fulfilled the thing that was required of him"[20]—and we must do the same.

Such a wrench came to John Taylor when he was asked to make known to his wife, Leonora, the principle of plural families. Notice how I have phrased it. The idea was, if I may put it in a single phrase, a form of divine eugenics. The purpose was to prepare the way for choice spirits to be born into a life of service and sacrifice and to give a divine format to family life. These children could then rise up and become gatherers of the gatherers in the modern dispensation of the fulness of times.

It wasn't a principle designed for ease or self-indulgence, on the part of either the man or woman. Speaking of how the principle first struck him, John Taylor said, "I had always entertained strict ideas of virtue, and I felt as a married man that this was to me . . . an appalling thing to do. The idea of going and asking a young lady to be married to me when I had already a wife! It was a thing calculated to stir up feelings from the innermost depths of the human soul. I had always entertained the strictest regard of chastity. I had never in my life seen the time when I have known of a man deceiving a woman. . . . I have always looked upon such a thing as infamous, and upon such a man as a villain. Hence, with the feelings I had entertained, nothing but a knowledge of God, and the revelations of God, and the truth of them, could have induced me to embrace such a principle as this."[21]

He went on to describe the struggle and how all of the Twelve postponed taking action. But the day came and with it, the response of Leonora. Samuel Taylor, who is gifted as a novelist and a creative writer (and who may therefore sometimes fictionalize), wrote a book on his famous predecessor. Samuel Taylor's account claims that when Leonora heard of the doctrine, she brought her hand down so firmly that she broke a cup or saucer, and the glass cut her finger so deeply that it had to be amputated. But in time those two as one began to honor and live this principle. Sometime later they were summoned by the Prophet himself into a sacred place—we did not yet have a completed temple—and were given, together, the highest blessings it is possible to receive on this earth.

But before that sealing, Wilford Woodruff's journal tells us that the Prophet required of John Taylor what he had also required of Heber C. Kimball. He actually asked John to let Leonora be sealed to the Prophet. John Taylor agonized over that. John Taylor, the man with a spine like steel, went to the Prophet and said, "Joseph, if *the Lord* wants Leonora, then the Lord can have her. If *you* are asking, NO!" The Prophet smiled, wept a little, embraced him, and said, "I just needed to know where you stood, John."[22] That was a terrible way to test a person (but so was it a terrible test for Abraham). Apparently, the Prophet needed to know, and so did the Lord, that the first thing in the lives of Leonora and John Taylor were God and his Christ.

They embodied the presupposition of any marriage performed in the temples of this Church. We never make a commitment to each other for time and eternity until after we have made an unconditional covenant with God and his Christ.

"TAKE CARE OF THE LITTLE ROOTS"

In due time seven good wives bore John Taylor children. Because of missions and travel and other responsibilities, he had to cherish every moment he was at home. One of his children said, "I have never heard him enter into any argument with any of his family; I have never heard him and my mother contend or disagree." He then added one qualifying phrase, "in the presence of the children."[23]

When someone in the family did something that hurt others in any way, they held a family council. The person involved explained what had occurred and why, and then the family agreed on what he was to do. Always the first procedure was to shake hands with each of them and say, "I'm sorry." Sometimes some kind of restitution would be required. John Taylor told his family over and over that there was no office in the Church greater than that of teacher, and he taught them that the most important teaching is done at home.

John had an experience similar to one we read about elsewhere concerning the home of Joseph Smith. He had home teachers. How would you like to be a young man assigned to visit the President of the Church and say, "I'm your home teacher"? When the home teachers arrived, John Taylor invited them in, then sat down and said, "We're awaiting your instructions."

The young visitor sat down as well and said, "I don't have instructions, I have questions. Brother Taylor, do you have family prayer?"

"Yes, I do."

"Do you have secret prayer?"

"Yes, I do."

"Do you have any trouble with your neighbors?"

"Not that I know of."

"Do you attend ward meetings?"

"Yes, I do."

"Are you in harmony with the authorities of the Church?"

"Yes, I am." When the young man was finished, President Taylor said, "God bless you. Continue in that spirit and you will be a great home teacher."[24]

In that era they paid tithing "in kind." A child of John Taylor recalls, "When gathering the fruit in the fall, father would come and inspect the baskets and selecting the largest and best fruit would say: 'Take the tithing out of this and be sure to pay it in full.'"[25]

"Take care of the little roots," he taught his family, "and the large ones will take care of themselves."[26] The first thing he did after the dedication of the Logan Temple was to call in two sons who had recently chosen their brides and perform, personally, their sealings in the Logan Temple.

WIDE-RANGING SERVICE

So far I've left out three important facets of John Taylor's Church service. He translated the Book of Mormon into both French and German, which were then printed in one volume, with alternating pages in French and German. He became editor, and that meant also a writer, of the *Times and Seasons,* which was the periodical newspaper of Nauvoo, from 1842 to 1846, and the *Nauvoo Neighbor,* another newspaper, from 1843 to 1846. His greatest frustration in that period, I believe, was that the papers weren't properly distributed. The Church had enemies who were so skillful that even when John's staff put the papers in the post office for delivery by name and address, somebody intercepted them and threw them in the Mississippi.

A comment about the *Times and Seasons*—which is itself a symbolic title for a newspaper. Having read most of the editions that John Taylor edited or wrote, I can see emerging over and over his threefold admiration of Nauvoo. First was his testimony of restored truth. He was constantly writing that the restoration of the gospel was occurring in Nauvoo and that it was where modern revelation was being poured down. Second, he described in a magnificent ode the brilliance of the converts, often from Britain, who knew how to hedge and build gardens and plant trees and so on. To him, the city was like the Garden of Eden. Third, related to the second, he stressed the beauty of the place. When "Nauvoo the Beautiful" became a popular phrase describing the city, it was no misnomer. John Taylor was convinced that the kingdom of God and Zion ought to be, and would be, nothing less than beautiful—and that the beauty of holiness would prevail, written on the bells of the horses and the doorknobs, and in the faces of the people themselves, who were there in purity.

John Taylor also had a key role in the exodus from Missouri. You know that Brigham Young and Heber C. Kimball were the main figures in bringing the refugees, thousands of them, out of Missouri. It's not as well known that President Taylor was instrumental in placating those who already lived in Quincy, Illinois, the destination of the Missouri Saints. Thanks in part to his skillful intervention—both in writing and speaking—the Saints had a warm and compassionate reception when they arrived in Quincy.

During this time when the Church was in exile, he asked again and again the questions: How could this happen in America? How could this happen in a land where religious rights are guaranteed? How could we be opposed both by officialdom in religion and officialdom in government?

He wrote, "If ever the latter-day glory, which we have so often spoken of, sang of, prayed about, and about which the ancient prophets have prophesied, is brought about, it will be done by this people; for there is not another people under the heavens that will listen to it."[27] That statement was prophetic.

JOSEPH'S LAST DAYS

John Taylor was an active participant in the last days of the Prophet Joseph. He was invited to the meeting that has come to be known in our annals as "the last-charge meeting," held on the upper level of the brick store in Nauvoo. Nine of the Twelve (the other three were already somewhat disaffected and never came back), along with their wives, gathered under the Prophet's instruction. In the morning the Prophet conferred sacred ordinances, confirming and reconfirming what they had earlier received; and then in the afternoon he spoke for nearly three hours. Here is an echo of what John Taylor experienced that day and in some prior councils: "Many a time have I listened to the voice of our beloved prophet, while in council; . . . his eyes sparkling with animation, and his soul fired with the inspiration of the spirit of the living God. It was a theme that caused the bosoms of all who were privileged to listen, to thrill with delight; intimately connected with this were themes upon which prophets, patriarchs, priests, and kings dwelt with pleasure and delight; of them they prophesied, sung, wrote, spoke, and desired to see, but died without the sight. My spirit glows with sacred fire while I reflect upon these scenes." And then he adds, "And I say, O Lord, hasten the day! Let Zion be established! Let the mountain of the Lord's house be established on the tops of the mountains!"[28]

In the Prophet's own discourses we find similar language about how all things are to be brought together in the last days, noting that many died without the sight, and testifying that we will have the privilege of participating and rolling on the kingdom. He used the phrase, "Generations yet unborn will dwell with peculiar delight upon the scenes that we have passed through."[29]

Joseph Smith, John Taylor said further, "introduced principles which strike at the root of the corrupt systems of men. This necessarily comes in contact with their prepossessions, prejudices, and interests, and as they cannot overturn his principles, they attack his character. And that is one reason why we have so many books written against his character without touching his principles, and also why we meet with so much opposition. But truth, eternal truth, is invulnerable. It cannot be destroyed, but like the throne of Jehovah, it will outride all the storms of men, and live for ever."[30]

Of all the men up to that time who held leadership positions, John Taylor was among the most cultured, the most educated, and the most traveled, which gives greater weight to his comment on the Prophet: "God chose this young man. He was ignorant of letters as the world has it, but the most profoundly learned and intelligent man that I ever met in my life, and I have traveled hundreds of thousands of miles, been on different continents and mingled among all classes and creeds of people, yet I have never met a man so intelligent as he was. And where did he get his intelligence from? Not from books, not from the logic or science or philosophy of the day, but he obtained it through the revelation of God made known to him through the medium of the everlasting Gospel."[31]

TRAGEDY AT CARTHAGE JAIL

It's common knowledge that John Taylor was present at Carthage Jail. But that wasn't always the plan.

The Church had more than its share of enemies. One was John C. Bennett, a politician and candidate for the presidency of the United States, who engaged in a campaign of disparagement against the Church, traveling around lecturing and slandering every element in Nauvoo. In response, some of the Brethren encouraged Joseph Smith to put his own name forward as a candidate for the president of the United States. Then, they said, we will go out by the hundreds, and while we are stumping for your election we will preach the gospel, maybe get a hearing, and perhaps be able to counter the effects of John C. Bennett's words. The Prophet wasn't at first enthused about the proposal, but finally he agreed to it.

Initially he planned to send John Taylor east, along with some others—obviously because of his gifts in persuasion, teaching, speaking, and writing. But as events played themselves out he did not send John Taylor. He sent all of the Twelve except John Taylor and Willard Richards. There were crucial reasons for doing so. In the case of Richards, it was that he had been working night and day to keep accurate records to bring up to date the history of the Church. They knew they were making history. They knew from the days the Twelve were organized they must keep records. The Prophet prophesied that their journals would be "sought after as history and scripture"[32] and that they must not be dilatory in this duty. Willard Richards had the historian's charge and was the Prophet's right-hand man in much else besides.

And what about John Taylor? He was the editor and publisher of the *Times and Seasons.* He had to stay and publish a paper. The others were sent away.

While the city council went with Joseph and Hyrum partway to Carthage, two of the Twelve, namely Willard Richards and John Taylor, went all the way. As John Taylor, the champion of liberty and constitutional rights, observed the noose tightening and the illegal procedures that went on, he said, "Brother Joseph, if you will permit it, and say the word, I will have you out of this prison in five hours, if the jail has to come down to do it!"[33] His intention was to go to Nauvoo and return with a company of men. But the Prophet refused. And so he stayed.

John Taylor was asked to sing that last afternoon, in his magnificent baritone, "A Poor Wayfaring Man of Grief." Recent research tells us the words were the same but the melody was somewhat different. Still it is poignant and plaintive and prophetic; and when he'd finished the first time Hyrum asked him to do it again. "I don't feel like singing," he said. His own record says, "Our spirits were all depressed."[34] But Hyrum said, "Oh, never mind; commence singing, and you will get the spirit of it."[35] He started and then the shooting began.

John Taylor left us a detailed description of what happened next. He said that when they saw the mobbers coming and heard the commotion, Hyrum and Brother Richards both instantly went up against the door and leaned against it. The door had a latch that was comparatively useless. While they were standing there, they heard first one shot and then another; one of those shots hit the left side of Hyrum's nose, and he fell backwards saying, "I am a dead man."

Under those circumstances, what was left for John Taylor to do? He had a large, strong hickory stick, left there by a Brother Markham. This stick was called a "rascal-beater."[36] When the muskets were thrust through the now partially opened door, Taylor pushed the barrels up with his stick so that the balls would be deflected toward the ceiling. He recalled, "Streams of fire as thick as my arm passed by me as these men fired, and, unarmed as we were, it looked like certain death. I remember feeling as though my time had come, but I do not know when, in any critical position, I was more calm, or unruffled, energetic and acted with more promptness and decision. It certainly was far from pleasant to be so near the muzzles of those firearms as they belched forth their liquid flames and deadly balls. While I was engaged in parrying the guns, Brother Joseph said, 'That's right, Brother Taylor, parry them off as well as you can.' These were the last words I ever heard him speak on earth."[37]

John Taylor went to the window and, in an effort to get out or having lost his balance, felt himself suddenly catapulted back into the room. Apparently he was hit twice from outside and twice from inside. He rolled, writhing in pain, under the bed. Later Willard Richards covered him with the mattress.

When we think of bullets today, we think of something out of a .22-caliber rifle, which has a small cap and then the pointed bullet. But the bullets at Carthage Jail were balls from muskets. To load a musket, you first put in the powder and then you tamp in the round ball, which is about the size of a "steelie" marble about a half-inch in diameter. The next day James W. Woods, Joseph's last attorney, examined the walls of the jail and counted thirty-six holes, places where the attackers had missed their targets.[38] In addition, five balls went into Hyrum, five into Joseph, and five into John Taylor. John Taylor, who lived another forty years, carried one of those balls just under his knee and sometimes encouraged his grandchildren to feel it.

Quoting from John Taylor: "It was with difficulty that sufficient persons could be found to carry me to the tavern, for immediately after the murder a great fear fell upon all the people, and men, women and children fled with great precipitation, leaving nothing nor anybody in the town but two or three women and children and one or two sick persons."[39] Why did they flee when no one was pursuing? They feared the Nauvoo Legion and the Mormons—even though the Prophet had instructed the Legion to stay home. That simple fact may have preserved the lives of Willard Richards and John Taylor.

John Taylor lived. They had to make a special carrier for him, a kind of sled, and they had to avoid the road and go as smoothly as possible over the prairie grass, and somehow he endured the pain.

At the eventual trial of members of the mob, in which John Taylor participated, no one was convicted. Among the Brethren it was then said, "We will leave it in the hands of God."[40] So it has remained.

SKILLED IN DEBATE

I turn now to one exemplary example of John Taylor's skill in debate. He was encountered by a social reformer from Europe, and they discussed the first principles of the gospel. After a long conversation this man said, "Mr. Taylor, do you propose to bring about a revolution in the earth . . . through the principle of repentance, of faith, and baptism?"

President Taylor could have said, "Well, there are other ordinances and powers included in the kingdom." Instead he said, "Yes, sir, that is the way we understand it."

"Well," said the reformer, "I wish you every success, but I am afraid you will not be able to accomplish anything."

"Said I," John Taylor continued, "you are trying to bring in a great reformation and you think you are going to accomplish something; we will compare notes. It is a number of years now since we left the city of Nauvoo; it was a large city then, and surrounded by a rich country, that we cultivated. In consequence of our religious views we could not stay there; we were persecuted and driven, and had to go into the wilderness. . . . You and your people came to our vacated city, lived in our houses already built for you; you came to gardens and fields, already in a state of cultivation; you had every facility for improvement and progression. Now, sir, what is the difference between the two people? In reading your communications from Nauvoo, which I frequently read, every time you issue your paper you call for more money and means to help them to carry out their plans, and to progress in building up their city. On the other hand, our people, situated far away . . . are sending out hundreds and thousands of dollars to help to gather the poor there. Now, which is progressing the most, you or they? 'Well,' says he, 'I have nothing to say.' I think he will have still less to say to-day than then."[41]

Here, as elsewhere, he was a little hard on philosophy. He said when he was in France that philosophy was "fried froth."[42]

TRAINING IN SUBMISSIVENESS

In the St. George Tabernacle you can see a dent on the pulpit. That dent came when Brigham Young, standing at the pulpit, slapped his cane down to make a point. What was the occasion? He was rebuking John Taylor. For what? We don't know for sure. But we do know that Brigham Young was known to rebuke others in public, and often the one receiving the rebuke was sitting with him on the stand.

Now that is medicine that most of us do not relish. Brigham Young himself had endured it. There is a family tradition that says that Brigham was sitting in an assembly, and the Prophet Joseph was at the pulpit. Joseph asked Brigham Young to stand, which Brigham did. Then the Prophet rebuked him in the presence of others for something he apparently had not done. Every eye turned to Brother Brigham. He was not known as a weak man. What would he say? He could have said, "You shouldn't do that in public, Joseph." He could have said, "You are wrong." He could have said, "What about Doctrine and Covenants 121, which tells us to deal with others in kindness, persuasion, and long-suffering?" What he said was, in a tone of voice everybody knew was genuine, "Joseph, what do you want me to do?" Then the Prophet burst into tears, came down off the stand, embraced him, and said, "Brigham, you passed."[43]

So Brigham gave medicine that he himself had taken. And what about John Taylor? He didn't like it either. As a matter of fact, there were moments, according to the story, when he had decided he was going to leave St. George and go home, not go to the afternoon meeting. One of the Brethren (one account says it was Lorenzo Snow, another says it was Wilford Woodruff) followed him out, knew how he was feeling, sat him down, and said, "Now, John, you're going to go back to the meeting this afternoon."

"Oh, no, I'm not."

"Yes, that's what you're going to do. You're going to go back, you're going to sit on the stand and smile, and this will all be worked out."

Well, he persuaded him, and John went back for the next meeting. In a short time Brigham Young had passed away, and John Taylor was his successor as the President of the Church.[44]

"I HAVE BEEN VISITED BY YOUR FATHER"

John Taylor's experience was widely varied before he became President of the Church. In Utah, he was elected to the territorial legislative council. For three years he presided in the early organization of the territory. For three years, he published in New York a paper called simply *The Mormon.* He set up his rooms between the two most popular dailies in New York and printed his own paper, constantly defending the cause of the Mormons in print. He was one of those serving military duty during the so-called "Mormon War." Not a shot was fired. He was the probate judge in Utah County. He was the speaker of the house when the legislature was organized. And in July 1880 he became the President of the Church.

After Brigham Young died, there were terrible struggles with his estate. Earlier, when the government came down hard and literally escheated Church property and said we could have only $50,000 in liquid funds, President Young handled it in two ways. One was that he took much of the Church property and put it in his own name; and second, as trustee-in-trust, he arranged for others of the Brethren to put Church funds in their names. That irritated our enemies a great deal, but it was an effective ploy to keep Church money in Church hands. But once Brigham Young was dead, there was a huge question about what belonged to the family and what belonged to the Church. And what would the family do about it all?

Leonard Arrington, our best economic historian, traced the issue and analyzed it thoroughly, and he demonstrates that the question was eventually settled ably and honestly. But the resolution did not come without some stress, and John Taylor had to bear the brunt of that.

Another challenge had to do with education. At one point a daughter of Brigham Young who had been working at the Brigham Young Academy, the predecessor of what is now Brigham Young University, went to Salt Lake City to see

President Taylor. She pleaded for financial help, because otherwise the Academy would have to close. "President Taylor took her hand in a fatherly way and said, 'My dear child'"—she was in her forties and so was hardly a child, but President Taylor must have had some fatherly feeling for her—"'I have something of importance to tell you that I know will make you happy. I have been visited by your father. He came to me in the silence of the night clothed in brightness and with a face beaming with love and confidence, and told me things of great importance. Among others, that the school being taught by Brother [Karl] Maeser was accepted in the heavens and was a part of the great plan of life and salvation; that church school should be fostered for the good of Zion's children; that we rejoice to see the awakening among the teachers and the children of our people, for they would need the support of this knowledge and testimony of the gospel, and there was a bright future in store for the preparing of the children of the covenant for future usefulness in the kingdom of God; and that Christ, himself, was directing and had a care over this school."[45]

Not just this school, however, was involved in this prophetic glimpse. John Taylor later said in a meeting in Sanpete: "You will see the day that Zion will be as far ahead of the outside world in everything pertaining to learning of every kind as we are to-day in regard to religious matters. You mark my words, and write them down, and see if they do not come to pass."[46]

That prophecy is coming to pass. John Taylor believed that Zion would someday have in it the greatest scholars, the greatest scientists, the greatest artists, the greatest political minds, the greatest legal minds—we could go on and on and on.[47] He said elsewhere that the Restoration isn't complete.[48]

It's a favorite saying of Protestants that the Reformation continues. The Latter-day Saint way of saying it: The Restoration continues. And so does the continuing advance of Zion in all things that matter most.

As Church President, John Taylor was plagued by the worst forms of legislative abuse we had thus far experienced. Since he lived the principle of plural families, he was constantly under suspicion and attack. Unlike some of the other Brethren, he did not go to prison—but that was only because he went into exile. He felt it his duty to continue to preside over the Church by contact through epistles and private meetings. In a place near the Great Salt Lake in Kaysville, he lived out two and a half years in exile. He had great stamina, but the exile eventually affected his health. He did not have sufficient exercise, he did not eat well, and eventually, at age seventy-eight, he was unable to cope and died.

A TEMPLE IN JERUSALEM

During his presidency John Taylor gave an interview that seems to me to have great significance. At one point he was visited by a Jewish man named Baron Rothschild, who was known at the time as the wealthiest man in the world. A glimpse of the dialogue: "I remember talking with Baron Rothschild when showing him our Temple. He asked what was the meaning of it. Said I, 'Baron, your Prophets centuries ago, when under the inspiration of the Almighty, said that the Lord whom you seek shall suddenly come to his temple.' 'Yes,' he said, 'I know they said that.' 'Will you show me a place upon the face of the earth where God has got a temple to come to?' Said he, 'I do not know of any such place.' But if your Prophets told the truth, then there must be a Temple built before your

Messiah can come.' Said he, 'Is this that Temple?' 'No, sir.' 'What is this then?' 'It is *a* Temple but not *the* Temple your fathers spoke of. But you will yet build a Temple in Jerusalem, and the Lord whom you seek will come to that Temple.' 'What is this for,' he enquired? Among other things that we may perform the sacred ordinances about which we are so much maligned, wherein we make eternal covenants with our wives, that we may have a claim upon them in the resurrection. Who revealed this? God our Heavenly Father. And because he has revealed these things, and because we are fulfilling these things, our nation, groveling in darkness, wrapped in midnight gloom, knowing no more about God and eternity than that piece of iron railing, makes it criminal for us to form associations . . . with our wives and children, with our fathers and mothers, with our friends and associates, so that when the last trump shall sound and the dead hear the voice of the Son of God, that we with them may come forth to obtain the exaltation which God has prepared for those that love him, keep his commandments, and are obedient to his laws."[49]

President Taylor was then visited by other Jewish people asking for help, some of them descended from Levi or from the house of Aaron. Said he: "I told them they had rather missed the place that they should have taken up in Palestine. They said, 'Well, that will be alright in its time, when the time comes.' I talked with them about a good many principles. I talked about our temples and said they would build one in Jerusalem. And I told them I had spoken to Baron Rothschild on this same subject some few years ago,[50] and that he would assist in gathering the people."[51]

Baron Rothschild became a major factor in preparing the way for what is known as the Zionist movement in the Holy Land. I have been to a place called Rosh Pina in the

Galilee, which was the first organized establishment of the pioneers, the *halutzim*. They had a terrible struggle, but they made it. He became a major contributor to further development over there, and his descendants and heirs have continued the work to our time. How much influence did President Taylor have on Baron Rothschild to do those things? We cannot know. But it is clear that in some ways John Taylor understood the future of the Jewish people better than the Jewish people themselves.

I once said as much to a man who had read the Orson Hyde vision. Notice I didn't say the Orson Hyde prayer. He had read that, too. Many Latter-day Saints have heard or have read the Orson Hyde prayer. But few also know that Orson Hyde, while in Nauvoo and before going to the Holy Land, had a vision—an all-night vision. This man had read it. He was then the editor of a major American publication, a professor at Harvard, and a former member of the Jerusalem Foundation. I said to him, "If you read it, how do you account for the fact that an obscure Mormon apostle anticipated more clearly the future of the Jewish people than the Jewish people themselves?"

He shrugged and then said, *"Mysterium tremendum,"* which means, in Latin, "tremendous mystery."

"THAT ZION MAY ARISE AND SHINE"

One of the great events in John Taylor's life took place on May 17, 1884. On that occasion he dedicated the second temple built in Utah. The St. George Temple was first completed, then Logan, then Manti; and only after those three was the Salt Lake Temple finished and dedicated, a place forty years in the making. By the time the Salt Lake Temple was finished, John Taylor was gone.

In a long and brilliantly insightful dedicatory prayer, a half-dozen paragraphs clarify what temples may mean to us and give clear expression to John Taylor's vision of the future of the kingdom of God on the earth. He first dedicated the Logan Temple for "the manifestation of Thy will, and the teachings and administration of ordinances, and the instruction of Thy people in all principles of science and intelligence pertaining to this life, and the lives that are to come."[52] It was a comprehensive vision of our learning more and more, or increasing in light, until the day comes when we may "comprehend even God, being quickened," as says the revelation, "in him and by him" (D&C 88:49). He spoke of the restoration of the gospel in its fulness, richness, power, and glory, and then prayed "that we . . . might be put in possession of the knowledge of Thyself and of Thy law, through the power of the Holy Priesthood, . . . [which] opens a communication between the heavens and the earth."[53]

Then he prayed that the temple will be a place "to purify and instruct Thy Church, and to build up and establish Thy Zion on the earth, which Thou hast decreed should be accomplished in the dispensation of the fullness of times."[54] He referred to the endowment as the preparatory power for all those who seek to teach the gospel throughout the earth, "that Thy servants may go forth to the nations of the earth endowed with power from on high"[55]—that last phrase a glorious Doctrine and Covenants phrase (D&C 38:32; 105:11).

Next he made a petition for unity between heaven and earth. The Prophet Joseph once said, "When you get the Latter-day Saints to agree on any point, you may know it is the voice of God."[56] John Taylor prayed: "We also pray . . . that

Thy Priesthood may be assisted by Thy Holy Priesthood in the heavens, that Priesthood which is after the order of the Son of God, after the order of Melchizedek, and after the power of an endless life, which administers in time and eternity, to impart unto us by Thy direction . . . a correct knowledge of all laws, rites and ordinances. . . . That there may be a perfect union and harmony, if we are counted worthy, between the Priesthood on the earth and the Priesthood in the heavens."[57]

Climactically, he prayed, "Thou hast ordained . . . that Thy presence may be with us"—but there is a condition—"if we are accounted worthy. We pray also that the presence of Thy Son, Jesus Christ, our Savior, may be here; and that the Holy Ghost, the Comforter, may be our guide and instructor, and that Thine angels may be permitted to visit this holy habitation and communicate with Thy Priesthood in the interests of the living and the dead."[58]

Then he made a petition for the government. If you read much about John Taylor, it sounds as though he were wearing a metaphorical hair shirt and constantly attacking the federal government. But in all cases he was attacking the abuse of the Constitution and the abuse of government responsibility. Here's evidence of the fact that he loved this country: "We ask thee to bless the nation in which we live and the rulers thereof." This request continues to our time. "For we are persuaded, O Lord, that while great wickedness and corruption abound in all grades of society"—yes, the high and the low, the leaders and the masses—"that there are hundreds of thousands of honorable men who are desirous to do right and maintain the principles of freedom and the liberty of men, and who do not and cannot acquiesce in the measures taken by the thoughtless and uninformed."[59] He concluded with this plea: "That Zion may arise and shine, that the glory of God may rest upon her. That thy people may be preserved from the errors of vanity, the follies and corruptions of the world; that they may progress and excel in every principle of integrity, intelligence, virtue and purity, until Zion shall become the praise and glory of the whole earth, and Thy will be begun to be done on earth as it is in heaven."[60] He saw clearly that Zion is both a condition of soul—it is the "pure in heart"—and a physical place. There is yet to be a central city of Zion, the place—a return toward the Garden of Eden, if you will, which had a glory that is transforming. John Taylor is one of those who led us to this vision and would never compromise it.

"LET THEM ALL BE ONE"

When John Taylor died, he received a tribute from his two counselors, George Q. Cannon and Joseph F. Smith, who had to endure and carry their own burdens while he was in exile. Among other things, they said that this man never sought for mammon. He never was anxious for money, for wealth, for prestige, for worldly approval. His only anxiety was to build the kingdom of God and be worthy as one of its citizens. He was given a revelation in 1882 that includes these words, "Let the Presidency of my Church be one in all things; and let the Twelve also be one in all things; and let them all be one with me as I am one with the Father."[61] He yearned for that; he prayed for that; he sought to bring it to pass.

At his death his two counselors said, as one, that he would go down in history as a double martyr—that he mingled his blood with Joseph and Hyrum at Carthage, and that he then went into exile as a living martyr, denied the rights of citizenship in a country dedicated by its Constitution to genuine freedom of religion. He had borne his witness both in life and in death.

Through his association with Joseph Smith, John Taylor came to the vision of the Lord Jesus Christ, who was going to transform not just individual people, but a whole community—the buildings, the gardens, and the whole surrounding civil and religious and cultural life. And finally, He was going to transform the entire earth so that it could be rolled back into the very presence of God. This is the joy of vision that John Taylor has handed on to us.

4

WILFORD WOODRUFF

Let me take you for a moment to the Holy Land, where some years ago I was privileged to be the guide for President Hugh B. Brown, then a member of the First Presidency. Somehow we began discussing the world's classical tradition about "saints" and the criteria that the Roman Catholic Church use when they investigate the possibility of canonizing a person as a saint. The rules come down to four. First, they must in many ways have a productive life; second, they must have faced unusual handicaps and difficulties; third, they must have complete and unflinching devotion to the religion; and finally, they must be *radiant*. He thought for a while, and then I said, "If we used those tests on our own history, who would you nominate as a 'saint'?" He instantly said, "Wilford Woodruff." Now, of course, all of those who have come to leadership in this Church have been saintly persons. But President Brown first thought of Brother Woodruff, in part because of those four rules.

Wilford Woodruff, like his predecessors, was reaching upward early in his life. He needed to feel completed. He speaks of walking to his mill at night, in his early twenties—he was a miller in Farmington, Connecticut—and pleading in prayer that he could find someone who could say, like Paul anciently, not simply "I know about Christ," but "I know Christ."[1] He longed for the spiritual experiences enjoyed by those of the first generation of believers after Christ as described in the New Testament. He did not find the truth in those around him, but once in great earnestness he prayed and at random opened the Bible to Isaiah 56, which speaks of a future gathering of Israel and of events that, by his interpretation, would occur prior to the final consummation of earth's history. Some peace of mind came to him from that, and he decided not to disturb himself further by investigating various other faiths.

Soon, for some reason, he was prompted to go to Rhode Island. He spoke to his brother about it and they both agreed. But then they decided not to go. Had they gone that year, they might have heard the gospel of Jesus Christ taught in its fullness by missionaries who were there at the time.[2]

In the following year, he did go to Rhode Island. At the same time, a missionary named Zera Pulsipher had an impression that he was to find a companion and go north. He did so, and they went under inspiration directly to the home where Wilford Woodruff was staying. They spoke of their testimony of the Restoration. Later, Wilford Woodruff and his brother attended a larger meeting where the missionaries spoke. At the end of the meeting, Wilford stood up and "exhorted" those assembled "not to oppose these men; for they were the true servants of God. They had preached to us that night the pure gospel of Jesus Christ."[3] He was baptized in icy water, and though his clothes clung to his body he said, "I did not feel the cold."[4] That was the beginning of his incredible growth in service and leadership.

There is a prologue to those experiences, which affected his life to its end. Early on in his life he had been the friend of a man known as Father Mason. He knew him for twenty years, but Father Mason had never mentioned to him his most crucial spiritual experience. Then, shortly before he died, Father Mason sat down with Wilford Woodruff and said, "The Church of Christ and kingdom of God is not upon the earth, but it has been taken from the children of men through unbelief. . . . But it will soon be restored again unto the children of men upon the earth, with its ancient gifts and powers, for the Scriptures cannot be fulfilled without it. . . . I shall not live to see it, but you will live to see that day, and you will become a conspicuous actor in that kingdom."[5] (The first person Wilford Woodruff acted as proxy for in baptism for the dead in Nauvoo was Father Mason, of whom he often spoke as a prophet.[6])

Later in his life, in setting apart a missionary, Wilford Woodruff said, "The Lord has chosen a small number of choice spirits of sons and daughters out of all the creations of God, who are to inherit this earth; and this company of choice spirits have been kept in the spirit world for six thousand years [meaning from the days of Adam] to come forth in the last days, to stand in the flesh in this last Dispensation of the Fulness of Times, to organize the kingdom of God upon the earth, to build it up and to defend it . . . and to receive the eternal and everlasting Priesthood."[7] It could have been said to him, "Wilford, you are one of them."

A MARKED MAN

Wilford Woodruff had so many accidents he came to believe he was a "marked man." The Prophet Joseph Smith once said, "Remember, brethren, that time and chance happen to all men."[8] There are in this world real accidents. A full-scale determinist would say they are inevitable, but sometimes we can correctly say, No, it's just the way things happen.

Consider this summary of Wilford Woodruff's struggle with every kind of mishap. When he was only three years of age he fell into a cauldron of boiling water. Though he was pulled out immediately, he wasn't out of danger for about nine months. When he was five years old he fell on his face from a great beam in a barn. Three months later he fell down the stairs and broke his arm. Shortly after that he broke his other arm. At six years of age he was chased by a mad bull but fell into a post-hole, and the animal leapt over him. The same year he broke two major bones of one of his legs in his father's sawmill. When he was eight a wagon of hay on which he was riding tipped over on him and he nearly suffocated. When he was nine he fell from an elm tree after standing on a dry limb fifteen feet above the ground and was, for a time, thought to be dead. When he was twelve he was nearly drowned in the Farmington River, in thirty feet of water, and finally was rescued by another young man. When he was thirteen he almost froze to death, having actually fallen asleep in a cutout part of a trunk. Somebody shook him and finally brought him back to consciousness. At fourteen years of age he split his instep open with an ax. It took nine months to heal. At fifteen he was bitten on his left hand by a mad dog. At seventeen he was thrown from an ill-tempered horse amid the rocks on a steep hill. The accident broke his left leg in two places and dislocated both his ankles. He spent eight weeks on crutches. When he was twenty, trying to clear the ice out of a waterwheel, he slipped, fell in, and plunged headfirst into three feet of water, barely escaping death. When he was twenty-four he was caught in a waterwheel twenty feet in diameter, but escaped with a few bruises. Also at twenty-four he had lung fever. At age twenty-six, only a few minutes after his baptism, a horse kicked the hat off his head, and if the blow had been two inches lower, he would not have survived. Ten minutes later he was thrown from a sleigh without a box and, lighting between the horses, was dragged about a half a mile. The list goes on.[9]

Years later, his son accidentally drank some lye, which nearly killed him. Wilford wrote, "If he follows my footsteps he will have many hard accidents to pass through."[10] Indeed so.

In his journal he copied one of the rules of Benjamin Franklin: "Be not disturbed at trifles or at accidents, common or unavoidable." At the dedication of the Salt Lake Temple he said in his prayer, "Nothing but Thy power could have preserved [Thy servant] through that which he has passed during the eighty-six years that Thou has granted him life on the earth."[11]

SEVEN THOUSAND PAGES

He wondered if he was "marked" because he would become one of the most conscientious journal keepers of this dispensation. Beginning almost from the time that he became a Latter-day Saint, he, under counsel from the Prophet, began keeping a daily journal, at least one entry every day for sixty-three years.[12] His record runs a total of seven thousand pages. He recorded at least thirty of the Prophet's sermons, often in his own form of Pittman shorthand. After recording a sermon, he couldn't sleep until he had gone home and transcribed his shorthand into readable English prose. And if he didn't have a notebook at the time he heard the sermons, he would go home and, from memory, outline what he had heard. He did the same for Brigham Young, recording a total of sixty of his sermons.

Besides that, Wilford Woodruff recorded crucial ordinances, including the ceremony we now call the temple endowment. He and Brigham Young, working together in the St. George Temple, systematized what the Prophet had introduced in an improvised way in Nauvoo—Brigham working from memory, Wilford from his journal. How many people have been influenced by that recording alone? We now have well over a hundred temples, and so far we have performed ordinances for one hundred million people. I suspect there was consternation in the lower regions of the devil's kingdom when Wilford Woodruff identified himself with the Latter-day Saints.

Though he had numerous mishaps and other sicknesses, he nevertheless lived to be ninety-one years of age, and he was never really disabled—although it sometimes required real courage to keep going in the face of injury. At one time he said, like Brigham Young, "A person possessed of the Holy Spirit never grows old."[13] There is a time, of course, when we do have to grow old. But there was a freshness and a rejuvenation throughout Wilford Woodruff's life. And he knew how much the Lord protected him. He said at one point, "I have many times had that Spirit manifested to me, and if I had not followed its whisperings to me, I should have been in my grave long ago."[14] He endured and overcame.

Of those who live a godly life, Wilford recorded the words of Orson Hyde: "Some person's atmosphere you like, others you do not. With some you feel safe, others you do not. It is so in meeting with families. . . . That person who dwells near the Lord and has an eye single to His glory, can tell whether he has the Spirit of God or not when he meets with him. . . . It sets him in a blaze, and the great light can see the heart. . . . Our character will be presented before God in its true light, and we shall see as we are seen and know as we are known."[15]

EARLY DAYS IN THE CHURCH

After joining the Church, Wilford immediately went to Kirtland to meet the Prophet. That must have been a strange moment, because when he arrived in Kirtland the Prophet was out tanning a wolf skin and asked Wilford to help him with it. Only a few days later Wilford attended the first priesthood meeting of his life in a little eleven-foot-square log cabin in Kirtland. That was the famous 1834 meeting when the Prophet asked each of those present to bear a five-minute testimony about the vision they had of the future of the Church. Wilford Woodruff's reaction: "It appeared to me there was more light made manifest at that meeting respecting the gospel and Kingdom of God than I had ever received from the whole Sectarian world."[16] He learned also from that point to honor the Prophet Joseph Smith.

Soon he was involved in the Zion's Camp march. As the march proceeded, some of those present, including some brethren, sisters, even some children, were not behaving as a camp of Israel should. Because they were wet and cold and hungry, and often walking thirty miles a day on bloody feet, there began to be bickerings and hostilities and even overt sin. Joseph warned them to repent. As Wilford Woodruff recorded it: "We were all well. There was no disease nor sickness in our camp. But he told us what awaited us. He gave us to understand that there was to be a chastisement visit our camp. He told us the reason. He had given counsel to the brethren with regard to many things, and a number of them had disobeyed that counsel. They did not understand and appreciate fully his position and standing as a Prophet of God. 'Yes,' says he, 'you think of me as a boy, like the rest of you'"—this is 1834, when the Prophet had not yet turned thirty—"'but you will understand soon that I occupy a position where God governs and controls me.' Those who were present know the feelings that we had. There was not a dry eye in camp. He stood upon a wagon and told us the judgments of God would visit our camp and we would be chastised. These things came to pass. The day that we landed the destroying angel visited our camp, and, of course, there was sorrow. I do not know the number that went to the grave, but somewhere about fourteen, I think."[17] Other contemporary records essentially agree—fifteen died of cholera.

A dozen or so years after that experience, there was a moment on another expedition when the people needed to repent. When Brigham Young's vanguard group was traveling west across the plains, Brigham had to rebuke the camp, and he called them anew to what they should be doing and feeling. Wilford Woodruff then stood and said that "he had not forgotten his journey in the Camp of Zion in 1834; and should he live to the age of Methuselah, he should not forget the hour when the Prophet and Seer, Joseph Smith, stood upon the wagon wheel and addressed that Camp and said that because they had not hearkened unto his counsel, but disobeyed and transgressed from time to time, judgement would come and that we should be visited by the destroying angel. And so we were, and more than twenty of our members fell by the stroke and we all suffered much in our feelings. I pray the Lord I may not see another such time."[18] The people hearkened, and that changed everything.

After Zion's Camp, Wilford Woodruff was called to be one of the Twelve. He was present for the glorious events of the Kirtland Temple. No one has chronicled them more carefully. His journal is a sacred record on this count. The Saints experienced an unprecedented outpouring of the Spirit in response to their unprecedented sacrifice. The outpouring of joy was so intense that many of the Saints thought for a while that the Millennium had come; and the Prophet had to arise and say, "Yes, brothers and sisters, this is of the Lord, but there will be trials, there will be a wrenching ahead and we must learn and prepare."[19] Wilford Woodruff did not, as did others, have any doubting as to the divine origin of these experiences. Some expected things to happen that didn't. Some were overwhelmed at what did happen. But Elder Woodruff recorded the fasting and prayer and preparation and then the jubilee that followed.

When the Kirtland Safety Society, the bank of the Saints, failed, some began to apostatize. Wilford did not. Let me give you just one glimpse of his kind of faith. By way of background, I give you words that William W. Phelps wrote that are no longer in the hymnbook, words Wilford Woodruff and other early Brethren sang:

> *We'll wash and be washed and with oil be anointed,*
> *Withal not omitting the washing of feet.*
> *For he that receiveth his penny appointed*
> *Must surely be clean at the harvest of wheat.*[20]

The last line is a reference to Jesus' parable about the wheat and the tares. Indeed, in Kirtland the leaders experienced washings of feet and anointing, and Wilford Woodruff participated. Here is just one excerpt from his journal: "I met at the house of Elder Hales at one o'clock with twenty-three elders, President Joseph Young was one of the number, for the purpose of attending to the ordinance of washing."

The Prophet's father, Joseph Smith Sr., blessed Wilford Woodruff. Two promises apparently meant a great deal to him, because he refers to them in his later writings. First, he was promised that if he had sufficient faith, someday, somehow, he would have the privilege of bringing all his relatives into the Church. That did not fully happen in his lifetime, but he had faith that ultimately it would.[21] The other promise had to do with the glory of the coming of Christ. He was promised that he would have the privilege of literally beholding the Savior in the clouds of heaven. He was also told that he will be numbered with the 144,000 who will stand on Mount Zion and sing the new song—the song none can know except by revelation (see D&C 84:98–102; 133:56). He did not live to see that happen during his mortal life. But his faith was that whether he first descended, as it were, the stairway of death, or whether he ascended to meet the coming of the Lord before dying, he would have the privilege of being with him. He lived for that and he died for that.[22]

HARVESTS OF SOULS AND FROM SOILS

The success of Wilford Woodruff's mission to Great Britain is well known. He was among those—Heber C. Kimball, Brigham Young, and others—who participated in the great harvest of souls.

While he was on a mission to England, he met a faithful sister who had had an experience she didn't understand. This was in the early 1840s, at least two years before the Prophet began to teach for the first time that there is such a thing as vicarious ordinance work for and in behalf of those who have departed this life. This woman—who had been a Methodist and had great regard for both John Wesley and Charles Wesley, who founded the Methodist movement—saw the Wesley brothers in a dream or dream-vision. They were dwelling in the life to come and were approached by a man in white. The man was an apostolic figure, and he taught them the principle of vicarious ordinances. In delight and great joy, they then taught it to others. She asked Wilford Woodruff, "What does this mean?" And he answered: "Well, it just happens that at the time you had the dream, one of our leaders named David Patten was killed, and he was the senior apostle in the Quorum of the Twelve. It may be that, as we believe, he is ministering in the spirit world, and you saw a glimpse of the consequences."[23]

Wilford had also served missions in Tennessee, Kentucky, and Missouri. And then in fulfillment of a promise that he would teach people "on the islands of the sea," he went to the Fox Islands, just off the coast of Maine. His first wife, Phoebe, accompanied him, leaving their children for a time with close friends and relatives.

He returned from his British mission to Nauvoo, where he had a home that was built with his own hands. Some refurbishing has been done, but today the home remains solid and sturdy. Wilford Woodruff had wonderful skills in manual labor. He was also a gifted horticulturist. He organized a horticultural society in Utah and was its president for many years. His journal is flecked with frequent references to his farm, to his plowing, to his sowing, to his harvesting. He speaks of hoeing corn, of investigating new kinds of plants and hybrids, a pursuit that continued through his life.

When he was in his eighties, he once greeted George Q. Cannon and said, "I'm getting old."

Brother Cannon answered, "What's the evidence? Why do you say that?"

"Well," President Woodruff replied, "today, for the first time in my life, my grandson hoed more than I did."[24]

A CAULDRON OF OPPOSITION

When Wilford Woodruff returned to Nauvoo, the place was a cauldron of opposition. The Prophet Joseph, who was motivated by a premonition that his days were numbered, called the Twelve and a few others together almost every day in the early part of 1844, holding council meetings and prayer meetings with them. In retrospect, Wilford understood that the Prophet was trying to convince them that he was going to die—but they did not want to believe it. "He told us that he was going away to leave us, going away to rest. Said he, 'You have to round up your shoulders to bear up the kingdom.'"[25] But they shook it off. They did not want to face it. Brigham Young later said, "We thought our faith would outreach it, but we were mistaken."[26] But it was not to be so. The last time Brother Woodruff was with the Prophet was after the great general conference in April 1844. The Prophet took his hand and asked, "Brother Woodruff, you are going on your mission?"

"Yes."

Then Joseph looked at him soulfully and said, "If you do not go you will die. God bless you," and hugged him.[27] Wilford felt that the Prophet had a premonition that they would not see each other again in this world, and it was so.[28] Where was Wilford when word of the martyrdom came? The Twelve were spread throughout the eastern part of the United States. Brigham Young was in Peterborough, New Hampshire; and Wilford was in Boston. They heard rumors, and there were some newspaper accounts. But they didn't believe it. Then Wilford received a letter from his wife, Phoebe, detailing what had happened.

His journal in this period is marked, again, with introspection. Brigham Young walked all the way from New Hampshire to Boston. Somehow he and Brother Woodruff had communicated that they would meet at the home of one of the few members of the Church in Boston, Sister Vose. Wilford recorded, "Until now I had not shed a tear since the death of the Prophet. My soul had been nerved up like steel."[29] They met at the home of Sister Vose, immediately went upstairs to a bedroom and closed the door, and then both of them for the first time burst into tears.

That is one of the times when Brigham Young slapped his knee and said, "The keys of the kingdom are right here with the Church."[30]

The next day a huge assembly gathered in a hall on Washington Street in downtown Boston. Apparently all of the Latter-day Saints who were in the area gathered, as did hundreds of non-Latter-day Saints who had heard the word and now were curious. The press at the time proclaimed, "Thus ends Mormonism."[31] Cut off the head, the body dies, they said. The kingdom of blockheads called "The Mormons" will disperse and that will be the end of it. These same people who did not believe in prophets did not hesitate to "prophesy."

Wilford Woodruff was assigned to speak at this assembly, but he didn't know what to say. He opened the Bible at random and read where John wrote in Revelation, "I saw under the altar the souls of them that were slain for the word of God" (6:9). Elder Woodruff took that as his text, and he bore his witness that two of the greatest prophets who ever lived had given their lives, just as had the ancient martyrs and prophets, and that their work had been established and the foundation laid, and it would continue to grow and flourish.

Orson Hyde spoke in that same meeting. Then Brigham Young said this: "Be of good cheer." And: "The testimony is not in force while the testator liveth; when he dieth, it is enforced. . . . When God sends a man to do a work, all the devils in hell cannot kill him until his work is accomplished. It was thus with Joseph. He prepared all things and gave the keys to men on the earth and said, 'I am soon to be taken from you.'"[32]

THE EXODUS

As the Saints were preparing to leave Nauvoo, Wilford Woodruff and Orson Hyde had a special assignment: to dedicate the Nauvoo Temple. It was done quietly, with no public announcement. The temple had already been in use—and in desperate use. They performed all the ordinances they could, day and night, before the exodus. But the Lord would have it formally dedicated by two of his apostles, and so it was.

Elder Woodruff gave us some glimpses of the journey west. For instance, he twice describes when the Brethren had meetings on the plains. You would suppose that they would talk only about fixing the wagons and fettering the stock and getting supplies. But also Brigham Young delivered doctrinal discourses out on the plains as comprehensive as those found anywhere. This was a group who were taking culture across the plains, not just wagons and a few possessions. They were reaching for daily sustenance from the Lord on the one hand, and on the other hand they were finding time for rejoicing and even for singing and dancing. The revelation given to Brigham Young at Winter Quarters includes the statement, "If thou art merry, praise the Lord with singing, . . . with dancing" (D&C 136:28).

After you've walked fifteen to twenty miles a day, how anxious would you be to dance? There's a humorous fictional depiction of this on film. Brigham meets with the Indian chief at Council Bluffs. The chief says to Brigham, "You can stay here as long as you want." And Brigham responds, "Those are the first kind words we've heard in ten years." He hastens back to the company and says, "They say we can stay! They say we can stay! Captain Pitt, break out the band, let's dance." Then Porter Rockwell says, "First he tells us we can rest, and now he tells us we have to dance."

One of Wilford's journal entries talks about Brigham's

prophesying of a temple that will be built in the West and then records this statement by Brigham: "Singing stimulates the whole system and the mental mind to such a degree that they want to dance. It's well enough in its place. Everything that is calculated to fill the soul with joy is ordained of God and is proper for the Saints, if they acknowledge God in all things and serve the Lord in it. But don't mingle with the wicked. The only lawful place to dance is a sacred place. You will never see any music or dancing in hell, neither joy nor gladness, but these things will be in heaven." Brigham Young elsewhere says, "There is no music in hell."[33]

Two additional journal entries by Wilford Woodruff give us a picture of life on the plains: "We spent the day in worship of God by prayer, singing and music, and going forth in the dance together before the Lord."[34] Sunday, "May 30, was set apart for prayer and fasting," Elder Woodruff wrote. "In the morning I shaved, cleansed my body"—notice he doesn't say bathed. Where would you bathe? Where's the bathtub?—"put on clean clothing, etc., read a chapter in the Book of Mormon, humbled myself before the Lord, and poured out my soul in prayer before Him, and His spirit descended upon me and I was blessed."[35]

THE GIFT OF DREAMS

Wilford Woodruff had dreams, sometimes apprehensive dreams, sometimes "I had too much for dinner" dreams. But often he had clearly inspired dreams. Here is one. "I dreamed last night we had arrived at our Journeys end where we were to build up a stake of Zion. As we came onto the place there was an open vision of a temple presented before me. I asked some brethren that stood by me if they saw it. They said they did not. I gazed upon it and it was glorious. It appeared as though it was built of white and blue stone. The sight of it filled me with joy and I awoke and behold it was a dream."[36]

While he was in Boston, fifty years before the Salt Lake Temple was finished, he had a dream in which he saw himself dedicating a six-spired temple. It was so vivid he was sure it would be built of cut granite, as it eventually was.[37]

Some of the granite from that same quarry, or nearby, was used for the new Conference Center. How would Wilford Woodruff feel if he knew we had constructed a building to hold twenty-one thousand officers and teachers, in addition to the eight or so thousand in the Tabernacle, in addition to those who can gather in the Assembly Hall—and still there won't be room enough? He would feel as George A. Smith did, who quoted the Prophet as saying, "You can build all the buildings you want but you will never get enough to hold the Latter-day Saints."[38]

INDIAN AFFAIRS

Brigham sent Brother Woodruff east from 1848 to 1850 as a missionary again. Then, shortly after his return, he began to serve as a legislator in the territorial legislature, which he did for twenty-one years. He was in Utah during the so-called Utah War—but in his journal we read of three wars. The first, of course, is the coming of Johnston's Army. Second is the Grasshopper War. You've heard of the crickets, but they also had a plague of grasshoppers. In one of his entries he writes about the terrible two days when they collected and destroyed 175 bushels of grasshoppers who were devouring their wheat. The third war had to do with the Indians. It wasn't really a war, but there were times when there were skirmishes. This was one of the great tensions in the early life of the Church and in Wilford's life specifically. On the one hand the Book of Mormon tells us that the Lamanites are going to have a day of great blossoming, that they will yet receive the fullness of the gospel, that they are going to become a delightsome people, and that they will be participants in the highest ordinances of the temple. On the other hand, in Wilford's era they were sometimes violent enemies.

Wilford Woodruff adopted two Indian boys. One of them eventually ran away and was killed in a railroad accident. The other neglected his duties in a roller mill, and Wilford Woodruff's five-year-old son, trying to do what the other boy hadn't done, got his hand caught in the mill and lost two fingers and mutilated two others. A nephew of Wilford Woodruff's, a son of the well-known Bishop Edwin D. Woolley, was killed in California by Indians, and his mule was strung up on a tree. How does one respond to the commandment to love and serve and teach while facing this kind of violence? He gave his heart and paid the price.

THE ROOM WAS FILLED AS WITH FLAMING FIRE

By 1874 Elder Woodruff was involved in helping with the temple building in southern Utah, and in 1877 he became the president of the St. George Temple. Wilford Woodruff had an innate love of temples, temple worship, and the glorious doctrinal background that teaches us that our destiny is to have influence throughout the entire universe.

When Wilford Woodruff was president of the St. George Temple, he was visited one night by the spirits of those who had put their lives on the line to sign the Declaration of Independence. He said that they pled as a man pleading for his life, seeking the ordinances of the temple. Wilford wrote that they said, "We did not apostatize," an interesting choice of words, "from the form of government God gave us. But we have no earthly representative in the Church of Christ to bring us these ordinances. Please, you do them."[39]

Not only did he proceed on behalf on those men, but also for most of the presidents of the United States, the Wesleys and other prominent religious figures, and at least seventy prominent women. A daughter of Brigham Young served as proxy for the baptism of the women.

How did he feel in the baptismal font in St. George? He said that it seemed to him that the room was filled as with flaming fire.

Among the number of prominent persons who were given the ordinances that day was one of the great writers in British history, Lord Byron. Wilford Woodruff was well read; he even did some work in Greek and Latin and Hebrew; and he was cultured, in part because of his missions, but also because he kept track of world events in the process of record-keeping. Lord Byron had a stormy life, and before his marriage to his wife (to whom Wilford Woodruff sealed him), he was hardly an example of a great and good man. Not only that, but once they were married, so far as the records tell us, they had a tempestuous relationship and eventually separated. Conclusion: If we take seriously the possibility that Elder Woodruff acted under inspiration in performing those ordinances, not just as guesswork, *hoping* that they might receive the ordinances, then we can take hope for others, because to receive those blessings Byron and his wife would have had to grow and come to deep understanding and become worthy.

Elder Woodruff later had "interviews" with George Washington and Benjamin Franklin and saw to it that they received further blessings. He wrote, "They were choice spirits, not wicked men."[40]

We have here a root of Wilford Woodruff's love of the

Constitution and the American way. He didn't just read the Doctrine and Covenants verses which say that the document was inspired. He actually conversed with some of the people who helped write it and who put their lives in jeopardy to do so.

Wilford Woodruff did a revolutionary thing while he presided over the St. George Temple. Up to that point the teaching was that you could perform temple work only on behalf of your own relatives, either blood relatives or in-laws. As he looked at the tremendous amount of work that had to be done, he had the inspiration to know that he could ask others to help him. He said, "This was . . . a key to me, a light burst upon my understanding. . . . I felt like shouting, 'Glory hallelujah.'"[41] Thus he found many to assist him in the temple, and the work proceeded and has continued much faster.

Another watershed decision was made in the Wilford Woodruff administration, having to do with the principle of spiritual adoption. The revelation he later published, titled "The Law of Adoption," says in summary that we are to trace our own bloodlines, regardless of the fidelity or faith or difficulties or problems of our forbears. We are not to short-circuit that by saying, "Well, I don't think much of my relatives, and maybe they don't think much of me, so I want to be adopted into somebody else's family, and then I'll do research on their lines." The whole point of the revelation was to abide with your own family. Do not give up on them.

DEDICATING THE SALT LAKE TEMPLE

Years later President Woodruff dedicated the Salt Lake Temple. I've mentioned his dream in Boston of the temple; later he had a dream in which President John Taylor gave him the keys to the temple (speaking symbolically) and told him to go and dedicate it.[42] That dream occurred before President Taylor died, and Elder Woodruff wondered after that if President Taylor would precede him in death, and in fact he did.

President Woodruff had another dream wherein Brigham Young said, in essence, to keep no one out of the dedication. If those who wish to attend are minimally worthy and if they have agreed to pray and come fasting, then let them attend the dedication.[43] President Woodruff had assumed the leaders would have to interview and prepare recommends for thousands of people. But after that dream he did precisely what he had been told. Many came. There were twenty-three dedicatory sessions, sometimes three a day, from April 6 on into the latter part of the month. For a couple of the sessions he was ill, but for most of them he was present. Two sessions were held just for children. More than sixty-five thousand people attended, and the spirit and power of the experience in some ways regenerated the Church. People returned from attending the temple dedication renewed in their faith, in their commitment, and in their love for the Lord Jesus Christ.

Wilford Woodruff often spoke of his experiences with the spirit world. On record is a conversation which I think typifies this man as a spiritual amphibian; it's as if he lived in two worlds simultaneously. He was walking down the street when he saw a friend. "Brother John, it's good to see you," President Woodruff said. Then after a pause he said, "You know, I don't think I've seen your father since he died."[44]

After the first day of the dedication of the Salt Lake Temple, Wilford Woodruff returned and said, "Last night, brothers and sisters, I saw that our Prophet, Joseph, and Hyrum and others had gathered the worthy in the spirit world. I saw that as we hold our dedicatory sessions here and as we shout 'Hosanna!' they shout 'Hosanna!' and they understand the significance of the temple far more than we, and it echoes to the very throne of God."[45]

He also bore testimony in the Salt Lake Temple that he believed that when Isaiah spoke of the "mountain of the Lord's house" being "established in the top of the mountains" (Isaiah 2:2), he was talking about the very mountains of the Wasatch Front, and that he had seen this six-spired temple, and the Tabernacle, and the wall around it all.[46]

AN IMPOSSIBLE CHOICE

Now to President Woodruff's timing of the Manifesto that put an end to plural marriage. Joseph Smith told the Twelve early on, "Fifty-six years should wind up the scene."[47] As we read in the Doctrine and Covenants, Joseph Smith had prayed about the timing of the Second Coming. A voice answered his prayer: "Joseph, my son, if thou livest until thou art eighty-five years old, thou shalt see the face of the Son of Man" (D&C 130:15). By doing the arithmetic, Joseph knew that he would be eighty-five in fifty-six years. Though Joseph died, which would seem to negate the promise, I believe Wilford Woodruff wondered if at the end of fifty-six years relief would come from the tremendous persecution and hostility and anguish the Church had suffered all that time. In 1890, the Church reached the fifty-sixth year and there was no coming of the Lord. That may have been a factor in President Woodruff's going before the Lord and pleading for guidance as to what to do next.

At this time the antipolygamy legislation had reached its height. Many of the Brethren were struggling under pressure from various sources to abandon their families or to escape to other places where they could openly practice their religion. For two years, Wilford was in a kind of exile in St. George, coming out only occasionally for meetings and to attend to other duties. We have record of a child who was told that the family had a roomer, or renter, who was staying upstairs in the attic. The child didn't know who he was and never saw him until the boy was leaving to go to Mexico and his parents introduced him to President Wilford Woodruff, who had been staying in the attic.[48]

It's clear in his own records that he understood that the Church had an impossible choice: Either we must let all of our temples become government property and let the Church become an entity subject to that government, or we must stop performing plural marriage. With historical perspective, I suspect there were some in Washington and elsewhere who were not really most concerned about plural marriage, but were concerned about temporal power, as the Saints seemed to be building a new nation. In any case, Wilford Woodruff received and presented to the Twelve a revelation stating that plural marriage was to end, and then he asked for their sustaining vote. George Q. Cannon stood up in a general conference and read it, and incredibly, considering all that the Church had gone through, there was nearly unanimous support for this decision.

Three questions remained unresolved. First, would the Manifesto apply to Canada, Mexico, and elsewhere in the world? Second, what would happen to those good fathers and husbands who now would be forced—or would they?—to abandon all except one of their families? And third, would we perform additional plural marriages in the future, when circumstances changed? Those issues were clarified eventually, but not without great turmoil and difficulty and not without tremendous foment at the national level. It was a courageous thing Wilford Woodruff did, and it becomes the symbol of accommodation with this country called the United States of America.

Speaking of Wilford Woodruff's submission to the word of the Lord regarding the Manifesto, George Q. Cannon said: "He was the embodiment of childlike simplicity of faith and, at the same time, a man of undaunted courage. It required a man of such peculiar gifts to do what he did. As natural men, neither Brigham Young nor John Taylor could have issued the Manifesto. They would have required to have been changed by the influence of the Spirit of God. Wilford Woodruff, because of his peculiar organization, could do it and did it. I think it one of the bravest acts a man could perform. I cannot believe that Brigham Young or John Taylor could have done it as he did, and it has always seemed to me that the Lord chose him specially to do this work, and he did it in a manner to please God and the people."[49]

Some historians have spoken of the Manifesto, the United Order, and so forth in terms of how much the Church has changed.

For instance, some have supposed that we gave up on the United Order once and for all, even though Wilford Woodruff and his predecessors tried to make it work. It's true that we are not as a people practicing the United Order today, but there are many Latter-day Saints who are giving most of their discretionary income to the cause of Christ and who would give everything if that were required. So, in a sense, there are people today living the law of consecration in spirit and in truth.

It has also been said that the Church gave up any notion of a political kingdom on earth, such as we had in a budding stage with the Council of Fifty. Joseph Smith said the Constitution was "a great ensign and a great umbrella, and a great guarantor of rights"[50]—but he also implied that it might need more teeth in it. He said, and Wilford Woodruff repeated it three times in his later life, "If he were the emperor of the world and had control of the whole human family, he would defend every man, woman and child in the enjoyment of their religion."[51]

Some people have been surprised to learn that the Prophet and his successors taught that in the Millennium there will be many faiths, many different points of view.[52] A pluralism will hold, even in the Millennium, and we will be among those who insist that this is the right of all people, conditioned upon the principles of the Constitution. Joseph Smith was the first to want to give to others the very right we ourselves had sometimes been denied.

SECULAR CONTRIBUTIONS

Let's talk about a few firsts. Wilford Woodruff was one of the first pioneers to enter the Salt Lake Valley. He was probably the first, aside from Indian tribes, to fish in this untracked wilderness. He was the first fly fisherman to float a fly down a Rocky Mountain stream. (He once went to Utah Lake, then fresh and clear and clean, and caught 1,500 pounds of fish.) He was one of the first to plant potatoes. He was one of the first to see some of the canyons of Utah's Wasatch Front. He was one of the first to go out to visit the Great Salt Lake. He was one of the first to get started building in Utah.

Elder Woodruff became president of the Deseret Agricultural and Manufacturing Association. In 1869 he dedicated the railroad. There is no room to detail the tremendous contributions he made in secular ways. The signs are still with us. For instance, he appointed two different committees to investigate the possibility of the Church becoming involved in the sugar industry. After both committees met, discussed, and analyzed, they reported, "No, we shouldn't." He called them in and said, "Well, we're going to go ahead, even if it breaks the Church." Well, it didn't, and for approximately a hundred years, the manufacture of sugar was a stable economic factor in industry, both in Utah and Idaho.

Wilford Woodruff directed the building and management of a number of water power plants. For many years, most Utahns have received an electricity bill from Utah Power and Light. Wilford Woodruff was the original founder and director of that electric company.

The list of his contributions goes on.

ORDINANCES AND STATISTICS

Wilford Woodruff was a statistician. At the end of each year he'd write, "I have attended so many meetings, I have preached so many sermons, I have visited this number of sick people, and so on." If you add together all those annual reviews, what do you get?

- 817 administrations to the sick
- 916 settings apart of missionaries
- 4,367 baptisms and confirmations
- 11,388 sealings of couples in the temple, both the living and the dead
- 23,269 total ordinances over forty-four years (not counting those times when he was simply assisting others), including some categories not listed above

He ordained many brethren to offices in the priesthood. He dedicated chapels. If you average his performance over the years, he was doing at least two ordinances a day every day of his life, including weekends.

With all that in mind, consider this staggering statement he made: "I have been a member of the Church of Jesus Christ of Latter-day Saints over sixty years, a member of the Quorum of the Apostles fifty-five years, and the President of the Church for a short time. During all these years, and in all my travels, I have never seen a moment when I have had the power to preach the Gospel of Jesus Christ or to administer in any of the ordinances of the House of the Lord, acceptably to God or to myself, only by the assistance of the Holy Ghost."[53] He may be saying that his very breath, his very life, his very ability to perform an ordinance is traceable, ultimately, to the power of God. But I suspect he's saying more; I believe he meant that he sensed, he felt, he experienced the flow of the Holy Spirit whenever he performed an ordinance.

I once asked my father, then in his nineties, "Has there been anybody in our history who fulfilled the sacramental prayer?"

He said, "What do you mean?"

I said, "That they may '*always* have His Spirit to be with them.'"

He thought a minute and said, "Well, some have come pretty close." Wilford Woodruff, I believe, would be among that number.

An additional mark of the Spirit in this man is that President Woodruff made a covenant with the Lord that he would say what the Lord inspired him to say in public meetings, regardless of the personal consequences to himself.[54] And so he did.

FINAL GLIMPSES

When President Woodruff had his ninetieth birthday, a celebration was held in the morning in the Tabernacle. In the afternoon ten thousand children dressed in white filled the Tabernacle and overflowed onto the grounds of Temple Square. As President Woodruff slowly ascended the steps to the lectern, the children stood and sang, "We Thank Thee, O God, for a Prophet."

Here is part of his response: "I want to say to my young brethren and sisters, . . . God bless you and I feel to bless you, as far as I have the power. I want to say that this is a scene before me today that has overpowered me. . . . I never in my life have been in a similar position to that of today. The scene before me has been a fulfillment to all my prayers from my boyhood up to early manhood. Eighty years ago I was a little boy ten years of age attending school the same as you are here in the mountains of Israel. I read the New Testament. I read of Jacob, I read of the Apostles and the Prophets. I could not find a man on the face of the earth who taught these principles or believed in them. I prayed to the God of heaven that I might live to see a Prophet. . . . Today I stand in the midst of ten thousand young men and women of Israel—sons and daughters of prophets, patriarchs and men of Israel. . . . I want to say to you as the rising generation, I never expected to see a day of this kind in my life, in my early days. I did expect as it had been promised me to see a prophet. I have lived to see him. . . . There has been, as it was stated by our brother, two powers, one to destroy me and the other to save me. And God in Heaven has willed to spare me to see this day."[55] (He said at the dedication of the Salt Lake Temple that the Lord had made known to him why he had been preserved to be the president: "Because he could not find a weaker vessel."[56]) He continued in his talk to the children: "He has given me power to reject every testimony and reject every example that leads to evil. I say to you children, do not use tobacco, liquor or any of these things that destroy the body and mind, but honor Him and you will have a mission upon your heads that the world know not of. May God bless you, Amen."[57]

In that same sermon, he said: "We cannot say the Bible is a novel—the Bible that contains revelation."[58] He had nothing against novels—novels are "true to life" but they are not the truth of history.

He knew it was part of his mission to bear testimony. In his later years, a man entered his office with a new contraption. The visitor said, "President Woodruff, if you talk into this, it will talk back." We belong to a generation where it's no great miracle to have a recording device, but then it was a miracle. They handed him a microphone and said, "Say something." What would you say? Our response might be "Testing, testing—1, 2, 3." No. He launched into bearing his testimony about the restoration of the gospel. "I know these are true principles. I received my own temple blessings under the hands of Joseph Smith, and I bear testimony that so did Brigham Young, Heber C. Kimball, Willard Richards, George A. Smith, John Taylor, and other brethren whose names I cannot recall; and also my wife, Phoebe, Bathsheba Smith, Leonora Taylor, Mary Smith, and others. The Prophet Joseph Smith laid down his life for the word of God and the testimony of Jesus Christ. And he will be crowned as a martyr in the presence of God and the Lamb. In all his testimonies to us the power of God was visibly manifest to the Prophet Joseph Smith. This is my testimony, spoken by myself, into a talking machine on this the nineteenth day of March, 1897, in the ninety-first year of my age."[59]

He went to California for his health and did not return alive. But he had left instructions: "I wish to say that at my death I wish the historian of the Church"—he had been

Church Historian for several years—"to publish a brief account of my life, labors, and travels." He left his journal in the hands of his trustworthy daughter, with the understanding that she would let the Church have it and use it as they saw fit.

"I wish my body washed clean and clothed in clean white linen, according to the order of the Holy Priesthood, and put into a plain, decent coffin, made of native wood, with plenty of room."[60] Eliza R. Snow records that the Prophet Joseph Smith taught earnestly against the use of black, or of mourning colors, in death. On the contrary, he said, "use white."[61] "I do not wish my family or friends to wear any badge of mourning for me, . . . for, if I am true and faithful unto death, there will be no necessity for any one to mourn for me. I have no directions to give concerning the services of my funeral, any further than it would be pleasing to me for as many of the Presidency and Twelve Apostles who may be present to speak. . . . Their speech will be to the living." That's an interesting comment. Why do we hold funerals? For the living.

"If the laws [an interesting phrase] and customs of the spirit world will permit, I should wish to attend my funeral myself, but I shall be governed by the counsel I receive in the spirit world."[62]

So ended the life of Wilford Woodruff. I come back to where I began: This man was a saint in the highest sense. This man fulfilled all of the requirements of a productive life, a life that had great hardships, and was still without stint faithful to the Lord Jesus Christ. And yes, through thick and thin, in the dull round of everyday life, through adversity and sickness, this man was radiant.

5

LORENZO SNOW

Several years ago I was assigned to teach a Special Interest class in Los Angeles. I wrote a friend in the Church Historical Department and asked for material on Lorenzo Snow. He sent a thick envelope, and when I opened it, Lorenzo Snow's patriarchal blessing literally fell out. I learned later that President Snow was so grateful for the explicit fulfillment of that blessing that he had it put on the wall of the Salt Lake Temple annex, so it became, in that way, public knowledge. I read it. I was so stirred and impressed that I sat there not wanting to move. And ever since that day I have been interested in the life and teachings of Lorenzo Snow.

That blessing was given by Joseph Smith Sr., first patriarch to the Church. Here are three promises: First, "Thou shalt have faith like the brother of Jared." (A related statement is that he would have "faith like unto Peter, the Apostle.") Second, "Thou shalt have power to stand in the flesh and see Jesus Christ." And third, "Age shall not come upon thee; thou shalt live to the age of Moses, but shall not be old."[1] (Only two days before his death at age eighty-seven, he spoke "vigorously"[2] in the tabernacle, without a microphone—and without glasses.) He had unique gifts.

He also received a blessing from Isaac Morley: "Thy Creator has given thee a mind capable of reflection and of expanding wide as eternity, and it shall be thy gift and blessing to receive the Comforter, even the spirit of truth, that shall guide thee into all truth."[3] He was known in his later life for his educated, cultured, but also brilliant use of language. He inherited, with his sister, great and poetic sensitivities. He was given, according to the blessing of Joseph Smith Sr., "intelligence and talent that thou mightest be useful in His cause."[4]

A word about his background. He was, along with his sister Eliza (they were two of nine children) and a cousin named Erastus Snow, descended from a man named Richard Snow, who was six generations before them. There is a tradition in the family that this Richard Snow was a descendant of Sephardic Jews who lived in Spain. When we hear "1492," we instantly think of Christopher Columbus and America. But any Jewish person in the world who hears that number winces, because that was the year of the beginning of the Spanish Inquisition, when Jews were either tortured or killed or exiled. Richard Snow reportedly came from Jews who suffered in that time and place; and Lorenzo Snow came from Richard.

By 1836 Eliza Snow had already joined the Church. Lorenzo Snow was a student at Oberlin College in Ohio, which had been created only about three years earlier. Oberlin was a liberal arts college with Presbyterian backing. Three things about it were unique. First, students had to do three or four hours of manual labor every day in addition to their studies. Second, the curriculum was oriented to some language skills (and Lorenzo had already become interested in Hebrew).

Third, the founders of the college hoped that it would eventually prepare people to serve in the ministry.

Lorenzo was not impressed with what he saw of religion there. His parents had been active in the Baptist faith. He wrote a letter to his sister and said, among other things, that if this was all there is to religion, then good-bye to religion.[5] Eliza, knowing of Lorenzo's interest in Hebrew and knowing that just that week Joseph Smith had arranged for a professor named Joshua Seixas to teach Hebrew in Kirtland, convinced her brother he should come to visit. That was his initial encounter, firsthand, with the Mormon community. Apparently Lorenzo had met the Prophet once before and in fact had heard him speak and bear testimony of the Book of Mormon in Hiram, Ohio. But he had also heard all kinds of stories about Joseph Smith, none of them complimentary.

"YOU WILL BECOME . . . AS GREAT AS GOD"

When he arrived, he was encouraged to attend a patriarchal blessing meeting that was held inside the Kirtland Temple. (In the early days of the Church, the temple was not restricted to those who came with recommends.) Blessings were given by Joseph Smith Sr., presumably to family or friends. Lorenzo already knew some of the people there, but he had never seen the patriarch. There was something about the patriarch's appearance that impressed him. Lorenzo said later that if one could picture how Abraham might have looked, it would give a sense of the personal presence of Joseph Smith Sr. There was such a "patriarchal feeling" about him.[6] But what most amazed Lorenzo was the variety and the magnitude, from his perspective, of the promises Brother Smith was making to those people. Lorenzo must have asked himself, Is he making this up, or is he inspired?

The meeting ended, and then, still speaking by the Spirit, the patriarch took Lorenzo by the hand and said two things; the first he understood but didn't believe, and the second was over his head. He said that "he would soon be convinced of the truth of the latter-day work, and be baptized." Second, he said, "You will become as great as you can possibly wish—even as great as God, and you cannot wish to be greater."[7]

Lorenzo Snow did in fact study the Church further, did find his way in, and was baptized. One account of what happened was given in court much later: "When alone, engaged in earnest prayer, the heavens were opened, the veil was rent from my mind, and then and there I received the most wonderful manifestations, grand and sublime, . . . beyond the power of language to describe. It was shown me in that vision that there truly existed a Son of God, that Joseph Smith was really a prophet of God. The first intimation of the approach of that marvelous vision was a sound just above my head like the rustling of silken robes." (This is before electricity so he didn't use the word "electric.") "Immediately the Holy Spirit descended upon me, enveloping my whole person, filling me from the crown of my head to the soles of my feet, which was a complete baptism, as tangible an immersion in a heavenly principle or element—The Holy Ghost—infinitely more real, physical in its effects upon every part of my system than was the immersion when I was baptized in water. That night after retiring to rest the same wonderful manifestations were repeated, and continued to be for several successive nights. From that time till the present"—some thirty years later—"on numerous occasions manifestations of the divine power have followed me and my administrations of the gospel ordinances."[8]

In another account he said, "I received a knowledge of the truth of this work by a physical administration of the blessings of God."[9] And he reported in a third account that whenever he began to think of that experience or talk about it in his later life, it was as if a taste of it returned to him, bringing something of the original power.[10]

"THE LORD WILL OPEN THE WAY"

Upon his baptism, Lorenzo gave up his strongest ambition, which had been to join the military. He had inherited some of the qualities of his forebears. Both of his grandfathers were active soldiers in the Revolutionary War; and he was stirred by the idea of serving in the military to the point that he was "wedded" to a gun. His sister made him a very beautiful uniform. When he joined the Church, he suddenly threw all that away, along with his intentions to further his education, and set out on his first mission, the first of five.

His mission was to travel in and around the Ohio area to try to convert his own family and friends. He had some success, but most of them simply said Lorenzo was sincere but deceived.[11] He eventually was called to go abroad—one of eight times he crossed the ocean in order to do missionary work. He had success, as did others of the Brethren, especially in England. As he traveled on the ship home, some 250 converts were with him aboard the ship. The steward on the ship, in order to while away the time, encouraged Lorenzo to speak about his faith and the faith of his people. Lorenzo eventually baptized several members of the crew.[12]

Maureen Ursenbach Beecher, a historian who has been working in these materials for more than a decade, has concluded that one cannot write the life of Eliza R. Snow without also writing about Lorenzo, their lives were so intertwined. Eliza R. Snow was ten years older than Lorenzo. Her decision to accept the Prophet Joseph Smith not only as a prophet but as a husband committed her to about forty years of loneliness. When the Prophet was killed, Eliza was so shaken and drained of any sense of meaning and purpose in her life that she fervently prayed that she also could die and go home. Her pleadings continued for some time until she had a spiritual experience with Joseph. He said to her from beyond the grave, in essence, "You must not mourn, but neither can you now come where I am. You have a great mission to perform. You must reach out and help others. You, who are crying for comfort, must now give comfort. You must lead, you must exemplify."[13] Her life then continued in single marriage (I say single marriage because she was married to Brigham Young and took his name but was never his wife in fact).

When Lorenzo returned from one of his missions, he noticed that his sister was living in the Prophet's home. That wasn't a great surprise because she had been the schoolteacher for the children of the Prophet in Kirtland. But there was a feeling that Lorenzo sensed between her and the Prophet. At that point he had not learned anything about the ideas of celestial and plural marriage. Eliza took the Prophet aside and said, "It's your assignment to talk to my brother, not mine."[14] So Joseph and Lorenzo went for a walk, and the Prophet taught him those principles.

Lorenzo noted later, "I remarked to the Prophet I thought he appeared to have been endowed with great additional power during my mission in England. He said it was true; the Lord had bestowed on him additional divine power."[15] (So much for the thesis that Joseph Smith became a "fallen prophet." It was the other way around. He lived his life "in crescendo,"[16] to use B. H. Roberts's phrase.)

Lorenzo's other comment was, "Joseph, I'm afraid I can't do this." He wasn't just talking about plural marriage, he was talking about marriage itself. Early in his career, Lorenzo decided he would not marry. He thought that if he really wanted to serve the Lord he could not marry and have the responsibilities and demands that come with fatherhood. "I'm not sure I can live the gospel of Jesus Christ and do this."[17]

The Prophet replied, "The principles of honesty and integrity are founded within you, and you will never be guilty of any serious error or wrong, to lead you from the path of duty. The Lord will open your way to receive and obey the law of Celestial Marriage."[18]

Before the Saints left Nauvoo, Lorenzo Snow walked into the temple with four wives to be sealed to him.

THE DREAM AT MOUNT PISGAH

While the Saints were crossing the plains, they stopped at Mount Pisgah, in Iowa Territory, to replenish their supplies. While they were there Lorenzo Snow became so critically ill that his family thought he was delirious, and therefore they couldn't trust what he was saying. But he was conscious and aware of his circumstances, and he had faith that he would emerge from his illness.

During this period he had a dream in which he experienced the most acute suffering that the heart can conceive. "I was led," he reported, "into the full and perfect conviction that I was entirely a hopeless case in reference to salvation, that eternities upon eternities must pass, and still I saw my case would remain the same. I saw the whole world rejoicing in all the powers and glories of salvation without the slightest beam of hope on my part, but doomed to separation"—and here we see his conviction about how crucial the family is—"from my friends and family, all I love most here, to eternity upon eternity. I shudder, even now, at the remembrance of the torments and agony of my feelings. No tongue can describe them, or imagination conceive. Those who were attending me at that time describe me as being in a condition of [death]. . . . My body was cool and my eyes and countenance denoted extreme suffering."

Then came the contrast. His exquisite pain of spirit was followed by what he calls "rapturous enjoyment." He said, "My spirit seemed to have left this world and [I was] introduced into that of Kolob. I heard a voice calling me by name saying, 'He is worthy, he is worthy, take away his filthy garments.' My clothes were then taken off piece by piece, and a voice said, 'Let him be clothed, let him be clothed.' Immediately I found a celestial body gradually growing upon me until at length I found myself crowned with all its glory and power. The ecstasy of joy I now experienced no man can tell. Pen cannot describe it. I conversed familiarly with Joseph, Father Smith, and others, and mingled in the society of the Holy One. I saw my family all saved, and observed the dispensations of God with mankind until at last a perfect redemption was effected. . . . My spirit must have remained, I should judge, for days, enjoying the scenes of eternal happiness."[19]

"DO YOU REMEMBER THE COVENANT WE MADE?"

In 1849 Brigham Young sat down with the other leaders of the Church, including Lorenzo Snow, who had been called to the Twelve. Said Brigham: "Brethren, do you remember the covenant we made in Nauvoo that we would not rest nor reserve our resources until every one of the poor . . . had been given opportunity to cross the plains? Now we must do the same for those who want to come across the ocean."[20]

Lorenzo Snow was assigned the task of overseeing what became known as the Perpetual Emigration Fund. Even though the Saints were threadbare and struggling without any resources, Church leaders went through the settlements and managed to collect a little money, which they added to until they had about $5,000. Over the next thirty years the Perpetual Emigration Fund raised over $2,600,000, and brought forty thousand people across the ocean and across the plains. This was one of Lorenzo's first experiences with developing financial savvy and managerial capacity as well as persuasive power with the Saints.

The Perpetual Emigration Fund was a great achievement; there is nothing else quite like it in our history. When the Church reached its Jubilee year in 1880, there were still some of these emigration debts remaining, and some of those debts were simply forgiven, or written off.[21]

BRIGHAM CITY AND THE UNITED ORDER

In 1853 Lorenzo Snow received another challenging assignment. Brigham Young called him in and said, "Brother Snow, we would like to have you go north sixty miles, where you will find a few cabins and there build up one of the cities of Zion."[22] Elder Snow gathered what he called the "silver grays"[23] to go with him, trustworthy, faithful families—fifty of them. When they arrived in the assigned area (which is now known as Brigham City), he asked the territorial surveyor, Jesse Fox, what could be done to divert the waters of the Bear River so the land could be made irrigable. Fox gave his opinion, but the project failed and those faithful ones who had followed Elder Snow were desperate.

So Lorenzo Snow called a meeting. They sat together in a log cabin on slat benches, and he gave what may have been the most important sermon of his life to that point. He said, in effect, "We cannot go on unless we unite in a cooperative covenant." He said, "Some of you [and there were few] have land. Others of us have none. Instead of your wanting to sell your land for the best price you can get to the rest of us, we are asking you to sell it for whatever we can pay; so it won't be according to price or what the market will bear. It will be according to what this person or that person can afford." Then he said, "I'll give you two weeks to deliberate." And he expounded on the idea of the honest consecration that is required of the Saints.[24]

Two weeks later the people returned to the appointed meeting, and Lorenzo was gratified to see that they had done exactly as he had asked. Such was the beginning of a thirty-five-year effort to build, literally, a community of Saints on the basis of cooperation, an effort that was very close to the United Order.

One of the impediments they faced was a doctrinal interpretation. When Lorenzo proposed they plant peach trees and apple trees and vines, some of the people asked why that was necessary—noting they would be traveling back to Jackson County soon. Elder Snow's response: "We are not going tomorrow, nor the next day, this week or next week."[25] They therefore needed to build up the place where they then lived.

And build it up they did. They built a mill. They started

developing a wool industry. They had a boot and shoe shop, a harness shop, a butchery. They built a sawmill and a carpentry shop. They had millinery and hats. They had a brush factory, and others for pottery, tailoring and clothing, a brick and adobe yard, and a mercantile store.

And they also had vexing problems. They had grasshoppers, they had drought, and the mill burned down. But overall Brigham City grew and flourished. And it came through the initiative of a man who had a financial mind, who was a poet, and who also bore the full load of an apostolic calling.

Brigham Young eventually turned Brigham City (which was named after him, of course) into the model for other efforts to establish the United Order and the law of consecration. He reminded the priesthood brethren and their wives of an essential principle: "The priesthood was bestowed upon you, as upon the Son of God himself, for no other purpose than that, through sacrifice, you might be proven, that, peradventure, at the last day, you might stand approved before God, and before perfect and holy beings: . . . it may be necessary to forget self and individual aggrandizement and seek the interest of your brethren."[26]

MISSION TO ITALY

Lorenzo Snow was next called abroad to open a mission in Italy. In a community known as Piedmont, with some of the other Brethren, he went up on a rocky mount and dedicated the land of Italy for the preaching of the gospel.[27] Then they went to work. The initial opening for conversions came through two events. The first was a remarkable healing. The people in the area had never heard of Mormonism, and they didn't even know who these ministers were. But a child was on his deathbed, and messengers ran to Lorenzo Snow seeking help, crying, "He dies! he dies!" Lorenzo Snow fasted and prayed and then blessed the child. The child was healed,[28] and doors began to open.

Second, he became acquainted with a traditional group known as the "Vaudois" or Waldenses, who had held onto certain original New Testament beliefs in defiance of the dominant churches in and around Italy. They sought to be more authentic, more true to the original New Testament church, which helped Lorenzo Snow and his companions to find common ground in teaching them.[29]

It was through Lorenzo Snow that the Book of Mormon was translated into Italian, and it was through his influence there that prophecies that seemed almost impossible began to be fulfilled. One such prophecy said that "thousands would . . . embrace the Gospel in Italy . . . and that from hence it should extend itself triumphantly."[30] So it began.

"AWAKE ANEW"

When Lorenzo Snow returned to Utah the Saints were in the midst of what was known as the "Mormon Reformation." In the mid-1850s, about a decade after their arrival, the Saints in their many settlements had become so preoccupied with coping with the elements and building forts and establishing farms that they had almost lost their identity. One day, Brigham Young said in effect, while meeting with the First Presidency, "Brethren, I don't know if I can stand to live another week unless something is done. We have lost the spirit and power of our calling. We are not building Zion, we are building little spots of self-aggrandizement."[31]

One of those who caught the spirit of the message was Jedediah M. Grant, who stood up and said, "I will go." He went up and down the Mormon corridor and held meetings and preached, telling the Saints, in essence, to "awake anew."[32] Many rebaptisms were performed in the early days in Utah. One of the explanations for this practice is that we had lost track of the records. In many cases that was true. But in the reformation period many were rebaptized who simply wanted to recommit themselves to the gospel. Even the First Presidency and the Twelve set the example.

Lorenzo Snow was influenced by this spirit of reformation, and he examined his own life. As he considered his own weaknesses, he and his colleague, Franklin D. Richards, became convinced that they had not fully magnified their calling. One day they went together to see President Brigham Young and said, "Perhaps we should withdraw. Perhaps we should no longer serve as Apostles. We are not fully worthy." Brigham Young began to weep and said, "Brethren, you have magnified your priesthood satisfactory to the Lord."[33] And so they went on.

"O JERUSALEM, JERUSALEM"

One day, after a Relief Society meeting in Nauvoo, Joseph Smith had said to Eliza R. Snow, "You will live to go to Jerusalem."[34] She went home and wrote it down in her journal—but then she forgot it. In 1873 when she was almost seventy and her brother almost sixty, Brigham Young called them in with George A. Smith of the First Presidency and Albert Carrington of the Twelve and said, "When you go to the land of Palestine, we wish you to dedicate and consecrate that land to the Lord, that it may be blessed with fruitfulness, preparatory to the return of the Jews in fulfillment of prophecy, and the accomplishment of the purposes of our Heavenly Father."[35]

In our generation a trip to Israel involves buying a ticket on a jet airliner and flying for about eighteen hours. But in the 1870s the trip included going through Europe, Turkey, and Jordan, and it took six months in all. After finally making their way by ship to the port of Jaffa, they had to use camels and horses. George A. Smith, who weighed over three hundred pounds and had arthritis, had to have a wagon. I've walked part of the way from Jaffa up to Jerusalem. It's about forty miles, and it's not an easy journey.

They kept a careful journal of their trip, and they sent dispatches to various newspapers describing their experiences. That paid for part of their expense. Their reports were read with great delight by people in Utah and elsewhere. Here is an interesting footnote: Because they were there in the 1870s, at least two decades before the full-scale development of Zionism and the beginning of the return of the Jews, their correspondence has now been published by Hebrew University in the Department of American Zionism and provides a precious documentary on the situation in the Holy Land in that time.[36]

They went from Jerusalem down to the Jordan River, which is a steep descent of four thousand feet, a painful fifteen miles, to the lowest point on earth. George A. Smith asked if he could be rebaptized there in preparation for the dedication day, on March 2, 1873. His record says it was "cloudy, breezy, cool."[37]

On the Sabbath they ascended the Mount of Olives. Geographic surveys and other maps, combined with the journals of those who went, indicate they traveled about seventy-five feet east and a few feet north of what's traditionally identified as the place of the ascension of Christ. That was the highest point on the Mount of Olives. They pitched a tent, then opened a meeting with prayer, dedicating the tent. A man named Thomas Jennings stood as a security guard outside the tent while the others prepared themselves to pray wearing their temple robes. They changed clothing, read aloud together the last few verses of Matthew 23, and then joined together in prayer.[38]

George A. Smith wrote, "The place of our tent was a few rods northeasterly. We concluded it to be as likely a spot for the Ascension as we could find. We had no doubt the mountain was correct."[39] An earlier entry indicated that he had stood just outside what is known as Stephen's Gate, or the Lion Gate, where tradition says Stephen was stoned. He looked east toward the Mount of Olives and remembered the prophecy in Zechariah about the coming of the Messiah to that mount, and he had a testimony that it surely would yet come to pass.

Orson Hyde was the first to go to Jerusalem years earlier, under instruction from the Prophet Joseph Smith; he had gone alone because his companion became disenchanted in New York and refused to go on. Several others went at various times after that, until a total of perhaps thirteen dedications occurred, either on the Mount of Olives or on Mount Carmel or both. Why so many? I suspect it was because they wanted to keep emphasizing our commitment to these prophecies and because they wanted to exercise the power of the holy priesthood with witnesses in making possible the glorious events of the last days.

They prayed that the land would become fruitful. When they were there it was barren; there was no flowing water at all in and around the temple mount, as there had been anciently and as the prophecies say there will be again. They prayed that the land would be tempered so it could be productive instead of a desert, and they prayed that the curse that had been resting upon Jerusalem over the centuries would be lifted.[40]

The Jordan River, according to Lorenzo Snow's journal, was then 80 to 150 feet wide and 10 to 12 feet deep.[41] It is now down to a trickle compared to that. The prophecies of fruitfulness have begun to be fulfilled.

You remember that Jesus stood somewhere overlooking the city and said, "O Jerusalem, Jerusalem, . . . how often would I have gathered thy children together, even as a hen gathereth her chickens under her wings, and ye would not!" (Matthew 23:37). I have done studies of the gathering of the Jewish people to Israel in the nineteenth century and have noticed two times when there seemed to be an increase of activity—more synagogues built, more people gathering, more foreigners coming. One occurred in the mid-1840s, after Orson Hyde's prayer, and the other was in the 1870s after the visit of the Snows.

Some time later Lorenzo Snow spoke in general conference about that trip. First he read from Doctrine and Covenants 110:12, saying it "describes one of the most important events of our day."

"'The veil was taken from our minds,'" he read, "'and the eyes of our understanding were opened. We saw the Lord standing upon the breastwork of the pulpit, before us'" (D&C 110:1–2)—and then he read the rest of the record of Christ's appearance to Joseph Smith and Oliver Cowdery.

Continuing, he said, "Years ago on my Palestine tour, I was one day upon the Mount of Olives, where Jesus left the earth and ascended to His Father, witnessed by persons that were there present, and I did not doubt that I was at the place where, as I read in the Testament, that Jesus took His departure from. While I looked around and gazed about, I believed that I was there at that place; I believed that Jesus did actually take farewell of the world and go to His Father, because certain individuals say and did make a declaration that that was the fact." Though he did not see those who witnessed the Lord's ascension, he nevertheless knew it was true.

Then he drew the comparison. "This that I have been reading in your hearing"—meaning Doctrine and Covenants 110—"occurred in *this* age. I was personally acquainted with the parties who saw this wonderful manifestation—intimately acquainted with Joseph Smith and Oliver Cowdery." And he implied that he knew as surely that Joseph Smith saw the Lord as that the ancient apostles had witnessed the ascension.

He concluded with this testimony: "There is no man that knows the truth of this work more than I do. I know it fully; I know it distinctly. I know there is a God just as well as any man knows it, because God has revealed himself to me. I know it positively. I shall never forget the manifestations of the Lord; I never will forget them as long as memory endures."[42]

He himself had come to know what the Prophet knew and in the same way.

"STRIPES OF SHAME"

In 1887 the Edmunds–Tucker Act passed Congress and became law. Under authority of that act, the government took over Church property and funds and denied polygamous members the right to vote. Those with more than one family were hunted down and arrested and imprisoned. There was also a "segregating of offenses" provision, which meant that each time a man was seen with his plural wife it was considered a single offense and could result in a six-month jail term. With the possibility of successive offenses and successive sentences, a man could spend a millennium in prison.

Lorenzo Snow was convicted under Edmunds–Tucker and sentenced to eighteen months in the old castle prison located in the area we now know as Sugarhouse. Approximately forty others who were known as "co-habs" were in the prison at the same time. They were mixed in with toughs who were there for a variety of terrible crimes. They wore what were known as the "stripes of shame." Some photographs still exist showing the prisoners, General Authorities Lorenzo Snow and George Q. Cannon among them, wearing black and white stripes with an ugly cap.

Elder Snow's attitude turned that experience from a disaster to a blessing. As the Prophet Joseph Smith said, "If they drive us to hell, we'll turn the devil out and make a heaven of it."[43] While they were in prison these men began to paint, to write, to sculpt, to hold classes in mathematics and languages, and so on. George Q. Cannon wrote a biography of Joseph Smith; in his dedication he says he had increased sympathy for Joseph Smith, who was also in a jail.[44] Lorenzo Snow felt blessed instead of cursed by his association with the Brethren in the prison.

In a blessing given to Lorenzo Snow earlier in his life we find a strange promise: "Prisons shall only cause thee to smile, to see the follies of men." I suppose you could read that to mean that if he's in prison, he'll recognize the terrible crimes that sometimes lead to such consequences. I read it to mean also that he would recognize that his incarceration was unjust and was being appealed at the time to the Supreme Court.

When general conference time came, they were unable to meet with the Saints. Rather than just feel downhearted, Lorenzo Snow called the Latter-day Saint prisoners together and said, "Brethren, we have learned in sacred circumstances to offer the Hosanna Shout. Now, we're being denied the privilege of attending conference. But we have the right, in this setting, to offer our Hosanna Shout to the Lord, to exalt and honor him, to express gratitude that our lives are blessed, even in these circumstances. All of you who would like to join me in this, raise your right hand."[45]

They all raised their hands. I don't know where they found the white handkerchiefs, but they performed the Hosanna Shout at the top of their lungs. It would be interesting to know what the other prisoners made of it. Rudger Clawson said at the funeral of Lorenzo Snow, "The shout ascended to heaven. I testify to you . . . that that great shout was acceptable to the Lord."[46]

While Lorenzo was in prison the Supreme Court finally ruled in his favor, and he was released in 1887, to the great joy of his family and friends.

We learn more about the prison experience from reading the life of B. H. Roberts, who was there and who became, shortly after Lorenzo left, sort of the chaplain of the group. On Sundays they had sacrament services, and B. H. Roberts taught a Sunday School class that even attracted some of the other prisoners.

"OUR EXPERIENCE HAS INCREASED OUR FAITH"

One of the advantages of passing through difficult trials is that afterward you have increased faith and increased confidence in your relationship with God. I once was with President Hugh B. Brown in Hebron in the Holy Land, where, according to tradition, Abraham and Sarah are buried. At one point I asked President Brown, "What are the blessings of Abraham, Isaac and Jacob?"

He replied quickly, "Posterity."

Then I said, "Why, then, was Abraham commanded to go up on a mountain and offer his only hope of posterity, namely Isaac?"

And he replied, "Abraham needed to learn something about Abraham. The Abraham and the Isaac who came down from Mount Moriah, after passing that incredible test, had greater faith in God and in the future than they had when they went up."

Lorenzo Snow taught this same principle. "If we had been made acquainted with the trials through which we have already passed, we would have been discouraged."[47] It's a good thing, he was saying, that the Lord doesn't give you a blueprint or a catalog of what you're going to be facing. It's much better to take it a day at a time. "As it is, our experience has increased our faith and so in regard to our future, it is wisely obscured from our view. I know what my trials have been. I know not what they will be. But on every emergency the Lord has given me needed succor. For this I feel thankful." And then he made this wonderful statement: "I have never seen the day when I was discouraged, as I could always see glorious blessings ahead."[48]

Several people went to see Lorenzo Snow in prison, including the governor. A reporter from the *New York World* visited and said in his subsequent article, "I expected to meet a man wearing a hair shirt and a rebel, sweltering in bitterness. Instead I found a saint, 'a Mormon Chrysostom.'"[49] He was referring to John Chrysostom, who lived centuries before and whose life paralleled Lorenzo Snow's. He was one of the great prelates of the Greek Orthodox faith. Like Francis of Assisi, he cared for the poor. He was imprisoned and finally gave his life.

A POETIC EXCHANGE

While Lorenzo was in prison, he wrote a poem to his sister, Eliza R. Snow, and then she wrote him a poem back. He said:

O Sister dear, could I define and write
A lovely measured line, my thoughts of thee.
A sister's love as burns in hearts of queens above.
Thy love to me, besides thy fame, now wafted o'er
the stormy main,
Thence spread almost to every clime.
And told in tongues of various chime.[50]

Then he wrote of how she was a potential goddess. He talked of their frequent converse, meaning their sharings of spiritual things.

She wrote back:

In your life record there is not one silent page,
Nor one foul blunt.
Eternal archives yet will tell your every page
Is written well.
Yes, those excelsior interviews
Refreshing as Mount Hermon's dews
Bade thought on lofty flights to soar
Beyond the reach of worldly lore.[51]

Eliza became the most faithful chronicler of Lorenzo's family. She defended him against the critics and against the slurs. She made the point that Lorenzo probably would not have married if his religion had not required it. When he did marry he remained, in some ways, a celibate because of his many years serving the Church away from home. Yet through the principle of plural marriage he ended up with forty-one children and three more whom he adopted. So this man who was reluctant to marry became a patriarch indeed.

His last child was born when he was eighty-two years old. The child was named Lucille Snow. At the time he was president of the Salt Lake Temple, the temple was her nursery. She learned reverence and patience. He sometimes stayed there for a week at a time and had a bedroom where she went and he taught her the gospel and told her stories. They were so close, and so loved by the temple workers, that the legend grew up that when he died she would die. But that did not come to pass.

When Lorenzo Snow was seventy years old, the entire family gathered in Brigham City. He said, "This is the last family reunion we have reason to expect this side of the spirit world." They had a three-day reunion, and he saw his children and grandchildren up close. They spoke, they sang, they performed, and then between the official meetings he, as patriarch, gave blessings to all of them.[52] Even though the Church has ordained patriarchs in every organized stake, a father is still the patriarch of his own family, and he has the right and privilege to give them blessings. So Lorenzo did, and his family came away rejoicing.

MIRACLES OF FAITH

The record tells of miracles that attended Lorenzo Snow's ministry, both in terms of healing and being healed. He raised a young woman named Ella Jensen from the dead. She was dead for two hours, and after his administration she remained dead (or appeared so) for an hour before she began to blink and breathe. She didn't, by the way, want to come back. According to her own account, she heard his voice commanding her to come back. And back she came.[53]

As for being healed, Lorenzo Snow didn't have great numbers of mishaps as did Wilford Woodruff, but he had poor health for much of his life. He was only 5'6" and weighed 140 pounds and had respiratory problems.

On the way to Hawaii on a mission he was convinced that he could get out of the ship, down a rope ladder, and into a dinghy. The boat capsized under a wave that was thirty to forty feet high. Others of the Brethren managed to hold on to the upside-down boat, but where was Elder Snow? It took them thirty minutes, with the help of the natives, to finally get his stiff body to the boat. By then he appeared to be dead. They got him on board and then to the shore. They pushed the water out of his lungs as best they could, and then somebody was impressed to give him what we would call mouth-to-mouth resuscitation, and he at last began to breathe and survived.[54] There is an interesting medical footnote to this story. Until that point in his life he had had what we would call migraine headaches. After that he never had another one.[55]

BECOMING LIKE GOD

One of Lorenzo Snow's most famous teachings is in the form of a couplet. He learned it by revelation in 1842, wrote it in a private journal, and then confided it to only two people: his sister, who treated it as a sacred communication, and

Brigham Young when they were in England together. It turned out that Brother Brigham himself had had presentiments of this same principle. The couplet is:

As man now is, God once was.
As God now is, man may become.[56]

To Lorenzo Snow, that was not only a revelation, it was startling. It was radically different from anything he had ever been taught or heard, even though he was a student of the scriptures. It was only after that experience that he began to find passages in John, in Paul, and from Christ himself that say that very thing. The early Christian fathers taught it, but it had been roundly and soundly suppressed since, and now it is considered by some Christians to be nothing less than a heresy.

Clearly, this doctrine does not mean that somehow man will replace God, as some distort it to say. It means instead that the Lord is to be taken at his word. The favorite verse of President Snow, which he recited to the Quorum of the Twelve on the very day he was sustained as President of the Church, was this: "Beloved, now are we the sons [and daughters] of God, and it doth not yet appear what we shall be: but we know that, when he [meaning Christ] shall appear, . . . we shall see him as he is. And every man that hath this hope in him purifieth himself, even as he is pure" (1 John 3:2–3).

There it is, a specific promise that the faithful will resemble the Christ in nature. The Christian world at large would not be as shocked if we said, "We can become like Christ," though even that is hard for them to bear. In Psalm 8:5 we read, "For thou hast made him a little lower than the angels." That's not what the original text said. In Hebrew the word for *angels* is *malacha*. The word for *gods* is *elohim*. This is the word originally found in Psalm 8. Thus we have in the original, "He hath made man a little lower than the Elohim, and crowned him with a physical body and with honor." That's the closest Hebrew transliteration of Psalm 8:5. Lorenzo Snow came to know and teach that in a revelatory way.

"FATHER, THY WILL BE DONE"

I was on Temple Square years ago to help with the tours. It was a wintry day and no one was coming. We sat in the President's Room, as it was known then, with portraits of each of the presidents, including the portrait of Lorenzo Snow. Sister Jean Dunn said to me, "I sat here one day with Milton Snow, son of Lorenzo Snow, and he told us that one night when the entire family was abed and asleep, the father, Lorenzo Snow, came home, waked everyone up, gathered them together, knelt down and prayed, and said, 'Help my family to understand what I'm about to testify about.' Then he unfolded to them the experience he had just had in the temple."

The background to his experience is this: A telegram had arrived from California, where Wilford Woodruff had gone for his health, saying the president was failing fast. Lorenzo Snow went to the temple and prayed earnestly that the life of Wilford Woodruff would be preserved. Lorenzo was then in his eighties. He knew the terrible financial condition of the Church and the other problems it was facing, with government prosecution and persecution. In effect, Lorenzo prayed that he would not have to carry this burden. Then another telegram arrived: Wilford Woodruff had died. Lorenzo Snow returned to a sacred room and prayed, saying in essence, "Father, thy will be done. Now guide me." But his prayer brought nothing he could recognize as an answer.

Disappointed, he finally left the room. He was walking

down the corridor in the Salt Lake Temple when, according to his last daughter, Lucille Snow, and his granddaughter, Allie Young Pond, he saw, in an open vision, the Lord Jesus Christ.[57] The Savior stood above the floor, as if something was under his feet. (We remember a similar description from D&C 110:2 of the Kirtland Temple manifestation: "under his feet was a paved work of pure gold.") President Snow described the magnificence of the Lord's personage and His countenance. Later he testified to his family that the Lord said to him, "Reorganize immediately and your counselors are . . ."[58] and they were named to him.

Soon thereafter the Twelve gathered in the upper room of the temple. Lorenzo Snow did not say a word about his experience, but opened the meeting and expressed in a humble way his feeling of being unfit and aged, and even his feeling that he could step aside. One of the Brethren, Elder Francis M. Lyman, said, "I feel impressed although one of the younger members of the quorum, to say that I believe it would be pleasing in the sight of the Lord if the First Presidency of the Church was reorganized right here and right now. If I am in error regarding this impression, President Snow and the senior members of the council can correct me." One by one the Brethren spoke, and they all were of one mind—that the First Presidency should be reorganized immediately, and it was the Lord's will that they sustain Lorenzo Snow as president.[59]

According to President Heber J. Grant, it wasn't until after that expression of his Brethren that Lorenzo Snow said, "Brethren, I'm glad to know you are inspired of the Lord. It has been made known to me from the Lord Himself that we are to reorganize and that I am to serve as President. And brethren, you will be surprised at my counselors. They are George Q. Cannon and Joseph F. Smith." Afterward President

Grant took a poll. He talked to each of the other brethren and said, "Were you surprised at the counselors?" Every person said "No." His conclusion: The only person who was surprised was Lorenzo Snow.[60]

Now I return to Lorenzo Snow's inspired couplet. The implication that is often drawn from this statement is that, if faithful, we can count on becoming fully like the Christ. But after his experience with the Master, Lorenzo Snow realized more than ever the long, long distance that he still had to travel, despite all of his efforts to live and honor the gospel. The promise is there—but it is up to us to seek to live up to our potential.

It was a joy for Lorenzo Snow to hear the doctrine taught publicly in April 1844, when the Prophet Joseph gave the last great discourse of his life. Lorenzo Snow shared another aspect of these teachings in one of his last addresses. Here are a few sentences: "When Jesus lay in the manger, a helpless infant, He knew not that He was the Son of God, and that formerly He created the earth. When the edict of Herod was issued, He knew nothing of it; He had not power to save Himself; and His father and mother had to take Him and fly into Egypt to preserve Him from the effects of that edict. Well, He grew up to manhood, and during His progress it was revealed unto Him who He was, and for what purpose He was in the world. The glory and power He possessed before He came into the world was made known unto Him."[61]

What was true of Jesus is also true of us: Neither do we know what greatness we attained before we came here.

Some conclude that belief in such greatness—past or future—stems from pride. But it is not, according to Lorenzo Snow, an effect of faith in this principle that you become arrogant and ambitious and power-hungry. That's the distortion in the world—the quest for power. That's the view of Nietzsche: The whole point of life is to gain power and, if necessary, tromp on the heads of those you put down. That's what Hitler attempted. Other people are simply slaves in your galleys. Power means domination. This, of course, is dead wrong. If we become like Christ, there is no domination. There is only persuasion. When you magnify the most powerful thing in the universe, namely Christ's priesthood, you can only do it with persuasion, longsuffering, gentleness, and meekness (see D&C 121:41). You serve and suffer for others instead of dominating them.

In that temple meeting where he was sustained by the Brethren as President of the Church, Lorenzo Snow said, "This principle has been a guiding star in my life since my early days in the Church." What principle? That we have within us the potential to become Christlike. And: "It has cleansed me of every improper ambition."[62]

It is the privilege of every faithful person in this Church to become truly great. That doesn't mean, as we sometimes suppose, holding an office or calling in a temporary Church position. We are talking about eternity. Lorenzo Snow was absolutely clear in teaching that there will be no form of government in the life to come besides family government. There is no God in eternity who has any governmental rights except over his or her own children. That's the meaning of the patriarchal order. All the efforts in this world to become an emperor or lord of the nations are a violation and distortion of that principle. Thus President Snow concluded in that speech to the Brethren, "The position I hold now means nothing to me compared to what I expect hereafter."[63]

MOUNTAINOUS CHALLENGES

There were four "alps" that Lorenzo Snow faced as president. First was the question of the financial obligations of the Church. The credit of the Church was zero. The debt of the Church was so extensive that the tithing collected annually was not enough to pay the interest on the loans. And we had lost much of our property to the government through the Edmunds–Tucker Act. The second alp was the whole question of the U.S. government itself and its making peace with us, and we with it, after the Manifesto. The third was the challenge to extend the gospel worldwide. And the fourth was President Snow's responsibility, as he saw it, to teach as the prophet with great clarity and power the distinctions of the restored gospel.

You know the story on tithing. He went to St. George, where he had a revelatory experience as he stood before the Saints. He then taught that the solution to the Church's terrible financial condition was for the Saints to pay their tithing, a full and honorable ten percent. He taught the same as he visited many towns as he traveled north. Then another meeting was held in the Salt Lake Temple. In that meeting he taught, again, "The Lord has told me plainly and clearly what we must do." In that setting, he taught Doctrine and Covenants 86, which has to do with our role as "lawful heirs according to the flesh" (D&C 86:9). The last verse includes the words, "blessed are ye if ye continue in my goodness"—perhaps referring in part to the goodness we received before this life—"a light unto the Gentiles, and through this priesthood, a savior unto my people Israel" (D&C 86:11). President Snow was saying, that's your identity. Magnify that calling by honoring the Lord's law, and pay your tithing. Within a short time the Church was back on a sound financial basis, and it has continued so ever since.

As for the government, some spoke in condemnatory

terms about the government, but he did not. He talked about the Supreme Court decision that had bearing on plural marriage and said we must demonstrate that we are thoroughly loyal, that we are part of the American community, diverse though it is.

As for extending the gospel in the world, while he was in Italy and later in other parts of the world (he had hoped even to go to India), his vision of how the gospel must go everywhere was never diminished. And here we are, a century later, established in 160 countries.

THE TEACHINGS AND THE TEACHER

Now a few words about his teachings. These are almost proverbs, lifted in one or two sentences from a magnificent set of discourses.

"The reward for righteousness is exaltation. . . . Godliness cannot be conferred, but must be acquired."[64] By that he meant that ultimately, if we are to become like the Savior, we have to give our all and he has to give his (which he has). "We approach godliness as fast as we approach perfection."[65]

"Before I die," he said, "I hope to see the Church cleared of debt and in a commanding position, financially."[66] It happened.

"If we are faithful, we shall at some time do our own work, but now we are doing the work of our Father."[67]

"Greater work was never done by man since the days of Adam than is being done here in the temple."[68]

"We have all the possibilities of God himself, and we should so act that every faculty shall be developed to the utmost."[69]

I wish there were space to expand on this one: "A mother

who has brought up a family of faithful children ought to be saved if she never does another good thing."[70]

"The glorious opportunity of becoming truly great belongs to every faithful Elder in Israel. It is his by right divine."[71]

"I would like to live to see the time when the old bitterness between Mormons and non-Mormons shall have disappeared."[72]

"The destiny of man is to be like his Father—a god in eternity. This should be a bright, illuminating star before him all the time, in his heart, in his soul, and all through him."[73]

Lorenzo Snow was a man who matched his message. A man named Prentis once visited him and said, "The face of Lorenzo Snow, next to only one"—and he didn't say who that other one was—"was the holiest face I had ever seen." Prentis added that if the Mormon church could produce even a few such men, it would not need a missionary system or "the pen of the ready writer."[74]

Another visitor said, "I found him a cultured man in mind and soul and body. His language was choice, diplomatic, friendly, scholarly. His mannerisms show the studied grace of the schools. The tenor of his spirit is as gentle as a child. You are introduced to him, you are pleased with him. You converse with him, you like him. You visit with him long, you love him. And yet, he is a Mormon."[75]

I testify that he was a true Mormon, meaning a literal latter-day saint. I return to my moment of truth in California, when I read his patriarchal blessing, which was significantly, fully, magnificently fulfilled. I have come to honor Lorenzo Snow for what he was—a modern prophet of the Living God, who spoke with Jesus Christ face to face.

6

JOSEPH F. SMITH

For background on the sixth President of the Church, Joseph F. Smith, I take you into the Kirtland Temple. There Joseph Smith and Oliver Cowdery were praying in the midst of others faithful in the Church—praying for a testimony that the dedication of the Kirtland Temple had been accepted by the Lord. The response was an open vision confirming that the temple was accepted and would be filled with the glory of God—and then there were successive appearances of ancient worthies who transmitted, or conferred, keys of authority. At one point a person called Elias restored "the gospel of Abraham, saying that in us and our seed all generations after us should be blessed" (D&C 110:12).

In regard to the seed or literal posterity of Joseph and Oliver, that promise seems to have been unfulfilled. It seems to have fallen to the ground. In the case of the Prophet Joseph, the record shows that his immediate blood descendants not only did not follow the Church into the Great Basin, but in fact withdrew from the Church and eventually organized their own. Only a few descendants of that original generation are now in what they call the "Utah Church."

As for Oliver Cowdery, he not only does not have a posterity in the Church, he does not have any posterity, period. He was married and did have one daughter, but she did not marry and had no children. So Oliver Cowdery can hardly be counted as a person whose posterity became a blessing to subsequent generations. Some might conclude that this was a false prophecy. But was it?

An answer can be found in Doctrine and Covenants 124. After Oliver Cowdery's decline and fall, "the same blessing, and glory, and honor, and priesthood, and gifts of the priesthood" that were "put upon him that was my servant" were conferred instead, in full, upon Hyrum Smith (D&C 124:95). The promise to Oliver that "in [thee] and [thy] seed all generations after [you] should be blessed" therefore applies to Hyrum and his dedicated wives. Has it come to pass? Well, therein hangs a tale, which we now undertake to tell.

In the spring of 1844, Joseph and Hyrum were free and clear of their enemies and had crossed the river, intending to go west. That story is well known. What is not so well known is that Hyrum had been told in a blessing early in his life that if he desired, he could give his life in the cause of Christ. In effect, the wording wasn't "you will be a martyr for the cause"; it was "you will be a martyr if you choose."[1] Moreover, he had been assured in a patriarchal blessing given by his brother Joseph that "faithfulness would be the strength of his loins."[2] As we interpret that phrase, it meant that he would have a very righteous posterity. At that point in his life, Hyrum had six children by Jerusha Barden, who had died, and one son and one daughter by Mary Fielding. The son was Joseph F., who in 1844 was not yet six.

Before Joseph and Hyrum proceeded on their journey,

they were approached by delegation after delegation from Nauvoo, all saying, come back, come back. Some reassured them (or tried to) that it would be safe. Others said, in essence, "You stood and said you would give your life for us and now you are the first to abandon us."[3]

Finally the Prophet said to Hyrum, "I will go back, but you don't have to."[4] Both expressed the desire to be with their pregnant wives when they would deliver the children they were expecting. I don't know how long the discussions lasted, but finally came the crucial, fateful moment when Hyrum gripped the Prophet on his shoulders, looked him in the eye, and said, "Joseph, in the name of Israel's God I covenant that I will live with you wherever you go, and I will die with you wherever you go."

The Prophet wanted to shake that off, but finally, hesitantly, said, "Amen."[5] So the decision was made that they would return together.

On three other occasions between then and Carthage the Prophet remonstrated, "Hyrum, you go back." All three times Hyrum said, "Joseph, I cannot leave you."[6] He didn't mean, "I don't have the agency or power." He meant, "I have made a covenant to the death."

On June 27 Mary Fielding Smith could not sleep throughout the whole night, sometimes reading the Bible, sometimes praying. Then early in the morning a knock came at the door. "Who is it?"

"George Grant."

"What is the news?"

"Joseph and Hyrum are dead."[7]

Little Joseph F. fainted and his mother wept. This was the same little boy who had run out to the horses—Hyrum was on his white horse, Sam—just as they were leaving for Carthage for the last time. Joseph F. later recalled, "Without getting off his horse father learned over in his saddle and picked me up off the ground. He kissed me goodbye and put me down again and I saw him ride away."[8] He never saw his father alive again. This was the same little boy who hid in the little brick outhouse of their home because the threat had been made that within thirty days the mob would not leave one Smith alive in Nauvoo. Young Joseph F.'s life therefore began in turmoil. He had been taken as a mere infant to the Liberty Jail and handed by Mary Fielding Smith down the stairway into the darkness of the dungeon so that his father could see him. He knew trouble.

But he was a child of promise. When the Church was barely organized Hyrum was given a charge: "Thy calling is to exhortation, and to strengthen the church continually. Wherefore thy duty is unto the church forever." And then the phrase that becomes more prophetic in light of his son: "And this because of thy family. Amen" (D&C 23:3).

CROSSING THE PLAINS

The story of Mary Fielding Smith on the westward migration is well known. She had oxen and a courageous young son who was a master driver at a mere seven years of age and who got them to Winter Quarters. Mary Fielding Smith was the woman who eventually administered to her ox in the pattern of faith and prayer and her ox stood up, was healed, and continued the journey. She was the same woman who was broken in health at the time that Hyrum died and was nursed back, in part, by a faithful woman who had also helped her in Far West, Missouri.

Young Joseph helped his mother a good deal at Winter Quarters, and they set out the following spring. One of his duties was to be a herdsman. "He never lost a hoof," as they say, meaning he took care of the cattle, protected them, properly fed them, and never lost one. Mary taught him a sense of duty, and he became very conscientious.

She also taught him to read. In many of the covered wagon trains, the wheelbox, or the box of the prairie schooner, became a school on wheels where children would sit, study, read, and recite. Joseph F. didn't have access to many books, but he did have access to the Bible, and his mother taught him from that.

His schooling stopped abruptly in his mid-teens, but he became self-taught and a master of English, with a prose style that shows clearly in his discourses and in his writings.

As an adult he was an inveterate letter writer—one almost wonders if he had time to do anything else. Four hundred of his letters addressed to one wife are now in the Church archives, and that's only a portion of thousands of letters. Most of his letters were to his family, but he also wrote his share of official letters. He had a very readable hand. From his youth on he kept up on vocabulary, kept lists of words that were not familiar, and looked them up. A book has been compiled of his letters to his missionary sons.[9] Sometimes he'd correct their spelling or grammar errors with a red pen. Joseph F. Smith is another proof that education doesn't have to be within academy walls and that one who is conscientious and persistent can become a master. He was a master of language.

Unfortunately, his mother's life and her health were fragile. It is correct to say that in two ways Joseph F. became an orphan. He lost his father at about age six, and he lost his mother, Mary Fielding, when he was fourteen. Yet that orphan fulfilled the promise made to his father, for from him came a numerous and consecrated posterity that now numbers in excess of six thousand.

"MAMA, MAMA"

Early in his life Joseph F. was known for his fiery temper. One day in a school class the schoolmaster threatened to either whip or use a cane on Joseph F. Smith's sister, and he loudly protested. He may have even added a threat. The schoolmaster went after him instead, and Joseph thrashed him thoroughly—and was expelled from school.

To channel his energies in another direction, he was called on a mission at the tender age of fifteen.[10] His mission? The Sandwich Islands, now known as Hawaii. As a mere boy he received the temple blessings in the old Endowment House and was set apart by Parley P. Pratt to be a missionary. Among other things, Elder Pratt promised him that he would learn to master the language, and quickly.[11] (He became adept and able in Hawaiian, with all the dialects and nuances of pronunciation.)

Joseph F. Smith was on the ship the day that Lorenzo Snow was almost drowned and then revived, as described in the previous chapter. Others told the young Joseph to get into the smaller boat, and, seeing the danger, he refused, saying, "If you, . . . by the authority of the Priesthood of God, which you hold, tell me to get into that boat and attempt to land, I will do so, but unless you command me in the authority of the Priesthood, I will not do so, because it is not safe to attempt to land in a small boat while this storm is raging."[12] He stayed on the ship. Then he had to stand there in terrible anxiety as he saw the little boat capsize and Lorenzo Snow disappear. Lorenzo Snow later said that when Joseph said what he did on that ship, he had the impression that Joseph would one day be a leader in the Church.[13]

Joseph F. struggled with the customs and the food in Hawaii. The only dietary staple was poi. He also had a period of great sickness. The natives themselves were often unclean and sick. And that was all very unpleasant. But he took seriously the commission to teach. Some missionaries who first went over with Elder George Q. Cannon, his predecessor, became so discouraged that they simply left and returned home. Even the mission president gave up.[14] George Q. Cannon refused to leave, however, and through prayer and inspiration he converted at least a hundred souls on the island of Maui. That was the beginning, the planting of the stake.

Elder Matthew Cowley once said that he had never felt the Spirit of the Lord more strongly than when he was near the little chapel up on the side of the mountain on Maui called Haleakala, where George Q. Cannon had first preached the gospel.[15]

The difficulties compounded during Joseph F. Smith's mission. During his sickness a woman named Ma Mahuhii took him in for three months and nursed him back to health, as if she were his mother. Years later, when he was President of the Church and she was ninety years old, he was with a gathering of the Saints. An elderly Hawaiian woman, almost blind, entered the back of the hall, limping, and carrying a little package of bananas. He recognized her, rushed down to embrace her, and called her over and over, "Mama, Mama, my dear old Mama!" and then kissed her. He turned to Charles W. Nibley, who was with him, and said, "She nursed me when I was a boy, sick and without anyone to care for me. She took me in and was a mother to me!"[16]

He had a head-on collision, as it were, with evil spirits on his mission, as had the first missionaries in England. He was in a place called Wailuku with a family of natives. Suddenly a woman was seized by evil spirits and went through all manner of contortions. Her husband was terrified, and Joseph, too, was troubled. But then, with faith, he faced the woman and said, "In the name of the Lord Jesus Christ I rebuke you," meaning the evil spirits. She fell limp to the floor. The husband thought she was dead and started to mourn. But soon she regained her strength and was completely relieved and healed.[17]

Joseph also experienced an earthquake in 1856. It was known as "The Great Volcanic Eruption." It started in a small area, but then the lava flowed for more than sixty miles. That's a lot of lava, almost ten percent of the area of the island.[18]

On his way home from his mission he crossed the Nevada desert as a teamster and learned that Brigham Young was organizing an army. Why? Because of what we now call "Buchanan's Folly," the coming of Johnston's Army. So Joseph F. became a horseman and literally stayed in the saddle, traveling back and forth toward and beyond Echo Canyon and Fort Bridger.[19] Finally, the conflict was resolved in a peaceful way.

"WILL YOU BE WANDERING?"

Then, instead of being able to stay home, Joseph was called on another mission. He traveled with a relative to Nauvoo and then headed for his first of three missions to England. It was during that journey that he saw Emma Smith in Nauvoo for the first time since his childhood. (It was also the last time he saw her.) She was stunned at how much he looked like Hyrum and said, in essence, "I would have known you anywhere."[20] As he was leaving she asked, "Will you be wandering?" which was her phrase for doing missionary work.

He said, "Quite a lot of that before I return home."

"Are you fond of it?" she asked, as if to say, are you really committed to this?

He said, "To be truthful, I would rather be at home."

And then with tears in her eyes she said, "Someday I hope

all of us will be able to stay home with our families." That says a lot about Emma's own struggle. (She and Joseph had moved something like fourteen times in fifteen years.)

In England he grew closer to George Q. Cannon and they became fast friends at every level—intellectually, spiritually, and in terms of joint commitment to the work. He anticipated then that they would later be serving as counselors in the First Presidency.

While he was in England he had a sacred dream. Notice that many of the dreams that one reads about from Joseph F. involve family relationships and kinships:

"Last night I had a glorious dream. I saw Uncle Joseph, father [Hyrum], Brigham, Heber and the Twelve, all dressed in their robes of white. They seemed to have an additional robe of pure white, without a seam, coming down to their feet and around the edge was a broad strip of pure white, down-like fur, dotted here and there with beautiful spots, which gave a richness to them beyond description. Uncle Joseph scolded me for being late, but I had been to bathe and felt I was clean, and his every word was life and joy, though spoken in reproof. Uncle and father blessed a child. I took the child from Uncle Joseph to return it to its mother and the backs of my hands touched his [Joseph's] bosom, which sent a thrill to my very heart that I cannot describe nor ever shall forget. The perfect order, the extreme joy and happiness that I saw and felt is past my power of expression. I can only write the words, the joy and bliss can only be felt."[21]

For him one of the messages of these dreams, as well as one of the outcomes of them, was: Never withdraw from duty. For him it was made clear that only when he was fully ready could he go back home amidst an eternal family.

"MY DARLING, HOW I MISS THEE"

Joseph F. Smith's family was remarkable. His first wife miscarried and then could have no children, one of the painful and difficult parts of his life. When he then took another wife, there was great frustration on the part of the first wife, and she later divorced him. Eventually he married six wives and had many children by each, except the first; but his joy in his children was tempered by premature deaths. He lost thirteen of those children before his own death. Knowing this and knowing he personally was denied a father and a mother at a young age helps us understand his tenderness for children.

Touching are the words he wrote when he lost a three-year-old daughter whom he had named Mercy Josephine. Mercy was the name of Mary Fielding's sister, and Josephine, of course, is the female version of Joseph. In the crisis he spent the entire night at her bedside. She was sometimes delirious and sometimes filled with uneasiness and anguish. The next morning he said, "My little pet did not sleep all night."

She replied, "I'll sleep today, papa."[22]

I have been to the Smith plot in the Salt Lake City Cemetery and pulled the grass back from Jodie's little grave. The inscription on the stone says, "I'll sleep today, Papa." She knew that she was going to die, and he knew. From that day he asked all his children to call him "Papa." And his most endearing term for his wives was "Mama."

Here is what he wrote after that tender parting: "Oh! Dodo, my babe, my love. I love thee, my ambition was to see thee shine pure and bright amid earth's noblest and best.

"I love thy innocent prattle and thy footsteps echoed in my heart. Thy voice was music, thy little cunning ways more pleasant than the voice of love. . . . Thou wert a heavenly gift directly to my heart of hearts. I loved thee more than tongue can tell, more than the soul can speak through mortal agency. Thou didst make me a better man; for thy sake I loved humanity, earth, and heaven, more; thine image drew me nearer unto God, and caused heaven to bless and flourish in my home. Thy bright spirit lightened all my cares and made all earth seem better. O thou wert all in all to my most fervent love; for thee I could brave life or death. . . . More dearly loved than life. Dodo, how I miss thee; but sleep my babe, in peace. . . . But in thy spirit visit me and as thou didst love to do my bidding do thou now in thy sleepless, immortal life, watch over us, thy papa and mama, baby sister Mamie, Aunt Sarah and brother Edward, and make us to feel that thou art near."[23]

We have another picture of how he dealt with others, especially his own family. One of his sons, Willard, was playing in the dirt road in front of the Beehive House. A bully came along and roughed him up, then pushed his face into the mud and held it there until he almost suffocated. This was in February and close to Valentine's Day. Willard went inside and wrote a valentine to the bully—and on the valentine he wrote every evil word he could think of, every one that he ever heard or read, and put the note in an envelope. But in the process he made a critical mistake. Unwittingly he sent the one he intended to go to the bully to an uncle and the one he intended for his uncle to the bully.

The offending valentine quickly reached the desk of Joseph F. Smith. That morning at family prayer, following his daily routine, Joseph F. kissed each of his children—but he didn't kiss Willard. Instead, he said, "I will see you in my office." Willard went in and waited while his father wrote for a while at his desk. Then Joseph F. Smith turned to a large Bible, opened it, and said, "Come close, Willard. What does that say?"

"It says, 'Swear not at all.'"

"Yes. Now . . . ," and he turned to another passage, "what does that say?"

"It says, 'Forgive seventy times seven.'"

"Yes, that's right." He turned to a third scripture. "What does that say?" This went on for twenty minutes. And then Joseph F. said, "Come here, Son." He embraced him and kissed him and that was the end of it. Willard said later, "I never used a bad word again."[24]

I have personal witness of the legacy of Joseph F. Smith as a father. I knelt as a guest in the home of Willard R. Smith, son of Joseph F. Smith, and listened to Willard's prayers, and watched him with his own family. When he was assigned to speak in church, he would ask his children "What should I say?"

"Dad, just say whatever you say when you pray, but only half as long, and everything will be all right."

Following the tradition of his father, Willard kissed all of his children on the lips whenever he met them—just a quick smack. It didn't matter if they were grown up or not, he kissed them all on the lips. Tender, sweet, and beautiful.

This same Willard R. Smith had a son named Heber who enlisted and flew in World War II with Britain's Royal Air Force. After one furlough visit with his son, Willard noticed that Heber had left his flight jacket at home. Willard took a copy of Heber's missionary Bible, opened it at random to "The Lord is my shepherd" (Psalm 23) marked it, put it in the flight jacket, and sent it to his son.

Before the parcel could arrive a telegram came: Heber had been killed in action. Their package was later returned unopened, as Willard and his wife prayed in anguish at the loss of their boy. They unwrapped the package; the flight jacket came open and so did the Bible. They then saw "Who shall ascend into the hill of the Lord? . . . He that hath clean hands, and a pure heart" (Psalm 24:3–4). He knew that that scripture was meant for them, as a comfort in the loss of their pure-hearted son.

CALLED AS AN APOSTLE

Joseph F. Smith was called as an apostle at the young age of twenty-seven. He had been in a meeting with Brigham Young. At the close of the meeting, as the participants began to leave, President Young said to himself, "Hold on. Shall I do as I feel led to do? . . . It has come to my mind to ordain Brother Joseph F. Smith to the Apostleship, and to be one of my counselors."[25] In that setting, Joseph F. Smith knelt while Brigham reached out his hands and ordained him. He was later set apart as a member of the Quorum of the Twelve by the great patriarch of that time, John Smith.

Joseph F. served as an apostle as well as a counselor to four successive presidents of the Church, Brigham Young, John Taylor, Wilford Woodruff, Lorenzo Snow—all of his predecessors except Joseph Smith. When he became President of the Church he had served as a counselor for seventeen years. His service as a Church leader totaled sixty-two years.

Early in Joseph F. Smith's presidency, the Church erected a monument near Sharon, Vermont, Joseph and Hyrum Smith's birthplace,[26] to commemorate the one hundredth anniversary of the Prophet's birth. The monument weighs forty tons and stands 38½ feet high—one foot for each year in the life of the Prophet. A small visitor's center was also constructed.

In December 1905, Joseph F. Smith traveled to Vermont to be present for the dedication. During the ceremonies the speakers reviewed the life of the Prophet and his brother and then presented President Smith with a gold watch that reminded him of those loved ones whose lives had begun here. He broke down so he could hardly speak and said, "My heart is like that of a child. It is easily touched, especially with love. I can much easier weep for joy than for sorrow."[27]

It is a tribute to Joseph F. Smith that he came on the scene as president after some of the turmoil over statehood and plural marriage had diminished. He had to issue a second Manifesto in 1905. He constantly said, "Let's not be vengeful, let's not be tearing down, let's not be destructive. Let us be among those who build up."

At one point Charles W. Nibley prevailed on President Smith to visit Carthage, where he had never been. They walked up the steps, turned into the room—and then one of the men present said, "That stain is the blood of Hyrum Smith." Preston Nibley, a son of Charles who also was there, told me that Joseph F. Smith walked over and sat down, put his hands over his face, and wept until the tears flowed through his fingers. Then he said, "Charlie, take me out of here." They got in the little horse and buggy and rode the twenty-odd miles from Carthage back to Nauvoo. Not one word was spoken.

Then while Charles Nibley took care of some business, Joseph F. Smith took Preston Nibley, a student from the University of Chicago, all over the city and pointed out the sights—that's where the Relief Society was organized, that's where the Prophet stood when he preached the King Follett discourse, this is where Edward Hunter lived when the Prophet was in hiding, and so forth. Preston, who had until then taken Church history all for granted, said, "That was the day I knew I had to go home and start being serious about Church history." He later wrote twelve books and became assistant Church Historian.

"WE HAVE BEEN PRAYING ALL NIGHT FOR YOU"

Once Joseph F. was walking with a friend—I think it was John Henry Smith—down Main Street and along came the editor of the *Salt Lake Tribune.* At that time the newspaper was hammering two main themes: The Mormon Church represented a dynasty of authoritarian control, and the Mormon Church did not believe in the separation of Church and state. When the two Smiths met the editor of the paper, John Henry Smith reached out and shook hands with him. Joseph F. Smith smiled, but did not shake hands. As they continued down the street, Joseph F. said, "I declare, John Henry, I believe you'd shake hands with the Devil himself." But Joseph F. was not an antagonist. Slowly, he achieved peace both with literary magazines and local newspapers and finally found himself praised.[28]

For a long time in Utah there was a People's Party, which actually was the Mormon Party. Most who really had commitment and faith in the restored gospel considered that the way to show loyalty was to belong to the People's Party. But when statehood was achieved the Church wanted to divide members along political party lines. So it happened that what they then called block teachers (now we call them home teachers) went out, knocked on the door, and said, "You're a Republican," went next door and said, "You're a Democrat," and so forth. Unfortunately, true divisions soon set in, along with opposition and deep feelings about which was the best party.

B. H. Roberts was a political animal from birth and was a fervent Democrat—some would say a pugnacious Democrat. As an independent spirit, and without asking anybody among the Brethren, he sought to be elected to the national House of Representatives and was successful. Then in the most incredible journalistic outcry I know about, he was unseated because he was a Mormon.

To avoid such freelancing in the future, the Brethren decided they would establish a rule that henceforth no General Authority would seek public office without first receiving the approval of the First Presidency. All of the Brethren agreed to the rule except B. H. Roberts. The Brethren labored with him. There is an entry in Wilford Woodruff's journal that says, "H. B. Roberts [the error in the name is in the journal], spent the whole day with him in the temple, but he is adamant and going to destruction."[29]

Finally the time came when they called him in to a meeting and said, "Brother Roberts, if you really can't feel to be one with us on this, we're going to have to drop you from your position as one of the seven presidents of the Seventy. You have until nine o'clock tomorrow morning to give us your answer." That night B. H. Roberts went for a long walk up and down the foothills of Salt Lake. The next morning he entered the office of the First Presidency just before nine o'clock and said, "Brethren, I am at one with you. Everything is resolved. I'm sorry I have caused you such distress." Then with a little bit of acid left in his voice, he said, "But, Brethren, it's taken me all night to arrive at this."

To that Joseph F. Smith said, quite calmly, "Yes, Brother Roberts, and so also with us. We have not left this room. We have been praying all night for you."[30]

Brother Roberts later became a chaplain to the major Utah division of the army and led them overseas in World War I. He had prepared a band that was part of the regiment, and on Pioneer Day (the twenty-fourth of July) they went to Salt Lake City. Brother Roberts struck up the band just outside the Beehive House and they played martial airs. President

Smith walked out onto the balcony and welcomed them, spoke to them briefly, and spoke in praise of B. H. Roberts. Then Brother Roberts went inside and they embraced. Brother Roberts said, "I have no root of bitterness left in my heart toward you."[31] That was the last time they saw each other in this life.

TWO SETS OF SMITHS

I come now to one other difficult part of Joseph F. Smith's life—the separation between the "Utah Smiths" and those who did not go west with the Church. Several years ago a conference of these two families was held in Nauvoo, Illinois, to renew their common legacy and heritage. For the first time in more than a hundred years the Utah Smiths, mostly descendants of Hyrum, met the "Reorganization Smiths." The president of the Reorganized Church (now renamed the Community of Christ) at that time was Wallace Smith. I was invited to attend the conference and talk about Emma Smith. When I received the invitation, I went to a member of the First Presidency and said, "I didn't ask for this, and I don't want to do it."

The answer: "You need to do it."

"Well, before I go, tell me: What is the feeling of the present leaders of their church about Emma?"

"Very positive," he said.

And so I gladly spoke of her virtue, her worth, her nobility, and her service in developing the greatest women's organization of this dispensation.

During the days of Joseph F. Smith, the relationships between the two groups were stressful. At one stage the Reorganized Church summed up the differences in tract form under the title "Differences That Persist." Ironically, these are now no longer differences. Their four points: One, that the church president after the Prophet's death had to be a lineal descendant of Joseph Smith. They no longer require that. Second, that the later discourses of Joseph Smith, including the King Follett discourse, were ascribed to Brigham Young. Their historians now acknowledge Joseph's authorship. Third, that plural marriage was neither taught nor practiced by Joseph Smith. But now it is recognized he did both teach and practice it. And fourth, that the temple ceremony was mostly the invention of the Utah Mormons and not authentically derived from the Prophet's teachings. Now they themselves have built a temple in Independence at great cost—a place for peace conferences. None of the ordinances that we understand are introduced there, but their historians tend to the view that Joseph Smith did introduce and did practice certain principles that are inherent in our temple work.

During his lifetime, Joseph F. Smith was an instrument in the process of reconciliation, a peacemaker, encouraging understanding and mutuality. Never have relationships been better in Independence, Kirtland, and Nauvoo.

"DIVINE HOMESICKNESS"

The teachings of Joseph F. Smith are marked by clarity and personal spiritual sensitivity. Once Orson F. Whitney, as a missionary in England, wrote a letter to Joseph F. Smith, musing on what he called "spirit memories." Here is the essence of Elder Whitney's comments and questions, as he recorded them on another occasion:

"Why are we drawn toward certain persons, and they toward us, independently of any known previous acquaintance?

Is it a fact, or only a fancy, that we and they were mutually acquainted and mutually attracted in some earlier period of our eternal existence? Is there something, after all, in that much abused term 'affinity,' and is this the basis of its claim? More than once, after meeting someone whom I had never met before on earth, I have wondered why his or her face seemed so familiar. [In our day, we have popularized the French expression *déjà vu*—already seen.] Many times, upon hearing a noble sentiment expressed, though unable to recall having heard it until then, I have been thrilled by it, and felt as if I had always known it. The same is true of music, some strains of which are like echoes from afar, sounds falling from celestial heights, notes struck from the vibrant harps of eternity. I do not assert preacquaintance in all such cases, but as one thought suggests another, these queries arise in the mind.

"When it comes to the Gospel, I feel more positive. Why did the Savior say: 'My sheep know my voice'? Can a sheep know the voice of its shepherd, if it has never heard that voice before? They who love Truth, and to whom it appeals most powerfully, were they not its best friends in a previous state of existence? I think so. I believe that we knew the Gospel before we came here, and it is this knowledge, this acquaintance, that gives to it a familiar sound."[32]

Joseph F. Smith replied, "I heartily endorse your sentiments." And then he went on to say that we were all present before the foundations of this world in the grand council. We saw the Savior chosen. He knew beforehand that he must come into the world and fulfill his mission. And Joseph F. Smith said, "If Christ knew beforehand, so did we." Then he noted that the veil of forgetfulness has been drawn so we can truly be tested. Yet he concluded, "By the power of the Spirit, in the redemption of Christ, through obedience, we often catch a spark from the awakened memories of the immortal soul, which lights up our whole being as with the glory of our former home."[33] I have a friend who sums up those experiences by calling them "divine homesickness."[34] Joseph F. Smith felt that.

In 1916 President Smith gave a discourse wherein he talked about those who have gone before, and he was overwhelmed with emotion. He said he felt that at that very moment, he and the Saints were in the presence of the Father and of the Son, along with others whose whole lives had been given to build the kingdom and to make possible healed and sealed family relationships. Then he said, "I hope you will forgive me for my emotion. You would have peculiar emotions, would you not, if you felt that you stood in the presence of your Father, in the very presence of Almighty God, in the very presence of the Son of God and of holy angels? . . . So I hope you will forgive me, if I exhibit some of my real feelings."[35]

Someone asked him point-blank if he believed in guardian angels. His own opinion was that in the spirit world we still have relatives who care as much about us as we presently care about them, and probably more, and that they are not far from us and have influence in our lives.[36] He taught that we are in the presence of heavenly beings.[37]

He often spoke in his discourses of a joyful reunion in the resurrection. He believed in a literal, complete, and (for the righteous) celestial resurrection.

He talked to Eliza R. Snow about how Joseph Smith had revealed to her that we have a Mother in Heaven, and Joseph F. sang that truth in "O My Father"[38] with great feeling. In a letter to one of his wives, he said, "Oh, . . . how I love and cherish true motherhood."[39]

He spoke of the Godhead, that "matchless governing quorum over all the creations of the Father."[40] That one word, *quorum,* helps explain what we mean when we talk about the three persons in the one Godhead. It's a quorum—three persons—who nevertheless are at one with each other in mind and in will.

He taught that the scriptures would bring new insights to us, even those with which we are presently familiar.[41] You know the experience. You may have marked a passage in the book, and then a year or two or longer later, you open your scriptures to that place, and there's the passage. You don't remember marking it, and this time when you read it, it has a deeper meaning. What we bring to the scriptures in large part determines how much we take from them.

He often spoke of the "mighty change" we must receive, referring to the experience recorded in Mosiah 5:2: Those who listened to King Benjamin's sermon not only listened, but were pricked in their hearts; they not only were pricked, but that day were reborn. He talked in his discourses about how this mighty change relates to the ordinances of baptism and confirmation and of the temple.[42]

VISION OF THE REDEMPTION OF THE DEAD

Doctrine and Covenants section 138 is Joseph F. Smith's vision of the redemption of the dead. What is in that vision that we don't find in prior revelations? It was made clear to President Smith that the "descensus," as it's called in classical theology (that is, the time Jesus spent after his death in the spirit world), did not mean that Jesus went in person to those spirits who had been awaiting the fullness of the gospel. Instead, he sent trustworthy, loyal, and faithful missionaries who had lived in this world and now were in the spirit world.

The full presence of Jesus Christ is a privilege for which one must prepare. We cannot truly enter into his presence unless we are purified. The implication, then, is that the Lord could not have gone personally to the unprepared in the spirit world because it would have been destructive rather than redeeming to them (see D&C 138:18–22, 36–37, 57–59).

At the time of the death of their mother, Joseph F.'s sister had a remarkable vision. She saw her father, Hyrum, who had gone before, and now Mary Fielding with him, and they both were veiled. When she inquired why, they answered, "If we removed the veil you could not endure our presence." One version reads, "You could not see us." She described the beauty and the glory and the whiteness shining from them.[43]

In the vision of the redemption of the dead, President Smith named many of what we might call the "worthies" of former dispensations and how actively they were engaged in the work of the Lord in the spirit world. He saw that the primary work of those who step through the veil is teaching and sharing the gospel, even in the classroom sense; and that in that place there's no such thing as a release. The release of death simply takes us into a new venue for continuing the ministry. It is true, we cannot escape ourselves. We are in a linear, temporal pattern. We go from one stage to another, and there is no backtracking. There is no way one can cease to be him or herself.

"WHO DO YOU MOST WANT TO SEE?"

We come to November 1918. World War I had ended, but there was a great influenza epidemic in the land. Joseph F. Smith did not have the flu, but his lungs were weakened and he had pneumonia. Heber J. Grant went to the Beehive House, unaware of how truly sick the president was. He found President Smith in his bedroom asleep and tiptoed back out. Then he heard a voice, a rather weak voice, say, "Tell Heber to come back." David A. Smith hurried to the front door: "My father would like you to come back."

President Smith reached out and took Heber J. Grant by the hand, and with a strength, Heber later said, that was hardly compatible with being on his deathbed, said the following exact words: "The Lord bless you, my boy, the Lord bless you, you have got a great responsibility. Always remember that this is the Lord's work and not man's. The Lord is greater than any man. He knows whom He wants to lead His church and never makes any mistake. The Lord bless you."[44]

Heber J. Grant had fasted and prayed for years that Joseph F. Smith, the son of the martyr, Hyrum, would be alive in 1930 when the Church would reach its first one hundred years. Elder Grant felt it would be a beautiful thing if President Smith could stand as the living prophet at the Church's centennial celebration. At that moment it was clear to him that it was not to be. Joseph F. Smith passed away that night.

Mary T. Schwartz Smith, the last living wife of Joseph F. Smith, loved and missed her husband so much that after he died she walked up to his portrait every night and kissed "Papa" on the lips. Someone once asked her, "What is the first thing you want to do when you step through the veil—who do you most want to see?" Her answer was, "I want to embrace the other mamas, and then Papa."[45]

I bear you this testimony that love in the family context is the glorious fulfillment of the life and atonement and death of Jesus Christ.

7

HEBER J. GRANT

Not everybody knows the names Jedediah M. Grant or Rachel Ridgeway Ivins Grant, but each of them has a story that bears directly on the life of Heber Jeddy Grant. Rachel Ridgeway Ivins was born in Hornerstown, New Jersey. As a girl, she was given both Quaker and Baptist training, but she became an orphan before she was grown. On a dare one night she went with a friend to hear two men talk regarding the restoration of the gospel. The two men were Erastus Snow and Joseph Smith. That night, according to the story, she went home and prayed for forgiveness for listening to false prophets on the Sabbath. Her minister learned of that venture and challenged her, saying, "If you ever do that again you will not have a pew in my church."

Apparently she had an independent spirit, and she responded, "How do you know they don't have the truth?"[1] Somehow speaking boldly in that manner opened her own heart. She studied and gained a testimony, over the protests of her uncle and aunt, who said she had disgraced the family name. In the spring of 1844, she gathered to Nauvoo.

Jedediah M. Grant was converted in his teens and was called to missionary labor. He had given something like forty sermons before he was out of his teens. In one of his missionary labors in the South, he once was challenged to attend a meeting where he was to stand up, receive on the spot a piece of paper that contained his text, and speak to that topic without preparation. Those sponsoring the meeting decided to embarrass him, and they handed him a paper that was blank.

He gave a marvelous sermon: "My friends, I am here today according to agreement, to preach from such a text as these gentlemen might select for me. I have it here in my hand. I knew nothing of what text they would choose, but of all texts this is my favorite one.

"You see, the paper is blank, (at the same time holding it up to view). You sectarians down there believe that out of nothing God created all things, and now you wish me to create a sermon from nothing.

"You believe in a God that has neither body, parts, nor passions. Such a God I believe to be a perfect blank, just as you find my text is.

"You believe in a church without prophets, apostles, evangelists, etc. Such a church would be a perfect blank as compared with the Church of Christ and this agrees with my text."

Some were not happy with the impact of his sermon, but others took up a collection to get him a new suit of clothes.[2]

Jedediah Grant was present the day the Prophet Joseph Smith left for Carthage. He heard him speak of the future in terms of the terrible wars that would someday occur in the United States of America, and he heard him say, "This is the loveliest place and the best people under the heavens."[3] Jedediah Grant led a company of a hundred in the second large group that followed Brigham Young to the Great Basin, and he became the first mayor of Salt Lake City.

After the death of the Prophet Joseph Smith, Rachel went home to New Jersey, assuming that perhaps Mormonism had come to an end. But in due time, despite her family's inducements to stay—they even offered to settle an annuity on her for life—she decided to gather with the Saints and went to Utah.

Now we bring the two together. Eventually, in her early thirties, Rachel married Jedediah M. Grant. In that era the "Mormon Reformation," as it was called, began; and Jedediah Grant went out, Brigham Young later said, "like an angel."[4] He traveled up and down the Mormon corridor, pleading with the Saints to renew their spiritual identity and live the gospel. Baptizing in sometimes icy water in November 1856, he developed pneumonia. Heber J., the first and only child he had through Rachel, was eight days old when his mother put him on the chest of Jedediah, who was dying. Jedediah passed away at the age of forty and she had to raise that one boy alone.

There were many heralds of his prophetic future. For many years Rachel Grant was the president of the Relief Society in the Salt Lake City Thirteenth Ward, and they often met at the home of William C. Staines. (Brother Staines, incidentally, later took care of all the flowers on Temple Square.) In one of those meetings Rachel Grant, who was slowly going deaf, heard Eliza R. Snow speak in tongues and then heard Sister Zina D. H. Young interpret. That often happened with those two remarkable women. Eliza R. Snow had pronounced a kind of blessing upon the sisters present. But then Eliza turned to the little boy on the floor, who was about two years of age, and said, in effect, that this little boy will live to be an Apostle of Jesus Christ. Rachel wrote that in her heart, and all through Heber's growing up stages she would remind him, "Behave yourself, Heber, and some day you will be an apostle in the Church." He would reply, "Mother, get it out of your head. I do not want to be an apostle. . . . I do not want to be anything but a business man."[5]

Heber C. Kimball, who was often prophetic, picked up Heber J. when he was seven or eight, put him on a table so that they were eye to eye, and said, "You should become an apostle of the Lord Jesus Christ and become a greater man in the Church than your own father."[6] He didn't remember that incident, but his mother did.

"THE LAZIEST BOY IN THE WHOLE WARD"

What were his advantages and what were his trials and what were his ambitions? He and his mother suffered extreme poverty, and his mother made a living by taking in lodgers and by sewing. He often helped her at the sewing machine late at night, pushing the treadle with either his feet or his arms. Once the bishop, Edwin D. Woolley, came by. When he saw six or more pans catching the leaks from the roof, he said, "Why, widow Grant, this will never do. I shall take some of the money from the fast offerings, to put a new roof on this house."

She gave him a Scotch blessing and said, "Oh, no you won't. No relief money will ever put a roof on my house. I have sewing here [to support us]. . . . This house will take care of me until my son gets to be a man and builds a new one for me."

The bishop "went away and said he was very sorry for Widow Grant, that if she waited for that boy to build a house she would never have one, for he was the laziest boy in the whole Thirteenth Ward."[7]

I've come to believe that Bishop Woolley was a master psychologist. Heber J. Grant overheard that remark, and he said to his mother, "I don't want to do anything but make money so I can buy you a new house." He eventually built her not just a better roof, but a new house—and guess who he invited over to dedicate the house? He said to his bishop, "I want to thank you for the remark you made some time ago about me; and I would like you now to dedicate this house."[8] Edwin Woolley knew what he was doing.

Later, when Heber J. Grant was called to be a stake president at the ripe old age of twenty-three, Bishop Woolley said to one of the Brethren, "Yes, you've made him a stake president. I want you to know that this boy is the peer of any man in the Quorum of the Twelve."[9]

When Heber was a boy he had four ambitions: first, he wanted to serve a mission; second, he wanted to have a fine education, perhaps at West Point or Annapolis, leading to a military career; third, he wanted to be a millionaire by thirty; fourth, he wanted to be mayor of Salt Lake City, like his father, then governor, and finally a United States senator. That's all he wanted. Each, in turn, could have happened.

When he wanted to go on a mission at age eighteen, Elders Erastus Snow and Daniel H. Wells objected. Heber was, they said, already performing "a very splendid mission" in providing for his widowed mother.[10] So there was no mission.

As for education, George Q. Cannon, then a territorial representative, told him he could have his choice: West Point or Annapolis. He stayed awake almost all night thinking of the opportunity and what a great step it would be in his life. But in the morning when he saw his mother, her eyes were bloodshot, and it was clear she had been weeping all night. He said, "Mother, I do not want a naval education. I am going to be a business man and shall enter an office right away and take care of you."[11]

We'll talk about his financial successes and failures later on.

He did have the opportunity to fulfill his political aspirations. At one point he went to President Woodruff and asked whether he should run for governor.

President Woodruff, seemingly with a little irritation, said, "What are you bothering me with your affairs for? Haven't you got enough inspiration as one of the apostles to know what your duty is?"

Heber said, "Thank you. If you had wanted me to run, you would have said so. Good-bye."[12] And he gave it up.

The story of his goal to become a U.S. senator is even more dramatic. Years later he received a telephone call. "So-and-so has withdrawn from the senatorial contest. Just tell me we can put your name in nomination and you're in."

He answered, "Wait just a minute."

He put the phone down and paced back and forth in conversation with himself: "Heber, why do you want to be a senator?" "Well, so that you can walk in on so-and-so [a man who had called him a brainless boy in his earlier life] and slap down a card saying 'Honorable Heber J. Grant, U.S. Senator.'" "Oh, so it's your dirty, nasty, stinking pride, is it?" "Yes, it is."

He picked up the telephone again. "Hello? No."[13]

That's the decisive Heber J. Grant. Of course, he could have served others by being a senator. There are legitimate reasons for public office. But at that point he was already involved deeply in Church administration, and the Spirit seemed to guide him to stay with it.

"DO YOU HAVE AN ABSOLUTE TESTIMONY?"

As mentioned, he was called at age twenty-three to be a stake president in Tooele. This was an assignment from President John Taylor, who interviewed, called, and set him apart on the spot. But when the "Amen" came after that priesthood blessing, one of the Brethren said, "Heber, . . . don't you know absolutely that this Gospel is true?"

He said, "I do not."

The brother then turned to President Taylor and said, "I am in favor of undoing this afternoon what we did this morning. I do not think any man should preside over a stake who has not a perfect and abiding knowledge of the divinity of the work in which we are engaged."

President Taylor laughed and said, "He knows it just as well as you do. The only thing he does not know is that he does know it. It will be a short time until he knows it."[14]

Well, he shortly came to that testimony,[15] but in the meantime there was another question. This is in the Grant family lore, and I'm not sure it's ever been written down. He was on the street, and a man who had heard about his calling approached him. This man knew that the boy Heber had been skinny, knock-kneed, and called "a sissy." He knew that Heber had been told that if he drank a little beer it would help him put on weight. The man said, "Heber, are you keeping the Word of Wisdom?"

"Yes, sir," Heber replied.

Skeptically, the other man said, "Since when?"

And President Grant replied, "Since right now." That was true.

In the language of his friends, Heber committed financial suicide by accepting that calling. It meant that he would live part time in Tooele but ride his horse to Salt Lake City a couple of times a week. His opportunities to work and make money would be greatly diminished.

He started in business as a young boy when he learned to play marbles. At first he lost every marble he ever played with, but he practiced on the rug in his house until he became better than anyone else around. He began to play for keeps, but he had to put up ten marbles for every one of his opponents' marbles. And still he won. He took the earnings from his marble games and used them to pay people to do his chores, chopping wood and hauling coal. So he was in business at a fairly early age.

Later, as a young adult and a married man, he had an opportunity to buy stock in the Utah Southern Railroad, which at the time (if I may sound skeptical) ran from nowhere to nowhere. The stock cost a penny or so a share. Then all of a sudden, either silver or coal was discovered nearby, and it became clear the railroad would be an essential artery in hauling—and the stock was going sky high. Instead of going home to his wife, Lucy, and saying, "Hurrah, hurrah, we're rich! Hello, I'm a rich man," he went home and prayed about it: "Heavenly Father, if having money is going to make me like . . ."—and then he gave specific names—"if that's what's pending, then I will sell the stock before it appreciates. Guide me."[16] (A phrase he often used was, "I have seen rich men and rich men's children; I've seen them go to the bad."[17])

At first no guidance came. So he thought of another way to approach the problem. He put two piles of the stock in front of him, one large pile and one small one, and asked, "Which one do I sell first?" The answer came in an impression,

"The big one." And so he sold the stock that was quickly going up in price.[18]

The people who bought it thought he was crazy. When he later sold the small pile, he still netted about $15,000, which wasn't bad. But he felt that if he hadn't made that prayerful effort and hadn't had the courage and integrity to honor the impression the Lord gave him, he might not have accepted the call to Tooele—and the course of his life would have been totally different. Heber J. Grant, then, was a man who knew about sacrifices.

As stake president in Tooele, he had an impressive experience where the Lord blessed him to speak with great spirit and power, and becoming proud about it, he took credit to himself. The next Sunday, he stood up and expected to make another wonderful performance—and ran out of ideas in five minutes and sat down. He was humiliated. He humbly knelt in prayer and pledged that he would never again go to the pulpit proudly. He would go only with one concern: Can I teach and lift the Saints?[19] And he kept that promise.

A great patriarch named John Rowberry lived in Tooele. Brother Rowberry visited Brother Grant one day and said, "I have a blessing for you." Heber sat on a three-legged stool in the probate judge's office in Tooele, and Brother Rowberry put his hands on his head and blessed him. He included a powerful commendation: "Heber, the monitor of your mind is honesty and integrity. Because of this you are beloved of the Lord, and you will become a pillar in His kingdom." Brother Rowberry hesitated for quite a few seconds, and then went on. When the blessing ended President Grant said, "Brother Rowberry, why did you pause?"

And he replied, "Heber, I saw something I dared not say."

Then Heber heard a voice—though he doesn't say he

heard it with his physical ear—that said, "He saw that you will become the President of the Church."[20] Heber didn't believe it, he tried to forget it, and in all the years that passed after that he simply refused even to credit it. But it was true.

There is a fascinating side note about Brother Rowberry. He had a dream in which he saw a series of General Authorities falling off a ship, swimming a short distance, and then entering a very beautiful place. At the end of the dream he saw himself go overboard. He wondered what it meant. When Orson Pratt went to Tooele to visit a stake conference, Brother Rowberry told him about the dream and asked if he could interpret it. Elder Pratt said, "I don't know, but I'll pray about it and before I go I'll tell you."

Some time later Elder Pratt returned to Brother Rowberry with the answer. He said, "Brother John, you write down the order in which you saw those brethren go off the ship, and you will find that that is the order in which they die. And when you get into the spirit world you tell the first man you saw fall overboard that his interpretation of your dream was correct." So Orson Pratt knew he was going to be the first to die.

Time passed, and Orson Pratt became very ill. Word was sent to Tooele (and elsewhere): "We are having a fast and prayer circle for Orson Pratt. Please join us." John Rowberry responded, "Well, I'm willing to fast and pray for him, but he's next." And Orson Pratt died.

Later still, Elder Grant was visiting Tooele and Brother Rowberry approached him and said, "Brother Grant, everybody has gone over except me. I will be next, and I just want you to know that when I get on the other side I will tell your father that you are doing well as an apostle."[21]

"YOU HAVE NEVER SEEN HIM"

How did he get to be an apostle? That happened only three years after his call as stake president. At age twenty-six, as a stake president, Heber J. Grant was walking down Main Street, just before going over to the Tabernacle for conference. He was approached by a man he knew, George Teasdale, who said, "Brother Grant, I am delighted to see you. You and I are going to be . . ." and then he went into a paroxysm of coughing and didn't finish his sentence. But President Grant got an impression of what he was going to say: " . . . sustained this afternoon as apostles of the Lord Jesus Christ to fill the vacancies in the Quorum."

Heber went to the conference, sat through the sessions, and went home. No one was called to fill the vacancies. He later said, "I do not believe that any mortal man ever more humbly supplicated God . . . to forgive him for his egotism than I did for thinking that I was to be chosen as an apostle."[22]

But ten days later a telegram arrived in Tooele: He and George Teasdale were summoned to meet with the President of the Church. In the meeting, John Taylor read from a written revelation which said, "Let my servants George Teasdale and Heber J. Grant be appointed to fill the vacancies in the Twelve."[23]

After the meeting Heber said to Brother Teasdale, "I know what you were going to say to me on the sixth of October when you happened to choke half to death and then went into the meeting."

"Oh, no, you don't."

"Yes, I do." And he told him.

George Teasdale answered, "Well, that is what I was going to say, but then it occurred to me that I had no right to tell it. . . . Heber, I have suffered the tortures of the damned for ten days, thinking I could not tell the difference between a manifestation from the Lord and one from the devil."[24]

Here are two stories that President Grant told about dealing with the devil. In one story, a man was asked to donate a choice ham that the ward could eat at their banquet. The man walked out to his smokehouse and chose a choice ham. Then he said to himself, "I don't have to give my best ham. I could give them any old ham and it would look all right. No one would know the difference." Then he began to realize where those feelings were coming from and said, "Shut up, Mr. Devil, or I'll give them two hams." President Grant's triumphant line was, "He was troubled no more."[25]

The other story was a personal one. President Grant once pulled up in front of a house on a Thursday morning, and a man came out with a huge bowl of Bing cherries out of the refrigerator—they had a little bit of frost on them in the summer heat—and thrust them through the open window of the car. "President, have a cherry." Heber's eyes lit up and he reached out. But then he stopped himself. "Oh, no, brother, this is Thursday. We always fast before our meeting in the temple." And then, as if he were turning to somebody sitting next to him, he said, "Knocked you out, didn't I, Mr. Devil!"[26]

After Heber J. Grant's call to the apostleship, he went through six months of great depression and struggle. He felt terribly young; he had never been a great student of the scriptures (he had a problem with astigmatism and found it hard to read); he felt unworthy (he had lived a clean life, but as he looked at the giants who were leading the kingdom and then at himself, he felt the gap was too great); and he was troubled further because one of the Brethren had gone around saying no man could serve in the Quroum of the Twelve who had not had an open vision of Christ, and Heber had not. Every time he bore his testimony, he said later, it was as if "Old Nick" (his favorite term for the devil) was hammering him, "You lie, you lie; you have never seen Him; you do not know." Several times he wanted to knock on the door of President Taylor and say, "I resign. I can't do it."[27] But then he recalled his testimony that he knew President John Taylor was a prophet of the living God and that he, a prophet, had had a revelation. So he didn't knock—but he did suffer intensely.

Six months later, he was journeying on a mule through northern Arizona, and at one point he was alone. He thought of his torments, of his sense of unworthiness. As he rode along, he stopped and knelt in the sand and prayed yet again for peace and assurance. Then, as he continued on his way, he saw in vision a council in the spirit world. He saw his father, he saw the Prophet Joseph Smith, he saw others of the worthies of his time, and he saw the Savior there. He said, "I understand what Lehi meant when he said, 'I seemed to see.' I was not seeing it with my eyes, but it was powerful. It was as if I could see it, and I could hear." Their concern was, "Since conference has convened and ended and they have not filled the vacancies, we must send a revelation."[28]

In the process of this experience, it was made known to him that because the Prophet Joseph Smith had given his life in his youth for the cause, and because Heber's father, Jedediah, had died as a martyr in the so-called "Reformation" and had died prematurely, their faith and worthiness was a factor in his call—he was called to honor them, not necessarily because of anything he had yet achieved in his life. But he further understood that they wanted him now, in the language of Joseph Smith, "to round up his shoulders and go forward"[29] and that it now depended upon him and him alone whether he made a success or failure of his call. "I sat there," he says, "and wept for joy." And never again did he question that his call was of the Lord. But, oh, the responsibility.[30]

"THE CHURCH IS BANKRUPT"

As a young apostle, Elder Grant asked the Church president, first John Taylor and then Wilford Woodruff, "Please, could I be like the other Brethren? I had no mission. I need to go to as a missionary."[31] For years the answer was no. They had him working day and night on pressing financial matters pertaining to the Church. He was told that was his calling. He was told he must stay home. But he yearned to go on a mission.

The Church was in terrible financial condition, with extreme pressures from the government and with a variety of internal problems. More than a million dollars of Church funds had gone into building the Salt Lake Temple and another million was invested in the Utah–Idaho Sugar Company. Elder Grant was one of those who had recommended against the sugar company. Wilford Woodruff appointed a committee of the brightest financial minds in the West to explore the possibility of starting such a company. They reported back: "It's not feasible. Don't do it." So he dissolved the committee and appointed a second committee. They also responded, "Don't do it." He answered, "Every time I think of abandoning it, there is darkness; and every time I think of building it, there is light. We will build the factory if it bursts the Church."[32] Following that feeling, they did establish the Utah–Idaho Sugar Company, and in the long run it turned out to be a great blessing to the Church and its people.

In 1891–92 and again in 1893 the country went through a financial panic, not only because there was a severe drop in the stock market and in the economic situation worldwide, but also because the banks then had a panicky run on them from depositors who instantly wanted their money out—and they could not meet the demand. So bank after bank was going down. Elder Grant walked into the office of President George Q. Cannon of the First Presidency and said, "The Church is ruined and bankrupt." And he was rebuked: "Don't talk that way."[33]

The Church was dependent on Zion's First National Bank and Utah State Bank. So he and George Q. Cannon were sent East (and, in the case of President Cannon, all the way to England to talk to Baron Rothschild) to see if they could get sufficient loans to keep the Utah banks from going under. President Cannon wrote a telegram saying, "Unsuccessful." Heber J. Grant was sent across the continent four different times to try to get loans. But people in the East, especially in New York, knew that the Mormon Church was in trouble in every possible way and, of course, didn't want to loan the Church money, even when it was given with security such as, for example, stock in ZCMI.

But there was one man that Elder Grant finally reached in a favorable way. One night Heber couldn't sleep. In his letters[34] is a comment about Wilford Woodruff, who had sent him on this mission to raise money. He wrote that President Woodruff "has the sweetest disposition of any man I know, but he is so at peace about everything; and he even says, 'If the Church is to go bankrupt, then let it be and thank the Lord for it.'"[35] Yet despite his love and respect for his leader, Elder Grant said to himself, "We cannot have another Kirtland Bank episode. We cannot."[36] Because he was so anxious to have success, that night Heber prayed through the entire night. In his prayer he offered his life to the Lord, offering that greatest sacrifice, if that somehow could make it possible to save the credit of the Church.

The next day he went to the office of a man named Claflin who had dealt with the Church before, and he committed to loan the Church $200,000 if he could have a $50,000 bonus upon repayment. Heber agreed. That one check saved the two banks and the Church was able to emerge from financial darkness. And even though he had had to offer a great price for his success, Heber returned home infinitely grateful.

Heber J. Grant was the man who kept saying all through the depression of the 1930s, as well as thereafter, "Get out of debt, and stay out of debt."[37] He knew what debt was, because he had dealt with it in the Church and he had dealt with it in his own life. He once said, "I got $30,000 of experience by investing in a lumber company in Oregon. I got another $30,000 of experience investing in a sheep company in central Utah, and another $30,000 of experience by signing on a note with my brother."[38] All three businesses failed and he found himself $90,000 worse off than nothing. In the 1890s, $90,000 was not just a piece of change, but if you calculate the effects of inflation in the intervening years, he lost about $3 million in today's money.

The result was a huge personal debt. He sat down with his family (ten daughters) and told them that if they all helped, earning money in whatever way they could, and if he did his best in his own businesses, they might be able to pay the debt off in thirteen years.

It never occurred to him to take out bankruptcy. That was not, from his perspective, an honest option. For some people, bankruptcy may become the only desperate escape, but

President Grant's attitude was, "I owe the money and I owe the interest on the money and I will pay it."[39]

Working together, the family slowly began to dig themselves out. At that point, just after the turn of the century, he again was walking down Main Street, on a Thursday. One of the Brethren met him and said, "Brother Grant, let's go to the meeting. I have a feeling that they're going to open a mission in Japan."

When Heber heard that, a quiet inner voice said, "You will be called to preside there." He went to the meeting in terrible suspense. After conducting other business, President Lorenzo Snow finally said, "We're going to open a mission in Japan, and we're calling Heber J. Grant to open that mission, provided his financial circumstances enable him to do so. Heber, what is your situation?"

Heber's response: "Oh, I owe a few dollars."

When he said that, the imp on his shoulder cried out, "You lie, you lie. You know if you tell them exactly your situation there isn't a man in this room that would call you to go to Japan."

Heber responded, under his breath: "Shut up, Mr. Devil. If the Lord wants me to go to Japan, I will go and if it takes me another ten years to pay my debts, I will go."[40]

The Brethren asked additional questions about his finances, and he indicated he needed some time to get his affairs in order, but yes, he would accept the call. The meeting ended and everyone left. Heber was feeling so limp and weak he couldn't get out of his chair. Then one of the Brethren, John W. Taylor, came back. "Heber," he said, "it's been made known to me that you made a financial sacrifice today that was comparable, financially speaking, to the sacrifice of Abraham. It's been made known to me that the Lord has accepted your willingness to go to Japan. And it's been made known to me that the Lord will open the way and you will leave for Japan a free man, financially."[41]

Elder Grant wept, and then Brother Taylor went on, "I have more to say to you. I'm going to tell you how to do it. You're not to plan to make money. You're to get out of bed every morning and ask the Lord to guide you that day, and He will put ideas into your mind, and you follow those and you will be out of debt."[42]

That conversation occurred at about two o'clock in the afternoon. He went home immediately and knelt down and said, "I do not want to wait until tomorrow." Six months later he was out of debt and went to Japan.[43]

"THAT WHICH WE PERSIST IN DOING . . ."

I'd like to be able to say that during those next two years he had great success in opening the gospel in the Orient. He did not. It was terribly difficult, and his struggle with the language was pitiful. He used to say that, yes, he had learned the language, but the Japanese people didn't understand it when he spoke it. It was a trial. This is the man who is famous all through the Church for persistence, for popularizing among us the axiom which is attributed to Ralph Waldo Emerson: "That which we persist in doing becomes easier for us to do; not that the nature of the thing itself is changed, but that our power to do is increased."[44]

His persistence in his youth is legendary. I've noted how good he got at marbles. He earned a spot on a baseball team, after being called a "sissy"—and they went on to win the championship. He was told that his writing was like lightning had struck an ink bottle, or like chicken tracks—yet he eventually taught penmanship at the university. Most amazing of all, he was successful in learning to sing when he was tone deaf. His tone deafness was so profound that if his back was to the piano and you hit the highest note and the lowest note, he couldn't tell the difference.

Many told him he'd never learn to sing. One man said, "I'd be glad to have you sing, but I would like to be forty miles away."[45] But he just loved the challenge, and he went at it. He read the statement in the Doctrine and Covenants that says, "The song of the righteous is a prayer unto me, and it shall be answered with a blessing upon their heads" (D&C 25:12). He wanted to pray in singing.

He once traveled in a carriage with Elders Rudger Clawson and J. Golden Kimball from Holbrook to St. Johns, Arizona, a journey of about sixty miles. As they went, Heber asked them if they objected to his singing one hundred hymns that day. They agreed.

"After I had sung about forty times, they assured me that if I sang the remaining sixty they would be sure to have nervous prostration. I paid no attention whatever to their appeal, but held them to their bargain and sang the full one hundred."[46]

It took him five thousand repetitions to learn to sing "O, My Father" and only be off tune once or twice. There is a recording of his singing "The Flag without a Stain." Once he was on a trip to Alaska with his family on a three-tiered boat. He was eighty years old at the time. He and some of his family were gathered around a piano singing, and someone said, "President Grant, would you like to sing a solo?"

The family's response: "Oh, no."

President Grant's response: "Oh, I'd be glad to."

He sang "The Flag without a Stain," and people began to gather even from the lower decks, listening, incredulous, not because it was so poor, but because it was so strong, and they applauded when he was finished.

Did he ever give up trying to learn to sing? I played touch football in front of his house on Eighth Avenue all through my high school days, and I still remember seeing the open front door of his house and President Grant at the piano, practicing. Even after he had had a stroke, he still tried to sing.

A MISSION IN JAPAN

He knew that if he persisted in something, he would improve. But he did not learn to speak Japanese. His only success in Japan, someone has said, was that he continued in the absence of success. After two years, he had made two primary contributions. First, he started on the translation of the Book of Mormon into Japanese, which was completed by Alma O. Taylor. The translation took a total of nine years. Second, he had offered a dedicatory prayer in Yokohama, opening that island and the county of Japan to the preaching of the gospel.

We do not have an exact transcript of that prayer, but we do have a summary written by someone who was present. We also have a letter he wrote home to his family about it. He was known to say, "I am not greatly blessed in prayer,"[47] and that he couldn't compare himself to many of the others of the Brethren when it came to prayer. Before he offered the dedicatory prayer, somebody handed him a copy of Orson Hyde's prayer in Jerusalem, to suggest some ideas he might want to use. He looked at it for a minute and then said, "No, I'm simply going to go under inspiration." In that particular experience the Spirit truly did burn in his heart. People would say in that day, when the Spirit helped the language flow, "I had great liberty of the Spirit." He did.

Patriarchal blessings given to the Japanese do not always say the same thing about their lineage. But somehow, either by adoption or by their lineal descent, the Japanese are a people who tie in with the same promises of Abraham and Ephraim. The promises are coming to pass. Since the beginnings established by Heber J. Grant, the Church in Japan has grown beyond all expectation. There are now well over one hundred thousand members in Japan. That doesn't count the many, many Japanese converts who are in other countries, including many in the state of Hawaii. As of this writing, Japan has thirty stakes, seven missions, and two temples. And the Church has had two General Authorities of Japanese descent, one from Hawaii and the other from Japan.

"DO YOU REMEMBER THAT MEETING?"

President Joseph F. Smith had said, "Thousands, and perhaps millions, will receive the gospel"[48] through the service of Elder Grant in opening the mission in Japan. But Heber didn't see such a breakthrough, and he must have been terribly frustrated. He wrote home and said, "Please, send me to another mission where I can have success."[49] They took him at his word and sent him to the European Mission, with headquarters in Liverpool, England.

In 1905, he conducted a three-day missionary conference (we would say zone conference) where all the missionaries from the surrounding European missions, including British, gathered in Liverpool; during the conference all had opportunity to bear testimony. One of those who did so was the late Hugh B. Brown, who eventually became a member of the First

Presidency of the Church. At the end of those three days Elder Grant arose and said three things. First, "Do not be discouraged brethren and sisters. The time is coming when the British people will queue up [that's a British expression for *line up*] to hear the gospel." That has come to pass. (I don't know how many hundred thousand came and waited in line at the open house of the Preston Temple.)

Second, he said, "We have been feasting upon the fat things of the Spirit, and we will never forget." President Brown has left on record that forty years later, when President Grant was almost on his deathbed, he took Brother Brown by the hand and said, "Hugh, do you remember that meeting in England?"

He could have said, "What meeting, President Grant? We had lots of meetings." But he knew exactly what President Grant was talking about, and said, "Yes."

Then President Grant said, "That was one of the greatest outpourings of the Spirit of my life."

Third, Elder Grant prophesied, "One of you in this congregation will someday hold the same position I hold."[50] And the missionaries fell to discussing who that might be. One position he held, of course, was president of that mission, and some of those brethren later had that calling. But he was also a member of the Quorum of the Twelve. One of his missionaries came to both callings. His name was Hugh B. Brown.

"DO YOU FEEL ANYTHING STRANGE?"

At home he had been a family man since 1882. Solicitous of his first wife, Lucy, he prevailed on President Taylor to bring her home from Tooele to his own mother's area in Salt Lake. Lucy didn't sleep well at night in Tooele, thinking of Heber going back and forth. His mercy and his love for her prevailed.

Later, Lucy went through three years of agonizing disease and finally died. In the meantime he had married Emily Wells, the daughter of Daniel H. Wells. He had four daughters by her and five daughters by Lucy. Each wife also bore him a son. One they named Heber, his namesake; one they named Daniel, after his second wife's father. Neither lived past age eight. One died of whooping cough and the other of what was known as tuberculosis of the hip. President Grant has left on record the statement, "I don't know why my name must die with me."[51] He loved and honored his daughters, but he had also hoped for sons. But he did have grandsons and great-grandsons who bear the name "Heber" and the name "Grant." His third wife, Augusta Winters, also bore him a daughter. When the other wives died, she cared for the expanding family and outlived her husband.

This leads us to a point about sorrow. When one of his close relatives lost a little boy, he wrote her a letter of comfort; later he used the letter in a discourse that has become a classic called, "When Great Sorrows Are Our Portion."[52] He described his own experience, after the loss of the first son and then in crisis with the second. That son was suffering greatly from hip disease, and Heber and his wife Emily took turns, day and night, caring for him.

At one point, while he was taking a catnap, he had a dream. (Later in his life he said this was the only dream in his life he was sure came directly from the Lord.)[53] He saw himself in the room with his son, and then he saw Lucy, the mother of this little boy, who had by now passed away, come into the room to take the child. He wouldn't let her take him, and they almost got into a kind of tug-of-war. Still dreaming, he found himself losing his balance and falling on his son. The boy began to scream in terrible pain; Heber had fallen right on the place where the boy hurt most from his hip disease. Heber couldn't stand it and ran out of the house covering his ears. There he met a friend, Joseph E. Taylor, and told him what had happened. Brother Taylor said, "Heber, if that boy's mother comes for the child, knowing as she does all about this life and the next, I would let her take him."

He woke and saw that his son was in critical condition. He turned to his wife and said, "Do you feel anything strange?"

She said, "Yes, I feel assured that Heber's mother is sitting between us, waiting to take him away."

Of this experience he said gratefully, "I sat by the deathbed of my little boy and saw him die, without shedding a tear. . . . [I] experienced a sweet, peaceful, and heavenly influence in my home."[54]

For the remainder of his life he was comforting to others who faced similar experiences, and he bore his witness of the reality of the spirit world.

One personal note: I was alone with Heber J. Grant, then President of the Church, only once in my life, when as a teenager I was supposed to visit him after his stroke and read to him. I was so impressed and in awe and nervous that I ran all the words together when I read. He finally stopped me and said, "Well, now, Truman, why don't I tell you some stories?" Thank the Lord! The only thing I remember clearly about the stories he told me was the sentence, "When I get on the other side, I am going to hug Ort Whitney and thank him for such and such." It was that "*when* I get on the other side" that hit me as a teenager. Not, *if* it turns out there is immortality, or *if* it is true that the spirit lives after the body, or *if,* as J. Golden Kimball reportedly put it, all these strange things we teach turn out to be true. He said "*when* I get on the other side," and that rang in me, and I never forgot it.

In that generation they didn't have this curious etiquette that's now grown up in the world, and even in the Church, that you don't talk to people about the reality and the possibility of death, even though they're getting close. On the contrary, in those days they would come in and say, "It's only going to be a few days, Mary. Would you say such and such to Hortense, and would you please carry a message to Aunt Ruth"—and so they had to sort of collect the "mailing instructions." That's intimacy with the spirit world, that's knowledge; it's just a step through the vestibule, and they're waiting for you. Well, he had that attitude. He had absolute certainty.

PRESIDING APOSTLE

Elder Grant became President of the Church in 1918. He was only sixty-two years old. A few months before, Elder Grant's half-brother (they had the same father but different mothers), having recently been called as a patriarch, said, "Brother Heber, I am told that as a patriarch I can give blessings to my relatives. I would like to give a blessing to you."[55] Elder Grant knew that his brother had not had much training in language or English grammar—and it showed—and so with his usual candor he said, "Well, Brother Hyrum, you know that you and I don't have much grammatical training, so you go ahead and give the blessing and I'll give it to the editor of the *Improvement Era,* Junius Wells, and he'll straighten out the grammar, not changing the meaning, and everything will be fine."[56] Hyrum agreed to that.

In his youth, as a student assigned to listen to conversation and write down grammatical errors, Heber went to hear an old-timer named Millen Atwood speak in his ward. Heber thought, "I am going to get here tonight, during the thirty minutes that Brother Atwood speaks, enough material to last me for the entire winter in my night school grammar class." But within five minutes Heber stopped writing down the mistakes, because that man knew the Lord Jesus Christ, and despite his broken English, the power of his testimony put Heber Grant in tears.[57] He never forgot that experience. So while he was grateful to those who knew correct grammar, he also knew the greater importance of the Spirit.

When Hyrum Grant put his hands on Heber's head to give him a blessing, he told him three powerful truths, which I paraphrase: "It is the will of your father, and through his life and sacrifice, that you are where you are." "You will become the Presiding Apostle." This repeated the words he had heard from John Rowberry in his youth. And a promise about his family: "Dear brother, if any of your children shall wander from the path of righteousness your faith, your righteousness, your persistence, and your love will eventually reach them and they will return, and you will have them all by your side."[58] He did have children who wandered, but he clung to that promise, and it gave him even greater motivation to be righteous and to be filled with love in his own life.

He served as president for twenty-seven years, from 1918, the end of the First World War, to 1945, the end of the Second World War. War was abhorrent to him. In 1939 he led the First Presidency in saying, "We affirm that all international controversies may be settled by pacific means if nations will but deal unselfishly and righteously one with another."[59]

I once went to the Punchbowl, a dormant volcano in Honolulu, where there's a military cemetery that has the names of all those who gave their lives in the Pacific in the Second World War and the Korean War. President Grant had fifteen grandsons who served in those wars, three of whom didn't come back. At the center of all those names is an inscription from Abraham Lincoln, quoting a letter allegedly sent to a mother who lost five sons in the Civil War. The inscription ends, "the solemn pride that must be yours to have lain so great a sacrifice on the altar of freedom." President Grant laid his family on that altar, and if any man sustained the Constitution, it was Heber J. Grant.

"I WILL BE AN ENEMY OF ALCOHOL"

In his sermons as Church President, Heber J. Grant gave prominence and sanction to the Word of Wisdom as perhaps no one before him. In response he got all kinds of anonymous mail: "Get off that subject and talk about something important." His counsel was publicly rejected when the issue was whether Utah was going to remain a dry state, as they called it, and whether Utah was going to repeal Prohibition. There were many arguments on both sides, all the same arguments we hear now about whether we should or shouldn't legalize marijuana. President Grant felt strongly that there needed to be some legislation and efforts at law enforcement or there would be an epidemic of addiction in this country. He was in New York City when he was shown the headline "Prohibition repealed." He slapped the paper and said, "We will pay for this in misery and suffering in this country."[60]

Why did he feel so profoundly that alcohol was a menace? One factor: He had a close childhood friend who got involved in drinking but then repented and went on a mission. After he returned home he went back to his old habits. Elder Grant stood at the graveside of his friend, who had died of cirrhosis of the liver in his early thirties, looked up at the heavens, and said, "I swear before the living God I will be an enemy of alcohol the rest of my life."[61] He was.

"WHO IS MELVIN J. BALLARD?"

Since the late 1880s, President Grant had had a lifetime friend whom he hoped might someday serve with him in the Twelve. The friend was a faithful, worthy man, a grandson of Brigham Young named Richard. There was even an instance when there were three vacancies in the Quorum of the Twelve, and Elder Grant hinted to his friend that he would likely be called. It didn't happen, and in the quorum meeting when there was a call for a vote (which always has to be unanimous), he was a little hesitant. President Woodruff said, "What is it, Heber?"

"Well, the truth is I told Richard W. Young that he might be called."

President Woodruff said, "Brother Heber, you're not supposed to do that."

When Heber J. Grant became president and there was a vacancy, those who knew of the close friendship assumed he would call his friend now that he was in charge.

One night he was praying about the change and the impression came, "Hadn't you better inquire of the Lord?"

In true humility, Heber answered, "Yes, so who should be called?"

"Choose my servant Melvin J. Ballard."

He replied, "Who is Melvin J. Ballard?"[62] According to one account he didn't remember he was a mission president.

He later said, "From the day that I chose a comparative stranger to be one of the Apostles, instead of my lifelong and dearest living friend, I have known . . . that I am entitled to the light and the inspiration and the guidance of God in directing His work here upon this earth; and I know . . . that it is God's work."[63]

After the call was made public, he went home and his family said, "Don't you know you have broken Brother Young's heart?"

And he replied, "Maybe I have broken my own heart, but I am not in charge here. The Lord is."[64]

In the 1930s the world experienced another financial panic, now known as the Great Depression. We weren't fully ready. But Melvin J. Ballard was a key to helping establish the welfare plan, to getting it out and getting it understood. Among other things, Elder Ballard visited with President Roosevelt in Washington about the plan and got some solid help and endorsement to see that it worked. Ironically, the time came when Brother Ballard became ill at a young age, by Mormon standards, and President Grant was almost of the mind to say, "I can spare almost any man before him."[65] But he passed away in 1939 at the age of sixty-six.

President Grant's influence on the Church welfare plan continues to this day. Not only did he oversee the establishment of the program, but he pressed into service others who had a lasting influence: Melvin J. Ballard, Harold B. Lee, Henry D. Moyle, Ezra Taft Benson, and Marion G. Romney—men whose names are synonymous with Church welfare.

President Grant was constantly an advocate of work—even of menial work. "I have never seen the day," he said, "when I was not willing to do the meanest work, (if there is such a thing as mean work, which I doubt) rather than be idle."[66] I've heard a story (though I haven't been able to verify it) that in his early life he was pushing a wheelbarrow full of manure up Main Street to his house. While he was en route, somebody stopped him and said, "Heber, you shouldn't be doing this. It's below your dignity!" Heber replied with perfect aplomb: "Why not? I paid for it."

STRAIGHTFORWARD ONE-LINERS

B. H. Roberts, who wrote in detail about President Grant's administration, said that we shouldn't expect a lot of high-flown poetic doctrine or philosophical discussion from Heber J. Grant. What we should expect—and what we get—is straightforward one-liners: "Keep the commandments" and "That is the law and the prophets."[67] That's exactly what needed to be said then and still needs to be said.

President Grant believed that intellectual reasons for refusing to investigate the Church or for leaving the Church are often "after the fact"—and the fact is behavior. When a person's life is out of harmony with the truth, he tends to find a rationale for his behavior. He has received some light, but he tries to suppress it and invents plausible reasons to do so. But he believed conscience will speak out in protest at our lives and our sins when we are out of harmony. On the other hand, our conscience will "kiss" us, as it were, when we honor the core of our hearts, which is truth.

Here are some examples of the straightforward teachings of Heber J. Grant:

On obedience: "Some spend nearly the whole of their time in hunting mysteries, while neglecting important duties."[68]

On child rearing: "No greater heritage can you and I leave to our children than a good name, and a good and faithful testimony to the gospel of Christ."[69]

On the temple: "The best inheritance that you can leave to your sons and your daughters is an investment in the House of

God. . . . It will . . . cause them to . . . think of those things that are eternal and perish not."[70]

On humility: "The royal blood among the Latter-day Saints is the blood of humility."[71]

"So long as we have God's Holy spirit, we will be found meek and humble in His sight."[72]

On pride: "I know of no disease as dangerous as that commonly known as the 'big head.' When persons get this they have lost the spirit of God."[73]

On flattery: When people complimented President Grant he would answer under his breath, "Devil talk. Devil talk. Don't listen! Make you proud. Make you proud."[74]

On teaching: On one occasion, Elder Grant went on a stake conference assignment to the Northwest. His traveling companion was Karl G. Maeser. (In those days a representative of BYU traveled with a General Authority for recruiting purposes.) In that weekend visit Karl G. Maeser was asked to teach a group of children. Heber J. Grant sat in the front row and watched his companion teach. Elder Grant said, in effect, "In one minute Karl G. Maeser had those children in rapt attention, and he taught them the power of the gospel, and I began to weep, and I said to myself, 'Here I am spending hours, hours every day in decision making and administration and going after the things of this world, and he is totally dedicated to lifting mankind.' I said to myself and to the Lord, 'I will not be worthy to black his boots in the life to come.' "[75] Now that's humility, as well as a recognition that teaching is what Christ did, and that it is an honorable profession.

On Jesus Christ: "Not only did Jesus come as a universal gift, he came as an individual offering with a personal message for each one of us." He said this in the context of people who were talking so much about civil matters, "the social gospel," and so forth. "His blood will conditionally save us, not as nations, communities or groups, but as individuals."[76] So it will—and, if I might add, if the individuals find the Christ, then the community will become a real church.

He also taught that Christ could not have been humanity's greatest moral teacher unless he was, in very deed, the Son of God. This was spoken in response to the liberal theology of his time, which claimed that although Jesus was a great moral teacher, he clearly was not divine. President Grant's response: "Permit me to deny the fact that he was a great moral teacher, unless he was the Son of God. He himself announced that he was the Savior of the world, that he was the Only Begotten of the Father in the flesh, that he was the Son of God; and therefore, if he was not the Son of God, he could not have been a great moral teacher, because the foundation of this mission was that he was God's Only Begotten Son. If he was not God's Son, he could not be a great moral teacher, because his foundation would be a falsehood."[77]

He owned a book by James Allen called *The Way of Peace* (James Allen also wrote *As a Man Thinketh*). President Grant wrote in the book, "When reading a book like this I thank God from the bottom of my heart for the testimony of Jesus Christ, that He was the Son of God, and the Redeemer of the world."[78] *On the law of the harvest:* "We would look upon a farmer as a natural born idiot [if he called] upon everybody who passed his farm to throw in a few seeds of weeds, to do this for a period of twenty-one years, and then expect he could sow a crop of grain and expect to get a good harvest."[79]

On tithing: "The great trouble with the majority of people is that when they get the ten apples, they eat up nine of them and then they cut the other in two and give the Lord half of what is left. Some of them cut the apple in two and eat up one-half of it and then hold up the other half and ask the Lord to take a bite."[80] (That's a little bit like the old story of the man who prayed and said, "God, give me a million dollars, and I'll give $300,000 to charity." There was no response, so the man said, "Okay, you don't even have to trust me—just give me $700,000.")

On the nature of man: President Grant made a great statement, in company with the rest of the First Presidency, on evolution. The basic point was this: "Leave it to the scientists to deal with this question, and let's get on with preaching the gospel."[81] But in that statement he also said something that's now beautifully written in our Proclamation on the Family: "[The doctrine of premortality] shows that man as a spirit was begotten and born of Heavenly Parents, and reared to maturity in the eternal mansions of the Father prior to coming upon the earth in a temporal body to undergo an experience in mortality."[82]

On fasting: He agreed with Wilford Woodruff: "If it makes my head ache by keeping the commandments of God, let it ache."[83]

On wealth: "A man's wealth consists in the number of people he loves and blesses, and who love and bless him in return."[84]

President Grant had a business mind that was quick as lightning, and he was very successful. But he also sought to make a difference in giving. There was hardly a single significant fund-raising project in his day to which he didn't contribute. People would say to him, "Heber, why do you give to these causes?" (He knew that the highest form of giving is anonymous, but people still found out.) They would ask, "Why do you give away all this money? Aren't you going to build up an estate for your family? You have a large family." His answer, with a twinkle: "I want my family to be sorry when I die."[85] He knew what true wealth was.

ONE OF THE GREAT MEN OF HIS TIME

Esteemed figures in the business world—Henry Ford, for example—thought President Grant was one of the great men of his time. As a matter of fact, near the end of his life, Henry Ford sent him a car as a gift—and it wasn't a Model T. It was a streamlined Lincoln.

For many decades the nation's newspapers had mercilessly cartooned Church Presidents. But because of contacts such as that with Henry Ford, and because his name was synonymous with being forthright, President Grant was able to gradually bring a change in the attitude of the media toward the Latter-day Saints. It would be an overstatement to say that he brought about an era of sunshine and goodwill—I suppose we'll never quite get to that stage—but he did lead many people of great influence to look again at the Mormons. They wrote letters of tribute, both to him and the Church, which are among the classics in our archives.

He also influenced others through music and the Tabernacle Choir. He was instrumental in getting the national choir broadcast under way. The choir broadcast has been continuously running now for more than seventy-five years. They are heard or seen around the world. President Grant believed that music could open hearts when all else failed.

I once served as assistant to the director of Temple Square, and one of my functions was to open the mail. It struck me as significant that the most frequent request from around the world was "Could we have the words to 'Come, Come, Ye Saints'?" (That was President Grant's favorite hymn.) The other frequent request was for the words to "O My Father." The Church began to put the words to those two songs (on alternating weeks) on the programs we distributed on Temple Square after organ recitals.

Later in his life, President Grant took a trip to California, where he had a stroke. The doctor called in some of President Grant's family and associates and said, "This is irreversible. He is paralyzed on his left side, and it will affect his speech." Then the doctor, who believed in honesty (and perhaps he knew that President Grant valued it as well), went into President Grant's room and said, "You're permanently paralyzed."

Characteristically, President Grant said, "Is there nothing I can do?"

The doctor said, "Well, you could send Willard out to a drug store for a little sponge. He could put it in your hand [for you to squeeze] and try to get a little movement back in your left hand."[86] (Willard was a son of President Joseph F. Smith, mentioned in the previous chapter.)

The president sent Willard to the store without delay. When Willard returned he put the sponge in President Grant's hand—and it rolled off. Willard R. Smith told me personally that he stayed up all that night with President Grant. He wouldn't go to sleep, and just kept saying, "Try again. Try again."

They kept at it for several days. Then one day the doctor returned for a visit. President Grant said, with a twinkle in his eye, "Doctor, I'd like to give you the Scout handshake." The doctor, knowing President Grant was paralyzed on his left side, reached out with his right hand. President Grant said, "No, no. I said the Scout handshake, and that's always with the left hand." So the doctor put his left hand out and President Grant reached with his own left hand and squeezed.

The doctor teared up and said, "Heber, I didn't know you could ever, ever get back that much strength in your left hand."

President Grant also worked with his leg. He did not totally regain his strength, and for the remainder of his life some would say he was somewhat physically incapacitated. But there was nothing wrong with his mind or his heart.

A SOVEREIGN TESTIMONY

As I have studied the lives of the prophets, I have noticed how each one was different—different in background, different in personality, different in experience. But I have also seen that all of them have one essential thing in common. They all, somehow, early in their lives, came to a personal assurance that the kingdom of God had been reestablished, and they identified themselves with the effort to build it.

Heber J. Grant was the first President who had not known the Prophet Joseph Smith. But he heard testimony directly from those who had. He personally knew every President, starting with Brigham Young, down to his own predecessor, and most of the Twelve. He also knew many of the great women who were natives, as it were, to the kingdom of God. From early in his life they surrounded him and filled him with insight. He mentioned specifically Emmeline Wells, Zina D. H. Young, and Eliza R. Snow. He said that Eliza R. Snow spent hours with him in his mere boyhood teaching him about the glory of the life of the Prophet Joseph Smith. "No greater prophet," she said once, "except Jesus Christ, ever lived on earth."[87] Because of that background, President Grant from boyhood couldn't believe any of the terrible and vociferous attacks against the Prophet and the Church.

People have said to me, "There are two Joseph Smiths out there, and you talk about only one." But the second Joseph Smith has been created by those desperate to put him down, and that image is not based on truth. Those who were firsthand witnesses give us a uniform testimony of the greatness of the man.

So President Grant, the first of the Church presidents to hear it rather than see it, nevertheless, had a sovereign testimony. I saw him up close in his later years. I was not truly sensitive at that time to the gospel, but had, as most young people do, other interests and many wonderings. Yet today I can say that I know Heber J. Grant was a prophet of God, and I know that the Lord raised him up for his time to do what he, in fact, did, building upon the foundation of apostles and prophets, of which he was one of the greatest.

8

GEORGE ALBERT SMITH

The late J. Golden Kimball is supposed to have said that if you want to live a long time, get an incurable disease and then take care of it. That would be one way to describe President George Albert Smith, who reportedly was frail all his life.

I was sitting as a mission president in an office in Boston when Elder Harold B. Lee walked in unannounced. His first sentence was, "You could stand a little weight."

I replied, "No, I am built for speed."

He laughed and said, "That reminds me of a story about George Albert Smith. When George Albert Smith was called into the Quorum of the Twelve, his father, John Henry Smith, was in the First Presidency. When others accused John Henry Smith of having orchestrated the call, his first answer was, 'No, I did not.' His second answer was: 'Well, he's not healthy. He won't last long.'"

Elder Lee told me of the time when President Grant set Elder George Albert Smith apart as president of the Quorum of the Twelve. On that occasion, President Grant quoted what

John Henry Smith had said, and then remarked, "You see, he has outlived all of the men who were worried about him."[1]

George Albert apparently did have a certain congenital weakness, both of heart and of breathing, that would eventually take its toll. But not until he had fulfilled his mission. He joined his brethren in the faith that the Lord has power over life and death. Men do not. Therefore, there cannot be any manipulating, maneuvering, or politicking when it comes to succession in the presidency of the Church. The Lord makes a decision and the man he chooses lives to become his president and his prophet.

A meeting was held at the home of George Albert Smith just after the appointment of Elder Melvin J. Ballard to the Twelve. Elder Ballard was invited, along with other General Authorities, to participate in a postconference banquet. In the course of the evening, Elder Ballard was invited to say a few words, and he said, "When I was only thirteen years of age I blacked the boots of a patriarch whose name was Zebedee Coltrin. Afterward he said he wanted to give me a blessing, which he did. In that blessing he told me that I would one day be a member of the Council of the Twelve. I have never believed it. But tonight I stand as witness of his inspiration."

Then Elder George Albert Smith stood up and said, "This is a remarkable coincidence. When I was thirteen years of age I was given a blessing by Zebedee Coltrin, and he told me that I would one day be a member of the Twelve."[2]

Present that night was the son-in-law of George Albert Smith, Murray Stewart, who became curious to read that blessing. He found that it didn't say just that George Albert Smith would be a member of the Twelve. It said that he would stand higher in the Church than his forebears. His grandfather had been a first counselor in the First Presidency and his father a second counselor. That left only one other position.

"THIS IS NOT A HANDSOME MAN"

To understand George Albert Smith, it is important to go back to his heritage. He was descended from several prominent men. First, he was a descendant of Edward Winslow, who was on the *Mayflower*.[3] That was a great distinction in the early part of this country's history. Edward Winslow was also an early governor of the Plymouth colony. George Albert Smith was also descended from a man named Timothy Chase, who was an aide to George Washington.[4] He had a strong heritage of liberty-loving Americans.

The Smiths were a poor family, but they had, of course, a distinguished background in the Church. At thirteen, George Albert was already hard at work at menial tasks. He put in a lawn in the front of their house. He then worked in a ZCMI factory, making overalls. A little later in his teens, George Albert Smith became a surveyor for the Denver and Rio Grande Western Railroad. The D&RGW Railroad, which advertised that they went "through the Rockies, not around them," went from Salt Lake to Denver and then on to Texas. On that assignment, working outside under the glaring desert sun, his eyes were affected and he lost almost all the sight in one eye. Ever after, his eyesight was a bit askew, which affected his ability to read, though he remained a constant student. As his own secretary once said, "This is not a handsome man like, say, David O. McKay."[5]

His schooling included a year, at least, at the Brigham Young Academy. One of his teachers there was Karl G. Maeser.

His classmates included Reed Smoot, who became a U.S. senator for Utah.

An interesting story is attached to Reed Smoot. When one ragtag group of arriving pioneers entered the Salt Lake Valley, somebody made a comment while Brigham Young was standing there welcoming the new arrivals. "Well, that's a motley assembly. They don't look like much; they won't amount to anything."

Brigham responded, "Do not talk that way. One of them will become a great legislator."[6] One of them did, Reed Smoot.

Others in George's school group were George Sutherland, who became a member of the United States Supreme Court, and Richard R. Lyman, who became a distinguished engineer and later a member of the Twelve.

In one of his lectures, Karl G. Maeser communicated the idea that we are responsible for our thoughts. George Albert Smith said later that he did not like that idea, did not want to accept it. Thoughts, he had supposed, come unbidden, and we have no full control over them. But he later became convinced that Brother Maeser was right.[7] As the German proverb says, "We may not prevent the birds from flying over our heads, but we can prevent them from building nests in our hair."[8] "I will be," he ended up saying, "when my life's labor is complete, the product of my thoughts."[9] "As [a man] thinketh in his heart, so is he" (Proverbs 23:7).

A LITTLE BIT OF EDEN

George Albert Smith met a young lady named Lucy Emily Woodruff, a granddaughter of Wilford Woodruff, while they were both young. He courted her and finally received a promise from her that she would marry him. But she was also being pursued by a competing suitor, who, in contrast to George Albert, was handsome, dashing, cultured, and rich. Lucy's heart was ambivalent. George Albert Smith continued his courting but wanted her to have a choice. Finally, and not completely convinced she was making the right decision, Lucy kept her promise and married George Albert. Later, when her other suitor turned out to be, in the language of a biographer, "a handsome man who lacked substance,"[10] her husband "got even" with him in a Christian way. Lucy later told her children that she had "almost made a terrible mistake."[11] But in the end she married the right man.

Shortly after their marriage, George Albert was called to go on a mission. In those days, you weren't excluded from mission service if you were married. The truth was quite the opposite. At the end of general conference, one of the leaders would stand up and say, "The following brethren will report on Monday for missions." Names would be read from a list, and the brethren named would show up on Monday to be assigned their field of labor. Many of these brethren had large families, and the strain and the difficulties that that imposed were well known.

George Albert Smith was called to the Southern States Mission, headquartered in Chattanooga, Tennessee. The Church's history in the South had not always been a peaceful one, especially for missionaries. In the early 1880s there had been what is now called "The Tennessee Massacre," where four men—two missionaries and two Mormon boys—were gunned down by the Ku Klux Klan.[12] The Southern States Mission was not the most favorable place to go on a mission.

George Albert kept in his house some splinters of wood he showed visitors. While serving in Alabama, he and his companion were surrounded in the home they were staying at—a log cabin—and were shot at several times by an armed mob. The hissing bullets knocked off pieces of wood from the logs. He brought those splinters home as souvenirs.[13]

His new bride, Lucy, was both worried about him and devastated by loneliness, so the First Presidency arranged for her to be called as his companion. Their labors together were effective. Following their release, they had a belated honeymoon visiting Niagara Falls.

After they returned home and had established a household in a little bungalow on Yale Avenue, Lucy and her home became legendary for at least two reasons. First, she was a talented gardener, famous for her tulips. In one season, for example, she raised 4,000 tulips, as well as 2,700 Shasta daisies. She gave them all to local hospitals. Second, her home became legendary because both to humble and world-renowned visitors it was a place of great comfort and tranquility. A home may be a "sanctuary of the Lord." Hers was. It was a little bit of Eden.

George and Lucy eventually had three children: Emily, Edith, and George Albert Jr., who became one of the deans of the Harvard Business School.

"I HAVE COME TO ASK FOR YOUR FORGIVENESS"

George Albert returned to a job at ZCMI and shortly he wanted to be the head of the Utah National Guard. He displayed brilliant horsemanship, he was in the cavalry of the guard, and he thought he would be elected. However, a rival spread some vicious rumors about him, and the rival, not George Albert, got the position. George Albert felt so frustrated, bitter, and angry that he decided he couldn't take the sacrament. Then, after praying about it, he received an impression that he should go see the man. The man was defensive, afraid George Albert was going to attack him. Instead, George Albert said, "I have come to ask for your forgiveness for the hateful feelings I have had towards you."[14] It bowled the man over. He became apologetic and warmly asked for forgiveness. They became fast friends and remained so for the rest of their lives.[15]

George Albert Smith's aspirations also included political ones. Had he had funding and a little encouragement he might have run for Congress. He had already distinguished himself in business, and service in Congress seemed to fit with the next step in his life. Had he run, however, he would have had to campaign in a way that would have jeopardized one of the candidates for whom he felt a great friendship.[16]

George Albert also became involved in the YMMIA—the Young Men's Mutual Improvement Association—which was also the origin of the monthly magazine, the *Improvement Era.* That word, *improvement,* became the key word for how to develop auxiliary programs for the young men and the young women. He was a major figure in youth programs for many years. He was superintendent of the YMMIA for more than thirteen years, and he was instrumental in the Church's adoption of Scouting as the activity program for boys. As a Scout, he received the highest awards—the Silver Beaver and the Silver Buffalo. It was his personal conviction that the Scouting movement in the Church enabled many young men to survive in World War II, because they had learned discipline and how to deal with emergencies in their youth.[17] The time came when Latter-day Saint–sponsored units constituted one-third of the total program of the Boy Scouts of America.

In business affairs, George Albert Smith had become distinguished enough that he was appointed by President

William McKinley, one of the six U.S. presidents he knew personally, to a position in the Department of the Interior, the first Latter-day Saint to hold such a position. At various times in his life he was a director or a member of the executive committees of Home Fire Insurance Company, Utah Savings and Trust Company, Utah–Idaho Sugar, the Heber J. Grant Insurance Company, Western Express (which became Western Airlines), Mutual Creamery, LDS Hospital, the Utah First National Bank, the Salt Lake Theater, and Decker Wholesale Jewelry Company.[18]

"YOU HAVE JUST BEEN CALLED"

On October 6, 1903, George Albert Smith was walking home from working at ZCMI and cut through Temple Square while general conference was in session. It was crowded and he couldn't get in, so he kept on walking home. When he arrived, family and neighbors were celebrating and congratulating and kissing each other. "What is this?" he asked.

"Don't you know?"

"No."

"You have just been called to the Council of the Twelve."

He said, "Oh, no, there must be some mistake."[19]

In those days there was no television, so somebody rushed back over to the Tabernacle to make sure they hadn't misheard. Sure enough, George Albert Smith had been called to the Quorum of the Twelve—and he hadn't even been informed.

He was uncomfortable with the idea. He was sure that people would say (and they did), "George Albert Smith's father is in the First Presidency. He wasn't called by revelation—he was called by relation." He didn't feel in any sense equal to the task. He knew that others in Church leadership were giants. Since a child he had been attending conference and sustaining these great men. Now this little pygmy, as he felt himself to be, was called? No, it couldn't be.

A story about William C. Staines is appropriate here. Brother Staines was a convert from Britain who was the gardener on Temple Square. He was crippled and double-jointed, which enabled him to stoop down and plant petunias better than anybody. In his work, Brother Staines saw men who were the great leaders of the Church—Brigham Young, John Taylor, Wilford Woodruff. Then he would go out into the community and see the roughness of many of the people there. "What will happen to the Church when these giants are gone and others take over?" The thought shook his faith; he could barely consider it. The problem continued to bother him, so he prayed about it. The answer that came was, in essence, "Those who will lead the kingdom of God on the earth are known unto the Lord and are already in the world, and in due time they will take their positions."[20] William Staines was comforted.

George Albert Smith felt that he did not measure up to his new calling—but he did feel he had one thing going for him: a moral life. He had sought diligently to live the commandments. So he accepted the call and went to work.

"YOU MUST GO ON PRAYING"

In about 1909, only six years later, George Albert Smith's congenital weakness made him particularly susceptible to what was then called "la grippe," an intensive form of flu. Weeks passed, and George Albert didn't recover. Finally he was sent to California, where it was hoped that the climate might assist his recovery.

One day while he was in California, he went out on the beach and into the surf, where he had a form of heart attack. For three years after that attack he was almost bedfast. When he experienced no genuine improvement in California, he was moved back to St. George to recover, but it didn't seem to help. The burden of his health finally seemed so heavy that he wondered if he should ask the Lord for a release from this mortal life, if that be the Lord's will. He counseled with his wife. She resisted at first, then finally relented. So together they prayed.[21]

Eventually he began to improve, and though he was not completely recovered, President Grant called him to go to England to preside for two years. Incidentally, on that trip he had one of his first adventures with a small airplane. He crossed the English Channel in a small plane, and his only comment was, "If I ever get back on the ground, I'll never do this again."[22] But he later became a great advocate of flying.

While in England, George Albert was asked to represent ZCMI on a tour of England and Scotland sponsored by the British Drapers Chamber of Trades, a kind of British chamber of commerce. A great number of British businessmen were on the tour, and one of them, whose suit was covered with medals, kept belittling and badgering George Albert and his family as Mormons. The chairman of the affair tried to keep the peace among the men. Finally, at a dinner during the tour, the man began pestering George Albert again. He sneeringly asked George Albert about the little button he had on his lapel, showing he was a Son of the American Revolution. "Mr. Smith, what's that funny little button you are wearing?" he asked.

Elder Smith replied, as only he could, "That little button,

my friend, represents the time when my great-grandfather whipped your great-grandfather."[23] The bystanders applauded, and there was no more badgering.

GEORGE ALBERT SMITH'S CREED

Throughout his life, George Albert Smith followed a creed. It is important to remember that The Church of Jesus Christ of Latter-day Saints has no final or fixed creed such as other churches do. We have the Articles of Faith, but they themselves say there is no single creed for the Church. George Albert Smith, however, had a series of personal convictions and self-commandments, if you will, which he tried to live by.

His creed was this:

"I would be a friend to the friendless" (somebody once summed up his life by saying that's what he was, a great friend) "and find joy in ministering to the needs of the poor.

"I would visit the sick and afflicted and inspire in them a desire for faith to be healed." (That phrase, "sick and afflicted," is in many Latter-day Saint prayers, and I have realized it's from the Book of Mormon [see Jacob 2:19; Alma 1:27; 4:12; 34:28]).

"I would teach the truth to the understanding and blessing of all mankind.

"I would seek out the erring one and try to win him back to a righteous and happy life.

"I would not seek to force people to live up to my ideals, but rather love them into doing the thing that is right.

"I would live with the masses and help to solve their problems that their earth life may be happy.

"I would avoid the publicity of high positions and discourage the flattery of thoughtless friends.

"I would not knowingly wound the feeling of any, not even one who may have wronged me, but would seek to do him good and make him my friend.

"I would overcome the tendency to selfishness and jealousy and rejoice in the successes of all the children of my Heavenly Father.

"I would not be an enemy to any living soul.

"Knowing that the Redeemer of mankind has offered to the world the only plan that will fully develop us and make us really happy here and hereafter I feel it not only a duty but a blessed privilege to disseminate this truth."[24]

That was his creed, and he lived it.

His gift for peacemaking is exemplified by a crisis that occurred in his family. At one point, George Albert's daughter was released from her position on the Primary general board, apparently because of some difficulties with the general Primary president. George Albert did all he could to defend her and to have her reinstated, but the decision was made and was not reversed. This man, who could have agitated his case (like Thomas B. Marsh, who eventually broke with the Church), became reconciled to the decision and pled with his daughter likewise to be reconciled.[25]

"A LOVING RADIANCE HE SHEDS"

George Albert Smith's life exemplified his creed in other ways. He was concerned to reach out to the downtrodden. He became, for example, the president of the Society for the Aid of the Sightless in Utah and helped develop a Braille system so that the major Church works could be read in Braille.[26] In 1940 Irene Jones, who was herself blind, shared at a seventieth-birthday reception for President Smith a poem she had written. In her tribute, she spoke of the book of Acts, chapter 13, verse 11, "There fell on him [a man who has been blind] a mist and a darkness; and he went about"—and this is the key phrase—"seeking some to lead him by the hand." Then she said, "The blind of this community have not had to seek far for someone to lead them spiritually out of their mist and their darkness." An excerpt from her poem includes these lines:

A loving radiance he sheds
That comes from God to man.
And we who walk in life-long night
Can see as others can.
Although his tender loving face
From us is shut apart,
We see the gracious wisdom
Of his understanding heart;
We feel peace within his soul
And know a peace our own;
We hear his silent prayer that tells
We do not walk alone.[27]

And what about the poor? One glimpse demonstrates his feelings. The doorbell rang, and workers from Deseret Industries picked up some clothing he was donating. At Welfare Square, while unloading the truck, workers found five shirts perfectly laundered and starched and wrapped in cellophane. "Oh, no, we picked up somebody's good shirts," they thought. They traced the shirts and discovered they came from George Albert Smith's house.

In haste, the workers went back and very apologetically knocked on the door. "President Smith," they said, "we're sorry but apparently when we were taking away some of your donations . . ." George Albert was very puzzled and said, "Those are my shirts."

"Well, yes, we picked them up by mistake."

"I intended to give those shirts."

"But President Smith, they're all laundered and starched."

He said simply, "Well, that's the way I like my shirts."

He believed the Golden Rule applied to the welfare program.

Then there was the thief. George Albert Smith had an old 1936 Ford with a very precious blanket on the front seat made by Navajo Indians; they had sewn the names of all the Twelve into the blanket, along with his own name. The car wasn't locked because it was in a guarded Church parking lot. But the blanket was stolen anyway. George Albert walked out from his meetings and found the blanket was gone.

He could have called the mayor of Salt Lake City and said, "What kind of a city are you running? I'll have your head if you don't get that blanket back." Or he could have called the chief of police and said the same thing. Or he might have said to the guard, probably a Latter-day Saint, "Are you blind?"

What did he do? He said simply, "I wish we knew who it was so that we could *give* him the blanket also, for he must have been cold; and some food also, for he must have been hungry."[28]

To help prisoners, George Albert Smith organized classes at the state prison. He also reached out to alcoholics. He helped a man who said, "I had to look up to see the gutter." Yes, he was drunk. Yes, he was an alcoholic. Yes, he was almost helpless in the addiction. George Albert Smith encouraged Latter-day Saints to encourage others in Alcoholics Anonymous. He contributed to the Salvation Army, and when people said, "Why?" he said, "Because they reach some we miss."

He also cared about the fatherless, the motherless, and the homeless. He saw people on the street and felt sorry for them. He came home one night and Lucy saw he was blue with cold. "What's the matter, you went to work with your coat. Did you forget your coat?"

"No. I gave it to a man on South Temple."[29]

George Albert was also concerned about those who were starving. Right after the Second World War ended, he went to see President Harry Truman and explained that the Church had stored food and clothing and quilts, and that we could raise cash besides, for those suffering in Europe. Eventually, with Truman's endorsement, we sent 127 carloads of goods to the distressed people in Europe.[30] I had the privilege once of asking President Truman in Independence, Missouri, "What about the Mormons?"

He responded, "I know they are honest and they pay their debts."

George Albert Smith's concern extended to people who had left the Church. In 1946 he went to Mexico and spoke to 1,200 people who felt they had been neglected during the war years and broke away from the Church. He told faith-promoting stories, expressed great love, and pled with them to return. Almost all of them did.[31]

MONUMENTS AND COMMEMORATIONS

George Albert was committed to Church history and to its commemoration more than any other person (excepting, perhaps, Church historian B. H. Roberts). He believed if you do not memorialize—if you don't put up monuments and mark significant places in your history—you will forget and neglect them. There's a phrase in the Book of Mormon about sacred records enlarging one's memory (see Alma 37:8). That was the rationale for hauling the golden plates through the desert.

Consequently, George Albert became a great trailmarker. That was partly due to his connection with Scouting, but it was also because of his commitment to memorialize events in Church history. The Sons of the Utah Pioneers and the This Is the Place monuments were developed and created under his influence and direction.

While in the Holy Land, a visitor commented to me that he was troubled that wherever there seemed to have been an event of biblical significance, somebody had put up a shrine. Echoing this sentiment, another said, "I thank the Lord they couldn't put a church up over the Sea of Galilee." That feeling is understandable, but the counterresponse should be, "If it weren't for the trouble someone has taken to designate and preserve these sites and sights, then today they might be gas stations or drug stores." We should perpetuate monuments, and George Albert Smith did.

In 1947, the year of the pioneer centennial, George Albert was the man who led the construction of the This Is the Place monument, unveiled that year after thirteen years of planning and construction. A great celebration was held. He also arranged an automobile caravan that retraced the travels of the pioneers all the way from Winter Quarters to the Salt Lake Valley.

The Mormon Trail wasn't as well-marked then, nor was the history clearly brought together. The caravan found a place somewhere east of Echo Canyon where it was assumed the handcart pioneers had had their adventure. The caravan decided to camp there overnight and simulated the pioneer experience by building an outdoor fire. There an old man the group did not recognize shyly approached, wearing rough clothes and holding a battered hat in his hand. He said, "I live not far from here, and some years ago I was working nearby and found what I thought were unmarked graves. Something told me them were Mormons." Standing there fingering his hat as he talked, he continued, "So every year in July I've come over and put a few flowers on the graves." This man wasn't a Latter-day Saint, but he understood about life and death and about how hard it was to get across the plains in "them days." There wasn't a dry eye in the camp.

My father was there that night, and the next day he went out and found a place where the wheels of the wagons had gone and gone and gone, until there was a bit of a rut in the stone itself. He got down on his stomach, put his chin in that little "V," and said to himself, "This is where they came." Eighty thousand of them came, with six thousand buried on the way. He could never hear any stories about the plains after that without weeping.

"NEVER PREPARE A SERMON"

After the death of George Albert Smith's wife, President Grant sent George Albert with Rufus K. Hardy to the islands in the South Pacific. This was, of course, long before there was a Polynesian Cultural Center. Prior to this trip, the only General Authorities who had ever visited that area had been David O. McKay and Hugh J. Cannon in the early 1920s. (Perhaps it was President Grant's way of getting George Albert away from all the familiar memories.) Elder McKay and Elder Cannon went together and had a royal welcome. People there know more than we've ever learned about how to welcome and honor visitors.

Several years after Elder Smith's trip, an incident happened that indirectly involved Elder Hardy, his traveling companion. Rufus K. Hardy loved the people of New Zealand and was much loved by them, but then he suddenly passed away. The Maori had a memorial service for him, at which Matthew Cowley was present. Brother Cowley had served in New Zealand as a mission president; he knew the Maori language and had translated the Book of Mormon into Maori. The people mourned that their representative among the Brethren, namely Elder Hardy, was now gone. Then a man stood up and said, "We don't need to mourn because Tumuaki [that was their name for Matthew Cowley, which means *leader*] will go home and he will be appointed to the Council of the Twelve and then we will have a representative again."[32]

After the meeting, the people came forward and congratulated Elder Cowley on the wonderful news and appointment—something they knew only through the Spirit. Elder Cowley did return home and soon he was called to the Twelve—by President George Albert Smith.

I remember clearly an address Matthew Cowley gave at the University of Utah institute describing how inadequate he felt when he was called. He said, in effect, "I sit in that room. There is David O. McKay, there is J. Reuben Clark, there is Stephen L Richards—giants; and I say to myself, Matt, what are you doing here?"[33]

Matthew Cowley tried to walk in the image of his hero, George Albert Smith. The first thing President Smith said to him when he called him was, "Brother Cowley, never prepare a sermon. Just stand up and say what the Lord inspires you to say on that occasion." Brother Cowley, telling the story, said, "That certainly is putting some responsibility on the Lord."[34] But Elder Cowley promised to heed President Smith's words, and he kept his promise. You can read Elder Cowley's discourses in Conference Reports and the collection of his discourses. There is formal preparation of a talk, and there is preparation of a life. Elder Cowley manifested the latter. His are not footnoted and prewritten discourses, but they are masterful and they are inspired.

"MUSIC HATH CHARMS"

I was present in the Tabernacle once when George Albert Smith was President of the Church. I was singing in a youth chorus, and we were sitting in the loft where the Mormon Tabernacle Choir typically sit. To my right and below me was President Smith, and over in another section was a group of children known as the Shepherd Strings. They ranged in age from three to nine, and they had all been taught to play violin by a talented woman, Mrs. Shepherd. During the program those children performed "I Think When I Hear That Sweet Story of Old" on the strings. I could see President Smith's profile as he turned to watch them, and tears dripped into his goatee and then down onto his suit. When they had finished, President Smith stood up and said, "Brothers and sisters, I know that this program has been prearranged and that there are speakers, but could I ask if the Shepherd Strings would please perform that again?" He sat down, and they played again. This time he wept even more, if anything, than the first time.

Someone has said, "Music hath charms."[35] Music can reach the soul and melt the heart when prose cannot. I don't know what touched him so profoundly, but my guess is that it was partly the innocence of those children. It was partly the sweetness of their harmony, which required discipline and application. And perhaps it was partly his sense of their tenderness as he thought of the life that they would have to face in this world. In any case, music was important in his life.

George Albert Smith reinforced what President Grant had started with the Mormon Tabernacle Choir, and new opportunities came to them. He traveled widely, and wherever he went, he tried to arrange for extending the broadcast to those areas. President Smith himself had a high-pitched tenor voice. When he spoke and sang there was an intimacy about it. He didn't have a stentorian voice. It was tender, and it had a great influence on the people who surrounded him. You just couldn't get him angry or hostile, no matter how you tried.

KINDLING HOPE

President Gordon B. Hinckley's father said of President Smith that "he has the priceless gift of rekindling hope in the hearts of the hopeless."[36] When people would say that President Smith was a VIP, a Very Important Person, he would reply, "Everybody is a very important person."[37] My daughter picked up on that as a little girl. She said, "Oh, I see, every Mister Nobody is Heavenly Father's friend." "We are all our Father's children," President Smith would have said.

He prepared for the dedication of the Idaho Falls Temple by fasting, and felt he should include in the dedicatory prayer a fervent petition in behalf of the Jewish people. He thanked the Lord for the beginnings of the gathering of the Jewish people.

A great Jewish novelist who received the Nobel Peace Prize, Elie Wiesel, visited Brigham Young University only a few years ago. Wiesel was at a luncheon, and we expressed our sympathy and identification. I said to him, "But you're aware that there are at least a dozen books now that say that the entire story of the Holocaust is a fiction, that it was all made up." He put his head down on the table and then looked up and said, "If that is believed, it will be worse than the Holocaust." President Smith prayed officially, as only he could in faith, for the return of the Jews and for their relief from the suffering that has haunted them from days of old.

"STAY ON THE LORD'S SIDE OF THE LINE"

President Smith's teachings were both heartfelt and impressive. He has been described as a Christlike man.[38] Matthew Cowley said, "He loved everyone because he could see the good in them. . . . I am sure that love found response in the hearts and in the lives of those he loved. . . . God is love. George Albert Smith is love."[39]

He would often say in his teachings, "Stay on the Lord's side of the line."[40] In one brilliant sermon, he said four things. First, "the majority of people . . . have been sidetracked by some of the men whose philosophies have taken the place of truth."[41] In the spirit of something John Taylor said, he continued, "We will lead all the world in knowledge and intelligence and in power, because we have all that the world has, plus the inspiration of the Almighty."[42] Then he said, "We talk about the philosophies of men. . . . When they conflict with the teachings of our Heavenly Father as contained in Holy Writ, they are valueless."[43] Finally, he stated, "Surely we will not be misled by the philosophies and the sophistries of men who pretend to know that which they do not know."[44] Those are all profound statements.

On scripture and great literature, he said, "What mattereth it though we understand Homer and Shakespeare and Milton, and I might enumerate all the great writers of the world; if we have failed to read the scriptures we have missed the better part of this world's literature."[45] So they are.

In a discourse on the home, George Albert Smith summed up his own lifetime aspiration by saying, "Let our homes be sanctuaries of peace and hope and love."[46] In the same discourse he also said, "Let us come into the sanctuary of the House of the Lord"—and he often spoke of the home as a temple—"and attune ourselves to the spirit that is always present when He is there. Then when we go out we can resist the temptations that sometimes threaten to destroy us, and in turn destroy our families."[47]

In another discourse, he spoke of those who are on the other side of the veil. He said they are just as anxious about us as we are about them, and they are praying for our success.[48] Talking about children, which he did often, he said, "There is nothing more precious to us than our children, and our eternal happiness will be largely conditioned by what they attain to."[49]

George Albert Smith also used to say over and over, "Give the Lord a chance."[50] He was talking about not making up your mind on your own or even proceeding in action on your own without consulting the Lord. That means, of course, being prayerful. No one can "talk" a prayer twenty-four hours a day, and if that's what "pray always" means, we're all helpless. But likely it means instead that even while we are active and our mind is generally focused on something else, in our core we can be acting and listening prayerfully. He did that and taught others accordingly and therefore was a "revelator."

"A SERVANT OF ALL MEN"

He never closed the door to friendship, even among those who had berated or attacked him. And he reached out to others, regardless of their background. Dean Wilson, who was the speaker when an honorary degree was given to George Albert Smith, said, "He has helped to build a living economy, devoted years to the handicapped, kept alive a devotion to the ideals and achievements of the pioneers, and invested his best efforts in the leadership of tomorrow." President Smith often spoke of how much growth and development lay ahead of us and how we are only in the infancy of the Church.

Dean Wilson continued: "He is a prophet to the members of his church, a counselor and friend to all. Being a servant of all men, he is in truth a man of God."[51]

President Smith didn't care for organizational walls. "I meet members of the Catholic, the Presbyterian, the Baptist, the Methodist, and all other churches, and I find in these men and women virtues that are most beautiful to me. But I find that they are so rooted in the organizations with which they are identified that when I try to explain to them what we are doing, they seem mystified; they are not able to understand. One man said to me, 'Would you have us give up all that we have had, all these blessings that we have enjoyed, to join your church?' I replied: 'Not a blessing, not one good thing would we ask you to give up. But we do say to you, we will be glad to divide with you, if you will permit us so to do, without cost to you, some of the blessings of our Heavenly Father that have been kept from you in the past which are now at your very door.' "[52]

In 1949 President Smith was the first Church President to appear on a telecast. He was the first president to visit Mexico. He was the first to become an honorary chief among many tribes of Indians; more than once he went to Washington, D.C., to plead the cause of the Indians. I heard President Spencer W. Kimball say President Smith had called him to be the supervisor of what was then called the Navajo–Zuni Mission. President Kimball said, "George Albert Smith was a good Indian."

I said, "What do you mean?"

He replied, "We once sat on a hard bench for forty-eight hours waiting for a chief to see us."

Indian chiefs have a way of testing you. That would be a hard task.

"I'VE LOST MY BEST FRIEND"

George Albert Smith's health began to decline in 1949. There were a couple of efforts to send him to better climates, including Hawaii. While there, he celebrated the centennial of the introduction of the gospel in the islands—but the change of climate had no effect on his health. Nothing seemed to work. When he returned to Salt Lake City after his last trip, he was chronically tired.

My father once sat at the bedside of President Grant, who was then in his eighty-eighth year. President Grant said, "Here's a piece of paper, and take a pencil and write what I tell you." Upon instruction, my father wrote down the names of all of the Presidents, leaving out Joseph Smith. President Grant told him to write their ages at death, which he did. Then he said, "Now average them." This my father did, and the average age of death was eighty-two. President Grant, then eighty-eight, smiled a satisfied smile and said, "Well, I will not bring down the Church average." But then he said, "But I worry about George Albert Smith." Already it was clear to President Grant that George Albert would become the next President. With a bit of irony President Grant then said, "He has enjoyed ill health all his life."

It is an interesting coincidence that President Smith died at eighty-one, but he was in his eighty-second year. So he didn't bring the average down. Since then, of course, the average has changed upward, as several Presidents of the Church have lived into their nineties.

In the last years of his life, George Albert Smith had a thrombosis, and his hearing was declining. President McKay visited President Smith in the last day or two of his life and said, in tears, "He failed to recognize me."[53] His son, George Albert Jr., spent many hours with his father in those final days. He said, "When people would ask Father, do you have any final counsel? [Father would reply,] 'Yes, I know that my Redeemer lives.'" As his son tried to help him turn over in bed, he heard his father say his final words, characteristically in concern for someone else: "Don't hurt yourself." With that, George Albert Smith died.

Two things happened when the word of his death went out. First, a phone call came from Washington, D.C.: "This is Harry Truman. I considered your father one of the country's great moral leaders. You have my sympathy." The second thing that happened was that the doorbell rang. The seven-year-old paperboy stood at the door. In tears, he said, "I've lost my best friend. Is there anything I can do?"[54] The family decided to ask him to be one of the pallbearers.

George Albert Smith died on his birthday, April 4, 1951, which happened to be exactly in the middle of general conference that year. Conference was extended an extra day, with the solemn assembly sustaining President McKay and a funeral for President Smith occurring on the same day.

One of the tributes to President Smith was given by Matthew Cowley, who ended by saying that President Smith had traveled at least a million miles in his ministry; and now on

April 4, he left this world for the next, the shortest journey he ever took.[55]

President McKay, having been sustained in solemn assembly, arose and said, among other things, "To the members of the Church: We all need your help, not your adverse criticisms, but your help."[56] But in asking that of the assembly, President McKay was saying, "We need you to be like George Albert Smith, who was the world's greatest reconciler, and who was a man of peace, and who set an example of embodied love." He not only made friends, he made warm friends.

I close this chapter with a comment about the issue of the calling of men and women to high position who obviously are related to, descended from, and genetically tied to great and prominent predecessors. George Albert Smith fit this category and was acutely aware of his own relationship as a kinsman to many in the leading quorums of the Church. He did not like nepotism. Reading about the original Twelve in the Old World, one finds there were brothers in that quorum. A study of those who were the Twelve Disciples in the New World reveals that there were three brothers in that first council, too. A pattern suggests itself: The Lord, long before we got into this world, asked the question, "Whom can I trust, and whom have I prepared with certain gifts and powers to go forward in the ministry?" In the long run these first families, these anchor families, as President J. Reuben Clark used to call them,[57] were, in effect, called in order to call others. These were gathered in order to go out and become gatherers of gatherers, and that will continue until eventually the so-called "chosen" or "elite" have made it possible for everyone to have all the blessings of the kingdom of God.

It is not a self-serving paradox to talk about the chosen people if, ultimately, the result of being chosen is to choose everyone else. Though it's true that only one man at a time can stand at the head of this Church, that should not trouble those who have been taught that the ultimate blessings of the kingdom will descend upon all who achieve what George Albert Smith himself called "the aristocracy of righteousness."[58] I bear my testimony that he was a prophet, that he was righteous, and that he was the embodiment of love.

9

DAVID O. MCKAY

David O. McKay was a General Authority longer than any of his predecessors in the history of the Church, more than sixty-three years. He was born in 1873 and died in 1970 at the age of ninety-six. He inherited a remarkable legacy, as has been the case with so many of our modern leaders. His grandparents were converts. One set was Scottish, the other Welsh, and both sets joined the Church at great peril. They weren't just persecuted, they were also ostracized from their families for disgracing them. Separately, they came to America just after the Willie handcart migration and were spared some of the terrible tragedies that occurred in that company.

The McKays (pronounced *McKie* in Scottish, with a long "i") faced particular difficulties coming to America. The family loaned money to a man who preceded them in crossing the ocean, with the promise that he would then repay them in full. When they reached New York, they found that their friend had absconded with their money. The McKays eventually made it across the plains and settled in Ogden, Utah, and later in Huntsville.

President McKay's father was deeply committed to the gospel. He served a mission, even after marriage, back to the British Isles. Later he served as a bishop for a total of twenty years. He was a man of great discipline.

The Welsh have the reputation for being fiery tempered, and the Scots are known as being parsimonious. Even farther back from the Welsh and Scottish in the McKay genealogy is their Celtic inheritance. The Celts had the reputation of being fierce warriors. Thus, it was all the more impressive that David O. McKay's father was a man of tremendous self-control and discipline. In fact, it was said of him that as the family sat around the table in Huntsville, if somebody began to make a disparaging comment about anyone—teachers at school, individuals in the Church, neighbors, friends—all Father McKay needed to do to alert them to stop was to raise his hand. That meant, "That's enough of that," and the family changed the subject.

In his boyhood, David, because of the death of two older siblings (one from pneumonia and one from diphtheria), emerged as the oldest child. When Father McKay was away on a mission, David took over the chores and hard labor of the ranch and farm. It was in this setting that he became a lover of animals and horses, which continued to the end of his life. It also accounted for his spiritual preparation, because he spent many hours in the saddle shepherding. Instead of simply "wool-gathering," he memorized things. He already was attuned to literature, especially British literature, and he memorized poetry, including whole segments of Shakespeare.

Two other aspects about his father should be mentioned. David's father served in political office, first in the territorial legislature, and then, after Utah gained statehood, as a state senator. He was also a man who strongly emphasized education to all of his children; David went through the typical schools and high schools of the time.

After public school, David went to Weber Academy, which has since been transformed and enlarged into Weber State University, where he graduated as valedictorian and was president of his class. His instruction at the academy, unlike secular education in our time, included much emphasis on character development, on ethics, on standards, and on ideals, as well as an emphasis on mastering specific fields. He flourished in that setting, and it nurtured his conviction that he must become an educator.

"WE HONOR YOU"

One historian of the Church, Preston Nibley, once asked President McKay, who was then in his eighties, "Who is the greatest man you ever met?" A list of those he met worldwide in every walk of life—including industrial leaders, educational leaders, and religious leaders—would tally at least 1,500 VIPs. But President McKay instantly answered, "My father."[1] The power of his father's commitment to the gospel and the quality of his exemplary life were things he never forgot.

In a tribute to his mother, he said that motherhood is "the greatest of all professions, the most beautiful of all arts."[2] Mothers are co-partners with the Creator,[3] he said, and indicated that he considered his mother to be the greatest inspiration of his life. President McKay once stood while presiding in the Tabernacle just after the Relief Society Singing Mothers had performed and turned toward the choir loft, and his face told it all. It was as if he were saying without words, "We honor you."

There is some irony here. David O. McKay was a man

who experienced a solid home life, but whose forebears had been rejected by their own families. The paradox of this modern Restoration movement is that sometimes people had to leave their families in order, ultimately, to bless them and that some of the enemies of the most faithful have been those of their own household. Unlike that which his grandparents had experienced, David was blessed with a supportive, powerful family life.

"HE THREW THE LETTER ACROSS THE TABLE"

After attending Weber Academy, David went to the University of Utah and became a guard on the line of the first University of Utah football team. From then on, he defended and encouraged sports. He grew to be very tall and strong, and even in his later years his posture was statuesque.

When he had finished college he went back to teach at Weber Academy. While there he was called on a mission. Thomas E. McKay—who has sometimes been called David O. McKay's Hyrum, a loyal, supportive brother—recorded that David was not enthusiastic about the call, that "he threw the letter across the table."[4] His response came because he felt he had finally become able to help support his family, and now the family would have to endure more hardships if he accepted the call. But he and they did accept it, he did serve, and he returned "bearing his sheaves."

"JUST THE SAME 'OLD BOY'"

It was while he was on his mission that his real testimony finally came. During the long hours working on the family farm, David had repeatedly prayed for divine assurance that the gospel was true. His father and mother had both shared their testimonies, but he wanted assurance himself, independently. He recorded that he often got off his horse and knelt down in the sod and petitioned earnestly and lengthily. Nothing he could interpret as an answer came. These experiences became the basis of his later teaching that prayers are answered, but not always as expected, and especially not always *when* expected. He pled and he pled. Once he was so discouraged at the lack of an answer that he said to himself, "No spiritual manifestation has come to me. If I am true to myself, I must say I am just the same 'old boy' that I was before I prayed."[5]

"IF YOU WILL KEEP THE FAITH . . ."

His mission call was to Scotland, where he served under the fine leader James McMurrin. One day in a special meeting, which was unforgettable to everyone, there was a rich outpouring of the Spirit. It was so uniting that one elder said, "Brethren, there are angels in this room." President McMurrin concurred, then made a prophetic statement about an elder there who later became a patriarch. Then he turned to young David, who was then in his twenty-sixth year. "Brother David, Satan has desired you that he may sift you as wheat. . . . If you will keep the faith, you will yet sit in the leading councils of the Church."

David later said that when he heard the warning about Satan and sifting, there flashed though his mind the boyish and youthful temptations and near misses of his life. He took that prophetic statement as an answer to his boyhood prayers, and he knew for himself that the Spirit of God had witnessed the truth of the Restoration.[6] He never turned back from that commitment.

About that missionary meeting that so transformed him, he said, "There was born a desire to be of service to my fellowmen; and with it came a realization, a glimpse at least, of what I owed to the elder who first carried the message of the restored gospel to my grandfather and grandmother, who had accepted the message years before in the north of Scotland and in South Wales."[7]

There was, in the time of President McKay's mission, a practice for the mission president to report on each missionary and put his comments in a permanent file. Years later, Gordon B. Hinckley, doing some research on the history of the Church in the British Isles, found the report on David O. McKay. It stated, "As a speaker: Good.

"As a writer: Good.

"As a presiding officer: Very good.

"Has he a good knowledge of the gospel? Yes.

"Has he been energetic? Very.

"Is he discreet and does he carry a good influence? Yes sir!

"Remarks: None better in the mission."[8]

So he impressed his mission president.

KINDNESS, COURTESY, AND TRUST

After the mission came courtship and marriage. It was in 1901 that he married Emma Rae Riggs. Her side of the story is that he was dashing and charming when he danced and when he quoted poetry, and she just couldn't resist him. His own version is that she was his queen, and he knew it.

As a General Authority, he performed well over a thousand

marriages. Among the counsels he gave, reflecting on his own home life, were these:

Never shout at each other unless the house is on fire.

Never let your wife's hand touch a doorknob. Always open the door for her.

Take your wife out once a week. Let her count on a night each week when you will be together to share feelings.

He did that for sixty-plus years, and when he was away and couldn't be with her, he phoned her and said, "I'll make it up to you." These were expressions of his motto: kindness, courtesy and trust.[9]

He did all these things himself. I saw him, for example, past age ninety taking steps of a few inches at a time to help Emma Rae sit down in a chair. President N. Eldon Tanner shared a similar glimpse. President Tanner had gone to the hotel where the McKays lived, helped the prophet into a wheelchair, and pushed him all the way down the hall to the elevator. Then President McKay said, "Oh, sorry, sorry, President Tanner, we have to go back." Why? He hadn't kissed Emma Rae good-bye.[10]

My family once drove past his home and we saw him out in front. We slowed and said to our children, "There is the President of the Church—that's President McKay." They couldn't see him well, so I turned the car around and parked a little to the west his house. As if he recognized us, he started to walk to the car. He leaned in and said to my wife, Ann, gesturing to an aged lady nearby, "This sister is disoriented. She has apparently wandered from a nearby rest home, and she doesn't know where she is, and she doesn't trust me. So would you talk with her?"

Of all the men on the planet that a woman could fully trust it would be David O. McKay! Ann took care of the situation, a phone call was made, and we found out where the woman belonged. As my wife started to get in the car, her gloves fell out of her purse. Before I could get around to pick up the gloves, President McKay was on his hands and knees, picked up the gloves, gallantly put them on his arm, and handed them to her. Kindness, courtesy, and trust.

"HE NEVER ASKED HIS BOYS TO DO ANYTHING HE DIDN'T DO HIMSELF"

President McKay said, "No member of this church . . . has the right to utter an oath in his home."[11] I have asked Robert and Edward McKay, two of his sons, "Was it really the case that he never raised his voice in his home or that he never shouted or said something a little bit angry?" They answered, "It was." (In some ways that can be more a burden than an inspiration to those of us who are not quite so controlled.)

At one point the Church was making a film on home teaching, which they showed to President McKay. In one of the early scenes home teachers were visiting a home and the family had left their television set on. President McKay said to the filmmakers, "No one would be that discourteous. Take that out of the film. That wouldn't ever happen." (Unfortunately, some of us do know people that discourteous.)

His wife said two things in a tribute to him. First, she said, "The President's ability to quote at any time the Bible, Shakespeare, Wordsworth, Burns, Pope, and other authors [and not just quote to be quoting, but doing so appropriately], helps exceedingly to make him an interesting companion."[12] She continued, "Many people have asked [me], 'How have you been able to instill enthusiasm for Church work in your boys?'

[And there are also two wonderful daughters.] The answer is that . . . Father never asked his boys to do anything that he does not do himself. Example is more forcible than precept. 'A father that whipped his son for swearing and swore himself while he whipped the boy did more harm by his example than good by his correction.'"[13]

CALLED AT A TENDER AGE

In 1906 he was called at the tender age of thirty-two with two other Brethren, namely Orson F. Whitney and George F. Richards, to become members of the Quorum of the Twelve. Shortly after, he was made the assistant general superintendent of the Sunday School, under Joseph F. Smith. He worked in that capacity until he had literally transformed the organization with two major programs that have remained influential in the Church to our day.

First, he developed teacher training for the entire Church, but especially in the Sunday School. He taught that there should be method and outline and manuals, and there should always be application of principles as part of every lesson.

I once attended a Sunday School board meeting when David Lawrence McKay, President McKay's son, was serving as the general superintendent. He told an anecdote about how someone came to President McKay worried that a particular Sunday School superintendent never started on time on the Sabbath. President McKay's answer was to "wait until he does it, even accidentally, and then praise him, fervently praise him for the one time he does it right, and you will see that he will keep doing it." They did, and he did.

Second, David O. McKay not only influenced teachers

themselves, but he also influenced the curriculum they used. The kinds of things he talked about in his sermons are the same things he sought to have the Church emphasize in lessons. For instance, as I reread all of his writings and sermons, I saw that he used words that now are too often forgotten. He talked about nobility, about character-building, about chivalry, and about lofty ideals. He talked about the sublime, and even uses the word "ecstasy" referring to the meaning of life. Such words permeate his sermons.

"DISFIGURED FOR LIFE"

In 1916, he drove a car that had a windshield and a soft top. One night there was a dangerous swelling of the Ogden River, and he was driving onto the bridge. A worker had put a warning rope across the road that, because it was dark, he did not see. He and his brother drove through the rope. It crushed the windshield, caught him on the mouth, severed his lip, knocked out his lower teeth, and broke his jaw. (His brother ducked at the last minute and was uninjured.)

Workers in the hospital said, "He will be disfigured for life." One of the nurses said, "Well, he can always wear a beard." One man said, "Well, the eyes are the same."

Heber J. Grant drove up from Salt Lake City. There was a sign on the door that said, "Visitors Not Allowed." But President Grant entered and said, "David, don't talk. I'm just going to give you a blessing." Among other things, he said, "I bless you that you shall not be scarred." Looking at him afterward, President Grant said to himself, "I've made a promise that cannot be fulfilled."

In due time they were together at a banquet. Elder McKay noticed that President Grant was looking at him very intently. "From where I'm sitting," said the President, "I cannot see a scar on your face!"

He replied, "No, President Grant, there are no scars—your blessing was realized completely!"[14]

DEDICATION OF THE CHINESE REALM

In 1921, Elder McKay undertook the first worldwide tour by a General Authority, traveling with Hugh J. Cannon, a son of George Q. Cannon. Their trip lasted six months, involved at least twenty-three sailing vessels, and literally circumscribed the globe. Elder McKay was prone to seasickness. In one of his letters home, he said that he thought he had given up everything he had ever eaten, even back to the preexistence.

One major stop was China, a country that then had about 500 million people. In Peking (now called Beijing), he looked for a place where they could appropriately dedicate the land for the preaching of the gospel. They found the place near a cypress tree. He felt instantly, "This is the spot."[15] There they proceeded to plead and pray to the Lord that this realm, the Chinese realm, would be visited by the Lord's Spirit and that superstition and error might diminish.

Elder McKay felt great regard and love for Buddhism and the Buddha, but Buddhism denies any personality in the nature of God. He prayed mightily that the people would come to a conversion to the living, personal God. He prayed that the truth would come powerfully and that the Lord would send people of broad mind and intelligent views, who had "the spirit of discernment and the power to comprehend the Chinese nature," to help the people recognize the glorious gospel truth.[16]

Millions of people were starving at the time he offered that prayer, and he was saddened by the suffering of this great people. Twenty-five centuries earlier, even before the Christian era, the Chinese had developed a high level of civilization. But now they were in abject poverty and often misery. He prayed that the famine and pestilence they were suffering would be stayed.[17]

Elder McKay's visit to China was a defining moment for that people, though they knew it not. Since then, new horizons have opened in bringing the gospel to Taiwan, Hong Kong, and now into what was known as Red China.

David O. McKay and Hugh J. Cannon left China and continued on their trip. One night while traveling, they were on a smooth sea. The sky that evening was tinged with pink. Because the ocean was almost without waves, placid like a mirror, the color of the clouds was reflected in the very ocean, and they were surrounded with 360 degrees of wonderment. David O. McKay pondered this scene until the moon appeared, and then went to his hammock.

"I then fell asleep, and beheld in vision something infinitely sublime. In the distance I beheld a beautiful white city. Though far away, yet I seemed to realize that trees with luscious fruit, shrubbery with gorgeously-tinted leaves, and flowers in perfect bloom abounded everywhere. The clear sky above seemed to reflect these beautiful shades of color. I then saw a great concourse of people approaching the city. Each one wore a white flowing robe, and a white headdress. Instantly my attention seemed centered upon their Leader, and though I could see only the profile of his features and his body, I recognized him at once as my Savior! The tint and radiance of his countenance were glorious to behold! There was a peace about Him which seemed sublime—it was divine!

"The city, I understood, was his. It was the City Eternal; and the people following him were to abide there in peace and eternal happiness.

"But who were they?

"As if the Savior read my thoughts, he answered by pointing to a semicircle that then appeared above them, and on which were written in gold the words:

"'*These Are They Who Have Overcome the World—Who Have Truly Been Born Again!*'

"When I awoke, it was breaking day."[18]

"PARTAKERS OF THE DIVINE NATURE"

If there was one phrase that President McKay reiterated more than any other, it was a phrase from Peter. He often said that Peter, the rough-hewn fisherman, was his favorite apostle. He greatly admired Paul, who was educated and brilliant. But Peter was his favorite. It was Peter who said in one of his epistles that we may become "partakers of the divine nature" (2 Peter 1:4). President McKay testified that that blessing is a process that happens through the sacrament and temple worship, and it ultimately will enable us to say of ourselves, "I have been born again."[19]

Part of his tour with Elder Cannon took them to the Holy Land. While there they walked out of St. Stephen's Gate, the place where tradition says Stephen was stoned, across the valley Christ himself would have crossed, and up on the Mount of Olives. On that special mount they prayed for seven things: First, that the seeds sown during their visits to the various missions would be blessed and multiplied. Second, that the Lord would accept their gratitude for the privilege of visiting the Holy Land when, as they began to feel, the prophecies were coming to pass. Third, that the outward semblance of worship that they had seen everywhere, which was often a worship without the heart, might be replaced by genuine and true worship. Fourth, that the opposition and hatred they had seen in some terrorist incidents would be diminished and rebuked, and that tolerance would replace hate. Fifth, that the members of the Church themselves might more fully manifest the gospel in their lives, and thus, by their good deeds, lead others to glorify their Father. Sixth, that the Church in general and their loved ones in particular might receive special protection and guidance. And finally, that they might be led by inspiration on their upcoming trip to the Armenian Mission.[20] They were so led.

They also visited the island of Maui in Hawaii, where they had a remarkable experience. Years earlier, Joseph F. Smith had served a mission to Hawaii, where he had life-shaping experiences of his own. Also years earlier, George Q. Cannon had a manifestation that led to his teaching in the native language in a little wooden chapel in Pulehu, Haleakala. Something close to 98 out of 100 people joined the Church after hearing just that one exalting and inspired sermon. That became the beginning of many conversions in what was then known as the Sandwich Islands.

Now David O. McKay stood on the very spot where that little chapel was, and offered a special prayer. Present with him were Hugh J. Cannon (son of George Q. Cannon) and Wesley Smith (then president of the mission and son of Joseph F. Smith). After the prayer one of the natives made an excited comment in his own tongue. The translation of his words was, "While you were praying I saw two men step out of line and shake hands with someone."

Elder McKay replied, "I do not understand the

significance of your vision, but I do know that the veil . . . was very thin."

Then Hugh J. Cannon, in tears, said, "Brother McKay, there was no veil."[21]

Some of those present were convinced that the two spiritual beings shaking hands were Joseph F. Smith and George Q. Cannon, both long since dead. President McKay and his associates lived close to the spirit world.

Elder McKay prayed that the seeds of that 1921 world tour would somehow bear fruit. The fruit has grown. Just one example. When he visited Halifax, Nova Scotia, in 1921, there were attempts to advertise that an apostle of the Lord was going to speak. The few local members even put placards on telephone poles. A man named Nelson Smith, who lived a hundred miles or so from Halifax, heard about the apostle's visit, was intrigued, and came that night. But he was so ashamed to be seen anywhere near a Latter-day Saint meeting that he simply stood behind a pillar and listened to President McKay without being able to see him.

That experience was the beginning of his conversion. His conversion led to the conversion of his family and friends, and others followed, and yet others. When President Hinckley visited Nova Scotia years later, there were enough faithful Latter-day Saints to justify a temple. He dedicated it in 1999.

"I WANT TO GO AND SEE PRESIDENT McKAY"

In 1922, Elder McKay was called to be the president of the European Mission. In 1934 he was sustained as a counselor to President Grant in the First Presidency. Elder McKay was then sixty-one years old. He was also made a trustee of Utah State University and a regent of the University of Utah. In 1951 he was sustained as President of the Church, and in 1952 he undertook another extensive tour of nine missions in Europe.

In 1955 President McKay went to the South Seas, visiting Tahiti, Tonga, New Zealand, and Australia. He left a deep and lasting impression on those he visited. I have a close associate, a convert friend, from Samoa, whose name is Sini. He received a patriarchal blessing one day in the Church offices from the Church patriarch. Afterward he said, "I want to go and see President McKay."

We shook our heads. "Brother, you can't just go and see President McKay. You would need to make an appointment. You need to talk to his secretary. And he's probably too busy."

He simply stared at us and said, "I'm going to go see him."

We finally decided to let him try it and find out for himself that visiting President McKay wasn't all that easy. About thirty minutes later he rejoined us. He was all smiles. He said, "This is the hand that shook the prophet's hand."

We said, "What happened?"

He said, "I walked into the building and walked past the front desk. I went to where his office was. The door was open about six inches. I looked in and he looked up and said, 'Come in, brother.' We had a fine discussion, and he shook my hand. I'm not going to wash it now."

The Polynesian people loved President McKay and honored him as only they can.

In 1956 he dedicated the Los Angeles Temple. In 1957 he spent some time trying to get the Book of Mormon into an audio book. In 1958 he dedicated the New Zealand Temple, the Church College of New Zealand, the Church College of Hawaii, and the Auckland Stake. In 1960, he inaugurated the

Churchwide youth fireside series. From 1960 to 1970, he saw that many visitors centers were developed, exhibits were set up, and more Assistants to the Quorum of the Twelve were called. In 1961, the uniform method of teaching the gospel was established for missionaries and the Swiss Stake was organized.

In 1962 the Mormon Tabernacle Choir sang at the Seattle World's Fair; it was broadcast by shortwave around the world. In 1963 President McKay dedicated the new Salt Lake Temple annex. In 1964 he dedicated the Oakland Temple. In 1966, the Granite Mountain records vaults were finished and opened. In 1967, the first Regional Representatives were called. In 1968, he added a third counselor to the First Presidency. In 1969, he presided over the dedicatory ceremonies for the David O. McKay Hospital. On January 18, 1970, President McKay died.

"ARE YOU A PROPHET?"

This was a man with the attributes of a prophet. Along with his prominence and spiritual development, he had a delightful sense of humor and could recite in the brogue many great Scottish stories. I remember attending an April general priesthood meeting in the Tabernacle. It was an unusually hot evening, and President McKay stood and said it would be appropriate for us to remove our suit coats, which we did. But the people in the balcony were still sweltering. I remember him smiling and saying, with twinkling eyes, "Brethren, I hope this is not prescient of your future state."

The blue eyes of President McKay were revelatory eyes. President Lee later said, "Tall and impressive was President David O. McKay, as he . . . looked at me with those piercing eyes, which always seemed to search my very soul."[22] When

President McKay was in Glasgow a reporter said to him abruptly, "Are you a prophet?" And he replied, "Look me in the eyes and answer your own question."[23]

During one world tour, Church members and other people mingled on one of the ships. A couple of worldly ladies were curious about this handsome man. How could he be identified with something as strange as the LDS Church? They had a conversation and at some point asked him about marriage. It was fashionable then to have a double standard in morality and in marriage—namely, that mother should be close to home and, in a measure, faithful. But the men—well, everybody knew men were wanderers.

President McKay replied with sincerity, "When one of our young men kneels at an altar in the temple to be married, it is expected that he is as pure as is his companion."

They sized him up, and then one of them challenged, "Ah, yes, but you couldn't have said that."

President McKay looked away for a minute, and then he looked her in the eyes and said, "Yes, I could." That ended the conversation.[24] His eyes were the windows of his soul.

President McKay had other godly attributes, which correlate with the priesthood. He taught that the source of the priesthood was Jesus Christ himself.[25] For him, the most powerful statement of what that means in our lives is in Doctrine and Covenants 121. He said, "No philosopher nor psychiatrist could give better advice than that."[26] It's the one we should memorize: Force or compulsion are never to be used in the authority of the priesthood. Christ's priesthood is to be used only as he used it. And how is that? With persuasion, long-suffering, gentleness, meekness, and love unfeigned. President McKay's secretary of many years said she never saw him depressed, and she never saw him strike out at someone. On the other hand, she said, she saw people come in an endless stream who were both depressed and sometimes angry, but when they left his presence they had been changed.

President McKay became known as a prophet of love. President Lee recorded that when he became President of the Church, he had an experience when he seemed to hear the voice of President McKay, which said, "If you want to love God, you have to learn to love and serve the people. That is the way to show your love for God."[27]

In his dedicatory speech at the Swiss Temple he said, "Love is as eternal as the spirit of man; and if man continues after death, which he does, so will love."[28] He said to one of his close friends, Joseph Anderson, "I never think of death: I am too busy thinking of life."[29]

A RADIANT LIFE

Sermons of President McKay's reflected his own personality. For example, he taught, "Man radiates what he is, and that radiation affects to a greater or lesser degree every person who comes within that radiation."[30]

On the "radiation" of David O. McKay, President Kimball provided this glimpse: "If I could live to merit the smiles of my Lord in the faraway future so that he might shake my hand or embrace me, then and only then would I be lifted into greater ecstasy than I was on Saturday afternoon when I felt your strong arms around me and heard a word of approval."[31]

Other prominent men who visited President McKay echoed this sentiment. One was Walter Reuther, labor leader in the United States. He said to Marion D. Hanks after an interview with President McKay, "I never met a man like that. I do not think our generation will ever produce a man like that."[32] Cecil B. DeMille, who gave an address at Brigham Young University on his film *The Ten Commandments,* was introduced by President McKay. When he stood to speak he said, "David McKay, almost thou persuadest me to be a Mormon!"[33]

When Elder John Longden met him one day in the Church Administration Building, President McKay inquired about his daughter, who had been stricken with polio and was in an iron lung (this was pre–Salk vaccine days). "How is your daughter?" the President asked.

Brother Longden said her spirits were high, but the doctors had said she would never walk again.

President McKay took his hand, looked him in the eye, and said, "She will walk. She will walk."[34] She did.

Elder S. Dilworth Young served as a member of the First Council of the Seventy during the entire time David O. McKay was Church President. At one point Elder Young was scheduled to have a meeting with President McKay, which Elder Young assumed was about one of his committee assignments. But then he had an impression that instead the prophet was going to call him to be a mission president. Elder Young went home and told his wife, "We're going on a mission."

He went to the meeting as scheduled—and President McKay called him to be the president of the New England Mission. Elder Young responded, "I know."

President McKay said, "What do you mean, you know?"

Elder Young then told him about his impression. President McKay sat back and said, "You know, I have called many mission presidents, and I have surprised very few."[35]

I was called (to my great surprise) by President McKay's

counselor, President Henry D. Moyle. "We're calling you to be the president of the New England Mission," he said.

Later we went to a paneled office in the Church Administration Building to be set apart. President Moyle set apart my wife, and President McKay set me apart. It was a sacred thing. President McKay said that as long as I was in the path of duty I would travel in safety, whether by air, sea, or land conveyance. We were traveling as far as Labrador in Canada. I cherished that promise, especially when airplanes were in trouble.

When President Moyle set apart my wife, he included a promise that our family would be blessed with health because we had accepted the call. Ann's mother jumped up in tears and said to President Moyle, "You don't know what you said. I have just been diagnosed with cancer." I thought President McKay and President Moyle might hesitate or would reconsider a moment. Instead, President Moyle simply took her hand and said, "Sister, you heard the promise." I'm grateful to report that Ann's mother overcame that cancer and still later another version of it and lived to be eighty-five.

President McKay was present at the Hill Cumorah Pageant during one of the rare times when it was rained out—and not just rain, but a hurricane. The mission home in New York was damaged. A testimony meeting was held in Palmyra out of doors because there wasn't room in any building nearby. In a discussion with the mission president, Sister McKay said, "Why, I think it is awful that we don't have a larger accommodation in Palmyra. I think we should have one immediately so that these people won't have to sit out in the rain when they have a testimony meeting!"

President McKay turned to the mission president's wife and said, "Now you can see why they name hurricanes after women."[36] That was his gentle, subtle way of saying something else we sometimes heard from him. He said, "I am president of the entire Church, except Rae." (President McKay called her Rae, rather than Emma Rae.)

When a cynic said to him one day, "I don't believe there is a happy couple in the world."

President McKay said, "Well, I know one."

"Who?"

"Rae and me."

The cynic responded, "Well, but you're always away from home."[37]

In his emphasis on self-control President McKay often advocated prayer and fasting, and he advocated teaching little children to fast, to learn early that sometimes you must do things you don't really want to do just because you don't want to do them. That little sacrifice will enable them, then, to face greater conquests and struggles as they mature.[38]

President McKay tried to spread the gospel as a mellowing force internationally from the day he became a member of the Twelve. He continued reaching out worldwide for the rest of his life. In 1968 one man asked him, "What was your greatest accomplishment?" He replied, "Making the Church a world-wide organization."[39] The sense of vision that reaches out to everyone is easy to give lip service to. But from the days of President McKay we have seen tremendous progress in that outreach.

"GIVEN TO HAVE ALL THOSE GIFTS"

The Doctrine and Covenants includes promises about spiritual gifts, and the scriptures imply that each of us should have at least one and that we should pray for them, even seek them earnestly (see D&C 46:8). It is also clear from the revelation that because no one has all of them, and because each of us has a different one, we need each other. But then the scripture makes an exception. It says, "Unto some it may be given to have all those gifts, that there may be a head, in order that every member may be profited thereby" (D&C 46:29).

Of the gifts mentioned in that revelation two are difficult to define. One speaks of knowing the diversities of operations. The other is knowing the differences of administration. What do those mean? President McKay seemed to have both these gifts. By one definition, "diversities of operations" may mean the power to discern those movements in the world that have profound influence and where they are coming from. Are they merely human? Are they from the "lower regions," meaning of the devil? Or are they ultimately of God?

President McKay confronted the diversities of operations. For instance, on the one hand, he was a strong and constant advocate of modern science and technology. But on the other hand, he was an avowed opponent of communism and especially of atheism and the attempt to diminish agency, as taught in dialectical materialism. He was also outspoken in a political way on those issues which he considered to be moral.

On the question of philosophical and literary currents, President McKay affirmed and advocated many of the gems of great poets and philosophers. On the other hand, he was deeply troubled and spoke out against the philosophies of Nietzsche, for example, who supplied the party cries and slogans of the Nazis. He saw clearly that such attacks on Christianity were not always attacks on authentic Christianity. Nevertheless, he was troubled that people weak in faith could be undercut and shaken by such diatribes. In one of Nietzsche's most extreme books, he wrote, "Everything Christianity has advocated is bad, and everything it's been against is good."[40] Nietzsche called this a transvaluation of values.

President McKay was the one who began the correlation program that has carried down to our time. Simply put, it was an attempt to avoid duplication of services, an attempt to reduce too elaborate programs to more basic ones, and to see that the auxiliaries resemble more what good and ideal priesthood support should be instead of becoming proliferated into entertainment.

President McKay was known in his time as a great reconciler. He was in charge of the Church's centennial celebration, for example, and was on a committee to bring disparate personalities, disparate outlooks, and disparate gifts into harmony in civic matters. That is an administrative skill.

That brings us back to the dedication of temples and, specifically, of the Swiss Temple. Until the Swiss Temple was dedicated, all other temples had been built in the United States (including Hawaii) and Canada. The Swiss Temple was the first "across the Atlantic" temple and the first in Europe. There had been prophecies under the administration of President Joseph F. Smith that there would be temples abroad. This was the first.

When President McKay opened the first dedicatory session, he offered a welcome to his predecessors, to those who had served and suffered and sacrificed before him, including Joseph Smith and others.[41] President Spencer W. Kimball was once questioned by a person who was both reverent and curious, "Well, how did you feel when you were there in that meeting?" And President Kimball shared his testimony that there were others there from beyond the veil.

The slogan "Every member a missionary"[42] was President McKay's. It has now been reiterated by President Gordon B.

Hinckley. Consider the numerical power of that idea, if it were actually carried out. Present membership of the Church is about twelve million. If, as President McKay pled and advocated, every person in the Church this year brought one other person into the Church, how many converts would we have in one year? Twelve million. If the next year everybody did it again, including the new 12 million converts, how many converts would we have? Twenty-four million. Now you do that approximately fourteen times, and by the laws of exponential growth you have converted everybody in the world. Then if each of the persons who had been converted went to a temple and did approximately forty names, you would have taken care of everybody back to Adam. That is how powerful, numerically, actually getting one convert per person per year could be, if we would only do it. President McKay envisioned that, and in doing so he exhibited another gift of administration.

SPIRITUAL REJUVENATION

Joseph Anderson, who lived to be 102, had known a whole series of Presidents and had been secretary to many of them. He himself was eventually called to be a General Authority. His comment about President McKay was that he was always present and focused on the issues at hand, and that he was a master of eliciting the best thoughts and counsel of his Brethren. "He was never afraid to make decisions when he felt those decisions were inspired of the Lord. Often as I listened to discussions he had with his counselors and with the Council of the Twelve, I heard him give his decision after first saying, 'I feel impressed.' There was never a time when decisions were rendered by him in such a manner that I was not certain that this great prophet had sought the inspiration to which he was entitled and the Spirit of the Lord had dictated the answer."[43]

Elder Anderson also said that in the prophet's later years, when many supposed that he had become ineffective, or, as the phrase goes, "outlived his usefulness," President McKay was often the first one at the Church offices, before six o'clock, and often there later than the others; and his pace did not diminish until he was in his early nineties. It was yet another witness of spiritual rejuvenation.

President Hugh B. Brown often said that President McKay was living evidence that there is a double meaning in the Doctrine and Covenants promise that says that our bodies can be renewed.[44] "Whoso is faithful," the scripture says, "unto the obtaining these two priesthoods [speaking of both Melchizedek and Aaronic] . . . , and the magnifying their calling, are sanctified by the Spirit unto the renewing of their bodies" (D&C 84:33). President Brown saw him, aged and infirm, stand up in the Oakland Temple dedication, and he seemed suddenly almost young again.[45] The deeper meaning of that sanctifying and renewing is a long-range purification of the soul, which gives not just energy for tasks in this world, but also is a preparation for a higher resurrection.

President Brown spoke of the burdens President McKay carried, and then he said, "I will give you an example. Recently my phone rang and President McKay said, 'Come in.' So I left my office and went into his. 'President Brown,' he said, 'I've been searching for a counselor.' [This was after the death of President Henry D. Moyle.] 'I have been praying but I have not received an answer. I'm going over to the temple. I'm going to that sacred room, and I'm going to get my answer.'"

The inference was that he wanted President Brown to pray for him, but he did not say that specifically. President

Brown continued, "Sometime later my phone rang again. President McKay said, 'Come in.' I went to the door and it was partly ajar and I could see him sitting behind his desk." Then President Brown said, "You know that when Moses descended from the Mount his face shone and 'he wot not,' which is to say he did not know that it shone. I saw that on the face of David O. McKay. When I sat down he said, 'President Brown, it has been made known to me in as clear a manner as anything I've ever received of the Lord that N. Eldon Tanner is to enter the First Presidency.'"[46]

President McKay taught about the Spirit as if it were sunlight. "The peril of this century"—and he said it is certainly to be more so in the next—"is spiritual apathy. As the body requires sunlight, good food, proper exercise and rest, so the spirit of man requires the sunlight of the Holy Spirit; proper exercise of the spiritual functions; the avoiding of evils that affect spiritual health, that are more ravaging in their effects than typhoid fever, pneumonia, or other diseases that attack the body."[47] He taught that without the Spirit we cannot overcome the worldly environment of our time.

David O. McKay was interviewed late in life by an earnest reporter who caught on to the idea that Latter-day Saints trust in the reality of modern prophets and apostles. The man directly asked President McKay, "Have you ever seen the Savior?"

President McKay replied that he had not, "but that he had heard his voice, many times, and that he had felt his presence and his influence. . . . Then he told how some evidences were stronger even than that of sight," and he recalled for the reporter the testimony of Thomas. In President McKay's mind, Thomas, after saying he wouldn't believe until he had seen and touched, "did not actually look up but knelt at the Savior's feet and said unto him, 'My Lord and my God.'"[48]

"ECSTASY"

The word *jewels* is used from time to time in scripture. The Lord says he's going to come some day and make up his jewels (see D&C 60:4; 101:3). The jewels are people. If you read the book of Revelation, you see the future of the Holy City, the New Jerusalem. It talks about a magnificent city, golden in its streets, and jeweled in its buildings (see Revelation 21:10–21).

President McKay often said that the greatest jewels of your life are your children, that we are jewels, and that this earth is the treasure box that has been given to surround these jewels.[49]

He spoke of delight and of beauty and used the word *ecstasy*. Here are a few sentences:

"To all who believe in a living, personal God and His divine Truth, life can be so delightful and beautiful. As a matter of fact, it's glorious just to be alive. Joy, even ecstasy, can be experienced in the consciousness of existence. There is supreme satisfaction in sensing one's individual entity, and in realizing that that entity is part of God's great creative plan. There are none so poor, none so rich, sick or maimed who may not be conscious of this relationship."[50]

For many of us, there are clouds in the sky, of trial and worry and perplexity. We do not often think it's glorious just to be alive. President McKay was trying to communicate that we need a perception of our possibilities of fellowship with the living Christ. That kind of relationship and that kind of fellowship can emerge from awe and reverence. Fellowship in the quorums and in the Church generally can bring about this kind of feeling. President McKay gave an entire general conference sermon admonishing us to look upon a chapel, especially the interior, as sacred ground, that we sing only appropriate music, that we pray in reverence, that we speak in the sacred moments of worship in whispers.[51] He himself did that.

President McKay visited the Sacred Grove. The trees that are there now perhaps were not even saplings 150 years ago. But while he was there pondering and meditating, two or three little boys started to climb the trees, standing on each other's shoulders, shouting and acting as boys do. His eyes flashed and he walked over and said, "Please, boys, please. This is the Sacred Grove. This is not a place for games; this is not for fun. Please, go over there if you want to climb a tree."[52] That was his perspective on reverence.

I have pondered the whole question of what it means to say a place or a thing is sacred. We are not in a tradition similar to some other major faiths that say that somehow an object may be magically infused with a power and that we should worship it. That for us comes close to idolatry.

On the other hand, we believe the earth is the Lord's, and there are places where the Lord has physically stood and walked, and these places are considered sacred. Ultimately the earth is going to be transformed as the home of the truly righteous. We further believe that the Spirit of God can consecrate specific places, and that those who enter there will be constrained to acknowledge that it is the house of the Lord and that his presence and Spirit are there. Without that sense of the sacred, we are not likely to come to a close relationship with Christ.

TWO PHILOSOPHICAL POINTS

Two other philosophical points. President McKay wrote and spoke on the subject of the Creation. Some scientists, of course, believe that the world as we know it, with all of its laws and complexities, came into being by happenstance. But President McKay's conviction was that you cannot explain life and creation simply as a matter of chance. Personality, according to one theory, emerged from protoplasmic slime with no prevision of what was intended. But personality is an essential element of the very ultimate nature of God and his Christ. And we are created in the image of their personality. Whatever one wants to say about the processes that led to our creation in this world, President McKay would insist it was not without divine intervention.[53]

The other point has to do with the three temptations of Christ. President McKay studied the life of the Savior and then taught that the three temptations he faced in the wilderness are prototypes of the very temptations we face every day in our own lives.

Not only are the temptations prototypes, but the escape from them, the overcoming of them, is the same for us as it was for him. Jesus reached directly to the Father and quoted scripture back to the adversary, who was using scripture in his own way. We have to reach through Christ to the Father.

The first temptation is that of appetite or passion. Personally having been in the Judean desert above Jericho, I don't see how anyone could be there for forty days and survive; to think of him looking back at the oasis and not be thirsting and hungering is beyond any mortal conception. The second temptation is what President McKay called "yielding to the pride and fashion and vanity of those alienated from the things of God." The third is "a desire for the riches of the world, or power among men."[54]

If those were temptations in the days of Christ they are still temptations today, and we are still buffeted by them. President McKay was one man who overcame them. And he would say, if he were here, that he did not overcome them alone but through the grace and power and blessing of the Lord Jesus Christ.

"A STEP-BY-STEP ASCENT"

Let us review his commitment to the temple. When I was a graduate student in Los Angeles, California, I attended a meeting presided over by President McKay. President McKay asked the Saints there to raise a million dollars to build a temple, saying that if they did, the Church would contribute three million dollars to finish the temple. Stake presidents arose one by one and made commitments on behalf of their stakes. I remember being startled at their faith. They raised $1.6 million, far more than what was requested, and during that same period the tithing in the Los Angeles area increased instead of diminished. Later, President McKay stood with tears in his eyes at the dedication and said, "You cannot get the Lord in debt."[55]

It was in that first meeting, after those pledges were made, that he gave what I consider one of the greatest discourses ever given on the temple. In shorthand I took down one paragraph that I have quoted over and over. It changed me. This is the summation:

"Brothers and sisters, I believe there are few, even temple workers, who comprehend the full meaning and power of the temple endowment. Seen for what it is, it is the step-by-step ascent into the Eternal Presence. If our young people could but glimpse it, it would be the most powerful spiritual motivation of their lives."[56]

I was staying at a cabin a distance away with an aunt who had abandoned the Church. In an earlier conversation, when I asked her how she felt about her previous temple experience, she was disparaging and even hostile.

I approached her with this question, "What do you think of David O. McKay?"

She replied, "I think he's one of the most Christlike men I've ever known of."

I then asked, "Would you be interested in what he said about the temple today?"

She said, "Yes."

And then I quoted the statement printed above. After looking at the stars for a while she said to me, "Well, maybe if I had listened reverently I might feel the same way."

When people have disparaged the temple ceremony in my hearing, I have often thought of that comment and of President McKay's impressive stature, and I have said to myself, How can anybody believe there is anything evil about temple ordinances when he looks at the prophet? President McKay was a man who had been in the temple every week for fifty years. And it showed.

"PAPA DADE HAD IT MADE"

Finally, we turn to his passing. He had requested that at his funeral the Mormon Tabernacle Choir sing "Crossing the Bar," Tennyson's famous lines put to music. The key line asks that after death there be no mourning by those left behind.

Then it says, "I hope to meet my Pilot face to face when I have crossed the bar."

I was there that day. I heard the choir. Someone quoted a grandson of President McKay, who, when he had heard that his grandfather, Papa Dade, had died, said, "Oh, Papa Dade had it made." I testify that that was surely the verdict of the Christ and of the Father, and that he did meet them face to face when he "crossed the bar," and that he left us with the testimony and the example of how we may do the same someday.

10

JOSEPH FIELDING SMITH

My first exposure to Joseph Fielding Smith—and to his wife—was during a high school football game. I was cheering heartily for a close friend named Milton ("Mitt") Smith, the star punter for the team. Suddenly I heard a shrill whistle from behind me, the kind made with two fingers and a curved tongue. "Go, Mitt! Go, Mitt!" a woman shouted—and it didn't sound like a high school coed! I turned around and saw that the voice belonged to Jessie Evans Smith, the third wife of Joseph Fielding Smith. She was there with him, supporting her youngest stepson.

All of that, of course, was much later in his life. Let's look at the familial roots of Joseph Fielding Smith. His father, Joseph F. Smith, sixth President of the Church, influenced him profoundly, of course, but Joseph Fielding himself often said that the spiritual legacy from his grandfather Hyrum Smith—whom he never knew—was also indelible.

Doctrine and Covenants 23:3 records instructions given through the Prophet Joseph Smith to his brother Hyrum in April 1830, the month the Church was organized. Hyrum was told: "Thy duty is unto the church forever, and this because of thy family." An earlier blessing Hyrum received from Joseph helps us understand that Hyrum was the patriarch of a line that would be a great strength to the Lord's Church: "Blessed of the Lord is my brother Hyrum for the integrity of his heart; he shall be girt about with strength, truth and faithfulness shall be the strength of his loins. His name shall be called a blessing among men. . . . He shall receive counsel in the house of the Most High that he may be strengthened in hope. . . . And the goings of his feet shall ever be by streams of living water."[1]

On one occasion Wilford Woodruff, pointing to Hyrum's son Joseph F. Smith, said, "Children, look at him. He, more than any man living, resembles the Prophet Joseph Smith and his brother Hyrum," and then made a prediction about Joseph F.'s contribution to the leadership of the Church.[2] Through Joseph F. and Joseph Fielding Smith, "faithfulness" has indeed been "the strength of [Hyrum's] loins from generation to generation."

On the day of Joseph Fielding Smith's funeral, President Harold B. Lee asked for President Smith's descendants to stand. Of the seventy-six that were present, the record shows that the great majority had been dedicated to the cause of Christ. This is a faithful family.

IMMERSED IN THE GOSPELS

In Joseph Fielding Smith's boyhood we see two strong tendencies. He began early—at age ten—to read serious literature and had completed the Book of Mormon twice before he was twelve. How many of us can say that? He soon was immersed, likewise, in reading the history of the Church. In all of his work—from herding and milking cows in Taylorsville to his job at ZCMI—he constantly carried with him his New Testament and became immersed in the Gospels. So here is a man interested in scripture and who studied for mastery, almost from day one.

In a sermon many years later, he said, in substance, talking about the scriptures, "Take it up if you want by topics or doctrines. That is good. But you're not going to understand the Doctrine and Covenants, you're not going to get out of it all there is in it unless you take it up section by section. Then when you do that, you will have to study it with its setting, and as you get into that, you will get into the history of the Church."[3] When he was appointed Church Historian, he carried into that assignment not only much preparatory study but that focus: we need to understand the scriptures in their setting.

Out of that focus came two axioms. One is that a text without a context is pretext. In other words, you need always to put a text into its context. And then further he learned that text in context without its historical setting is probably only a partial truth. Joseph Fielding Smith became known in his time as our primary doctrinal writer and teacher, as well as our primary historian.

He became known for his willingness to answer gospel questions, a reputation that was both a privilege and a burden. Jessie Evans Smith sang for years as a contralto with the Mormon Tabernacle Choir. One day during a break, another member of the choir went down into the Tabernacle loft where there was a telephone and saw Sister Smith pick up the receiver, dial a number, and then put the receiver down on the table and start to read. After several minutes she picked it up again and said, "Hello, Daddy," her term for Joseph Fielding, and they began to talk.

The choir member later asked her, "What was going on there?"

Sister Smith said, "Well, people all over the Church expect Daddy to answer their questions, so they telephone day and night. We have an agreement now that only if the telephone rings thirty-two times or more will we pick it up. Daddy feels that if a person holds on that long, maybe it really is urgent, so then he answers."[4] Thirty-two times!

And of course there were thousands of letters. Joseph Fielding would often simply return a person's letter with a clear, brief answer of one or two lines and the initials "JFS." Rarely did he keep copies, so if somehow we could gather back into one place all of those letters with all of his comments or answers, they would be precious.

He was committed to two passages of scripture that he sometimes said were his absolute favorites. I heard him give discourses on these scriptures, once in the Salt Lake Temple Annex and once when he gave a lecture on temple marriage in the old Eighteenth Ward in Salt Lake City. The talk in the temple annex focused on Doctrine and Covenants 50:24: "That which is of God is light; and he that receiveth light, and continueth in God, receiveth more light; and that light groweth brighter and brighter until the perfect day." He wrote that ultimately you and I, if we are faithful, will have bodies that shine like the sun.[5]

The other favorite—one that also had been a favorite of President Lorenzo Snow—was from 1 John. When Christ shall appear, "we shall be like him; . . . and every man that hath this hope in him purifieth himself, even as he is pure" (1 John 3:2–3).

"I BEAT THE SOCKS OFF HIM"

Elder Smith was an accomplished handball player—and he was ambidextrous. If you are a good handball player you can swing on the ball with either hand. You sometimes have to hit it very hard, so you wear a small leather glove. He became an expert and continued playing into his seventies. He could often just hit the ball from one position until his opponent—who had run until he was dog tired—had missed the ball. And then he would smile. The phrase he would use to describe his victory: "I beat the socks off him."[6] Playing handball was great exercise for him and perhaps had something to do with his longevity.

He also enjoyed flying, especially in jet airplanes. On one occasion he flew over territory he and his father had traveled by land. Going to St. George and back had taken them about three days. In the plane it took thirty minutes. He liked to fly with the National Guard and eventually was given honorary brigadier general status. One day a visitor entered Elder Smith's office and said, "I came to see Brother Smith."

The secretary said, "Step to the window here and maybe you can see him." There was a jet going over.

The visitor said, "You mean he's in that plane?"

"Oh yes, that's him all right," came the answer.[7]

These hobbies helped to bring balance to his life.

He often attended his children by their bedsides when they were sick. He had hardly any sickness in his own life, and he frequently said that was because he kept the Word of Wisdom. B. H. Roberts used to say that the Deseret Gym's location situated close to the Salt Lake Temple symbolized the uniting of the spiritual and the temporal and the Latter-day Saint belief that one must take care of the body as well as the spirit.[8]

President Smith didn't eat much meat. He wasn't a vegetarian, but he took seriously the Word of Wisdom admonition to eat meat "sparingly." He didn't drink even decaffeinated coffee because he felt that one should avoid even the appearance of evil.

"DADDY, CAN I TELL HIM THE STORY?"

Joseph Fielding Smith was married three times. He married his first wife, Louie, in March 1898. She bore him two beautiful daughters, but after ten years of marriage she died. Then he married Georgina Ethel Reynolds, a daughter of George Reynolds, well-known compiler of the *Concordance to the Book of Mormon.* (This work was done—down to the *ands* and the *buts* and the *ors* of the 522-page Book of Mormon—while Reynolds was in prison for plural marriage.) She bore Joseph Fielding Smith five sons, all of whom served missions and all of whom served in World War II (one son, Lewis, was killed in that war), and also four daughters. After nearly thirty years of marriage, she died in August 1937. Then he married Jessie Evans.

One day I was in the Historical Department of the Church. Jessie Evans Smith recognized me (she had known my father well) and said, "Let's go see Daddy." I knew who she meant, and I was intimidated in the presence of this man. But she pushed me into his office. He was sitting there studying, as usual. He looked up, smiled, and said, "Brother Madsen, you can have two questions."

I was equal to my opportunity. My first question was, "Do you believe that marriages are made in heaven, Brother Smith?"

When he hesitated (I've learned since that his stark answer would have been, "No"), she poked him and prompted, "Daddy, Daddy, don't you think marriages are made in heaven?"

Now this was a completely honest man, and he wanted to honor his wife, so he said, "It's in heaven now."

Then she poked him again and said, "Daddy, can I tell him the story?"

He said, "Go ahead."

She began, "I was the city recorder in Salt Lake City, and I phoned Joseph Fielding Smith's office and told him that a document needed to be signed and that we would bring it to him. But shortly I heard one of my clerks say on the telephone, 'All right, Brother Smith, we'll have it here for you.'

"When she hung up, I said, 'Was that Joseph Fielding Smith?'

"'Yes,' she replied.

"'You don't ask him to come down here,' I said. 'You go up there.'

"She phoned him back, but he had already left. He came and signed the document."

That evening, she said, as Jessie left in her car she was stopped by a policeman, who happened to be a Latter-day Saint, at the corner of Fourth South and State Street. He held up the rest of traffic, walked over, and said, "Jessie, did Joseph Fielding Smith come to see you today?"

She said, "Yes."

"Did he ask you to marry him?"

She said, "No! Don't be funny." She put her car in gear and drove off.

Soon after, there was a general conference, and Jessie sang in the choir as usual. A longtime friend of Joseph Fielding Smith from Idaho took him aside and said, "Joseph, I had the impression today that you're going to marry Jessie Evans."

At this point in the narrative Sister Smith poked her husband again. "Daddy, can I tell him what you said?"

"Go ahead," he replied.

She said, "Well, Daddy says it isn't pretty but we *had* to get married."

In that same conversation she said, "Truman, do you know the phone number of the Garden of Eden?"

I said, "No."

And she said, "Adam 8–1–2."

They certainly had a twinkle in their relationship.

The marriage to Jessie Evans occurred within the same year as the death of Joseph's second wife, and some people criticized that. President Heber J. Grant overheard one such comment at a dinner. He turned to the speaker and said, "Yes, he married soon after his wife died. He did it because I told him to."[9] Apparently President Grant believed that it is not good for man to be alone.

All of Joseph's sons served missions, and all of his children had temple marriages. A sermon he gave at Brigham Young University after he had become President of the Church was not just about eternal life, but about what he called "eternal lives," a scriptural phrase in Doctrine and Covenants 132:24, 55, that we sometimes ignore or downplay. Eternal life, singular, can no doubt apply to any one of us and describe the kind of life we aspire to. But eternal *lives* refers to the creation and procreation of families into eternity. And it also applies to the lives of our children and their children. He taught that we have a responsibility, because life does not begin or end in this world, to bring spirits into this world and then to care for them with profound and lasting concern.[10]

Perhaps this perspective was second nature to him because of his long experience serving in the temple. He was a counselor in the temple presidency for nearly twenty years and was president of the Salt Lake Temple for four years. On behalf of Eve and of all women he wrote: "The most noble, exalting calling of all is that which has been given to women as the mothers of men. Women do not hold the priesthood, but if they are faithful and true, they will become priestesses and queens in the kingdom of God, and that implies that they will be given authority. . . . They do reap the benefits coming from that priesthood."[11]

He took that very seriously, and of course he honored his wives, as had his father before him, with persistent love and concern. "The Lord . . . ," he said elsewhere, "offers to His daughters every spiritual gift and blessing that can be obtained by his sons."[12]

INTERNAL RUMBLINGS

Because of his long life of continual service, and because of the multiple responsibilities he carried for so long, Elder Smith provided a kind of continuity, a kind of institutional memory to the Church that no one else, perhaps, could have. Let me give some examples. He was made a missionary in the England Nottingham District at age twenty-two—a year into his first marriage, so his dear wife had to wait for him at home. When he came home, he was made a stake missionary and continued in that calling for nine years. That makes eleven years of specific "in the trenches" missionary work. In 1901, at the age of twenty-five, he began working in the Church Historical Department, then known as the Historian's Office. In 1906, at age thirty, he was appointed Assistant Church historian, and from then on for sixty-four years he was involved in the leadership of the Historical Department. At the age of thirty-one he was given an assignment from the U.S. Department of Commerce to collect statistics of the Church for its religious census, and so he became involved in record keeping, one of the constant themes of his teaching thereafter. He was director and librarian of the Genealogical Society at age thirty-two and became secretary in 1910, when he was thirty-four, serving in that role for twelve years.

He was given assignments in editing both the *Utah Genealogical and Historical Magazine* and the *Improvement Era.* At the same time he was assigned to educational posts in the Church Board of Education and General Board of Religion Classes. Church education and working with youth became a central concern and continued to the end of his life. He became president of the Council of the Twelve at the age of seventy-four, serving in that role for nineteen years, longer than any man in our history. No man came to the presidency at a more advanced age (ninety-three). He served as President of the Church to the age of ninety-five.

When he was called into the Quorum of the Twelve in 1910 at age thirty-three, there were rumblings about Joseph F. Smith's appointment of his own namesake son to the Twelve. Archibald F. Bennett, our great genealogical leader, related to me that Susa Young Gates, the outspoken daughter of Brigham Young who had thirteen children and who wrote 1,300 articles, walked in on President Joseph F. Smith and said, "Joseph, how dare you! How dare you!"

Part of her objection was that Joseph F. Smith had earlier, with the unanimous consent of the Twelve, called another son, Hyrum Mack Smith, to the quorum. And now he had appointed another of his sons—two were serving in the Quorum of the Twelve simultaneously. "That's just going too far," Sister Gates had said. (Hyrum Mack died prematurely, at the beginning of 1918. He was only forty-five years old. The father, Joseph F., died later that same year.)

President Smith's answer was, "Sister Susie, every time I thought of calling anyone else I had darkness. I had to call him. I knew in advance what would be said. I had to call him."

In retrospect, I think no one would say that he made a mistake.

"IT'S IN THE BAG"

In his later role as a member of the Twelve, Joseph Fielding Smith had a renowned partner in his third wife, Jessie Evans. He loved music, and his wife taught him to sing duets with her. An accomplished contralto, she had turned down an operatic career after touring one year with a light opera company. Her "signature" song was based on the twenty-fourth Psalm: "Who shall ascend into the hill of the Lord? . . . He that hath clean hands and a pure heart" (Psalm 24:3–4). She and Elder Smith delighted the Saints wherever they traveled. Sister Smith would promote their singing together in stake conferences. He would say, "Well, it's not going to be a 'duet'—it's going to be a 'do it'"; he said he had to do it whether he wanted to or not.[13] Joseph Fielding Smith wrote several hymns, two of which are "We Are Watchmen on the Tower of Zion" and "Come, Come, My Brother."

Elder Smith was an early riser, and he insisted that his family be likewise. He was dedicated to the proper use of time. Somebody asked him once how he managed to get so much done, and he said, "It's in the bag."[14] He explained that he had never taken an hour off for lunch but had always brought a brown bag lunch, had a sandwich, kept working, and thus saved at least three hundred hours a year.

On one occasion at the Historical Department he said to me with a smile, "Brother Madsen, I hold the distinction of being the only General Authority who ever dedicated a jail." He had gone to Missouri as a senior member of the Twelve, and, along with President David O. McKay, had dedicated what is now the visitors' center at Liberty.[15]

"ONE OF THE MOST IMPORTANT DUTIES"

He attended the funeral of a woman who had been a bedfast invalid almost all of her mature life. Instead of pining the time away, she had scrupulously studied and copied genealogical and family history records in a clear, impeccable hand. He paid tribute to her that day, saying that though he was Church Historian and Recorder, he had not had time to do justice to his own pedigree and family group sheets. She helped him with that, and he said he and his family would bless her name forever.

He often said, probably because of his genealogical experience, "The matter of record keeping is one of the most important duties devolving on the Church."[16] He pled for accuracy; he pled for adequacy. A mission president who returned after his three-year assignment had an interview with President McKay, and then was asked if he would meet with Joseph Fielding Smith. Joseph Fielding Smith asked him if he had kept records of his ministry. He said he had kept a journal. Elder Smith said, "Would you consider pulling out excerpts of your journal that pertain to spiritual experiences of your mission?"

The man replied, "There are too many, Elder Smith. Every page of my journal is somehow connected with such experiences."

"Well, send us some of them," Elder Smith replied.[17]

He encouraged three kinds of record keeping. He wanted recorded everything that showed the hand of the Lord in modern Church history. But he also wanted complete and accurate records of ordinances performed. (Parley P. Pratt once noted that in addition to other entries in his journal, he kept a faithful and accurate record of his every use of the priesthood.) And third, Elder Smith wanted histories of nations and peoples, a broader history of the world. There is in the Historical Department a fifteen-hundred-volume set of books—thick, sizeable, tall volumes—titled "Journal History." For every day of the Church's existence there are inserts pertaining to anything that happened on that day, not just in the Church's history but in related world events. The books also include references to personal histories or journals, diaries, or letters. Joseph Fielding Smith was responsible for much of that record. Someday that may all be available on microfilm or the Internet.

As Church Historian Joseph Fielding Smith was responsible for dividing the labors of the department. His assistant was a meticulous historian named Andrew Jenson, who wrote both a four-volume biographical encyclopedia and another volume called *Encyclopedic History of the Church.* He said, "I have sometimes spent a whole week to find out if something happened on Thursday or Friday."[18] That's how painstaking he was. B. H. Roberts and Joseph Fielding worked side by side with him for many years.[19]

"I'M NOT SURE ABOUT THAT MAN"

President Smith's temperament was sometimes misunderstood. People thought of him as austere and severe. According to one story he went to a stake conference in Wyoming where he bore down hard on their need to repent.

He finished by saying, "Brothers and sisters, if you do not repent, few of you will be saved in the life to come."

He had barely reached home when letters began coming from that stake, saying, "This man didn't inspire us at all. He condemned us. He was harsh. We would like something done about this."

So he was assigned to go back to the stake and speak again. He went back—and repeated his words from before. He then said, "Brothers and sisters, the last time I was here, I said that unless you repented there would be few of you saved. I have changed my mind—none of you will be."[20]

This story may or may not be true, but his whole life was indeed given to teaching repentance, which is not a pleasant subject—especially for those of us who need it most.

I was once with an assembly of Temple Square guides at a banquet where the speakers praised and admired the guides and said how wonderful the work was that we were doing on Temple Square. Then they called on Elder Smith, and he read a section of King Benjamin's discourse that says, in effect, that no matter what good you do through your whole life, you will still be an unprofitable servant (see Mosiah 2:21). Well, that fell with a dull thud on the proceedings. But as we all thought about it and talked about it, we decided that that was exactly what we needed to hear. We needed to recognize our great debt to the Savior and be more articulate and humble in our calling as his witnesses on Temple Square.

But Joseph Fielding Smith was also a very kind, caring man. He used to talk often about "the yoke" of this life. When Christ made the statement, "My yoke is easy, and my burden is light" (Matthew 11:30), his point was not that he took away either the yoke or the burden. He said that "*through me* your yoke can be light; it can be easy." Otherwise it's burdensome.

Elder Smith loved that concept, but noted that we, in our vanity and sometimes our pride, suppose that we can do it all ourselves.[21]

He observed two kinds of people in the world, which encouraged his addressing this point in his sermons. One was those who were frittering away their lives in superficial things. The other was the people who came to him in anguish, the people uttering what he called the "pitiful cries"[22] of those who had not only broken commandments, but had deliberately violated covenants, and who now were pleading with him to somehow help them. He said, in interpreting the concept of a broken heart, that a broken heart in the scriptures doesn't mean a person who's been jilted romantically, or who is keenly disappointed. "A broken heart [is] one that is humble, one that is touched by the Spirit of the Lord, and is willing to abide in all the covenants."[23]

Brother Smith was once approached by a young woman, a convert, from the east coast. She said that her bishop had asked her one day, perhaps in a temple recommend setting, if she sustained the authorities of the Church. She had said, "Well, I'm sure that Joseph Smith was a prophet, but I'm not sure about *that* man," speaking of Joseph Fielding Smith.

Then she noticed in a publication that President Smith was going to speak at a BYU devotional in the Marriott Center. She fasted, went to the building, and afterwards approached him. She said, "As his hand touched mine I felt tremendous spiritual strength. I was almost overwhelmed by it. Immediately I thought of the story about the sick woman in the New Testament who thought that if she could but touch Jesus' robe, everything would be all right. I felt something go out of him and into me. I knew then, without a doubt, that I was shaking the hand of a real prophet."

She said, "Brother Smith, I'm a convert," and he replied, "Well, I'm a convert, too."[24] And he smiled.

Of President Smith's compassion, Elder Harold B. Lee once said, "If I had committed crimes and could receive counsel from anyone in the world to defend me in court, I would choose President J. Reuben Clark Jr. But if I had committed crimson sin and could choose anyone to be my advocate before the Lord, I would choose Joseph Fielding Smith."[25]

A Salt Lake Temple worker walked into the temple one day weighed down with a severe family problem. He walked past the office of President Smith, not thinking the president was there. Many steps later, the worker felt an arm come around his shoulders and heard his name spoken. "It's pretty tough going, isn't it?" President Smith said to him. The worker explained briefly what was happening, and President Smith embraced him and said, "The Lord bless you, brother."[26] That one moment changed the temple worker's life.

I believe one root of Joseph Fielding's sense of reverence was his temple experience. While my wife and I were in New England (I had been called as mission president), we had a monthly publication that we thought could be appropriately called *The New England Prophet* because, after all, that's where the Prophet Joseph was born. I received a kindly letter from Elder Smith saying, "I suggest"—he didn't say *command* or *order*—"that you change the name because the term 'Prophet' is a sacred term." We changed it to *The New England Advocate.*

In the same spirit he said something that became a quotation on the wall of the Temple Square Bureau of Information (the precursor to the visitor's center): "The supreme act of worship is to keep the commandments."[27] There has been a lot of discussion about what worship is and whether Latter-day Saints have the proper spirit of worship, whether our meetings are not reverent enough, and whether we're too social. In the above quotation President Smith seemed to be saying, "Yes, there should be reverence and especially in a sacrament meeting and the temple. But the supreme act of worship, the way you prove you love and worship the Lord, is to keep His commandments."

It is said of him that he was always punctual, that he never came to a meeting late. Sometimes he spoke out about the undue length of some meetings, and he was a great organizer and a great expediter. But his punctuality wasn't all about efficiency. I learned from a man who was with him on a trip to Missouri that Joseph Fielding Smith was always the first one back to the car—and he sat on the hump seat in the backseat so the others could be more comfortable. That may be a little thing, but it shows thoughtfulness.

This was a man who, of course, was known as a man of integrity. The word *integrity* is related to the words *integration* or *integral.* It means pulling things together harmoniously and being consistent and persistent in putting principles into practice in your life. Many examples could be given of this quality in President Smith. On one occasion, the *Improvement Era* staff wanted to take his picture for their cover. Someone handed him a pen and said, "Brother Smith, pretend you are signing a letter."

He said, "No, I won't pretend." He found a letter he needed to sign and said, "Now, I will actually sign a letter."[28]

DO THE PEARLY GATES SWING OR ROLL?

The same integrity led him to focus on the first principles of the gospel, to stay "close to the trunk of the gospel," as the

Prophet put it,[29] and not get out on the branches in speculation. There has been a notion in the Church that you can count all the sons of perdition on one hand. Someone asked him if that were true, and he said, with a twinkle in his eye, "Yes, five, ten, fifteen, twenty."[30]

At least two of his discourses warn us that we should avoid pursuing the "mysteries."[31] He did not mean the mysteries of godliness, which are centered in the house of the Lord and which are sacred and which we are encouraged to try to understand. He was talking about speculating on such fruitless topics as whether the pearly gates swing or roll. "Pursue a steady course," he would say.[32]

In the same vein, more than once he spoke about what he called "bending the gospel to fit"[33] the issue of the moment, perhaps the latest scientific theory. Scientific facts do emerge, but most scientists will say about things that are not yet established as facts, "We remain open. These are hypotheses. Until further notice, this is how we see it." In physics, for example, before Einstein, everybody thought that certain axioms were established. Newtonian physics carried the day, but every one of those theses has now been exploded. Elder John A. Widtsoe speculated for a time that perhaps what scientists were calling "ether" was really what Doctrine and Covenants 88 describes as the pervasive light of Christ (D&C 88:6–13). The scientists' hypothesis has since collapsed. Section 88 has not.

President Smith's point was, in essence, "Don't bend the gospel to fit fads, because the fads may not last long." In the same way, he took a strong position on the crucial question of whether man is descended in the Darwinian pattern or is descended from heavenly parents. Some may insist that our spirits were indeed begotten of God, but that the process whereby our mortal bodies became prepared as the living tabernacles of our spirits is another matter. President Smith might have phrased it this way: "You'll find that the latest best guess of the scientists is not as good as the word of the Lord."[34]

Even scholars in the Church can, of course, disagree on how to interpret scientific discoveries. B. H. Roberts, for example, wrote about a geological theory that was then called "catastrophism." According to this theory, fossils found in modern times do not correspond to those of the human family since Adam. He tried to make sense out of the Cro-Magnon and Neanderthal men and even wondered if there had been an entire race of human beings prior to the advent of Adam.[35] Catastrophism, of course, is no longer carrying the day in science, and B. H. Roberts's science has been criticized for being obsolete.

President Smith was patient with, and tolerant of, members who were critical of the Church. Joseph Fielding Smith invited a very prominent man, a somewhat disaffected member of the Church, to chat with him and one of the other Brethren. After nearly an hour, as this man was leaving, Joseph Fielding Smith said, according to the man's own record, "In spite of your telling us of your disbeliefs and heresies, . . . we want you to know that you have the Holy Ghost."[36] That kind of discernment was typical of Joseph Fielding Smith. Later on, when he became President, concerned that this man might be anxious about his status in the Church, Joseph Fielding asked his wife, Jessie Evans, to call the man and say, "Joseph wanted me to tell you he doesn't want you and your wife to take us off your list." And he replied, "You tell President Smith that as long as you keep us on your list, we'll keep you on ours."[37]

A potential BYU faculty member needed to be interviewed by a General Authority in order to teach at the Church's university. His field was a rather controversial one, and so he hoped that he would be interviewed by somebody who wouldn't raise too many questions about it. When he was assigned Joseph Fielding Smith, he said, resignedly, "Well, there it goes; I'll never get to BYU."

The first question Elder Smith asked him was, "What do you think of my book?" The book, sitting there on the desk, was *Man: His Origin and Destiny*.

The man thought to himself, "Well, I might as well be honest." So he said, "I don't like it."

Elder Smith said, "Well, tell me why."

The man said, "I think some of your science is misleading and even obsolete."

Elder Smith said, "Fine. Show me some." So the man opened the book and read him some things. Then Elder Smith said, "Well now, what will you teach when you are at BYU? Will you teach some of these things that I have said here I don't agree with?"

Again the man said to himself, "I might as well be honest—there's no hope here." So he said, "Yes, I would. If I were in a university setting, those are the things I would teach; at least I would give exposition of them, and somewhat defensively."

Then he almost fell off his chair when Elder Smith said, "Well, I suppose that's what you'll have to do. But I think you'll enjoy teaching at BYU. The Lord bless you."[38] The man was stunned, and he is teaching at BYU.

CAN YOU FORGIVE MY HUMAN WEAKNESS?

President Smith was quick to forgive. One man taught in the Church Educational System. Elder Smith spoke at an institute graduation ceremony, coming down hard on some things that he said had crept into the manuals of the Church.

Disturbed by these remarks, the teacher wrote a letter to the First Presidency, saying, "I don't think it's appropriate for a General Authority to come to an institute graduation and say something negative about the manuals of the Church."

One day this faculty member was walking down Main Street and saw Joseph Fielding Smith going along on the other side. The man tried to avoid him, but Elder Smith saw him, crossed the street, called him by name, and said, "Brother, you have prejudiced the Brethren against me with your letter. But I have come to tell you that I bear you no ill feeling, and all is well between us."

The faculty member said, "How can you help loving a man like that?"[39]

Joseph Fielding Smith's brother David walked into Elder Smith's office with another man and said, "This brother has been offended by you. He was going—"

That was as far as he got. Joseph Fielding jumped up, walked over, took the man by the hand, and said, "Brother, can you forgive my human weakness?" He did.[40]

President Smith honored the unique qualities of his Brethren. The June 1970 *Improvement Era* records what he said about his counselors when he was called to be President of the Church: "President Harold B. Lee is a pillar of truth and righteousness, a true seer who has great spiritual strength and insight and wisdom, and whose knowledge and understanding of the Church and its needs is not surpassed by any man. President N. Eldon Tanner is a man of like caliber, of perfect integrity, of devotion to the truth, who is endowed with that administrative ability and spiritual capacity which enables him to lead and counsel and direct aright."[41] Those are words that could have been said of him. It must be true that "it takes one to know one" in spiritual matters as well as other things.

LITERAL WATER AND LITERAL FIRE

He wrote a book called *Signs of the Times,* which was actually a collection of discourses he gave in the old Barrett Hall (which was just east from the Salt Lake Temple) about the last days. He was constantly reading the prophecies. He loved Matthew 24, especially in the Joseph Smith Translation.

In one of his lectures he spoke of the prophesied cleansing of the earth, saying, "It will be cleansed by fire."

Someone in the audience said, "Brother Smith, do you believe that will be literal fire?"

And he replied, "Not any more than I believe it was 'literal' water in the flood."

To his great amazement, that became a matter of Churchwide discussion. What did he mean, "literal water" and "literal fire"? So he had to put a footnote in his book that said, in effect, "I don't know of any other kind of water except H_2O, the kind we drink, the kind we bathe in. And by the same token, I don't know of any other fire except the kind that burns. So yes, I believe it will be literal fire."[42]

Another theme that recurs in several of his books, such as *The Way to Perfection* and *The Progress of Man,* is that of our divine potential. He said, in sum, "I think if all men knew and understood who they are, and were aware of the divine source from whence they came, and of the infinite potential that is part of their inheritance, they would have feelings of kindness and kinship for each other that would change their whole way of living and bring peace on earth."[43]

President Smith also wrote often about the priesthood. "With regard to the holding of the priesthood in the preexistence, I will say that there was an organization there just as well as an organization here, and men there held authority.

Men chosen to positions of trust in the spirit world held the priesthood."[44]

He talked often about the fulness of the priesthood. In the Doctrine and Covenants the word *fulness* is used in other connections—the fulness of the earth, for example, the fulness of truth, the fulness of the Holy Ghost, the fulness of the glory of the Father (see, for example D&C 59:16; 93:26–27; 109:15; 132:6). The phrase "fulness of the priesthood" is in conjunction with the fulness of the glory of the Father, blessings that can come only in the temple.[45] He repeatedly made the statement that this fulness comes as the climax of all our preparatory steps and that to receive a fulness of the glory of the Father is to receive what is called "eternal lives." This power requires both a man and a woman to be sealed to each other and sealed together to the living God.[46] Joseph Fielding Smith, as a temple president and as President of the Church, envisioned that truth as perhaps few in our generation have.

When doctrinal questions arose, President Smith would sometimes simply quote from his books, but he always tried to encourage people to go to their knees and search their own copies of the scriptures instead of writing a letter or making a phone call. He said, "If there is any doctrine or principle connected with the teachings of the Church that we do not understand, then let us get on our knees. Let us go before the Lord in the spirit of prayer, of humility, and ask that our minds might be enlightened that we may understand."[47]

Of the atonement of Christ, he wrote, "I am sure if we could picture before us (as I have tried many times to do) the solemn occasion when the Savior met with his apostles, if we could see them there assembled—the Lord in his sadness, sorrowing for the sins of the world, sorrowing for one of his apostles who was to betray him, yet teaching these eleven men who loved him and making covenant with them—I am sure we would feel in our hearts that we would never forsake him.

"If we could see them there assembled and realize the weight of the burden which was upon our Lord, and after their supper and the singing of an hymn"—and, he could have added, the washing of their feet—"their going forth, the Lord to be betrayed, mocked and scorned, the Disciples to forsake him in the deepest hour of his trial—if we could understand all this (feebly though it be and feebly it must be, I am sure, my brethren and sisters), we would forevermore want to walk in the light of truth. If we could see the Savior of men suffering in the garden and upon the cross and could fully realize all that it meant to us, we would desire to keep his commandments and we would love the Lord our God with all our heart, with all our might, mind and strength, and in the name of Jesus Christ, would serve Him."[48] That's his witness and his experience and his testimony.

In a discourse in 1966 Elder Smith affirmed anew his great testimony of Christ, and said, "Do you think it will ever be possible for any one of us, no matter how hard we labor, or even if we should suffer martyrdom, to pay our Father and Jesus Christ for the blessings we have received from them? The great love, with its accompanying blessings, extended to us through the crucifixion, suffering, and resurrection of Jesus Christ is beyond our mortal comprehension. We never could repay. We have been bought with a price beyond computation—not with gold or silver or precious stones, 'but with the precious blood of Christ, as of a lamb without blemish, and without spot.' (1 Pet. 1:19.)"[49]

ONE HUNDRED PRESENTS

The Joseph Fielding Smith family held annual reunions at a local park for his birthday every July. On one occasion Joseph

Fielding gave one hundred presents for each of the family members' birthdays during the previous year. He treated the day as his birthday and their birthday all rolled into one.

There is a tangible sense of love that seems to emanate from the prophets of God. When you're in their presence, when you see them with their families or at a celebration or a reunion, their love is something you can almost feel on your skin, like sunshine. They have learned, somehow, the power of the love of Christ and how for them it infuses everything. It all begins with family and culminates in the glorifying of family life.

Bruce R. McConkie was married to Joseph Fielding Smith's daughter Amelia; it was Elder McConkie who compiled Joseph Fielding Smith's sermons and writings into three volumes called *Doctrines of Salvation.* Elder McConkie said of President Smith that he could not give a sermon, write a letter, or even counsel with his family without bringing in the scriptures. Elder McConkie, of course, followed in the footsteps of his famous father-in-law.

Joseph Fielding Smith has left us a heritage of principle and integrity. I bear my witness that he was sustained by the Lord through an immensely long career. There was a moment, when he was in his eighties, when he confided to one of his daughters that he had come to know that he would become President of the Church, but for only a short time. He served as president only two and a half years, and he packed those years with fervent activity, including organizing missions all over the world and dedicating two temples. He was the Lord's choice, a prophet who kept the scriptures sacred, and who reminded us that we must, whatever else we learn and whatever else we do, return to them again and again as the fountain of our testimony.

11

HAROLD B. LEE

Those who knew Harold B. Lee, in looking back on his life, said that it seemed he was always moving fast, always ahead of himself, and seemingly ahead of schedule in many different ways.[1] For example, he began his schooling one year earlier than most because he had already learned to read. He was a deacon before he was twelve. He was a missionary before he was nineteen. He was a high councilor when he was twenty-seven and a stake president when he was thirty-one. He was on the Salt Lake City Commission when he was thirty-three and was already being touted by some as a candidate to become either governor or senator, or both. At age thirty-six he was called by the First Presidency to be the full-time coordinator of a Churchwide welfare program.

He was called to the apostleship when he was only forty-two, and when he first met with the Twelve in the temple, he realized that he was at least twenty years younger than any other man in the room. He was associated with the Church correlation program from its beginnings when he was in his fifties, became a counselor in the First Presidency at seventy-one, was sustained as Church president at seventy-three—and was gone at seventy-four. He served as president fewer than two full years, but in the long span of his life his contribution to the programs and policies of the Church was immense.

HERITAGE AND FAMILY

Historian Leonard Arrington did a study of President Lee's background. Brother Arrington would have had a special interest in his life because his own professional career was as an economics historian, and the name of Harold B. Lee became the synonym for the Church's security program, as it was called (later the welfare program).

President Lee's heritage included Americans who served, and some who died, in the War of Independence, as well as pioneers and early converts to the Church. He often said he came from a little town in Idaho, but before that he lived in Panaca, in the southern part of Nevada. His grandmother had eleven miscarriages and finally bore only one child, a premature boy, and then she died. That child was Harold B. Lee's father, Samuel Lee.

As a young boy, Harold bit off what looked like a piece of candy—but it turned out to be lye. His grandmother records that if they had not had the priesthood in the home, and olive oil that was often used both externally and internally, he would not have survived. When people lived on the frontier, a long way from any sort of help, they learned a kind of sterling independence, as well as a greater dependence on the Lord. It's now known, medically, that olive oil is an antidote for more poisons than any other single substance we know. This is rather interesting in light of our use of olive oil for healing in "the household of faith" (Galations 6:10; D&C 121:45).

Harold attended the "normal schools" of the time—schools that were designed to train teachers. He did well and was promoted a little ahead of schedule, graduated, and aspired to become an educator. He did teach school and became the principal for a short time. But then necessity forced him to turn to other means of livelihood.

Harold married and, unlike any of our other presidents, never had a son, but he had two outstanding daughters and ten grandchildren. He was married for most of his life to Fern Tanner; about a year and a half after she passed away he married Joan Jensen. He spoke of both of them in sermon and in conversation, not just with love and affection, but with reverence. Fern died in 1962, and three years later one of his daughters, Maurine, who was expecting a child, died suddenly at age forty. President Lee was in Hawaii at the time and rushed home for her funeral. I still remember him saying at the funeral, "The Lord keeps stirring me up."[2] It was not an easy time for him.

"IS A RADICAL INNOVATION NEEDED?"

Harold B. Lee was a young stake president during the Great Depression when he was called in to visit with the First Presidency about the welfare effort in his stake. Close to 60 percent of the more than 7,000 people in his huge stake were unemployed. Yet he had been so successful with administering to the needs of those members that the First Presidency wanted him to lead the welfare effort for the entire Church.

Some time after that meeting he took a walk up what is known as City Creek Canyon to Rotary Park at the very top.

He was burdened with questions about his weighty new assignment. He wondered, "Is a radical innovation needed?" He recorded that as he was praying, there came down on him the assurance that the Church itself held the Lord's perfect organization and that what he needed to do was to extend the activities of the priesthood.[3] He proceeded on that premise.

In time, people's economic situation began to improve, and they began to say, "The crisis is over" or "Why do we need to be talking about bishops' storehouses?" or "Why do we need to be discussing welfare and mutual aid?" Brother Lee prayed about it. Early one Sunday morning, he said, he had an impression that had two parts: first, that no one really knew yet the real reason for the Church welfare program and, second, that when that reason became apparent the total resources of the Church would be needed. He said, "Since that day that feeling has driven me on, night and day, hardly resting, knowing that this is God's will, this is His plan."[4]

Reactions to economic crises can produce two extremes—both of which we have witnessed in our lifetime. One reaction is to suppose that you must put in a ten-year supply, to bring in guns to defend your supply against marauders, to put in a nuclear-proof bomb shelter, and so forth. The other extreme is to shrug it off and say, "I don't have any problems or needs now, so why should I get involved in this?" Elder Lee wanted us to understand that our living leaders will give us guidance, and if we will trust them they will alert us to both when and how to be prepared, both temporally and spiritually.

Shortly after Harold B. Lee was ordained an apostle by President Heber J. Grant in the Salt Lake Temple, he was asked to give a radio address on a national hookup. To prepare for this assignment, he reread the entire four Gospels. He said that as he read, it was as if he were no longer simply reading words on a page. It was as if he could see, as if he were witness to, the events in the last week of the life of Christ.[5] That became the core of his testimony that Jesus is the Christ, that he did live and die for us. That testimony infused his life from then on.

"DO NOT BE PROUD OF YOUR HUMILITY"

The constitution of the state of Utah includes an interesting phrase: "a constant recurrence to fundamentals is essential to the welfare of this political unit,"[6] meaning the state. As I have reviewed all of the discourses of President Harold B. Lee, it seems that his undergirding theme was to come back to the basics.[7] His talks are consistently real and clarifying and simple to understand. They constitute "a constant recurrence to fundamentals."

In a discourse about educators—and he had been one—he quoted President Joseph F. Smith, who said that the proud "read by the lamp of their own conceit."[8] There is such a thing as intellectual narcissism—to be in love, as it were, with your own words and your own brilliance. In one discourse, President Lee noted that most truly great scientists, such as Sir Isaac Newton, believe that they know a little bit—but they look out at the vast ocean of the unknown and are humbled. On the other hand, many know a lot more than others and they're proud to say so and have a measure of contempt for the realm of faith. President Lee affirmed that the "best intellects" can teach us, but they cannot teach us the deeper things. He himself tried to teach the deeper things.

(At the same time President Lee, in his blessings and counsels, attempted to move and motivate scholarship in the entire educational enterprise. He often observed that in the Church we have had many people of sterling dedication and faith who have been denied—or who deny themselves—the rudiments of education. We likewise have many people of distinction and talent and intellectual strength who have limited religious enlightenment or dedication. His point: The future of the Church will depend more and more on those who bring to their service the best of both worlds.)

I recall his focus on the relationship of genuine faith and humility. A group of us, returning from what was then called "country work" (going out "into the country without purse or scrip") under Elder S. Dilworth Young, attended a mission conference. Each testified that he had been blessed that summer and had been humbled by the experience. Elder Lee was sitting on the stand. He stood up afterward and said, "Brethren, it's a wonderful thing to be humble. But brethren, do not be proud of your humility."

Someone told me that when a stake was organized in Maine for the first time, Elder Lee attended, and after the business was taken care of, he sat down and said, "These are my kind of people." They were humble people. New England is ribbed with higher education—colleges and universities and the Ivy League. But Maine people typically call themselves "Mainiacs," and they are close to the realities of daily earning and the hard work of farming. He respected them. Elder Lee loved them. He had much in common with them.

His father had been a bishop and was a man who did not flinch in accepting severe challenges. His father taught him that enduring is not quite the same as overcoming, and that religion should not be simply a matter of submission to events; it should also include challenge and overcoming. The gospel of Jesus Christ is a combination of those things. We cannot change certain things outside of us, but we can always make changes inside. It was President Lee's conviction that "in order to gain entrance into the kingdom of heaven we must not only be good, but we are also required to do good and be good for something."[9]

Characteristic of Harold B. Lee's understanding of the welfare program are these statements: "A house burns down. The ideal is to teach your new priesthood members how to rally round rather than turn the whole job over to some public relief agency."[10] "Encourage the putting aside for a rainy day in individual homes. That means teaching thrift, frugality, and avoidance of debt. Certainly that is a program that we ought to foster everywhere."[11]

Some people asked him if this were the beginning of living the United Order. His answer was no—but "our present welfare plan could well be the 'setting-up' exercises" for the United Order.[12]

Some asked him if the welfare program was socialistic. "No," he said, "in that private ownership and individual responsibility will be maintained."[13]

He said, "I found . . . in one mission something that was ingenious." (He didn't give this as universal counsel, but it shows his thinking.) "In one of these areas they had worked out a two weeks' suggested food list for an average-size family. They had two varieties in case the taste were different. They had an A variety for two weeks' supply and a B variety. Whenever the branch president would find a needy family, he would call upon the John Doe family to give up their two weeks' supply of the A variety and maybe the Bill Smith family to give up their two weeks' supply of the B variety and put them together, and there was provided a month's supply [for the needy family]. That was their contribution to the welfare program, and they of course replenished their own stock."[14]

Years ago, a welfare meeting was traditionally held prior to the opening session of general conference, at which Elders Lee, Marion G. Romney, Henry D. Moyle, and others often spoke. One of the often-quoted phrases in those meetings was that in the last days, "the poor shall be exalted, in that the rich are made low" (D&C 104:16). I can remember wondering what that meant. How are the rich made low? Are they stricken? Are they humbled? Do they give up their excess possessions? These Brethren interpreted it to mean that the rich will become cooperative servants to others, that they will dedicate time and means and talent to the general welfare of their brethren, which is the spirit of a good quorum.

"THE KID"

Elder Lee was the youngest member of the Twelve at the time of his call, and President J. Reuben Clark Jr., with whom he was closely associated, affectionately called him "the kid." President Lee told a story of the early days in his calling when he was concerned about the opposition he faced. President Clark responded, "Look, kid, you continue to follow the course and it won't be long before they will all want to jump on the bandwagon."[15]

Many years later, as the mantle of directorship of the Union Pacific was transferred from President Clark to Elder Lee, they traveled east together on a Union Pacific train. President Clark was nearly ninety, and after that trip Elder Lee said, "I learned from him then that once you have gone that far in your life, all of the distinction and honors that you thought were so important, and that you clamored for, lose their meaning, and the two questions that most concern you are: Have I truly lived the gospel? And second, What about my family?" He passed that advice on to several people. He said, "Life is for living."[16]

He was soon assigned the chairmanship of the Music Committee, the General Priesthood Committee, and the Servicemen's Committee. He became managing director of the General Church Welfare Committee, was advisor to the General Board of the Primary, and a member of the Publications Committee. Then he was assigned as one of the trustees of BYU.

Elder Lee played the piano. In his childhood and youth he loved to play marches. Both his daughters inherited his love of music; Maurine played the piano and Helen the violin. They sometimes performed with him in meetings around the Salt Lake Valley.

Early in his ministry he had an assignment to address the youth of the Church in a series of radio programs. These addresses were published first as individual talks, but later were compiled into a book called *Youth and the Church*. These addresses blessed many lives. They became the linchpin of preparation for missionary work and for service in the Church. One talk, called "A Constitution for a Perfect Life," expounded on the Beatitudes. One was titled "'Successful' Sinners."[17] The obvious argument was that there weren't any, but in arriving at that conclusion he made a distinction between indulging in the "rapture of the moment," as he called it, and holding on for the peace of the years that comes from self-control.

President Lee was the first man to visit the Holy Land while serving as President of the Church. He visited the Mount of Beatitudes, where those marvelous verses of the Sermon on the Mount might have been given. We don't know for certain that it is the exact place, but it is at least evocative of the place, and it became a favorite spot of his successors when they visited the Holy Land.

He visited with the mayor of Jerusalem, Teddy Kollek, and discussed what was then the embryo of the idea of the Orson Hyde Park. Mr. Kollek told President Lee that there was a piece of property on the west side of the Mount of Olives that his Jerusalem Foundation had decided to divide up between several churches. Each would have a small space for a monument, a memorial garden, or whatever they chose. To Mayor Kollek, President Lee seemed almost unimpressed by this offer. The mayor called in a man who was familiar with the Latter-day Saints and told him, "I don't understand it—I just offered Harold B. Lee and his church a piece of property on the Mount of Olives, and there was no reaction."

His friend said, "Well, Mayor, you have to understand: the people called Mormons came into being because they were told in what they consider to be a divine theophany to 'join none of them,' meaning the other churches. If you want the Mormon Church to be interested in a piece of property on the Mount of Olives, you're going to have to give it *all* to them."

Mayor Kollek called President Lee back and offered him access to all of the property. That was the beginning of the 3.5-acre Orson Hyde Memorial Gardens that were finally dedicated by President Kimball, due east of the very gate Orson Hyde passed through on the day he dedicated the land for the return of the Jews.

"TAKE THAT STACK AND DO IT AGAIN"

Early in the 1950s, Elder Lee received a letter from the First Presidency assigning him the task of simplifying and correlating the curriculum, the auxiliaries, and even the basic program of the Church. Each of four General Authorities (Elders Lee, Marion G. Romney, Richard L. Evans, and Gordon B. Hinckley) was assigned a secretary or acting executive aide, these aides being B. West Belnap, then dean of the Division of Religion at Brigham Young University, who was Elder Lee's right-hand man; Antone K. Romney, Daniel H. Ludlow, and Reed Bradford. These secretaries met hour after hour, day after day, week after week, to effect changes to avoid duplication within and enhance the program of the Church.

Elder Lee invited Brother Ludlow into his office one day. On the desk was the entire catalog of report forms for the Church: priesthood quorums, Relief Society, other auxiliaries, and so forth. Elder Lee said, "Take these forms and eliminate half of them. Then bring back the ones you think we still need to have." Brother Ludlow accomplished this task, and Elder Lee thanked him sincerely. Then he said, "Now take this stack you've created and do it again."[18]

Years later, President Lee met with J. Thomas Fyans (director of internal communications) and Daniel H. Ludlow and said to them, "This year, for one of the first times in Church history, we want all of the manuals for the year's curriculum sent out and in place by the beginning of the curricular year, which is September. That is your responsibility. Would it motivate you if I tell you that if it doesn't happen, you will be shot?"[19] Brother Fyans and his staff met the deadline.

The correlation committee separated the membership of the Church into three age-groups—adult, youth, and children. The consequences of those changes continue to this day. Now seventeen handbooks have been replaced by two, and those two are relatively thin. These are now used Churchwide, and all preceding handbooks are considered obsolete and have been discarded. That's the spirit of correlation.

There has also been a renewed emphasis on the priesthood, on priesthood direction of the auxiliaries, and the need for the priesthood to work arm in arm with the auxiliaries. Early in this century, President Joseph F. Smith made the statement that if the priesthood quorums would magnify their callings we someday would not need the auxiliaries.[20] That day has not yet come, but a new focus has: auxiliaries are to be viewed as an aid to the home, under the direction and cooperation of the priesthood.

TESTED TO THE CORE

President Lee was a longtime close associate of Elder Marion G. Romney, who eventually became a counselor to President Lee. These two Brethren served for a time as advisors to the Primary and to the Primary Children's Hospital, which has since been expanded to be part of the medical complex on the University of Utah campus.

In his discourses President Lee often said that we must face trials in order to prove ourselves. On the day that Elder Romney was called as an Assistant to the Twelve, President Lee said that he knew there were men sitting on the stand who had been tested to the core and who would not be sitting there unless they had passed such tests. He was speaking of Elder Romney, among others.

Elder Romney, like President Lee, had once run for public office and was quite aware that his election hung on the coattails of the national election. The president of the United States at the time was Franklin D. Roosevelt, who, in the language of the journalists, had "packed the Supreme Court" with his supporters. There was a four-column, front-page editorial in the *Deseret News,* a newspaper owned by the Church, that blasted this move by President Roosevelt.

When Brother Romney read the column he knew that, as a Democrat, his chances of being elected were over. He described his turmoil as he went to bed that night. He prayed, "O Lord, I feel all right about it and I'm going to sleep now." Then he got into bed and thoughts started going through his mind: "Why can't the Church lay off matters political? Why do they have to turn these issues into moral issues? Why . . . " He got more and more upset, so he got out of bed and prayed again: "Father in Heaven, I want to forgive the Brethren if there's anything here amiss, and I want you to forgive me for my feelings, but . . . " This debate with himself went on all night.

The next day as he walked down Main Street he saw Elder Lee. "Good morning, Brother Romney."

"Good morning."

"How are you, Brother Romney?"

He gave the standard answer: "Fine."

"Did you read the paper last night, Brother Romney?"

"Yes, I did, Brother Lee."

"Well, what did you think?"

"Well, Brother Lee, I've had a bad night, but I'm determined to sustain the Brethren."[21]

It wasn't long before Elder Romney was chosen for a more important position than an elected one.

"YOU PERFORM THE SURGERY"

President Lee had struggles with his health. We've seen over and over how none of these great leaders, men or women, has been spared the vicissitudes of life. Midway through his ministry, Brother Lee received an impression that he should return home early from an assignment. Twice on the airplane he felt hands on his head and turned to see who was behind him. No one was there. When he returned home the doctors found bleeding ulcers. He was convinced that had he not received these heaven-sent blessings on the way, he would not have remained alive.[22]

Elder Spencer W. Kimball developed a tumor in his throat and underwent surgery to remove all of one vocal cord and much of the other. The problem later recurred, and Elder Kimball went back to the same hospital in New York. They proposed removing his entire voice box in order to save his life, but leaving him unable to make a sound. His subsequent ministry would have to involve writing rather than speaking.

When that prognosis was announced to him, Elder Kimball phoned President Lee in Salt Lake and asked him, "What shall I do?"

President Lee said, "Spencer, put on your clothes and walk out."[23]

That is exactly what he did, to the great consternation of the staff and doctors. The hospital sent his records to Walter Reed Hospital in Washington, D.C., saying, "Please send us a second opinion, and we may be able to save this man's life."

The second opinion was less than helpful: "If this man will give up smoking there is a possibility we could postpone surgery."[24]

He returned home and was given a blessing by all of the Twelve. When the question was asked, "Is his cancer gone or is it arrested?" the answer was, "It is gone."[25]

Elder Kimball had had a heart attack in the 1940s. Years later his heart physicians learned he was increasingly short of breath. After performing all the proper tests, his doctors were reluctant to perform surgery; at his age and in his condition, they didn't feel he would survive the procedure. Elder Kimball asked if he and his doctors could meet with the First

Presidency to discuss the matter. One of the physicians was Russell M. Nelson.

During the meeting Elder Kimball said, "Brethren, I'm an old man. I've lived a long life. We have young and promising leaders coming along. Now, why don't we just let nature take its course?"

President Lee banged his fist on the desk and replied, "Spencer, you were called of God and you have got to live as long as you can live. Now, brethren, tell me what his chances are." The doctors explained the seriousness of the situation, emphasizing the great risk surgery would pose. After hearing them out, President Lee turned to Russell Nelson and said, "You perform the surgery."

Elder Kimball had heard Russell M. Nelson's medical opinion on the one hand and the counsel of the man he sustained as a prophet of the living God on the other. He agreed to the procedure. But Dr. Nelson felt inadequate. He said, "President Lee, if you will give me a blessing the night before, I'll try."

He received the blessing. They began the surgery, which involved 2,500 manual procedures from the first cut in to the last stitch out. Brother Nelson was aware that usually one percent of these procedures goes wrong; in other words, there was a possibility of twenty-five mistakes being made. But that was the only perfect operation Brother Nelson ever performed.

The moment of truth came when the patient was taken from the heart-lung machine. The screen showed within sixty seconds whether you had won or lost. Within thirty seconds they knew they had won.

During the surgery, Dr. Nelson received a strong spiritual impression. As he recounted years later, "I shall never forget the feeling I had as his heart resumed beating, leaping with power and vigor. At that very moment, the Spirit made known to me that this special patient would live to become the prophet of God on earth."[26] It was a most surprising impression: President Lee was young and vigorous and looking forward to a long presidency. Most people had never entertained the possibility that Elder Kimball could outlive President Lee. But of course something very different happened.

What if President Lee had not recommended that Elder Kimball avoid the surgery on his throat? And what if he had not insisted that Elder Kimball have heart surgery?

"THERE IS NO BOMB IN HERE—RELAX"

President Lee was close to the Spirit. As a little boy he was working on the farm, with his father far away. Beyond a fence was a barn that aroused the young boy's curiosity. He started to climb the fence to go exploring when a voice said, "Harold, do not go over there." He climbed down and never went to the barn—and never knew what the danger was.[27] (Perhaps one of the first questions he asked when he entered the spirit world was, "What was there?")

One of the Brethren said of him, "Brother Lee is as intuitive as all get-out."[28] He did have the gift of insight. A young man I knew went to general conference after coming home early from his mission. He kept looking at Elder Lee and was overwhelmed with a desire to talk to him. In his office Elder Lee, after shaking the young man's hand, said, "You're coming to confess a transgression committed during your mission." The young man admitted that Elder Lee was right, and they counseled together.

President Lee relied on inspiration in many situations. During one session of general conference, the City Commissioner of Public Safety received a phone call: "There is a bomb in the Tabernacle and it's going off in twenty minutes." Click. He sent the bomb squad to the Tabernacle.

A policeman came down through the choir loft, leaned over to President Lee, and said, "We've had a tip that there is a bomb in the building set to go off in five minutes."

President Lee sat for a moment, then turned to the man and said, "There is no bomb in here. Relax."

The policeman went out of the choir loft and reported, "He says there is no bomb in there."

The head of the bomb squad said, "*He* says there is no bomb? Who is *he?*"[29]

President Lee had not only put his own reputation on the line, but also the lives of about eight thousand people in the Tabernacle. What if there *had* been a bomb? But he was certain there was not.

POWER AND COMPASSION

For years Elder Lee had the assignment of meeting in the temple with missionaries to instruct them about the temple before they departed for the mission field. This was a great privilege for him and for those who heard him. He answered questions with clarity, always referring to the scriptures, especially the Doctrine and Covenants. Elder Lee arranged with a printer to put quotations and clarifications of various scriptural passages on tissue paper, which he inserted into his standard works. His listeners would see him open the Doctrine and Covenants and teach things they had never understood before.

I experienced President Lee's great power and compassion during a crisis in my personal life. I had just emerged from my second back surgery. I had received a bone graft and was helpless in a corset in bed. My wife was expecting our second child, I was in the third year of my graduate program—still very unsure of the future—and we were penniless. My wife's father was dying of cancer and living with us in our home.

The doorbell rang. An aunt of mine, who knew my situation and who had worked with President Lee in the Church, had phoned him and said, "Please go and give a blessing to my nephew." I don't have words to describe how this great man pulled me from despair to confidence, reassurance, and comfort. Even my pain, which had not yielded even to morphine, began from that time to diminish. All that he promised me in that blessing came to pass. I am one of hundreds, and perhaps thousands, who can testify that he always began a blessing with a prayer, always acknowledged his limitations as a man, and then proceeded to pray and bless.

On one occasion President Lee was about to ordain a bishop (a procedure he called "lighting another candle"). He told those present that he kept in his drawer a record of miracles that he had witnessed since his appointment to the Twelve some thirty years before. He did not often talk about these miracles or boast about them. He knew where the power came from. But that day he told about the healing of a little boy in Brazil who had never walked in his life. The boy understood that priesthood holders can give blessings, and President Lee gave him a blessing. By the time he was back home in Salt Lake City a photograph had been sent to him showing the boy walking. That same day a family brought a little girl with Hodgkin's disease. Her faith was that if she could just shake President Lee's hand she would be healed. She shook his hand and was healed.[30]

West Belnap, dean of religion at Brigham Young University and Elder Lee's secretary in the correlation committee, went on a stake conference assignment with Elder Lee. They held interviews all day and into the night and finally were able to go to bed about 2:00 A.M. Elder Lee prayed, saying, "Father in heaven, we will begin interviewing again in three hours, so we pray that thou wilt bless us through our sleep that our bodies will be sufficiently renewed to continue tomorrow."

Brother Belnap commented, "The Lord may have answered that prayer for Brother Lee, but he didn't answer it for me." He marveled at the stamina of Brother Lee.[31]

One Sunday Daniel Ludlow went to Brother Belnap's house to pick him up for a meeting. Brother Belnap said, "Dan, what are you doing here? It's Monday." It was not Monday; it was Sunday—and that was the first sign of what was soon diagnosed as a brain tumor. Brother Belnap had two surgeries, but neither was successful in removing all of the tumor. He asked for a blessing, not to be healed, but to receive assurance as to whether or not he would live to bless his son, who was to be born about four months later. Brother Belnap was given the blessing, and he did live long enough to bless his son.

Harold B. Lee spoke at his funeral. Those of us associated with BYU who were there that day heard him bear his witness that, in addition to the great and good secular teaching that BYU accomplished in the arts and sciences, the cream that should top it all is the environment and the teaching of the fundamentals of the gospel of Jesus Christ. Otherwise, he said, we have no business operating a major university, and we should close the doors. Brother West Belnap held that same conviction.

"STAY WHERE YOU ARE"

The day Harold B. Lee became President of the Church, he held a press conference. The reporters asked questions such as, "What are you planning to do in your administration? What changes do you foresee?"

President Lee said frankly, "I am like Nephi of old. I am proceeding without knowing in advance what I will do."

They asked him about the priesthood and the blacks. His answer was concise: "If one believes in revelation, then the reason is clear; if he doesn't, then there is no adequate explanation."[32] The question, of course, was not *whether* the priesthood would eventually be made available to all; the question was *when*. And that question has now been settled, as he said, by revelation.

President Lee gave many public addresses, of course, in general conference and to many youth groups, but he also did a good deal of writing. President Kimball said that there is more autobiography in President Lee's sermons than in most others.[33] He often referred to intimate details of personal experiences, opening his heart to the public.

In his teaching, he also often used comparisons. On the west tower of the Salt Lake Temple is a depiction of the Big Dipper, with the pointer stars leading the eye to the North Star. President Lee often quoted temple architect Truman O. Angell, who said this was symbolic. Just as those who are physically lost can find their way through learning where true north is, those who are spiritually lost can find their way through the priesthood of God.[34]

President Lee anticipated the great future gathering of the priesthood at Adam-ondi-Ahman. He pointed out that perhaps it was not coincidental that David W. Patten, the senior member of the Twelve and our dispensation's first martyr, died not far from Adam-ondi-Ahman. The Doctrine and Covenants teaches that "the land of Zion shall not be obtained but by purchase or by blood" (D&C 63:29).

President Lee and his Brethren reversed a traditional approach to the gathering of Israel. For many generations, converts to the Church were encouraged, either by missionaries or by the Spirit or both, to gather to "Zion," meaning primarily to Utah. President Lee gave a classic discourse saying that it is no longer *where* we live but *how* we live that expands the kingdom. The new instruction became, "stay where you are."[35]

Concerning Latter-day Saint soldiers who died in World War II, President Lee taught explicitly that many of them would be called in the spirit world to teach the gospel to others not of the Latter-day Saint faith who had been killed.[36] Concerning war itself, he, like President Kimball, said over and over, "Safety can't be won by tanks and guns and the airplanes and atomic bombs. There is only one place of safety and that is within the realm of the power of Almighty God."[37]

"YOU WILL NEVER BE RELEASED"

He also spoke, as did Joseph F. Smith before him, about the nearness of the spirit world. He assured us that those on the other side of the veil can see us, they are concerned about us, and they bless us with guidance and protection.[38] He taught that to grow unto godhood ultimately enables you to rule over your own—but only your own—progeny.[39] This includes man and woman, husband and wife, patriarch and matriarch. And he pointed out that "home teaching, bishopric's work, and other Church duties are all important, but the most important work is within the walls of your home."[40]

President Lee spoke of the atonement of Jesus Christ, of having our garments washed, as it were, in his blood, and even of being bathed in his blood,[41] a metaphor found in the scriptures. He taught that the phrase, "an eye single to the glory of God," is connected to the definition in Moses of the glory of

God, which is "to bring to pass the immortality and eternal life of man" (Moses 1:39).[42] If, then, your eye is single to the glory of God, you serve his children, adding to his glory and theirs. He taught that the light of Christ, which we often identify with conscience, also applies to reason, rationality, and clarity of thought.[43] Pure thinking is an outcome of the light of Christ, which is given to everyone in the world. He said that the light of Christ extends even to animals, through their instincts.[44]

President Lee would often say, "Be close in your homes. Invite people to your homes and see that the spirit of the home is a spirit of love and outreach. They will feel it; they will trust you; they will befriend you."[45]

At one time there was much discussion about a naturalistic book about Joseph Smith entitled *No Man Knows My History*. President George Albert Smith was speaking in general conference about another topic when, just as he was about to conclude, he paused and said the following words, "Many have belittled Joseph Smith, but those who have will be forgotten in the remains of Mother Earth, and the odor of that infamy will ever be with them; but honor, majesty, and fidelity to God exemplified by Joseph Smith and attached to his name will never die."[46]

President Lee said, "No truer words were ever spoken."[47]

"MUST THERE ALWAYS BE PAIN IN THIS LIFE?"

President Lee had a living testimony of the Book of Mormon. He was impressed by an experience of German Ellsworth, a mission president in the Eastern States area. Brother Ellsworth one day went up on the Hill Cumorah in New York. Alone in the morning hour, standing near the place where the monument now stands, he heard a voice that said, "Push the distribution of the record taken from this hill. It will help bring the world to Christ."[48] President Lee agreed.

There was a period when the seven presidents of the Seventy were the entire quorum. It was established that these men should be ordained as high priests so they could call stake presidents, ordain patriarchs, and perform sealings in the temple. A man went to President Lee and said, "Was it not true that the Prophet Joseph Smith had said that it was contrary to the order of heaven that a high priest should be in that position?"

President Lee replied, "Had you ever though that what might have been contrary to the order of heaven in the early 1830's might not be contrary to the order of heaven in 1960?"[49] It had not occurred to that brother.

President Lee attended a meeting in the Carthage Jail, where the story of the martyrdom was told. The speaker related that "'when the Prophet Joseph Smith was martyred, there were many saints who died spiritually with Joseph.' So it was when Brigham Young died: so it was when John Taylor died."[50] Those who had been able to uphold the living prophet did not transfer their support to his successor. President Lee considered this a tragedy because he knew that the keys of authority are properly passed in the Lord's Church. He fully sustained those who preceded him, and he and President Kimball often said they wanted to honor the prophets while they were alive and not wait for their funerals to do so.

President Lee testified of mighty prayer. He told of speaking to a woman in his office about Enos, who had knelt down and cried unto the Lord in mighty prayer all day and all night long. The woman said, "Just imagine a man praying all day and all night."

President Lee replied, "Maybe one day you'll be in a

position where you will have to pray all day and all night." President Lee described a time when he had "been in that circumstance where it wasn't all one day and one night, but the next day and the next night, and the next day. I'd fast until my strength was fast going, then I'd get a little nourishment and I'd go on fasting. I wasn't always on my knees, but I was praying."[51]

A young mother, whose child had just been killed in an accident, came seeking a blessing of comfort. She asked, in tears, "Must there always be pain in this life?"

President Lee had heard this question before, when he visited West Belnap in the hospital. Brother Belnap's quandary was, "Do I take more medication, numbing the effects of the illness, or do I avoid what could soon become addiction and struggle through in pain?" President Lee counseled and encouraged him.

He shared the words of James L. Barker with the young mother: "'The Apostle Paul said of the Master, . . . "Though he were a Son, yet learned he obedience by the things which he suffered" (Heb. 5:8.). I suppose that the answer is yes, there must always be pain in this life of travail and sorrow and there is a purpose in it all.' . . . God helps us to understand how we shall develop sometimes through heartache, sorrow, and tears and those spiritual qualities except for which none of us can achieve to the place of kinship to him who suffered more than any of us may understand."[52]

President Lee once used this analogy in explaining the restoration of the gospel: "If a scientist were in possession of fragments only of a scientific instrument, with many parts altogether lacking, he would be unable to reconstruct the instrument. However, if after having studied the fragments, he were given a complete instrument in perfect condition, he would be able to identify each fragment with the corresponding part of the perfect instrument."[53] We can, he explained, read in the scriptures of fragments of the organization and the doctrines of Christ's church. But without a new dispensation to clarify the big picture, it would be difficult to fit those fragments together.[54]

"HOW DID HE LOOK?"

President Lee was involved in preparing for the building of the temple in Washington, D.C., but he passed away before its completion. President Spencer W. Kimball and Elder Hugh B. Brown arrived for the first dedicatory session. Elder Russell M. Nelson recorded that he stepped into the elevator, in which Elder Brown was sitting in a wheelchair. On the next floor Sister Joan Lee, widow of Harold B. Lee, stepped in. Elder Brown looked up and said, "Hello, Joan. I talked with Harold last night."

She said unhesitatingly, "How did he look?"

"He looked wonderful."

"I hope," she said, "he will be with us today."

Elder Brown replied, "He will be."[55]

It seems that these men who serve in the highest councils of the Church have a relationship—in dreams, in visions, or in impressions—with their predecessors. No one would have been more interested in seeing the temple in Washington, D.C., completed than Harold B. Lee.

HARMONY AND UNDERSTANDING

President Lee was a strong supporter of the United States Constitution. He struggled, as we all do, to comply with the counsel in the Doctrine and Covenants to seek good and wise men to uphold our government. It's hard enough to find good men, let alone wise men, and to find both seems to be increasingly difficult. But we believe that the Constitution and the land of America was "redeemed . . . by the shedding of blood" (D&C 101:80), and this church is committed to uphold it. During the sesquicentennial celebration of the Constitution, the LDS Church was selected by the Smithsonian Institution to create a year-long exhibit demonstrating our religious understanding of the document. To have a temple in the nation's capital was a magnificent step, both for the Church and for the vision of President Lee.

Harold B. Lee had a specific view of how to encourage understanding between religious faiths. One non-Mormon man listened to a Church of the Air radio broadcast one Sabbath day and heard the calming voice of Richard L. Evans affirming that "man is not alone in life."[56] That man wanted to meet Richard L. Evans, and they became closely associated in International Rotary, of which Elder Evans became president. When Elder Evans died at the relatively young age of sixty-five, this man came forward and said, "I want to do something at the university level to perpetuate Richard L. Evans' work."[57] Thus was created an endowed chair at Brigham Young University called the Richard L. Evans Chair of Christian Understanding. Its purpose was to carry the distinctive Mormon heritage to the world and to invite opinion leaders, scholars, and other leaders to the institution itself, thereby creating a two-way communication to increase understanding.

President Lee encouraged this interchange, making two statements that shone like neon to those in charge. One was that the answers to the world's perplexities are, in fact, found in the gospel of Jesus Christ. And the other was that the more we can bring others to see the gospel in action, the more they will be willing to at least tolerate us, then to encourage us, and eventually to cooperate with us.

THE MATURE PRESIDENT

On the day that President Heber J. Grant passed away, the first person to reach the Grant home was Harold B. Lee, at that time one of the junior members of the Twelve. As he entered, someone suggested that Elder Lee lead them in prayer. As the family knelt together, Elder Lee was kneeling facing the front door of the house, which was still opened inward. During the prayer, President J. Reuben Clark, first counselor in the First Presidency, arrived and could look directly into the face of Elder Lee, whose eyes were closed, and who prayed, "Oh, Father, the burden of the kingdom will now be heavy upon the shoulders of President J. Reuben Clark, pending the reorganization of the Church. We pray for him. We pray that thou wilt magnify him."[58] When he said, "Amen," he looked up and saw President Clark, who was moved to the core. Here was the "kid" who had become mature in his calling.

Before the last day of Harold B. Lee's life, he had given eighteen successive addresses during the Christmas holidays. His death, from a hemorrhage and then cardiac arrest, occurred a day after Christmas. His close friend, President Marion G. Romney, was in President Lee's hospital room. They had been bound together in service to the Lord. And now President Romney said farewell to the mature president, who was about to step into the spirit world. Both of them were conscious that this was a temporary departure, and the love between them was tangible. After President Lee passed away, President Romney carried on in honor and in love.

The Church members were stunned at President Lee's sudden death, but the will of the Lord was apparent. I testify that he, like his predecessors, was raised up to the exact mission and the exact teaching and the exact example that the Church of Jesus Christ needed at that time.

12

SPENCER W. KIMBALL

One day in the office of the First Presidency a couple arrived who had come all the way from Hong Kong. Their two children had just been sealed to them in the Provo Temple. Spencer W. Kimball had been President of the Church just a short time. He held these little girls on his lap and said to their parents, "Learn Mandarin, because the Church will be going to China someday." Then he looked at the little ones and said, "There will be a temple in China someday."[1] Today there is a temple in Hong Kong. At the time of President Kimball's prophetic words, Hong Kong was not a part of China as it now is. The prophetic vision of President Spencer W. Kimball led the Church in giant strides internationally.

ROOTS

Spencer W. Kimball was an avid genealogist. Others have become interested in his lineage, producing an entire volume called *A Noble Son.*[2] These researchers found that he is related to many prominent men and women: to four presidents of the

United States, for example—John Adams, John Quincy Adams (son of the first John Adams), Franklin Pierce, and Chester Arthur—and to famous men in American industry, such as B. F. Goodrich, of Goodrich Rubber. And there are others.

If a Church patriarch had laid his hands on one of President Kimball's ancestors named John Lathrop (also spelled Lothrop), he might have said, "Out of your loins will come many presidents of a future country known as the United States; and out of your loins will come several modern apostles of a modern religious movement." Approximately 25 percent of the first generation of Latter-day Saint converts were related to John Lathrop.

Spencer W. Kimball was born in Salt Lake City, but the family soon moved to Arizona and remained there for most of Spencer's early life. His mother, who died when he was only eleven, was a marvelous woman, a descendant of Edwin D. Woolley, financial advisor to President Brigham Young and one of the most famous bishops in the Church. He was known in the nineteenth century as being "contrary." But he was tested once in Nauvoo when the Prophet Joseph Smith asked him to surrender all of his store goods to the Church, put them in boxes, and prepare them for removal. When Joseph went to check on Brother Woolley, Brother Woolley asked "whether you will send teams to take the goods away, or wish me to deliver them."

The Prophet said, "Is it true then, Brother Woolley, that you are willing to give up all of your store goods to the cause of the Lord?"

"Yes."

"Fine. You passed the test; now put them back on the shelves."[3]

When his mother died, young Spencer was inconsolable

for a time. She had been his inspiration through his childhood. He was the one in the family who did the hardest chores, including milking the cows. His older brothers would arrange with their parents to be paid twenty cents for a task, then say to Spencer, "We'll give you a nickel if you'll do it." They were making fifteen cents and he was making a nickel. He finally caught on to their strategy and told his mother it was unjust. "Spencer," she replied, "you will get extra blessings for helping me."[4]

His hard work—carrying huge buckets of milk and laboring around the farm—may have stunted his growth. He was stocky, but never tall. But he was a little giant. In athletics he was able to hold his own. Records show that he got in a few fights and scrapes, but he grew out of that. He was good in basketball and was strong enough and healthy enough that he could have gone into the army. President Kimball did not complain about his small stature or become overly competitive to compensate for it. He was a humble man, even when he became well known. He always, for example, invited others to go through doors before him.

He was filled with the faith of the gospel and seemed to aspire early to emulate the nobility and sacrifice of his grandfather Heber C. Kimball. (This grandfather, with the consent and the specific direction of his first wife, Vilate, arrived in the Salt Lake Valley with a family of one hundred members, if one counts many stray and bereft people they adopted. They had so many "sons" that they used almost every biblical name to name them. In prayer he actually went through the Old Testament in perfect sequence, mentioning all his "sons.") President Kimball was named Spencer at the request of his mother, but, interestingly, his father wanted to name him

Roberts Kimball, after B. H. Roberts, one of his heroes, the most eloquent orator he had ever heard.[5]

A SELF-TAUGHT MAN

Spencer's formal education ended when he married his wife, Camilla, who was a schoolteacher. Elder Kimball once spoke to an institute gathering at the University of Utah just after he had suffered a serious heart attack. He said, "I am in my grave tomorrow, brothers and sisters. So I leave you my witness that you should never let anything, *anything,* ANYTHING"—now that's emphatic—"get in the way of your relationship with Jesus Christ." He pointed across the street to the university and said, "You're too impressed, you young people, with education and the university degree program. Twenty years from now no one will care whether you got A's or E's."[6]

But he did know the value of a good education. His own children—three sons and a daughter—were well-educated. One of his sons became a Rhodes scholar and was the first American to take a "first" in law at Oxford. A second son received the highest grades ever given in the western states on what was called a V-12 examination for the Navy Air Force. The third son received the highest grades in his law school. His daughter attended college on a scholarship and served as a school officer.

I asked him once, "How do you account for this display of brilliance in your children?"

He smiled and said, "Camilla."

Spencer Kimball himself was self-taught through his teens and into his adult life. He even taught himself, after a very few lessons, how to play the piano—partly motivated by the fact that his father excused him from some farm chores if he would practice the piano. (He took over from Harold B. Lee as official organist when the Brethren sang hymns in their temple meetings. He once said that most of the General Authorities were basses, and the song they sang best was "We Are Sowing."[7])

He attended one semester at the University of Arizona. Then he married in 1917, toward the end of the First World War. He was a very avid reader and student of the scriptures. While recovering from heart problems in California, he was not out of his pajamas for nearly three months. He created an Old Testament timeline on a long paper that he rolled around a large spool. The timeline listed every major event and person in the Old Testament and when unrolled, it reached all the way across the room.

His study of Moses and the Ten Commandments may have influenced his great sermon called "The False Gods We Worship,"[8] in which he said that the prime transgression of our time is the violation of the first commandment, "Thou shalt have no other gods before me." He said that our gods nowadays are shining automobiles and supersized houses, stocks and bonds, and other distracting things that have nothing to do with our relationship with the Lord, except to cause us to neglect our relationship with him. We must guard against being an idolatrous people, even while we claim to serve the one true and living God.

"WHY DON'T YOU BALANCE?"

He turned, briefly, to making a living in banking. He worked extra hours, saved scrupulously, and then watched his life's savings be totally wiped out by the Depression. He later said, according to his son, "I will set up a peanut stand before I will go back to being an employee in such jeopardy."[9] Later, he was once more confronted with terrible debts because of a failing bank.

During this period he gave many kinds of civic service. The Kimball family heritage was not an "intellectual" one—they neither wrote nor thought nor spun philosophical or political theories. But they emerged over and over as the most reliable and trustworthy members of their communities. Spencer W. Kimball was active in library elections, in the city council, the Red Cross, the Boy Scouts, and the local college. He helped organize a radio station.

He became a stake clerk, perhaps the only General Authority to serve more than twenty years as a clerk at one level or another. He was, in fact, given the option of being a counselor in the stake presidency or being the clerk—and he said he would prefer to be the clerk. So he was given that responsibility.

As a banker, he had learned to balance the books to the penny. When he first began his employment at the bank he was shown the "Over and Under Box." When he asked what it was for, the reply was, "We're never exactly correct in our attempt to balance the books, so we put whatever amount we're 'over' in the box. Eventually our balance will be 'under' and then we'll take money out of the box and put it wherever it's needed."

He said, "Why don't you balance the accounts?"

The reply: "It would take too much time." Spencer took the challenge and balanced the books.

Eventually Brother Kimball was called to be president of the Mount Graham Stake. He was a gifted stake president. A flood came and he was in charge of helping his bereft, struggling people. Years later, as President of the Church, when the

Teton Dam in Idaho broke and a wall of water wiped out whole communities, he went to give counsel and comfort and instruction. His message: "You can't work all day, every day, in the effort to recover. Put in a good workday and then stop, and in the evening break out the violins and sing and live life."[10] They took his counsel, and it was a strength to them.

A SENSE OF TERRIBLE UNWORTHINESS

His call to the apostleship came as a great shock to him. One day in Arizona he received a phone call from J. Reuben Clark Jr. of the First Presidency. He said (and I don't know if there were any preliminaries), "The brethren have just called you to fill one of the vacancies in the Quorum of the Twelve Apostles."

One account records that he said, "Not me, Brother Clark! You can't mean that!"

His feeling was that he was totally inadequate and could not do it.[11]

He looked back on his life and remembered practical jokes that he was sorry for, vandalism that he had witnessed and had not tried to prevent (even though he had not participated in it). There were business transactions where perhaps he had been a little too pressing or had asked more than was justified. So he took his checkbook to every person whom he had had serious financial dealings with and said, "I have been called to a high calling in my church. I cannot do it in good conscience unless we are square. If you have any misgivings about any business I had with you, I want to make it right." Three or four of them said they thought he owed them some money, and he wrote them checks. But most of them said, "If anything, Spencer, *you* should have had more." One refused to let him have satisfaction. But he had done his best.[12]

The announcement of his call was made several weeks before general conference. He was in Denver, Colorado, and went up into the mountains in fasting and prayer. His journal records that as he climbed he felt a sense of terrible unworthiness. At one point along the trail he saw a coiled snake, which suggested the adversary. He prayed more fervently and earnestly than he had ever done, and finally he had a sense of the presence of the Spirit. He also felt the nearness of his grandfather Heber C. Kimball, one of his heroes, whom he knew had served the Lord unstintingly through his entire adult life. It was made known to Elder Kimball that his call was of the Lord, and he must accept the call and go forward.[13]

A statement ascribed to J. Golden Kimball was applied to Spencer Kimball when someone said to Spencer, "It's clear the Lord must have called you—no one else would have thought of you."[14]

Heber J. Grant was President of the Church at that time and had had a stroke. The president could not stand, so Elder Kimball knelt facing him. President Grant put his hands upon Elder Kimball's head to ordain and bless him. Before doing so, President Grant hugged him, kissed him, and said, "It was your grandfather's black eyes that pierced into me when I was a boy when he stood me on a table and prophesied over me."[15]

When Elder Kimball gave his first address as an apostle, he said, "I lean heavily on these promises, that the Lord will strengthen and give me growth, and fit and qualify me for this great work."[16]

So he did. One colleague said, "He was the embodiment of the Energizer battery. He just went on and on."[17] The only rest he had, aside from a few hours' sleep at night, came from short naps. He could often be found flat on the floor in a chapel or Relief Society room or in a mission home. Those who walked in on him sometimes thought he had had a heart attack. After such catnaps, he was right back to full energy and power.

His health challenges were staggering. Everyone knows that he had troubles with his heart, and that in the last years of his life he had two surgeries because of brain hemorrhages. But not everyone knows that he had boils and sometimes carbuncles on his body for a period of some twenty years. If he took his coat off, blood could be seen around his waist from those boils, which never were completely cured. We don't know if Job's boils lasted twenty years, but the Lord eventually gave Job, as I'm sure President Kimball was given, "twice as much as he had before" (Job 42:10).

LOVE FOR THE LAMANITES

Early in his calling as an apostle, he was given the assignment from President George Albert Smith to work with the Lamanites. He had given a sermon in conference that responded to a letter he had received. It was a bitter letter that the writer did not have the courage to sign. (Describing this letter and others like it, Elder Kimball coined a new word: he said it was written to him "with anonymosity.") The letter said, "I never thought I would live to see the day when the Church would invite an Indian . . . to go through the Salt Lake Temple." Elder Kimball said, "Generally the wastebasket receives all such messages . . . but [this one] gives me the theme for the words I wish to say today."[18] He pled for charity on behalf of our Lamanite brothers and sisters.

Shortly after that address, he spoke to a group of couples in Springville, Utah, who had been invited as potential foster parents for Indian students. He said to them, "You and you alone can give these young people a chance at education, and the warmth of normal family life. You can pull them away from their terrible situations on the reservation."[19]

My wife and I took that invitation seriously, as did many others. We had a young foster Navajo boy in our home for nine years. He loved President Kimball. He had many of the same conflicts that they all face, and his life had not been easy. But he said when he came to our home for Christmas some years ago, "If it hadn't been for this program, I would be dead." Thousands of others could say the same. In two decades the Lamanite placement program grew from one child to nearly five thousand a year.

Once in Colorado, at a conference where Elder Kimball was speaking, an unkempt Lamanite father and mother came in with a sick little boy. As they struggled down the aisle, people cleared away, almost as if the boy were a leper. The child's parents asked the apostle in broken English to give their child a blessing. Elder Kimball instantly understood, grasped the child, kissed him, hugged him, and gave him a blessing. A witness of the scene said, "If I'd heard that story, I'd say he was just trying to impress onlookers. But I could see his face. I could read the love he has for these people."[20]

NEVER GIVE UP

He was soon assigned to the missionary committee and traveled all over visiting all the missions of the Church. He circled the world in 1960. For four years he was in charge of missionary work in South America. In far-off Asia, an elder with emotional problems was being kept in the mission home. One night the mission president and his wife woke to see the young man with a knife, standing over them as they lay in their bed. When the elder left the room, the president phoned Elder Kimball, explained the situation and then said, "What do I do?"

Elder Kimball said, "Save him. The Lord bless you."[21] He never gave up on anyone.

When I was serving as mission president, three missionaries said to me that they were going home—period. They would not stay any longer, even if I pushed them in front of a truck. Elder Kimball was visiting the stake, and I asked him if he would briefly talk to these young men. All three of them came back looking as if they had been changed—and they had. He inspired them each to write a letter that day to their parents telling them they were going to stay. Elder Kimball had faith and he had spirit, and he was able to touch them personally where I could not.

Missionary work expanded, following his trademark phrase, "Lengthen Your Stride." An employee in the missionary department walking down Main Street one day saw President Kimball walking toward him. The man suddenly began to limp and drag his foot. President Kimball stopped him and asked with great concern, "What's the matter, Ned? What's the matter?"

"Well," came the reply, "I was trying to lengthen my stride and I tripped."[22]

It was President Kimball who reminded us that the mission of the Church has three main parts: Preach the gospel. Perfect the Saints. Redeem the dead. When he taught this concept, he would draw a circle around all three statements on the blackboard, and at the top would write, "Temple." He said, "You think your responsibility, you parents and you leaders, is to lead young people to go on missions. It isn't. It's to get them to go to the house of the Lord, and then they go out in the world to enable others to go to the house of the Lord. Everybody knows you cannot perfect the Saints without the temple. And as for redeeming the dead, of course that's in the temple." Everything, therefore, comes to the concentric center—to the temple.

There is something in his life and ministry which I think is simply matchless. He began early, in individual one-on-one counseling, to take on the most difficult, the most incorrigible cases, and he never withdrew from that responsibility, even after he became President of the Church. He worked, for example, with many different homosexuals, and he kept in touch with them with personal phone calls and by correspondence.

He gave them hope and he changed lives. Whether it's hereditary or not, you begin by changing behavior, and then you work on changing the inner life that has led to the behavior. That was his strategy.

THE MIRACLE OF FORGIVENESS

Concerning President Kimball's book, *The Miracle of Forgiveness,* a friend said to me, "Having read that book, I am convinced that if I am forgiven it *will* be a miracle." The book is uncompromising. It is unyielding on principle. But then come the last chapters on finding the way back through Christ.

A lad came out of the Haight-Ashbury district of San Francisco. Early in his life he was baptized a member of the Church, but then went downhill into drug addiction and worse. After he had come back through repentance, I saw him standing with an inspired expression on his face. He had read *The*

Miracle of Forgiveness and had decided to go on a mission. He loved President Kimball.

Once as we were driving through New England, Elder Kimball asked me the question, "Would you like to know my favorite story in *The Miracle of Forgiveness?* It's when a woman came to me after a stake conference and said, 'Brother Kimball, do you remember me?'

"I said, 'Sister, I meet so many, I don't remember.'

"And she said, 'Oh, thank the Lord,' and she explained, 'Years ago I came to your office and I poured out to you a story of terrible sin, and you started me on the way back through Christ. And if you have forgotten *me,* maybe the Lord has forgotten my sins.'"[23]

That was the compassion of a man who never gave up on sinners.

President Kimball often encouraged journal keeping, a principle he lived. His house was a humble brick cottage with no ostentation. The light was often on in his study until 1:00, 1:30, 2:00 A.M. What was he doing? Writing his journal on an old manual Olympic typewriter.

Why did he keep a journal? Because he had the strong conviction that it was important to his family, that his posterity would read it someday with great joy—and so would others. Not only did he keep a journal of dates and places and objectively viewed events, but he also opened his heart. In thirty-three black binders he put flesh and blood on the skeleton of events.

When the question arose concerning the writing of his biography, he assigned his son and his grandson to do it, giving them his journals and saying to them with complete candor, "There it is. Do with it what you will."[24]

The book is a high-water mark in biography, precisely

because of his candor, his openness, and his conviction that we needed to know his history. He had nothing to hide. In his counsel on keeping journals he said, "What could you do better for your children and your children's children than to record the story of your life, your triumphs over adversity, your recovery after a fall, your progress when all seemed black, your rejoicing when you had finally achieved?"[25]

"INTO THE HANDS OF CUTTHROATS"

When Elder Kimball went to a major hospital in New York to be operated on for throat cancer, he joked that he had "fallen into the hands of cutthroats." A famous doctor in Salt Lake City had found a spot on his larynx. It was confirmed to be cancer. The New York specialists removed all of one vocal cord and a third of the other. They gave him little hope that he would be able to speak again, and certainly not with the resonant voice that he had had before. In time, a small fold or polyp grew in place of that cord that had been removed, enabling him to emit sound.

When he returned to the ministry, for a long time he had to communicate by writing. Then he was assigned to go to Texas with Elder Harold B. Lee on a mission tour. As he sat on the stand, Elder Lee called on him to speak. He pointed to his throat and gestured as if to say, "I can't speak."

But Elder Lee insisted that he come to the pulpit. "Oh, yes, Brother Kimball," he said, "they need to feel your spirit." Elder Kimball, in attempting to speak, made only a terrible sound, and then sat down in embarrassment.

When this occurred a second time he put his hands over his face and wept as he said to himself, "I'm through. My ministry is over."

On the road to Texarkana, he wrote a note to Elder Lee, saying, "Brother Lee, I hope you will not embarrass me again."

"Oh, it will be fine, Spencer," Elder Lee replied. "I want the Saints to feel your spirit."

In his journal Elder Kimball wrote, "They say we should sustain the Brethren. Well, darn him, darn him."

And sure enough, in Texarkana, in a long hall, Elder Lee called on him again. To make matters worse, as he stood up, the sound system failed. In a raspy voice, Elder Kimball spoke his first words in public since the surgery: "Brothers and sisters . . ." He spoke for ten minutes, and when he sat down Elder Lee reached his hand over to him and said, "That's right, Spencer."[26]

The throat cancer recurred, and he returned to New York intending to have the whole voice box removed. A letter dated February 24, 1970, is evidence of his faith: "We spent Monday and Tuesday at the clinic, and though the doctor said that there should be a total laryngectomy, he was finally persuaded that no serious damage would come immediately, and that we might postpone any action. Accordingly we have come home and have asked Dr. Cowan to watch it closely. We intend to let the prayers and faith of our numerous friends hold sway; and I believe the Lord will, or has already, arrested the growth of this trouble."[27] (For President Lee's perspective on this story, see the previous chapter.)

Through his faith, coupled with a cobalt treatment, he continued speaking to the end of his long life.

President Kimball did feel the faith and love of those who prayed for him, and he was grateful. I met a man who received twenty-seven thank-you letters from President Kimball. The man said President Kimball was the most thankful man he ever met. President Kimball spent the last part of each day in his office, with his manual typewriter on his lap or desk, answering personal letters—even letters from children—and thanking everyone for anything they had done for him.

Though President Kimball's voice was reduced to a monotone without any inflection, you could still feel his calm, compassionate spirit. He was given a microphone on a headset that fit close to his mouth that then enlarged and expanded the sound into the regular sound system. One physician told me that it took President Kimball five times the energy to speak as it would take for you and me. If he spoke for an hour, for example, it was the equivalent of speaking for five. This is a man who worked and worked and worked to serve.

HEART AND LUNG SURGERY

When Dr. Russell M. Nelson performed heart and lung surgery on Elder Kimball in 1972, he said it was the only perfect operation he ever performed—one in eight thousand.[28] During that operation Dr. Nelson had a spiritual impression that Elder Kimball would become President of the Church. This seemed preposterous because, first of all, he was four years older than President Lee, who had just been appointed President. Second, he had had severe health problems all his life.

While Elder Kimball was in recovery, Dr. Nelson poured out his heart to him about his impression, and they wept together. But Elder Kimball didn't believe it. At the funeral of President Lee he said, "I never thought it could happen." He explained that he and Camilla had prayed harder than anybody in the Church that President Lee would outlive him. The Lord answered that prayer, but not in the way they had anticipated.[29]

On September 7, 1977, Dr. Nelson was in surgery and received an urgent call from President Kimball's secretary,

Arthur Haycock. President Kimball had just been carried in distress from a meeting with the Brethren. Dr. Nelson explained he could not leave his patient and recommended another doctor. Later he counseled with that doctor, who said that President Kimball was critically ill but that no diagnosis was possible at that time.

When Dr. Nelson was able to come to President Kimball's bedside, he did some preliminary tests and said, "We'll have to wait for the results, but hold on."

President Kimball said, "Brother Nelson, would you give me a blessing?"

Arthur Haycock anointed and Brother Nelson sealed the anointing. The power of the priesthood came strongly, and Brother Nelson said with confidence that President Kimball would recover completely, that his time had not yet come, that he would regain all of his functions, and that he would be well so quickly that he would not miss any major appointments. That is not what the medical judgment of Dr. Nelson would have been. Soon President Kimball felt so much better he asked to go home, and within four days he was on his way to Canada to set apart a new temple presidency.[30]

HE STAYED

When the father of my wife, Ann, developed cancer in the nasal passages, President Kimball administered to him and promised him that he would be totally healed. He was. But later he developed cancer in other parts of his body. President Kimball was out of town on the last night of my father-in-law's life. He returned a call from Ann's mother and went directly from the airport to the hospital. This was not for just a brief "Hello" and "We're praying for you." He stayed at my father-in-law's bedside all night until he died at about 6:00 A.M. Then President Kimball went directly to the Church Administration Building, shaved, and went on with his day.

A woman named Louise Lake had contracted polio before the Salk vaccine became available. Paralyzed from the waist down, she then lost the use of most of her upper body except for two fingers on each hand. Her husband abandoned her after that, leaving her with a child to raise. She raised the child, earned a living from the confines of a battery-powered wheelchair that she could manipulate with her two fingers, kept a beautifully clean apartment, and became a guidance counselor. People came to her home, ostensibly to help her, but she usually helped them. Her story has become legendary in certain parts of the Church.

She told me that President Kimball visited her apartment one day, walked through and chatted with her briefly, then said, "Oh, Louise, how you shame us!" In my opinion, he was just as courageous and strong as she was. He had a record of coping with illness comparable to hers, and he, too, continued his work anyway. Someone said of him, "If it was for the kingdom of the Lord Jesus Christ, pain meant nothing to him."[31]

He never asked, "Why me?" He came out of pioneer stock where duties always prevailed over rights. Our culture seems to have reversed that concept. Today we hear little about obligation and duty—we seem to be more concerned about "rights." But there has never been a "right" that did not have a corresponding duty. On the other hand, there has never been a duty or an obligation that did not come with a corresponding blessing. President Kimball knew that. He spoke of my father-in-law's struggle with cancer as "his Gethsemane," and he knew what he was talking about.

"AMONG THE NUMBER"

President Kimball gave remarkable counsel concerning love and marriage in his sermons titled "An Apostle Speaks about Marriage to John and Mary"[32] and "Love or Lust."[33]

I was present in the Salt Lake Temple when he performed a sealing for one of his own posterity. He said to the couple, "The main problem with marriages today is selfishness. You should reach out to help and to care about each other. That will build love. If you go on talking about your own needs and insist that they be fulfilled, and then talk about divorce if they are not, you will be among the number who find themselves divorced." He taught that divorce is rarely justified and that marriage involves lots of struggles.

In a sermon at Brigham Young University, he spoke at length about husbands' respect for their wives, about budgeting, and about the three Ds: diapers, drudgery, and difficulty. He noted that "while marriage is difficult . . . yet real, lasting happiness is possible, and marriage can be more an exultant ecstasy than the human mind can conceive."[34] Ecstasy! I quoted him later in a commencement talk and got a phone call saying, "President Kimball would never use a word like that." Thanks to the computer system, I confirmed that he did.

Speaking of how two people can relate to each other, he drew two oblong circles overlapping. He said, "You see this middle part? This is where Camilla and I totally overlap. But you see these two extremes at the end? Those are places we don't overlap. So we don't get into them very much. I let Camilla do her thing there. I do mine here. And we get along fine."

Camilla Kimball was a brilliant woman. She had intellectual curiosity and a very active mind. The sister of Henry Eyring, one of the world's great chemists, she was very inquisitive, always wanting to know the "why" of things. President Kimball would say, "Well, what we know is this. I take the rest on faith."[35] He did not worry about "why."

Someone asked him about the reference in *The Life of the Prophet Joseph Smith by His Mother* to several important visions experienced by Joseph Smith Sr. Some thought that lessened the credibility of Joseph Jr.'s vision, saying that Joseph claimed to have had a vision only because his father did. President Kimball's comment was, "I don't know that there's anything wrong with visions."[36]

When I told him of some of my colleagues' intellectual objections to gospel issues, he said, "Well, Brother Madsen, if only they had the Spirit they wouldn't talk this way. If only they had the Spirit." President Kimball had the Spirit.

Elder Kimball gave a watershed talk at BYU titled "A Style of Our Own: Modesty in Dress and Its Relationship to the Church."[37] He sermonized against what had become all the rage for dances—strapless evening gowns. My wife-to-be went home and asked her mother to make her a stole to cover her bare shoulders, which she did. Some others did the same. Others rebelled and said he had no business talking about the topic.

Shortly after, Ann went with a group of girls on a long trip to California. She stood up for Elder Kimball's words and eventually they organized a study group, most of them became active in the Church, and most of them decided to throw away their strapless evening gowns.

"THE FACE YOU DESERVE"

President Kimball often said, "Men's thoughts and lives are engraved on their faces."[38] Many would say he was not handsome, because he was short, balding like his grandfather, and had a receding chin. But when he was under the influence of the Spirit his face and his eyes were beautiful.

Someone once said to me that "the face you're born with is the face you deserve." I disagree. The face you're born with is the face you can't do anything about. But after you've lived forty years or more, the face you have is the face you deserve. Your life is written there. President Kimball's face was the face of a man of God.

While visiting the Holy Land, he taught anew that Jesus was the Christ. He went back seven times to the Garden Tomb, where the beauty and power of the Resurrection is palpable. He organized the group that established the Orson Hyde Memorial Gardens, and he gave the dedicatory prayer there. He was taken to seven of twenty-three possible sites for a BYU Jerusalem Center and then, last of all, to a place on Mount Scopus that he was told was utterly impossible to procure. He walked there with Elder Ezra Taft Benson, Jeffrey R. Holland (then president of Brigham Young University), and President N. Eldon Tanner. Standing there, he said, "This is where the Jerusalem Center should be." They all gasped. And then he said, "All in favor, raise your right hand."[39] After many miracles, the Jerusalem Center was built there on Mount Scopus.

He stood on the Mount of Transfiguration (we cannot prove that location as the correct spot) and bore his witness that not only was the Christ transfigured and filled with light, but that his three disciples were also. He defended Peter, saying that while he did in fact say, with an oath, "I do not know the man," he never said, "Jesus is not the Christ." Peter became the President of the Church and was filled with light and power on the day of Pentecost. President Kimball taught that perhaps Peter's denying his acquaintance with Jesus was part of God's plan, enabling him to live to carry on as the prime witness of Jesus' life and death.[40]

President Kimball taught that the welfare program of the Church is not just a program, but the essence of the gospel of Jesus Christ.[41] He did much to move the program forward. He was troubled when he heard people murmur about making sacrifices for the Lord. He, like Melvin J. Ballard and Marion G. Romney, often said, "A person cannot give a crust to the Lord without receiving a loaf in return."[42] Or, like Brigham Young, he said, "Can you call it a sacrifice if you give up a handful of dust in return for a whole earth?"[43]

He taught that eternal marriage is one of the hidden mysteries that Jesus taught in his parables,[44] and that we will ultimately understand that mystery of how two become one. He taught the Latter-day Saint understanding of Adam and Eve, defending them as wise and inspired individuals, and not, as much of the Christian world believes, terrible, degenerate people who brought upon us all the evils we now face.[45] He said that women have the privilege to create, with their husbands and God as their partners.[46] He taught that those who do not marry in this life will, if they are worthy, have the blessings of marriage in the world to come.[47] He taught that the disintegration of the family is the greatest tragedy of our times and that if we do not reverse certain social trends, the Church itself will be in serious trouble.

"What will we do in eternity?" he was asked.

"That life will be a busy, purposeful life with accomplishments and joys and development.

"If you can think of the greatest real joys that have ever come to you in this life, then think of the next life as a projection of this one with all the purposeful things multiplied, enlarged, and even more desirable. All in these associations of our lives here have brought to you development and joy and growth and happiness. Now when life ends, we shall return to a situation patterned after our life here, only less limited, more glorious, more increased joys."[48]

He taught that no affluence can compensate for the higher achievements of spirituality and the knowledge that comes through spirituality.[49] He reverently spoke of the name of Jesus Christ and taught that we shouldn't say "in the name of Jesus" in our prayers, but should use the full name.[50] He admonished the use of the proper language of prayer. It is not appropriate, for example, to use "you" and "your" in speaking to God, but rather to use "thee," "thine," and "thou."[51] He, like every prophet of our time, beginning with Joseph Smith, taught that the Lord's prophets will not lead us astray.[52]

"I'LL STAND BETWEEN YOU"

He had a great influence on others. A young Japanese convert had grown shaky in his testimony. Someone encouraged him to stay after a conference long enough to shake hands with President Kimball. President Kimball shook the young man's hand and then, as only he could do, kissed him and hugged him. The young man said later, "Is that what the celestial world is like? I felt the Spirit so strongly, testifying to me that our Heavenly Father is like President Kimball. I almost missed the glorious opportunity of staying in the Church."

President Kimball called a Japanese brother to be a General Authority. The brother broke into tears and couldn't control them, so President Kimball said, "Brother, I'll be back in a few minutes." He came back ten minutes later and the man was still crying. President Kimball left him again, and when he came back, the man was still crying. He could not get used to the idea that he could have the same relationship with President Kimball that other General Authorities had.[53]

Elder Marvin J. Ashton tried to talk him out of visiting the state prison. The trip was postponed, but President Kimball insisted on going—and he insisted on going into the high security compound to talk to the inmates there. He sat down in a room facing two men, one who had been convicted for manslaughter, one for murder. His first question to them was, "Tell me about your mother." One of them broke into tears. After the interview they asked if they could have their picture taken with President Kimball. Brother Ashton wanted to prevent that. He didn't like the idea of this little man standing between two such criminals. But President Kimball said, "Let's see. I'll stand between you, right here. You go ahead and take the picture." The picture was taken. He later wrote letters to these men and, I suspect, they to him.[54]

In New Zealand, President Kimball was stricken with the worst kind of flu, suffering around the clock with either fever and perspiration or with chills. Three thousand young people were waiting at a local stadium to hear him speak, but were told, "Tonight you will hear from President Tanner, because President Kimball is ill." Thirty minutes before the meeting was to start, President Kimball, still limp, spoke to his physician, Russell M. Nelson, who was waiting with him, and said, "Tell Camilla we're going."

They had to practically carry him to the car. At the stadium, a young man giving the opening prayer said, "We are three thousand New Zealand youth. We are assembled here, having prepared for six months to sing and to dance for thy prophet. Wilt thou heal him and deliver him here?" As he said "Amen," the car drove into the stadium. Three thousand voices cheered that the prophet had come. He stood, strengthened even in his illness, and bore his witness to them.[55]

In part because his son, as a missionary in New England, had come to love the Lamanites, he was assigned to go to the Old Town Maine reservation of the Penobscot Indians. This son wrote President Kimball a letter in which he said, "Everyone we meet seems sincere in their faith or even their unfaith. I wonder if my testimony is deep enough. Do we really have something to give these people?"

The letter his father wrote back has since been published. Among other things, he quoted Paul and said, "'Quench not the Spirit,' but whenever the Spirit whispers, follow its holy promptings."[56] He described how he had given blessings to missionaries, promising them life and healing and a safe return home—and then thought about it later and worried whether he had done the right thing. Sometimes after making promises in blessings, he said, "I have literally trembled in my shoes afterward when I realized what a responsibility I was under, but long ago I have come to the conclusion that I shall speak what I seem inspired to say, having asked the Lord for that inspiration, and any effort on my part to curb the Spirit would be rank folly and unappreciativeness and unresponsiveness to the moving of the Spirit."[57] A family eventually came into the Church through Elder Kimball's son's ministry.

His son, Ed, contracted polio early in life. The child was placed in the hospital and cried for his parents, but they were forbidden by hospital officials to come to his side. Eventually Ed recovered but was left with a radical limp in his left leg. Though his parents wanted to assist him, they knew from doctors' advice that he needed to struggle on his own to strengthen his legs. Ed has lived with that handicap all his life, but he never failed in his faith, a faith learned from his parents.

One of the sad phone calls I received as a mission president was the voice of President Kimball saying, "Will you go to Connecticut and perform the marriage of a close relative out of the Church?" I performed a civil rather than a temple marriage. Yet the faith of this man who never left the trenches but had vision as from Mount Olympus was that faithful parents can have an influence in the long run on even those who wander. When they do not yet see eye to eye, there may be differences and wounds, but the story is not over yet.

"WOULD YOU GIVE YOUR LIFE FOR JESUS?"

In his book *Faith Precedes the Miracle,*[58] it is clear that we can't expect divine intervention unless we have first fulfilled certain conditions. Signs given to those without faith don't really convert or spiritually influence. Faith must precede the miracle. A man was greatly surprised, and not pleasantly so, at being called to a certain position.

President Kimball, after smoothing the man's feathers a bit, said, "Well, now, brother, you've already agreed to this, you know."

The man said, "Brother Kimball, I had not the slightest idea."

"Yes, I know. But in a sacred place and time you said . . ." and he paraphrased one of the covenants of the temple.

The man thought about it, and said, "Well, yes."

"So you did agree to it?" President Kimball prompted.

"Yes, I guess so," the man finally agreed.[59]

President Kimball believed and taught that we can make some decisions once and for all, and that applies to our covenants.

There are two ways to give your life. One is to be a martyr, to forfeit your very life rather than betray your covenants. That's how the Christian church began. I heard President Kimball say, "There will be martyrs in this dispensation, in the future."[60]

Someone asked Jeffrey R. Holland, "Elder Holland, would you give your life for Jesus?"

He thought a minute and then said, "I thought that's what I was doing."[61] That is the other way to give your life: you give your energies, your time, your gifts, to the cause of Christ. And that is what Spencer W. Kimball did.

I think it's safe to say that the gospel is a matter of life and death. President Kimball's life and teachings show us how a person who considers himself diminutive and without real influence or power can become an arrow in the Lord's quiver and be magnified in the pattern of Jesus Christ. Against all the doctors' predictions, he lived to age ninety, and for decades he gave every breath of his life to the cause of Christ and to the building of the kingdom of God. May we also be moved to that kind of humility and that kind of service.

13

EZRA TAFT BENSON

Ezra Taft Benson almost did not survive his birth. He was the first of eleven children, and when he was born the doctors gave up on him as a stillborn, turning instead to save the life of his mother, which was in jeopardy. But Ezra's grandmothers were present, and they wouldn't give up on the boy. They dipped the baby alternately in hot and cold water, until suddenly he began to cry—a most welcome sound—and he lived.

Ezra Taft Benson was named for his great-grandfather, a man who came to Nauvoo on an impression—perhaps he had heard stories about the Mormons. While in Nauvoo, he was touched by a prayer offered by one of the leaders, Elder John E. Page, and like one candle lighting another, Brother Benson felt the spirit of the meeting. Later, when a controversy arose among the priesthood bearers, someone asked him what he thought of the Mormons now. And Brother Benson replied, in effect, "Well, the Church can be true even if the members aren't."[1] The first Ezra T. Benson eventually became an apostle.

Ezra Taft Benson grew up in Whitney, Idaho. The town was named after Orson F. Whitney, who later became a member of the Council of the Twelve and Ezra's mission president. Ezra felt a deep attachment to Whitney, Idaho, and he chose to be buried there. He is the only president—with the exception of the Prophet Joseph Smith—to be buried outside of Utah.

By our current standards, Whitney in the early 1900s was a primitive town. Ezra, who early in his life acquired the nickname "T," lived in a small stucco house on a forty-acre farm where the Benson family raised livestock; planted sugar beets, potatoes, and wheat; and ran a dairy. Both the parents and the children were dependent on each other for their living. Among other chores, Ezra had to clean the chimneys of the oil lamps and pump water to use in the house. The family had no telephones, and when they switched on their first electric light, they were absolutely thrilled.

When Ezra was about fifteen years old there was an editorial in the *Deseret News* saying that all faithful Latter-day Saints should have family home evening. This advice is familiar to the Church now, but it was innovative then. Instead of saying, "That's not for us," Ezra's father said, "This is the word of the Lord."[2] So the Benson family often spent home evenings engaged in three activities: reading the scriptures together, singing together (whether they were talented or not), and enjoying some recreation together. In the days before television and radio, people knew how to make their own entertainment.

Early in Ezra's life, his father gave him some advice about prayer. "Remember that whatever you do or wherever you are, you are never alone," he said. "Our Heavenly Father is always near. You can reach out and receive his aid through prayer." Years later when Ezra was in Washington, he related that advice during an interview for *Reader's Digest* for an article on "The Best Advice I Ever Received."[3]

INFLUENZA AND COURTSHIP

Ezra Taft Benson graduated from the Oneida Academy in Idaho when he was about nineteen years old and then enrolled at Utah State University. It was the end of World War I and a critical turning point in America's history. The influenza epidemic of 1918 covered the United States and parts of Europe. Many men who had gone to war died without ever shooting a gun—they died in that flu epidemic. It was a fast-moving disease. A man might be wrestling or doing calisthenics and then, fifteen minutes later, that same man could be fighting for his life on a cot.

One of Ezra's associates, Ernest L. Wilkinson (who later also served as his counselor when Ezra was a stake president in Washington, D.C.), often told in testimony meetings of being bivouacked in the old Karl G. Maeser building at BYU because there wasn't room in the hospital. He would relate his experience of almost dying of the flu and his promise to the Lord in prayer, "If only I can live I will give my life to the cause." Brother Wilkinson even prayed that if he could live he might someday return to Brigham Young University. Apparently the Lord took him at his word, because he eventually became president there.

During that same period of time, Ezra met a young lady named Flora Amussen. He was, in his own eyes, a mere country bumpkin, while she came from a wealthy and prominent home and family in Logan. When he expressed his interest in her to his cousin, the cousin said, "She won't even look at you."[4] But she did look at Ezra, and they dated for a time before he went on a mission. Before he left, he told her that if she was still around on his return they would take the relationship from there. When he returned she was still there, but then she announced she was going on a mission and offered Ezra the same terms. So he waited for her as she had waited for him. When they were married, their patience with faults and foibles and their focus on emphasizing the positive in their relationship became an example to the whole Church.

CALLED TO SERVE

Missionary work became important to Ezra's life at an early age. When Ezra was only twelve, his father was suddenly called on a mission. Ezra remembered that when his parents returned from the post office with the letter labeled "Box B" that contained his father's mission call, they were crying.[5] (In those days, "Box B" was stamped on all letters from Church headquarters that contained mission calls.) To finance the mission, the family had to sell part of their dry farmland and rent out another portion of land; they essentially retained only their pasture land with their dairy herd. One might suppose that such an experience could lead to some rebellion against missionary work. Instead, the entire family was filled with the spirit of the work and all eleven children eventually served missions. The Bensons became, in every way, a missionary family.

When Ezra was twenty-two years old he was ordained an elder and called on a mission. We, in our generation, don't comprehend the level of anti-Mormon sentiment that swept throughout England and elsewhere in the world in the early part of the twentieth century. Elder Hugh B. Brown, who served in the same mission as Ezra and about the same time, was first assigned to an area where the people had declared, "If another Mormon elder comes within the jurisdiction of this city, we will kill him."[6] The practice in the nineteenth and early twentieth centuries was for a mob to link arms and rush the victim, trampling him to death or critically injuring him. Since all of them were involved, no one could point a finger or blame any one man for the death or injuries. Sometimes the mob tried to capture missionaries and throw them in the river.

Ezra Taft Benson and his companion were mobbed on one occasion, though Ezra was saved by a police officer who somehow knifed through the crowd and pulled him to safety. When the officer returned Ezra to his home, he forbade the missionary to go out again. Ezra's companion suffered a severe head injury from the attack and was fortunate to be reunited with Ezra.[7]

MARRIAGE, FAMILY, AND NEW OPPORTUNITIES

After his mission, Ezra Taft Benson enrolled at Brigham Young University, where he received a bachelor's degree. In 1926, when Ezra was twenty-seven years old, he married his sweetheart, Flora. The sealing of their marriage was performed by Elder Orson F. Whitney. The newlyweds left for Ames College in Iowa in a Model T Ford truck. They had to sleep in a leaky tent at night. When they finally settled in Iowa, Ezra's salary during that first year was $70 a month, $22.50 of which went to rent a dingy apartment that lacked space, style, and a shower in the bathroom. He knew, therefore, from his early experience, the sacrifices demanded of a struggling and grubbing student, and so did his dear wife, who had left behind a prosperous home to marry a man who was somewhat in debt. If any man hated debt and worked for self-sufficiency, both in the Church and in the government, it was Ezra Taft Benson.

The Bensons hoped to have twelve children, but instead they had six; and Flora often joked saying, "If we could have had twins each time, then we'd have reached our goal."[8]

After Ezra received his degree from Ames College, the

family returned to the farm; a short time later he was hired by his county as an agricultural agent. Just before the Great Depression began in 1929, the University of Idaho hired Ezra to head their newly created department of agricultural economics and marketing. Ezra eventually became the leading proponent of farm cooperatives. When Ezra was thirty-nine years old, he took a leave of absence from his work for a year of graduate study at the University of California, Berkeley.

By then it was the eve of World War II, and big changes were in store. In 1939 Ezra became executive secretary of the National Council of Farmer Cooperatives, one of the four largest such organizations in the country, with about 5,000 cooperatives involving over 2.5 million farmers. During his application for the position, he announced that if he took the job he would live his standards, and that meant he would not hold cocktail parties nor would he wine and dine government officials. Instead of disqualifying him from the job, his sense of integrity actually encouraged the council to hire him.

Ezra also became the first stake president in Washington, D.C. He called Samuel Carpenter and Ernest L. Wilkinson as his counselors.

When he joined the executive committee of the American Institute of Cooperatives, his name became well known. One day a man from Chicago visited Washington and said, "We need young men with integrity, men who live a clean, moral life. But then," said the man, "there aren't many Mormons in Washington." Someone recommended he talk to Ezra Benson. "The man did so, and asked Ezra if he could supply the names he needed. Ezra replied, 'Not only can I give you three or four names, but I can give you dozens.' Often thereafter Ezra commented that 'it pays to maintain the standards of the Church and be true to the faith.'"[9]

In July 1943 Ezra stopped in Salt Lake City as part of an extended business trip. While there, he was informed that President Heber J. Grant wanted to speak with him. I suppose he assumed that President Grant had counsel for him concerning his job in Washington. Ezra met with President Grant at his summer cabin in Brighton. President Grant, who by this time was in the aftermath of a stroke and weak, simply pulled Ezra's hand close to him and said, "Brother Benson, with all my heart I congratulate you"—and Ezra probably thought he was going to say "on this new appointment"—"and pray God's blessings to attend you; you have been chosen as the youngest apostle of the Church."[10] President Benson later said, "The whole world seemed to sink. I could hardly believe it was true."[11] He had had no premonition of the calling—but his wife had.

The total Church membership worldwide was 837,000 members when Ezra was called as an apostle. The total number of stakes was 146. There was not one stake outside the continental United States. Missionary work abroad had been suspended because of the Second World War. General Authorities usually traveled in pairs, often by train and seldom by plane. In those days stake conferences typically involved two visiting General Authorities, who held a priesthood meeting Saturday night and then conducted two two-hour conference sessions on Sunday. Today, by comparison, stake conferences are attended by only one General Authority; and there are many in the Seventy and other General Authorities to facilitate the annual stake conference schedules.

TRAVELS TO EUROPE AND ISRAEL

Elder Benson was immediately called to London to assume the presidency of the European Mission. He and his secretary immediately got to work trying to open doors with local leaders, the International Red Cross, and other organizations to help the Saints who were in desperate straits after the war. Many were literally starving to death, surviving only on what we would call synthetic foods. Other people were nearly naked. Thousands of shoes were shipped but never used—so many people in the war had gone without shoes for so long that their feet had swelled and could no longer fit in shoes.

While Elder Benson was in Europe, he stood in two places which he never forgot. One was in a Jewish ghetto in Warsaw, Poland, where Hitler's purge began. When the purge ended, 200,000 Jewish people had been buried in the ghetto; not one person escaped. The other place he stood was near a warehouse where the Church had finally been able to bring and stack a tremendous amount of wheat in huge boxes. A man who had survived the bombing in Germany wept and said, "It is hard for me to believe that people who have never seen us could do so much for us."[12] The ragged, the hungry, and the sick came to various chapels that had been set up as refugee camps.

On one occasion I was present to hear Elder Benson's associate, Fred Babbel, who was his traveling mate during these rugged days in the aftermath of the Second World War. Brother Babbel spoke in detail of their experiences of how, against all opposition, they arranged for supplies of food and clothing for refugees of the Church in western Europe. He later wrote a book called *On Wings of Faith.*[13] Time and again, Brother Babbel said, they came up against a stone wall where they faced sure defeat in their relief effort. But faith and prayer and fasting and pleading opened the door, and success came.

In less than a year Elder Benson traveled sixty thousand miles all over Europe. He rededicated Finland for missionary work. He authorized the printing of five thousand copies of the Book of Mormon. He organized branches. Elder Benson's general demeanor, his faith, and his testimony could be summarized in three words, "Do not despair." That was his message in Europe and his message to missionaries. That was his message in other parts of the world. It became his message to the Saints throughout his time as an apostle and as President of the Church. "Do not despair; there is always a way." He rejuvenated the Church in Europe.

Elder Benson also eventually traveled to the Holy Land, where his knowledge of agriculture, grazing practices, irrigation, and desalinization benefited the state of Israel and indirectly Jordan. On one trip he spoke in detail to Prime Minister Ben Gurion, who had retired and was working on a book about the rise of Israel. Elder Benson shared with Prime Minister Gurion the story of Orson Hyde and the miraculous drama of the return of the Jews in fulfillment of ancient prophecy. Orson Hyde had, as Ben Gurion learned for the first time, "scooped" the rise of Theodore Herzl, who was the advocate of modern Zionism, by fifty years.

A JOB OFFER FROM THE PRESIDENT

Now we bring Dwight D. Eisenhower into the story. During the Second World War, Eisenhower had conducted the greatest military invasion in human history and was an international hero. The success of D-Day enhanced Eisenhower's run for president of the United States. He was elected overwhelmingly.

After Eisenhower's election, a U.S. Senator from Utah contacted Elder Benson and asked if he would be available to accept a Cabinet appointment as secretary of agriculture. And

Elder Benson said, as only an apostle would, "Well, I'll have to talk to the Brethren about that."

Knowing the kind of controversies that such an appointment might generate, and knowing what it would do to his family and even to the reputation of the Church, Elder Benson prayed about it and then sought direction from President McKay.

President McKay said to Elder Benson upon meeting him in the Church Administration Building parking lot early one morning, "My mind is clear. I know what the Lord wants you to do."[14] Elder Benson was still wary of the appointment. When he mentioned his concerns to Eisenhower, the president said, "You can't refuse to serve America!"[15]

Elder Benson proposed two conditions, "I will not defend a policy that I do not believe in, and I will not compromise my religious principles."

Apparently Eisenhower said, "That's it. You're in."[16]

Within a year of Elder Benson's appointment, journalists were writing that he would be the first man to be fired from the cabinet. The evidence, they claimed, was that Eisenhower never called Benson by his first name. In a subsequent interview the president was asked about that and he replied, "I wouldn't think of firing Ez."[17]

During the next elections, criticism mounted against Elder Benson, and Eisenhower was asked, "Is not Benson a political liability?"

Eisenhower replied, "Ezra is the shining star in the firmament of my administration."[18] When Eisenhower was later accused of being soft on communism, Russell Kirk wrote in an editorial, "Eisenhower's not a Communist. He's a golfer." Eisenhower suffered a heart attack in 1955; in due time his second term ended and Elder Benson returned home.

Elder Benson had agreed to serve for two years, but his original commitment was renewed for a total of eight years, the entire time Eisenhower was president of the United States.

There isn't room to detail all the innovations that Secretary Benson made in agriculture during his service to President Eisenhower. But the basic premise of all he did was "conservative conservatism." He was against paying farmers millions of dollars to plow under their crops, robbing the farmer of his own self-control, or developing subsidies beyond the creation of what was known as a "soil bank."[19]

PRINCIPLES AND POLICIES

Elder Benson advocated two ideas from day one, which immediately called down the wrath of various senators in various states. Elder Benson believed that the main test of any government policy, agricultural or otherwise, is to ask how it will affect the character and well-being of the people. "Character? What's that got to do with anything?" his opponents challenged. "Character!" Elder Benson also made statements that America was strong because of its spiritual values and that if those values diminished, America would become weak. In that, he was echoing the conclusion of the famous Alexis de Tocqueville, who came to America and wrote a book entitled *Democracy in America,* which said, "I sought for the greatness and genius of America in her commodious harbors and her ample rivers, and it was not there; in her fertile fields and boundless prairies, and it was not there; in her rich mines and her vast world commerce, and it was not there. Not until I went to the churches of America and heard her pulpits aflame with righteousness did I understand the secret of her genius and power. *America is great because she is good, and if America ever ceases to be good, America will cease to be great.*"[20]

Elder Benson's beliefs and integrity were revealed in an experience he had with one of his employees. He oversaw a huge department: 78,000 employees in 10,000 locations, who were responsible for the food needs of 160 million Americans. One of his employees was, he believed, showing disloyalty and representing counter-philosophies. I suspect, though I don't know this, that the employee was sympathetic to dialectical materialism and to Marxism, which everyone knew Elder Benson opposed. At any rate, he was fired. A few days later, after an investigation, Elder Benson learned that the employee did not harbor those sympathies after all. "How do you account for this?" Elder Benson was asked. "You, of all people, you who have been persecuted, you who have been misunderstood, how could you do this to this man?" Under such questioning, Ezra said simply, "Gentlemen, I made a mistake." And he set about rectifying it.[21]

A TOUCH OF RELIGION IN THE GOVERNMENT

Elder Benson insisted in his own meetings with his staff that they open the meetings with prayer, and he asked President Eisenhower to do likewise in their Friday morning cabinet meetings. Many of those men were not religious, though they had sometimes allowed for silent prayer. Elder Benson prevailed, and from then on the cabinet had vocal prayer each time they met.

In 1953, Texas had had a serious drought for four consecutive years, and Elder Benson, who went down to visit, suggested that the governor do what the President of our church once did: proclaim a day of fasting and prayer. Fast and pray for rain? Yes. When two inches of rain fell on San Antonio, the headline in a Texas newspaper was "Benson apparently has contacts that are literally out of this world."[22]

Word leaked out in Washington that the Benson family did a strange thing every Monday night. They had a "home night." President Eisenhower and his wife wanted to know what that was and asked the Bensons if they could participate. So the Benson family invited them. They built a fire. They took turns with the entertainment—musical numbers, comics, and skits. They did readings and sang together and finally got the Eisenhowers to join them.[23] That experience had an impact.

YEARNING FOR FREEDOM AND FAITH

During the election campaign in 1956 the Hungarian revolt took place. The revolt will be more understandable as we consider what has happened more recently: We have seen the fall of what had been an impregnable wall separating East and West Germany, the collapse of communism on economic grounds, and the rise of independent governments in satellite countries that were often buffer states to dictatorships. Such a revolt of so-called "freedom fighters" against communism arose in Hungary in 1956, but it was put down in the same ruthless way that China put down the revolt in Tiananmen Square in 1989.

Secretary Benson, troubled at American apathy toward the communists' response to the Hungarian revolt, wrote a statement that was slightly revised and then issued by President Eisenhower to protest the total brutality that attended the revolt. The article spoke of the orgy of brutality, and described those who rose up as the courageous liberty-loving people of Hungary.[24]

One thing that concerned Elder Benson was the question

of once the fight for freedom was won, then what? What does one do with one's freedom? Is it not remarkable that people who had limited access to written scriptures still maintained their faith east of the Berlin Wall? Is it not remarkable that now they have their own temple? Yes, it is. And that now they have their freedom? Yes, it is. But now, what will they do with it? Elder Benson felt that the ultimate question is how we hold on to our faith in God and that the greatest crisis in the world is forgetting the Lord.[25]

Elder Benson's faith in the Lord influenced others. When Secretary of State John Foster Dulles was told he had terminal cancer, he sat with Elder Benson, who spoke to him of prayer and of the practice of Latter-day Saint prayer circles. Shortly before his death, Dulles said, "Ezra, you know that I regard prayer as a priceless help."[26]

Elder Benson also influenced others who had no faith at all, including Andre Gromyko, Russia's representative at the first peace conference that was the genesis of the United Nations. Gromyko protested every step that led toward the formation of the United Nations. Elder Benson had conversations with him and Nikita Kruschev, who visited the United States and announced, "We will bury you." Kruschev had faith in the unwinding of a deterministic chain that would destroy all forms of capitalism. He believed it was the predetermined outcome of history.

When the Americans were present at a meeting in Moscow's Red Square, a little pocket of Christians—people caught in the terrifying, almost schizophrenic struggle between faith and atheism—sang to Elder Benson, "God Be with You Till We Meet Again."[27] And he, that day, felt the oneness, he says in his journal, of mankind in their unquenchable yearning for freedom.[28]

"THE CHURCH WORKHORSE"

Elder Benson was present for the dedication of the Swiss Temple in 1955. When President McKay finished the dedicatory prayer, he said that he had felt impressed to welcome an unseen audience to that dedication. Ezra Taft Benson had genealogical roots in Switzerland. Not only that, but he had a deep love for the great teacher, Karl G. Maeser, who was a native of Germany. Elder Benson had a dream in which Brother Maeser pled with him that a temple be built in Germany. Eventually President Benson was instrumental in developing and then building the Frankfurt Temple. And, of course, even before the Iron Curtain dropped, a temple was also built in East Germany.

Elder Benson became known as the Church workhorse. Though he was in his early sixties, he was laboring full time in the Church. Four major assignments came into focus. He hadn't yet had much experience in welfare work and in what was called the Church Security Program, but he set up offices in Frankfurt, Germany, and then combined all of the many functions of the Church: an information service, Presiding Bishop's office, genealogical society (now called Family History Department), building department, legal counsel, translation, German-language magazines, and so on. During his period in this assignment in Europe, nineteen chapels were built and over two thousand converts came into the Church. He also began, afresh, a mission in Italy.

He also visited Asia during the terrifying events of the Vietnam War. He was a vocal critic of U.S. policies in Vietnam, saying it was a war we did not intend to win and therefore should never have entered.[29]

Elder Benson visited the 1964 World's Fair in New York. The Mormon Pavilion was built with a facade that looked like the eastern spires of the Salt Lake Temple. It had within it a replica of the great *Christus* statue of Thorvaldsen and the film *Man's Search for Happiness,* written and produced by Elder Richard L. Evans. Many, many people from around the world visited the pavilion. Also at the fair was the Catholic Pavilion, which presented the fabulous Michelangelo sculpture, *The Pieta,* showing in classic marble the Mother Mary holding her Son after his death. After seeing both pavilions, one visitor commented to G. Stanley McAllister, president of the New York Stake, "At the Catholic exhibit we have the dead Christ—the *Pieta.* But the Mormon Pavilion has the . . . living Christ."[30] Elder Benson would not want to be misunderstood, but he did feel strongly that we have something to say when we speak of a living Christ who speaks to us now and not just then, who blesses us now and not just then.

FROM APOSTLE TO PROPHET

At age seventy-four Elder Benson became the nineteenth man to preside as the senior member of the Quorum of the Twelve. Several of the Brethren have said that no group of men has ever worked more closely or with such brotherhood as did these men. I am reminded of a statement made by the Prophet Joseph Smith, speaking of leaders in Zion, "There should exist the greatest freedom and familiarity among the rulers in Zion."[31] I believe he meant that the greatest openness of thought and feeling should exist among the leaders in Zion, the greatest trust, even in sharing one's intimate thoughts, the greatest familiarity in matters of joy or sorrow. These men were close, and whatever their differences they would lay down their lives for each other.

The Church continued to grow under the direction of the First Presidency and the Twelve. The First Quorum of Seventy was organized. The expansion of the Church in Asia—Japan, Taiwan, the Philippines—was almost explosive and likewise in Central and South America. As recently as twenty-five or thirty years ago, there was only one member of the Church in Manila. There are now more than 500,000 members in Manila and the rest of the Philippines, and a temple as well.

Elder Benson attended the inauguration ceremonies of U.S. President Ronald Reagan, as did the Mormon Tabernacle Choir. Later, when President Reagan visited Utah, he toured Welfare Square, saw the welfare program running on the power of volunteerism and brotherly organization, and understood a phrase that President Benson loved to quote from Orson Hyde, "There is more salvation and security in wheat than in all the political schemes of the world."[32] This is a Church that knows the importance of food and drink and a roof over our heads, just as we care about strengthening our spirits and souls. President Benson sometimes said, "The revelation to produce and store food may be as essential to our temporal welfare today as boarding the ark was to the people in the days of Noah."[33]

At times Brother Benson, during the foment of criticism, used a phrase applied to him to the end of his life: "No weapon formed against [thee] shall prosper" (D&C 109:25). Clinton Larson, who could have been called the poet laureate of the Church, knew President Benson and wrote a poem about him. It was Brother Larson's opinion that, for all President Benson's public notoriety, he was as guileless and self-effacing a man as he had ever known.

Elder Benson served as an apostle for forty-two years and under six presidents: Heber J. Grant, George Albert Smith, David O. McKay, Joseph Fielding Smith, Harold B. Lee, and Spencer W. Kimball. At age eighty-six, he became the second oldest man to be called as President of the Church (Joseph

Fielding Smith was ninety-four at the time of his call). President Benson chose as counselors Elders Gordon B. Hinckley and Thomas S. Monson.

AMERICA AND ATHEISM

President Monson often said that he thought it was symbolic and fitting that Ezra Taft Benson would be President of the Church when the U.S. Constitution reached its bicentennial birthday.[34] He was a firm defender of freedom and constitutional principles. When the question is asked, "Which of the two main political parties in the United States is closest to the vision of the founders of the United States?" the proper answer may be "Neither." Over the years there has been a shift from the basic principles on which America was founded and, in spite of all efforts to the contrary, an infiltration of ideas that are not true to the original vision. Among the areas that have been neglected, ignored, or opposed are the fundamental commitments to religious freedom.

Elder Benson did not increase his popularity when he pointed out in stark terms that atheism was about to become the state religion in the United States.[35] The Church was put on trial for permitting state funds to be used for religious purposes. Students who went to school also went across the street for released-time seminary. Critics argued that the same bus that took the students to school, which was paid for by state funds, also indirectly got the students to seminary; therefore, the bus was being used for religious purposes, which was a violation of the Constitution. They won the suit.

Robert N. Bellah, a brilliant sociologist from the University of California, Berkeley, visited Utah and testified that he required his students to memorize certain passages for world religion classes at Berkeley, including many Buddhist sutras. He said that he didn't see any significant difference between that requirement in a university and the opportunity for a student to cross the street from a high school and memorize biblical verses. President Benson said, "Atheism is becoming a state religion and I'm determined to do all I can to stop it."[36]

President Benson's point was that we have a right, according to the original vision of the Founding Fathers, to any religious position we desire, including a position against religion. What we don't have a right to is to say in the name of separation of church and state that we cannot have churches represented in public debate and in other places.

Some people felt that in order to be a faithful Latter-day Saint while President Benson was president, you had to be a Republican. He kept saying it wasn't true. He was once interviewed by a newspaper reporter and asked the question, "Do you believe a man can be a Democrat and still be a faithful Latter-day Saint?" When he was reported as saying, "No," President Benson called the reporter, asked for another interview, and corrected the quote.[37]

Many of President Benson's political attacks—some of them in writing—were against atheistic communism. He wanted it replaced, as did President David O. McKay, with faith in the living God. He was equally concerned about the destruction of freedom and the violation of human rights in any of the powerful dictatorships that remained in the world.

MAJOR THEMES AND TEACHINGS

The guiding principle of Elder Benson's life was, "Always . . . do what is best for the kingdom."[38] The results of that resolve became some of his most prominent teachings.

America. President Benson frequently spoke of America and pled for retaining its strength. As he put it, America is the Lord's base of operations.[39] It is the conviction of many Church historians that the only country where the Restoration of the gospel of Jesus Christ could have succeeded was America. It was prepared through the original struggle for freedom and from the countless people from all over the world who came to America, desperate for religious freedom. But even here the Restoration movement barely survived. The Rocky Mountains are the place where we have our headquarters and from where we send out representatives worldwide. If America becomes corrupt, that will affect, in ways we cannot fully foresee, the power, the influence, and the strength of the Lord's Church.

Atonement. In one discourse, Elder Benson spoke of Christ's atonement and said that only a God could atone for our sins. "Because He was God—even the Son of God—He could carry the weight and burden of other men's sins on Himself. . . . That holy, unselfish act of voluntarily taking on Himself the sins of all other men is called the Atonement. How one could bear the sins for all is beyond the comprehension of mortal man. But this I know: He did take on Himself the sins of all and did so out of His infinite love for each of us."[40] He spoke of how Christ descended below all things. It's not always recognized that the condescension of Jesus the Christ was indeed below all, but it was. There is no place you can go, in the experiences of life, bitter or sweet, that he did not himself reach to and even go deeper in.

The Book of Mormon. Elder Benson was the one who emphasized, first as a member of the Twelve and then as the President of the Church, that we must study the Book of Mormon daily.[41] He quoted the Doctrine and Covenants verses that say that the whole Church is under condemnation because we have treated the Book of Mormon lightly.[42] Under his tutelage and under his influence, the Book of Mormon became far more central in our curriculum, in our private reading, and in our missionary program. I suspect that in no administration have more copies of the Book of Mormon been printed, translated, and distributed than under his influence.

Home and family. Another great emphasis was on the home, the cruciality of the home, and the importance of the parents in the home.

President Benson could be called the "To" president because many of his sermons' titles begin with "To": "To the Youth of the Church," "To the Humble Followers of Christ," and "To the Missionaries." He focused his thoughts and his prayers on specific groups and addressed them.

One of his "To" talks, "To the Mothers in Zion,"[43] was one of the most controversial up to that point. He pled with mothers to stay home as much as they could, even if that meant stopping their employment or sacrificing their budgets, in order to be with their children. One woman, a social worker, who was at the time very sympathetic to the women's movement, said in my hearing, "When he gave that talk I thought he was an old man who simply didn't 'get it.' Now I say, 'He was a prophet and I wish I had listened more carefully.'" That may be the sentiment of many others. "Strengthen your families" was a theme he emphasized all through his Church service.

Joseph Smith. I was present once in a meeting with Elder Ezra Taft Benson and was overwhelmed by his spirit and his testimony. It was during one of the famous August Palmyra pageants, and the cast had gathered that afternoon in the Sacred Grove. I still remember Elder Benson standing at an improvised pulpit. The only sentence that sticks in my memory—but it is indelible—is this: "I testify that Joseph Smith was one of the greatest prophets who ever lived." That went into me like liquid fire.

Priesthood and the law. Again and again he spoke to the priesthood brethren about their dignity, their honor, and their responsibility. He often said that no civic honor can match the honor that comes to a man when he is given the Melchizedek Priesthood.[44]

He spoke often of Jesus Christ as the living law. He pointed out that Jesus Christ not only introduces the law, interprets the law, and records the law, but also that Jesus *is* the law.[45] That means that we must seek and honor his present will, which we learn through modern revelation.

Elder Benson was present in the Salt Lake Temple during the administration of President Spencer W. Kimball when all precedent, all tradition, all prior explanations were wiped away and revelation established that men and women of all races would be given the privileges of the temple and the blessings of the priesthood. Elder Bruce R. McConkie said that when the meeting ended, all of the Twelve were in tears, and he heard Elder Benson say that he had never "experienced anything of such spiritual magnitude and power" as this revelation.[46] Elder Benson had then been in the Quorum of the Twelve for thirty-five years.

Elder Benson also spoke often of how the Lord deals with this Church and with each of us individually by giving us guidelines, expecting us then to fill in the details.[47]

Pride. President Benson also discussed the great sin of pride. He alerted us that pride is the cloven hoof that leads us to idolatries and takes us away from the influences and powers of the Lord Jesus Christ.[48] It is a popular vice of our generation (and all generations). He also warned about popularity, another version of "look out for pride."[49] He said again and again, "Beware of pride."[50]

The temple. He taught extensively about the temple, emphasizing how the richest blessings of life are generated there. He taught that the ordinances of the temple, especially the ordinance of sealing, are the highest blessings of life.[51] He taught that the holy places we are to stand in are the temple and the home.[52] Second to the temple, the home is the most sacred place on earth.

He often spoke of the law of consecration, not as an economic experiment, but as a celestial law that points us toward the house of the Lord and our covenants therein.[53]

Scouting. From his early days President Benson was active in youth activities, becoming one of the great advocates of Scouting. Many years later, when he was more than ninety years old, he was awarded the Bronze Wolf, the only international award given by the World Scout Committee, for "outstanding services given by the individual to Scouting in his own country and internationally."[54]

A TRIBUTE

In 1960, Sumner G. Whittier, National Administrator of Veterans Affairs, was invited from Washington, D.C., to attend a typical Latter-day Saint general conference. He was quietly enjoying the meeting when President McKay arose and said, "Among our honored guests present this morning [is] Sumner G. Whittier. . . . Would you please come forward. . . . Just say a word to the audience." Mr. Whittier stood up there in the Tabernacle with all of the klieg lights and the cameras and came forward without having been given any warning. The clarity and brevity of his statement summed up President Benson's ministry from the point of view of a non-Latter-day Saint.

Mr. Whittier said, "Mr. President and all of those assembled here, I was sitting in this tremendous auditorium listening and being inspired and all of a sudden I find myself at this platform. But I must say to you that coming in last night by plane to this tremendous city, thinking of the great struggle that men went through to achieve this mighty thing, knowing as I do the dedication and the devotion of those who are members of this Church, for Reed Benson was an administrative assistant in my office, knowing the integrity of his father working for a great President of the United States, seeing this kind of strength, this devotion, this dedication, listening to the inspiration from this great pulpit here this morning, listening to the rising power of song as I listened to it in great Constitutional Hall in Washington when the Choir came there, knowing the love of the Benson family—and one of them can do nothing without the other joining—I tell you for one who comes from a long way across this continent, this is a moving[,] a thrilling, and inspiring moment, the greatness of America, the strength of Christianity here represented. I have a faith in all of our tomorrows."[55]

A LEGACY

In general conference, President Benson once referred to the time when he was facing the call to be a member of the Twelve and then later in Washington, when he was alone and without his family for a few days. On both occasions, he literally sank to his knees and wept aloud, feeling inadequate to his depths.[56] But he also had the experience of being lifted to the point that he did do it. That is one of his great legacies to the ongoing and growing Church.

President Benson, out of his missionary experiences in England, understood both the strength and the weakness of the opposition in the world. His familiar phrase "Do not despair" has a corollary: "The Lord has provided [many] ways which, if followed, will lift our spirits and send us on our way rejoicing."[57] Those convictions came out of his faith in Christ and the forward-moving dynamics of the restored Church.

There is no question that there will be increasing polarization in the world. Light stands against darkness. There will be increasing and organized opposition to the expansion of this kingdom and especially to our building of sanctuaries. There will be individual opposition in the lives of people who abandon their traditions and their sinful lives and find their way into the Church; often they will be told by their friends and family, "We are no longer yours and you are no longer ours." That will happen over and over. We talk about the painful history of the Church being past, but the history of this Church is being repeated all over the world every day.

President Ezra Taft Benson stands as Exhibit A of a man who faced the opposition, who did not tremble, who held to the Lord Jesus Christ, and who therefore could look back and say, "I have fought the good fight because, and only because, this is the work of the Lord." He lived, as did his predecessors, to become worthy of all acceptation.

14

HOWARD W. HUNTER

The Council of the Twelve was gathered for their usual Thursday meeting in the Salt Lake Temple. Elder Howard W. Hunter was absent and, for the first time, late. They waited, and then they heard a kind of ***kahlump, kahlump.*** It was Brother Hunter pushing his walker from the elevator to the room. He usually crossed that distance in a wheelchair. Elder Hunter entered the room and almost collapsed in a chair. Elder Maxwell recalled, "We do not often applaud in the temple, but we all stood up and applauded that day, and then one by one went around and kissed him and hugged him. The doctors had said that he would not walk again, but he had overcome that verdict."[1] That anecdote is the crisp typology of the life of Howard W. Hunter, who was afflicted often and especially in his later years.

A SERMON IN NAUVOO

Most of Howard W. Hunter's forebears on both sides of his family were Scandinavian. They were agrarian people, humble people, and eventually came to America, but not to anything resembling a Mormon community. They came much earlier than the Restoration, but in 1842 his grandmother, a devout Methodist, came to hear the Prophet Joseph Smith in Nauvoo. I have occasionally wondered if the Prophet sat down on a Sunday morning and asked himself, "What will I speak about today near the temple?" Did he occasionally say to himself, "I think the people need such and such?" Well, on that occasion he chose to speak about the second coming of Christ.

Elder Hunter's grandmother had written in her journal that she was troubled about her church, that to her it seemed that it "has not only lost its holiness and purity, but its power and strength. Where do we find that mighty, powerful faith, with all the gifts of the Spirit, that was once enjoyed by the infant church under the gospel dispensation?"[2] That day in Nauvoo, Joseph's sermon so moved her that she asked for baptism. She had found the church she was looking for.

She went west with the other Saints from Nauvoo, met on the plains the man she later married, and after their arrival in the Salt Lake Valley, settled in Idaho.

EARLY YEARS

Much of Howard W. Hunter's youth was spent in and around Boise, Idaho. He had a normal and even happy childhood. When he was five months old, he was taken to a fast meeting in the Boise Branch where the branch president, Heber Q. Hale, gave him a blessing. Howard's father, though sympathetic to the Church, had not joined. He is supposed to have said on one occasion that the Mormon Church was all right, but it seemed to have too many meetings. It wasn't until later that he finally decided to join the Church.

In the meantime, Howard's mother taught him the gospel. Though he was baptized and at the proper age became a deacon, a teacher, and a priest, he wasn't much of a student of the gospel. He was athletic and gifted in music. His mother insisted he take music lessons, and before he turned twenty years old, Howard could play seven instruments. He eventually became a band leader and his group, the Croonaders, toured the Orient and attracted international attention.

He had two narrow escapes from accidents during his youth. The first happened when, as a child, he ran through the house, tripped, and fell—and his right arm went into a pot of boiling water that had been left on the floor to cool. His mother called a doctor, who recommended that she wrap the burned arm first in mashed potatoes and then with a bandage. That might be unorthodox medical treatment, but it worked, though Howard had the scar the rest of his life.

The second experience came when his older sister was learning to drive. They were coming home from church, and it wasn't until she was in the driveway that she asked, "How do you stop this thing?" Before anybody could answer, she crashed through the garage door. The only comment Howard made about the event was that his father came out and surveyed the damage and was not pleased.[3]

Howard also contracted polio early in his life. One of his close friends was left with serious paralysis, but in Howard's case the only lasting effect was a stiff back. He was never after able to bend forward and touch the floor.

A LOVE FOR WORK AND ANIMALS

Among Howard's chores was pumping water, which was then heated on the stove and poured in a galvanized tub for

Saturday night baths. He had to tend and irrigate the garden. He raised potatoes. He had to handle the grain used for chicken feed and clean up the roosts and pens.

As a boy he loved animals. One time his rabbit escaped, and during the chase, one of his neighbors grabbed the bunny and accidentally pulled its tail off. Howard's journal says, "It made me sick. I went in the house crying. Mother came out to help me catch her." Seventy-five years later he called that experience "a tragedy in my young life."

On the other side of the coin, though, he was told that if you put a drop of turpentine on a cat's tail, it would do tricks. So, as boys will do, he put a drop or two of turpentine on the cat's tail. When it didn't respond, he dipped the entire tail in the container. "All was quiet and then suddenly the cat arched its back, jumped into the air with a screech, cleared the fence with a leap, and took off through White's wheat field. I could see the ripple of the wheat heads as it raced through the stems of grain. . . . For several days I was deeply troubled," he said, "but this turned into joy when the cat forgave me and came home."[4]

He was also a kind of naturalist. He collected birds' eggs: pheasant, meadowlark, bluebird. His sister records that he would never take an egg unless there were several already in the nest. Then he would pierce both ends with a pin, blow it out, and put it in his collection, kept in boxes lined with cotton.

YOUNG ADULT YEARS

When World War One ended in November 1918, Howard was a young man of eleven years. To celebrate, he and others went up and down the center of town shooting off hundreds of firecrackers. "Then we came home," he recalled, "and built a big fire."[5]

He became a Scout and, eventually, in 1923, he earned enough merit badges to become an Eagle Scout. The local newspaper wrote an article about his achievement. He wore his merit badges proudly and lived to endorse and support Scouting as a Church leader.

He also worked for a time as a caddy at the Idaho Country Club. He became an assistant in a pharmacy, and he also earned money by playing gigs with his Croonaders. He played his last engagement with his band in the Virginia Ballroom in Huntington Park, California, on June 6, 1931. With all of his work, he earned enough money to help with the family expenses and also to prepare for school.

It was at this time in his life that Howard moved to San Bernardino, California, where he was employed by the Bank of Italy, which eventually merged with the Bank of America. It was a job that in some ways shaped the rest of his life.

While he was in California, he also spent long hours studying the gospel. B. H. Roberts used to say of some young people who were indifferent, if not outright hostile, to the Church, "Ah, they have not yet met a great interpreter."[6] In the Adams Ward in Los Angeles, Howard met a great interpreter, a man named Clayton, who started teaching and tutoring him in the scriptures and other gospel-related books. Howard wrote in his journal, "I think of this period of my life as the time the truths of the gospel commenced to unfold. I always had a testimony of the gospel, but suddenly I commenced to understand."[7]

Howard's patriarchal blessing also indicated great blessings in store for the young man. He was told that he was one of those whom "the Lord foreknew," that he had shown "strong leadership among the hosts of heaven," and that he had been ordained "to perform an important work in mortality in bringing to pass [the Lord's] purposes." He was promised that he would receive "intelligence from on high" and would be "a master of worldly skill." He would be a "teacher of worldly wisdom as well as a priest of the Most High God." He would serve in the Church, sit in its councils, and be known for wisdom and righteous judgments.[8]

COURTSHIP AND A CRASH

By this time he had met a beautiful girl named Claire, but because of poverty and having to work full time to afford school, he didn't think he had a foundation for marriage.

He and Claire wrote often, and they both asked their parents if their families could take their vacations together during the same two weeks in July 1929. So the two families went down to Newport Beach and Balboa and took a three-day cruise near Ensenada, Mexico. His journal says, "Neither of our families liked the idea but we convinced them that it was all right." He explained that their cabins were "on different decks."[9]

In October of 1929 the stock market crashed. The bank Howard worked at had a net worth that was much more than other smaller banks, and thus it survived—but only by merging with another bank and by lowering the salaries of its employees. Howard was offered a position in the Hawthorne branch of the new First Exchange State Bank, a result of the merger. At this point he and Claire were talking seriously about marriage. He had not thought about serving a full-time mission. When Claire offered to help support him, he declined, saying, "It would be better for us to get married and at a later time, as soon as conditions might permit, we would go on a mission together."[10] Little did he know the service they would be performing together in the years to come.

MARRIAGE AND LAW SCHOOL

Because his father was not a member of the Church (he joined when Howard was nineteen), Howard had never quite developed a testimony of the law of tithing. As a result, when Howard sought a temple recommend and the bishop asked him if he had been a full tithe payer, Howard had to say no. He then promised the bishop that henceforth he would pay a full tithing. The bishop filled out the recommend, and Howard and Claire began their marriage in September 1935 living the law of tithing.[11]

At the same time, Howard entered law school and burned the midnight oil. When he sat for his test for admission to the bar, his law professor said that "when they sat down to write the examination, they should 'take a good look at the man on the right and the man on the left, and realize that out of the three, only one would receive a passing grade.'"[12] After the test, Howard and Claire waited for the results. Howard knew that if the envelope was thin, it meant he failed. If it was fat, it meant that he passed; the envelope would also contain information about possible jobs and various clients. On December 12, 1939, the letter came. His wife called and told him the letter from the Committee of Bar Examiners had arrived.

He asked, "Is it a thick or a thin letter?"

"A fat one," she replied.

He said, "A surge of blood went to my head and I closed

my eyes and waited for her to open and read the letter." He had passed.[13]

Of the 718 applicants who took the exam, only 254 passed. Howard was soon sworn in at the Supreme Court and began his law practice.

INCREASED CHURCH SERVICE

Howard was called to be the bishop of the El Sereno Ward when he was only thirty-two years of age. He didn't think of himself as much of a father (even though he had children) and even less as the "father of the ward." The ward didn't have a chapel, so they negotiated to meet in a lodge. Members would go to the lodge before sacrament meeting every Sunday morning and clean up the rooms and the spittoons and the beer cans left from the previous Saturday night. He started as a bishop in humble circumstances, but despite the wartime challenges that began in 1941, he was able to build a chapel and was an effective fundraiser.

He was soon asked to teach the young adults who were attending the "Deseret Club" at college. Colleges wouldn't permit an institute class unless they were off-campus and had a qualified sponsor. Brother Hunter agreed to be the sponsor and taught every Wednesday at noon. They studied carefully and prayerfully James E. Talmage's book *Jesus the Christ*. Perhaps Howard's interests in the Middle East, the Holy Land, and eventually the Jerusalem Center were nourished by that experience.

He served six years as bishop and then was called to be a stake president. As president of the Pasadena Stake, he inspired a bishop in Alhambra. I have a letter that bishop wrote saying, interestingly, that Howard W. Hunter "may be headed for the Council of the Twelve." It is a glimpse of the esteem many had for him.

STATEMENT OF HIS AIMS

Howard once wrote a profound statement of his aims in life: "It is my aim to find pleasure and enjoyment in life by seeking after those things which are good and worth while, that I may gain knowledge and wisdom with each passing year; to carefully plan my allotted time so that none of it will be wasted; to give my family the benefits of education, recreation, and travel; to conduct my life in obedience to the Gospel of Jesus Christ; to so manage my business affairs that I will have an income adequate to provide my family with their wants and the advantages of some of the finer things in life; and to set aside a portion for investments to provide an income for retirement."[14]

Later, President Hunter often quoted a statement of Napoleon Hill, who wrote the best-seller *Think and Grow Rich:* "Riches cannot always be measured in money. To some, riches can be evaluated only in terms of lasting friendships, happy family relationships, understanding between business associates, or peace of mind measurable only in spiritual values."[15] That quotation epitomizes his aspirations.

CALLED AS AN APOSTLE

After the rush of the holidays in 1959, Howard Hunter recorded, "We have traveled extensively the year before. I am now asked to go to see President McKay."[16]

One of his counselors in California met him on the street and, knowing that Howard had an appointment with President

McKay, said, "You know there is a vacancy in the Council of the Twelve."

Howard replied, "I know you are joking with me. The First Presidency has asked me to secure some information for them, and I presume they want a report."[17]

Clare Middlemiss, President McKay's secretary, ushered him into the office of the President, who offered him a smile and a warm handshake before saying, "Sit down, President Hunter. I want to talk with you. The Lord has spoken. You are called to be one of his special witnesses, and tomorrow you will be sustained as a member of the Council of the Twelve."[18]

Howard's journal entry reads: "I have never felt so completely humbled as when I sat in the presence of this great, sweet, kindly man—the prophet of the Lord. He told me what a great joy this would bring into my life, the wonderful association with the brethren, and that hereafter my life and time would be devoted as a servant of the Lord and that I would hereafter belong to the Church and the whole world. He said other things to me but I was so overcome I can't remember the details."[19]

Elder Matthew Cowley once observed in his candid way that when he was called to the Twelve, he was called to become a delinquent father.[20] Now that's not the intention of the call, but General Authorities are dedicated to Christ and the work of the Church first, and balancing family and Church duties is not always easy.

When the sustaining vote was taken the following day, Elder Hunter wrote in his journal, "My heart commenced to pound as I wondered what the reaction would be when my name was read . . . I have never had such a feeling of panic."[21] He was sustained, and soon enough came the flashbulbs and the whole weight of the world on his shoulders. That afternoon, Elder Kimball took him to the temple, showed him the council rooms, and explained to him the procedures of the meetings. Elder Hunter was the seventy-fourth man in our dispensation to receive the apostolic charge and the conferral of keys.[22]

GETTING TO WORK

I was once present when a whole group, up to seventy people, were set apart by Elder Gordon B. Hinckley as General Sunday School Board members. When he was finished, Elder Hinckley smiled and said, "Well, brethren and sisters, it's all over now except the work."

One of Elder Hunter's first assignments was to be involved in the clarification and, if need be, the cancellation of sealings—a tremendous burden. In every case where a husband or a wife wrote to say, "We are divorced. I want cancellation of the temple sealing," Elder Hunter, as a judge in Israel with discernment and inspiration, had the responsibility to answer the questions: "Is it appropriate to grant the cancellation? Is it appropriate to approve another marriage? And if so, after what period of time?"[23]

In 1970, Elder Hunter was taken by surprise when he was called as Church Historian and Recorder, a calling that Elder Joseph Fielding Smith had served in for forty-nine years. At the time, the Historical Department had a staff of only about fifty people, but it had more than a million documents, pamphlets, photographs, motion pictures, slides, and tapes. Elder Hunter was also responsible for the record-keeping of the Church—the temple records, ordinations, and patriarchal blessings. Though he felt overwhelmed, he set to work classifying and caring for the records.

While Elder Hunter was Church Historian, he was involved with the restoration of Nauvoo. He was present for a special experience at Carthage Jail when a grandson of Willard Richards recounted the details of the martyrdom of Joseph and Hyrum Smith. Brother Hunter recalled, "In the dimly lighted room we could see the stains on the floor from Hyrum's blood, and near us was the window from which Joseph fell after the shots were fired. We sang all the verses of the song, 'A Poor Wayfaring Man of Grief,' which the Prophet loved. . . . I will never forget this occasion with the Brethren in the upper room. President Carroll W. Smith . . . gave the prayer and we retired. . . . I slept in the inner jail behind the iron bars."[24]

PERSONALITY AND CHARACTER TRAITS

Comments and writings from the Brethren and others of President Hunter's associates paint a composite portrait of some of his personality and character traits.

- "He has a way of making people feel at ease. He doesn't dominate them. He is a good listener."
- "When you travel with him, he's always watching to be sure that everybody is taken care of and that nobody is being inconvenienced or put out."
- "He is tough when he needs to be tough, and gracious when he needs to be gracious, and forgiving when he needs to be forgiving."
- "He has extraordinary patience that comes from great inner peace. You have to have the feeling of love and

support from our Father in heaven and the Savior to live a life as selflessly as he does."

- "We have never seen him distraught or excited or unhappy with anything."[25]

Whether it was being trapped in an elevator in the dark in a wheelchair, or having the chorister faint in the middle of a meeting, President Hunter was always calm, even in the middle of a storm. The most extreme example happened in the Marriott Center. A man stood up to the pulpit with a briefcase and threatened President Hunter that he would detonate a bomb unless President Hunter read a statement.

President Hunter stood before a full Marriott Center audience and said, "I won't."

"You will," threatened the man again, "or I will set off a bomb."

President Hunter refused; he was both steel and velvet.

The audience began to sing "We Thank Thee, O God, for a Prophet," distracting the man, and the authorities took him away. President Hunter then continued his speech with barely a pause.[26]

He had a way of seeing that everything was done in the right way, according to the scriptures and Church policy. One day he was asked, "We would like to have three counselors in this presidency. May we?"

He calmly said, "Well now, brother, if you want to change the Doctrine and Covenants we could probably go ahead with that."[27]

He had a charitable and forgiving heart. He was loyal to his leaders. He was a student of the gospel, of mankind, and of human nature. He was a regular reader of the quarterly publication *The Biblical Archaeologist,* he was a member of the

Archaeological Society of Meso-American Studies, and he had a huge collection of historical books that he read.

Elder Hunter once visited the basement of the Rockefeller Museum in Jerusalem, where all the fragments of the Dead Sea Scrolls that have not yet been translated are housed. Emmanuel Tov, a world authority in Hebrew and Aramaic, showed Elder Hunter a clay ostracon from about A.D. 130 with the writing, "I convey my land to Alma ben Yehuda" on it. "Alma" is a Latin name and can apply to both women and men; but in Hebrew "ben" means son; and "Yehuda" means Judah. That simple ostracon reveals that Alma was also a Semitic name for a Jewish man. Emmanuel Tov made Elder Hunter a photostat of the ostracon for his office.

THE POLYNESIAN CULTURAL CENTER

In February 1955, President McKay spoke at the ground-breaking ceremonies for a new Church college in Laie, Hawaii, and said a striking thing, that Laie would become "a missionary factor, influencing not thousands, not tens of thousands, but millions of people who will come seeking to know what this town and its significance are."[28] At that time about 100,000 visitors came to Hawaii every year. Under the direction of Elder Hunter, the Cultural Center was developed and brought people from all around the Pacific Rim to participate in a production that has become a marvelous tourist attraction. And after twelve years, more than a million people had visited the Polynesian Cultural Center, well on the way to fulfilling President McKay's prediction.

EXPERIENCES IN ISRAEL

Elder Hunter had a powerful experience on one of his early trips to the Holy Land, when he attempted to climb a mountain called Sinai. It may not have been the very mountain that Moses climbed; it is also called "Horeb" in the Old Testament and there are at least five huge mountains in that chain that could qualify. Elder Hunter rode a camel for two hours up the mountain and then climbed over the rocky ground until he reached the seven hundred uneven steps leading to the summit. Partly because of the cold and the wind, and partly because he was not as hardy as some of the young men with him, his ascent ended there. He recorded, "We noticed it was getting light, and we stood in a crevice in the rocks and watched the sun gradually come into view over the rugged mountains at six o'clock—a sight I will never forget. [The guide] asked, 'Shall we put our feet on the summit?' I replied, 'I've seen it, that's enough. I can't believe that Moses went beyond this point.'"[29] Brother Hunter, a man like unto Moses, had climbed Moses' mountain.

Elder Hunter was also instrumental in building bridges between the Palestinians and the Israelis. There is no more inflammatory, no more ancient, no more apparently insoluble chasm in the political world than that which exists in the Middle East, and at its root it is religious in nature. The extremists of all three parties in the controversies—the Jews, the Christians, and the Arabs (or Palestinian Moslems)—are absolutely convinced that not only is God on their side, but also that he is either going to destroy or help them destroy their enemies. Though the extremists are in the minority, their influence is enough to keep the Middle East situation constantly unsettled.

Elder Hunter once gave an address at Shepherds' Field, which is in or near Bethlehem. The essence of his address was that "all are alike unto God," and he pointed out that even the genealogy of Jesus, through David, is mixed. Ruth, a Moabite woman, not an Israelite, married Boaz. His point was that we must eventually come to understand that the children of Abraham are of Abraham either in lineal ways or are adopted. But in either case, all blessings are promised to all individuals. Elder Hunter taught that in past dispensations the Lord has raised up prophets precisely for their own times.

He later wrote a statement declaring, "As members of the Lord's church, we need to lift our vision beyond personal prejudices. We need to discover the supreme truth that indeed our Father is no respecter of persons. Sometimes we unduly offend brothers and sisters of other nations by assigning exclusiveness to one nationality of people over another.

"Let me cite, as an example of exclusiveness, the present problem in the Middle East—the conflict between the Arabs and the Jews. We do not need to apologize nor mitigate any of the prophecies concerning the Holy Land. We believe them and declare them to be true. But this does not give us justification to dogmatically pronounce that others of our Father's children are not children of promise. . . .

"Both the Jews and the Arabs are children of our Father. They are both children of promise, and as a church we do not take sides. We have love for and an interest in each. The purpose of the gospel of Jesus Christ is to bring about love, unity, and brotherhood of the highest order."[30]

That belief became the creed of the operation of the BYU Jerusalem Center, which has an almost equal enrollment between the two main camps, and an unspoken philosophy that says, "If we cannot have peace here in this place, brother to brother, where will it ever occur?"

I would like to share as an example a story that happened while I was director of the Jerusalem Center. A young Palestinian man was supposed to be at the guard station at five o'clock one day, but he never arrived. His father, who also worked there (they were the only father-son employees at the Jerusalem Center), was very anxious and asked to be excused to search for his son. He had heard sirens over in the Old City and wondered if there was a connection. Late that night the father learned that a huge retaining wall had collapsed on a restaurant in East Jerusalem, killing twenty-seven people, one of them his son. The father had to identify the body. The next morning all of our staff—Jew, Christian, Moslem, Latter-day Saint—went up on the Mount of Olives and had a small funeral. The father's nerves were like steel and he didn't shed a tear as they lowered his son's body into the ground, put in a few palm branches, and then put on the covering soil. When he looked up, the first person whose eyes he met was one of our security men, who was Jewish. The father stood and walked directly to him; they embraced, and the first tears on his Arab cheeks were Jewish tears. Elder Howard W. Hunter was a force and influence that made that possible.

The Jerusalem Center

In connection with the BYU Jerusalem Center, the Orson Hyde Memorial Garden was first announced by Elder LeGrand Richards, who became the chairman of the committee. With Elder Hunter at his side, they raised one million dollars to select and landscape the 3.5 acres on the west side of the Mount of Olives. The land faces the Lion's Gate, or St. Stephen's Gate, which is the very gate Orson Hyde came through in October 1841 to dedicate the land for the return of the Jews. Elder Hunter was present at the dedication of the garden; he was also present when President Kimball visited the various sites proposed for the Jerusalem Center. In October 1983, Elder Hunter and Elder Mark E. Petersen had their picture taken on the site that was eventually selected for the Jerusalem Center.

The opposition and the outcry that arose when the Jerusalem Center was announced was unbelievable. But so were the blessings that came. When the mayor, Teddy Kollek, first recommended that the center be built, everyone around him "went down their mouse holes" and he was left entirely alone. He was the one person who, on principle, said, "Jerusalem is an open city. Jerusalem should be available to all faiths. This center will go forth."[31] And it did go forth, along with a promise from Howard W. Hunter that there would be no proselytizing in Jerusalem by the center's students.

Some years later, someone asked the mayor, "When did you first begin to trust Howard W. Hunter?"

And the mayor replied, "Oh, you cannot *not* trust Elder Hunter." That's a great tribute.

One more example of the challenge that faced the center: A rabbi walked in to see Jeffrey R. Holland, who was then president of BYU, and said, "I have come from New York. I have brought my checkbook. If you will specify how much you have spent so far on the construction of your Jerusalem Center on Mount Scopus, and if you will add to that any sum you want, I will write a check, you will stop building your center, and the Mormon problem in Jerusalem will be over." Brother Holland didn't give him a figure.

Before the rabbi left, he said to Brother Holland, "You have to understand. We Jews are post-Holocaust Jews. Only two-thirds of us survived Hitler's crematoria. We are nervous—even paranoid—about losing any more. For us a converted Jew is a lost Jew. Are you willing to face violence?"

Brother Holland spent some sleepless nights after that conversation, but peace of mind came to him when he opened the Doctrine and Covenants at random and read, "I, the Lord, am well pleased that there should be a school in Zion" (D&C 97:3). Brother Holland could certainly appreciate the double meaning of "Zion." And thankfully, there wasn't much violence during the building of the Jerusalem Center.

I happened to be in the Jerusalem Center the day Elder Hunter, Elder James E. Faust, and President Holland returned from signing the lease. Years had been spent trying to make it final, and the signing itself had been postponed at least a half-dozen times. It was a difficult position to be in—our building was almost completed and occupied, but we still hadn't signed a lease. It was finally time, and a huge check was handed over for the leasing of the property on which the Jerusalem Center stands. The man who accepted the check then tried, in a roundabout way, to unethically avoid responsibility for the check and its use. Elder Faust says Elder Hunter came up out of his chair like a shot and said, "You will do *what?*"[32] Elder Hunter could be tough when he needed to be.

When they returned to the center, bowed down and weary but successful, I overheard one of them say, "We need to go somewhere and pray." I heard someone else say, "The Garden Tomb." The three apostles immediately went together to that beautiful place, where so many other leaders and presidents had found such an intimate feeling for the Lord Jesus Christ. And they prayed in gratitude.

The Jerusalem Center is a magnificent building, an architectural marvel involving both a Jewish and an American LDS architect. The styles and visions of the architects run together like two rivers. Israel's former mayor, Teddy Kollek, has said that the Jerusalem Center is the most beautiful building in Jerusalem, with the exception of the Dome of the Rock, which has been there for centuries.[33]

When Elder Hunter dedicated the center with only a small group of fifty people present, he said, "We pray that all who come into this building to study, to teach, or for any other purpose may be constrained to acknowledge that it is thy house and that they may feel thy Spirit." Since the dedication, a guest book has been kept at the center. In many different languages, people have almost universally said the same thing: "Here we feel peace." I remember one rough-looking man saying one day as he walked in the hall near the upper room and its glorious overview of the Golden City, "You know when I walk by that room I feel like praying, and I'm an atheist." He's not the only one.

I have a picture of Elder Hunter sitting in his wheelchair overlooking the city from the Jerusalem Center and fingering the key which Robert C. Taylor had given him. Brother Taylor served for many years as the head of BYU Travel Studies and was the one who pioneered the initial efforts to build the center. Inscribed on the key were the words, "A city set on a hill cannot be hid." The center *is* set on a hill, and it is illuminated at night with magnificent, subdued lighting. It is so beautiful that anyone in the city who looks in that direction will see it. It cannot be hid, and it is indeed a monument to Elder Hunter and his vision.

The Mormon Tabernacle Choir in Jerusalem

Elder Hunter was involved in the meeting where the mayor issued an invitation to the Mormon Tabernacle Choir to visit. Elder Hunter said to the mayor, "We will take the proposal home. We will present it to the president, and you will hear from us." All the profits from the ticket sales were donated to the Jerusalem Symphony.

The choir's climactic moment was the day they

received special permission to lip-sync a performance of the hymn "When I Survey the Wondrous Cross" at the Garden Tomb. Approximately one hundred feet from the tomb is the place some people mark as the ancient Golgotha—the place of the cross. Elder James E. Faust and his wife and Elder Jeffrey R. Holland were present. Jerold Ottley stood in front of the open tomb directing the choir. Whenever they would break for a few minutes, someone would come to me and say, "Ask Brother Ottley if we can really sing it. We want to really sing it." So I was bold enough to go down and whisper the request to Brother Ottley. Then I heard him say, "Choir, this is the last take. Really sing it." To those who were there, the difference is audible on the CD and visible on the videotape. The last stanza builds in unison before breaking into harmony:

> *Were the whole realm of nature mine,*
> *That were a present far too small,*
> *Love [meaning Christ's love] so amazing, so divine,*
> *Demands my soul, my life, my all.*[34]

The choir sang "all" at full volume in harmony before ending the song with one glorious "AMEN!"

I believe that song was heard for a half-mile in every direction. And I wished that Elder Hunter had been there. It could not have happened without him.

A Last Look

I once took Elder James E. Faust and Elder Jeffrey R. Holland on a tour of Jerusalem and showed them many different perspectives of the area. The last stop on our tour was a place that presented a magnificent view of the center. Elder Faust said, in a voice I cannot forget, "Jeff, if ever Brother

Hunter gets back, for pity's sake, bring him here. Bring him here." Elder Hunter was ill and unable to join us. At that time I didn't know that I would be director of the center, but I remembered the request. And when the time came that Elder Hunter could return for a visit, I made arrangements to take him (again with Elder Faust) to that same place. Driving past the university and along the road, I asked Elder Hunter to close his eyes. He responded, "Don't close yours, Truman!"

I had arranged in advance to have every light in the Jerusalem Center turned on. We arrived at our destination, the very place where Elder Faust had made his request. I reminded Elder Faust of the conversation and then said to Elder Hunter, "Now, open your eyes." They wept. I wept. I have never forgotten the powerful, silent testimony given to me that night of Elder Hunter's love for Jesus Christ.

When Elder Hunter came to visit the Jerusalem Center with Mayor Kollek, who had never seen the inside of the building—in fact, the mayor had deliberately avoided visiting the center lest there be adverse publicity—we were able to sing for them the song, "The Holy City." The lyrics to the last chorus are:

Jerusalem! Jerusalem!
Sing for the night is o'er!
Hosanna in the highest!
Hosanna for evermore![35]

Though we were, in some ways, intimidated even to be in the presence of these great men, I can tell you how Elder Hunter's face looked. I can tell you that his love for Jerusalem was deep because it was the home of the Savior.

CLAIRE AND INIS

In her later years, Claire was bedridden after developing at least two different debilitating diseases—one that affected her nervous system and one that affected her memory. Elder Hunter cared for her ceaselessly. Sometimes the effects of these diseases were such that she would turn on the very people who were there to help her and love her, her husband included. Elder Hunter refused the repeated recommendations of the doctors that she be put into a hospital or a nursing home and instead cared for her himself. When Elder Hunter was introduced at a faculty meeting on BYU's campus, Elder Jeffrey R. Holland spoke of Elder Hunter's five years of devotion to his ailing wife—unmurmuring devotion—which he gave while at the same time bearing the full burden of his responsibilities as a General Authority.

Some years after Claire's death, Elder Hunter was meeting with the Twelve on a Thursday and, after the official business had concluded, asked, "Brethren, how would you feel if I remarried?" Though surprised, each person in turn said that would be fine. Elder Hunter then said, "I'm grateful to hear that. I'm being married this afternoon at two o'clock. None of you is invited. It will be a private service, no reception. President Hinckley will perform the sealing and then we will go away."[36] And so Elder Hunter married his second wife, Inis, and they spent their honeymoon enjoying a Nile cruise. Inis had served as a hostess in the Church Office Building for many years, but had met Elder Hunter many, many years before when he was her stake president in California.

AFFLICTIONS

Elder Hunter suffered a staggering number of afflictions, among them bleeding ulcers, lower back pain, and eventually bone cancer. He underwent surgery, which resulted in semi-paralysis. He exercised everyday at a swimming pool in an attempt to make his paralyzed legs move a little. Eventually, and against all odds, he regained some movement in his legs and was able to walk with braces and two canes or, sometimes, a walker. When he got the mumps at age sixty-nine, he wrote in his journal, "Everyone seems to think it is funny that I have the mumps, but I don't think so. President Kimball says maybe I haven't yet grown up."[37]

For one general conference, a special table was arranged for him and when it was his turn to speak, the ushers simply pushed his wheelchair forward to the table. He said with a twinkle in his eye, "Forgive me if I remain seated while I present these few remarks. It is not by choice that I speak from a wheelchair. I notice that the rest of you seem to enjoy the conference sitting down, so I will follow your example."[38] During another conference, he attempted to stand at the pulpit. He was doing fine until he leaned back about an inch and fell backwards. Instantly Brother Packer and someone else helped him stand back up. President Hunter continued his talk without missing a word. Though he broke three ribs in the fall and sustained a goose egg on the back of his head, he did not complain.

Despite his many health problems, he nevertheless remained tender and active and faithful. Each minor victory that he had in coping with his afflictions was shared by his Brethren and by his dear wife, Inis. His journal entries reflect the ups and downs of his trials: "This was the most quiet day of all. I was home alone. I've had surgery, a heart attack. The next may be a nervous breakdown for not being allowed to do anything." One week later: "Nothing to do. Nothing was done all day." By the end of August: "Becoming unbearable." He finally writes about a red-letter day: "Back to the office, if only for two hours each day. Each weekday morning I get up at 5:30, go for a walk at least a mile. Not because I enjoy it but because the doctors insist."[39]

Knowing what he had been through, one would expect that there would be age lines and wrinkles on Elder Hunter's face, as well as the lines that come from scowling or from constant pain. Yet, looking at pictures of him, even in the last month of his life, there are no such lines. There is something very Christlike about that.

TEACHINGS OF HOWARD W. HUNTER

President Hunter's mandate, which was issued the day he was sustained as President, was to "invite the members of the Church to establish the temple of the Lord as the great symbol of their membership. . . . I would hope that every adult member would be worthy of—and carry—a current temple recommend, even if proximity to a temple does not allow . . . frequent use of it."[40]

He addressed Church Educational System teachers in the Assembly Hall and spoke of not confusing emotionalism for genuine spirituality. He pled for them to be calm in their spirituality and not to be only cheerleaders.[41]

Here are a few one-sentence, brilliant insights:

"While true godly sorrow leads to repentance of sins, our reflections on the past should not be self-debasing nor generate self-doubt."[42]

"God is usually more willing to forgive us than we are willing to forgive ourselves."[43]

"The direction we are moving in is more important than a particular degree of perfection."[44]

"The covenant made with Abraham and his seed was

sealed by the ceremony of circumcision as a sacrament."[45] The Joseph Smith Translation makes it clear that the eight days that should pass before the newborn boy is to be circumcised (as prescribed in the law of Moses) is symbolic of eight years. Not only does that put the responsibility of teaching the child before eight on the parents' shoulders, but it also reminds them that the child must become, in Jewish terms, "a son or daughter of the covenant," and he or she is responsible.

"If Jesus lays his hands upon a marriage, it lives."[46] In other words, don't try to go through life, and especially married life, without Christ.

"The resurrection will again unite the spirit with the body, and the body becomes a spiritual body, one of flesh and bones but quickened by the spirit instead of blood."[47]

"We cannot continue to walk forward when at the same time we are looking backward. . . . The backward glance commences the backward turning, and may be the beginning of our disendowment in the kingdom of God."[48]

"[Christ] knows perfectly every problem through which we pass because he chose to bear the full weight of all our troubles and our pains."[49]

"To judge righteously is to judge with fairness, compassion, and charity."[50]

"The meek shall inherit the earth, a pretty impressive corporate takeover—and done *without* intimidation!"[51]

Late in his life, President Hunter gave a great sermon in the Tabernacle about the opening and closing of doors. "Adversity," he said, "touches many, many lives. What makes the difference is how we accept it. It's important to know it's all within the purposes of the Lord, whatever they are for us. If we can submit ourselves to that, we can go forward in faith and understanding. . . . I've learned patience. I've learned to have confidence. I think I've learned something about the principle of faith. I've learned compassion. Those 30 years, as far as I'm personally concerned, have been a refining influence in my life."[52]

15

GORDON B. HINCKLEY

Both Gordon B. Hinckley's father, Bryant S. Hinckley, and his grandfather, Ira Hinckley, were strong members of the Church. They were among the Saints who found their way across the plains and then settled in the central portions of Utah. The Hinckley history is connected to a famous place, Cove Fort, which has been turned into a memorial and visitors' center. The fort is a small rectangle, about eighteen feet high, and was built not only for protection, but also to encompass the totality of their culture. The wife of Thomas L. Kane summarized life at Cove Fort when she observed the following things: Here were women who were refined; here was a telegraph station constantly bringing in newswire messages in Morse code from New York; here were people who were teaching and educating each other; and here were remarkable signs of culture—pianos, other musical instruments, and choice books.[1]

I have heard it said that the people at Cove Fort were "a ragtag bunch," but Bryant S. Hinckley once said in a sermon, "Every jack man of them could stand up and say 'I know God lives,' and 'I know Jesus Christ is our Redeemer,' and 'I know Joseph Smith was a Prophet,' and when they said it, it shook the earth. They were men and women of fiber and testimony."[2] Someone said that when a famous Jewish rabbi prayed, "the water in the barrel trembled."[3] Well, when the men of Cove Fort testified, it was as if the ground on which they stood shook. That is the quality of the people and their faith.

Bryant S. Hinckley soon distinguished himself in his quest for education; he held degrees in business and soon was dean of LDS Business College. During that same period, he was recruited as a writer for the Church, and for twenty-five years he served on the General Board of the Young Men's Mutual Improvement Association. It is said that no one wrote more manuals than he did. Later, manuals were created and refined by committees, but in those days one person would write a course of study for an assigned class.

Brother Hinckley had a gift for writing and teaching—he amassed a great wealth of stories about the early history of the Church. He also served for a long time as the president of Liberty Stake, one of the three largest stakes in the Salt Lake Valley. The average membership of his stake was 18,000 to 20,000 members. Yet even with tremendous responsibility and the burden of counseling all those people, he was a family man.

His first wife died suddenly. They were driving to Provo one day and she began to feel unwell. Within two days, she was gone. He then married Ada Bitner, who inherited the task of raising his eight children. (Ada eventually had five children of her own, of whom Gordon was the oldest.) Gordon and his younger brother, Sherman, were nearly inseparable. Because of their relationship, Ada sometimes referred to Gordon and Sherman as the "twins," even though they didn't look alike.

Gordon B. Hinckley grew up in a home of nurturing, loving, and even tender care. But rock-ribbed assurance of the gospel is not developed by osmosis. The first time he felt through the Spirit a certainty of the truth of the Restoration was when, as a mere boy of twelve, a deacon, he reluctantly attended a stake priesthood meeting. At the meeting the men all stood up and sang "Praise to the Man." And Gordon said, "There came into my heart a conviction that the man of whom they sang was really a prophet of God."[4] That was a crucial, defining moment in his life.

"THE MOST STINGING REBUKE"

Gordon was a typical boy in a typical grade school and involved in the typical kinds of mischief—dipping the pigtails of a girl in a bottle of ink, for example. But when he joined a group who went on strike and didn't show up for school one day, he crossed the line. His mother the next day wrote a note to the principal: "Dear Mr. Stearns, Please excuse Gordon's absence yesterday. His action was simply an impulse to follow the crowd." Gordon's comment was that "it was the most stinging rebuke she ever gave me. . . . I determined then and there that I would never do anything on the basis of simply following the crowd."[5]

In one of his sermons, he talked about raising children and said, "You don't need to beat your children, you only need to talk to them."[6] He made it a principle that corporal punishment will only intensify rebellion and bitterness. Better to use words than the rod. His parents were Exhibit A of that principle.

Gordon was frail in his boyhood and had severe hay fever, asthma, and allergies. The doctors recommended clean, fresh air, so his father built a little cottage at the mouth of Millcreek Canyon where the family lived during the summers. During the winters, the family moved back to the city, which was hard on Gordon's allergies. In those days, homes were heated with coal furnaces, and that meant a kind of miasma coated the atmosphere and covered clean, white snowfalls with soot. Not only that, but the wallpaper of the house had to be cleaned every spring with a special chemical preparation.

When he was eleven years old, Gordon B. Hinckley received his patriarchal blessing. The patriarch said something remarkable. He said that this boy would bear his witness and testimony to the nations of the earth.[7] When Gordon B. Hinckley as a young man returned from his mission to England, he had borne his testimony in four world capitals—London, Paris, Washington, and Berlin—and he figured his blessing had been fulfilled. Now he has borne his testimony in practically every major city worldwide and in many rural communities. His blessing was literally fulfilled.

An additional note: Gordon's father had been given a blessing that promised that not only would he achieve greatness in the Lord's service, but also that his posterity would do likewise, and that the name of Hinckley would be known (and praised) to the ends of the earth. That blessing is also fulfilled.

AN "APPRENTICESHIP IN DOUBT"

The Great Depression wasn't just about failing banks and a ruined economy. It was also psychological and spiritual depression, and more than one person in this country thought of suicide. In that dark era, Gordon was in the midst of his university schooling when he experienced what could be called an "apprenticeship in doubt."[8] Some people are not disposed, spiritually and temperamentally, to raise the ultimate questions about life. They somehow live from day to day and manage to keep going. But Gordon was studying ancient Greek literature and philosophy, along with British poetry and literature, and was asking himself the hard questions. Why do some people suffer? Why do faithful people in the Church not prosper? Have we truly been given a full restoration? How do we cope with this depression, which has devastated not just our own country, but the world? Thankfully, he had the wisdom to talk with his father. He was not a dogmatist answering all questions with a quick, clipped response and then expecting conformity. He was, instead, a person who listened, sympathized, and counseled. Over the year or two of Gordon's college career, that continuing association made a great difference.

Three educators were instrumental in developing Gordon's skill with language and literature, which was his major. First, there was a bright—but strict—grammarian at the University of Utah who taught him how to diagram sentences and how to utilize the intricacies of grammar in writing. Second was Louis Zucker, a brilliant Jewish scholar who had mastered *The Iliad* and *The Odyssey* in Greek. He knew Homer inside and out, and he taught in a way that required meticulous responses. The third teacher expanded Gordon's interest from classical languages into some of the sciences, encouraging him to round out his liberal arts studies with anthropology and sociology—a remarkable combination. He dreamed of attending Columbia University, which was renowned for its English department, but events guided his life in another direction.

Under that rigorous tutelage, he learned to love language. He has often said to missionaries, "If you be called to a foreign language mission, you will be better equipped if you have studied the language. If called to an English-speaking mission, you will understand your own language better."[9] Those ideas reflect his own experience.

In the end, his very impressive mastery of communication was both studied and inherited. He had gifts from his birth and from his environment; his mother, after all, had been a teacher and a master of precision herself. His literary skills were even noted by Prime Minister Margaret Thatcher when she visited Utah and Brigham Young University. She admired not only President Hinckley's skill with words, but also his understanding of Wordsworth, Tennyson, and the great British poets. The Church has truly benefited from his skill and love of language.

"FORGET YOURSELF"

Gordon B. Hinckley often speaks of the time of his initial call to serve as a missionary to England, specifically Preston, as "the bottom of the Depression."[10] It is well known in the Church that he went on his mission in part because of the faith and commitment of his parents, and in part because he had two close friends who accepted mission calls at the same time. One of them was George Homer Durham, who later distinguished himself in political science, was a university president, and finished his career as an Assistant to the Council of the Twelve and as an historian at the Church Historical Department.

Because Elder Hinckley went partly out of social reasons, he had some misgivings about whether he would succeed as a missionary. He became discouraged in the first few weeks and wrote home, saying, "I don't think what I'm doing can justify the cost. I think I should come home." And his father simply wrote back, "Dear Gordon, I have your recent letter. I have only one suggestion: forget yourself and go to work."[11] That was a defining moment in his life. He realized that he had been selfish and even self-serving. From then on things changed and Elder Hinckley distinguished himself in the work of teaching and preaching.

He was called to serve in the mission office under the tutelage of a great man and mission president, Joseph F. Merrill, who was also a member of the Quorum of the Twelve. Brother Merrill was an austere man, a scientist trained in engineering, and a man whose habits were very modest. The mission home was an unpretentious bungalow, but when Brother Merrill saw it for the first time, he wrote home and said simply, "We'll have to sell it. It is too lavish."[12] Brother Merrill's role as a disciplinarian and his care as a mission president were a good influence on Elder Hinckley, becoming part of his admired ideal pattern of leadership.

WORKING FOR THE FIRST PRESIDENCY

It would seem logical that after Elder Hinckley's mission he would return home, finish his education, and receive his degrees. That was not the way it was to be. Joseph F. Merrill was convinced that changes needed to be made in the distribution of missionary materials, in the preparation of tracts, and even in the superstructure of the mission organization. He wrote down his recommendations and charged Elder Hinckley to take that report to the First Presidency. It was a daunting assignment.

After Elder Hinckley finished his mission and a brief tour of Europe (which was the standard practice in those days), he made an appointment with President Heber J. Grant, David O. McKay, and others. He was given fifteen minutes to make his report, but the meeting actually lasted an hour and fifteen minutes. He did his best and then breathed a sigh of relief. Only two days later, a phone call came from President McKay: "We have organized a committee consisting of six members of the Twelve . . . to address the needs you outlined. We would like to invite you to come and work with that committee."[13] The committee became the Church Radio, Publicity, and Mission Literature Committee and was designed to be the clearinghouse of all attempts to communicate the gospel through all kinds of media.

Brother Hinckley's first office was in the catacombs of the Church Administration Building. He was sometimes called "The Slave" because he would emerge from the basement office looking like one. From his efforts, though, came a set of records for radio and selected uses called *The Fulness of Times*. These were huge wax records that had to be played on a special turntable with a special needle. If the rate of speed changed because the motor was weak, then so did the inflections of the speaker. The records dramatized the history of the Church and were circulated widely. Gordon B. Hinckley's fledgling efforts were an acorn that has grown to be an oak. Gordon B. Hinckley has been involved in publicity and the outreach of the Church ever since.

When the Second World War broke out, Brother Hinckley was rejected from the service. Classifications were required for all young recruits to evaluate their health and their preparation for military service. The lowest ranking was "4F"; if you were ranked "1A," then the joke was that you could hear thunder and see lightning and you were qualified to enter the military.

Brother Hinckley gathered around him writers who were

skilled and who could communicate clearly, and they went to work on developing tracts and books. In 1947, Brother Hinckley authored *What of the Mormons?* which was his attempt, first, to briefly tell the story of the Mormons, including the epic trek west; second, to outline the fundamental precepts of the Restoration; and third, to clearly portray the Church not as a primitive or provincial sect looking to escape into a private cloister, but as a thriving church seeking to bring the gospel of Jesus Christ into all levels of culture and all areas of the world. It is a brilliant book that had a wide distribution and multiple printings.

"MY DARLING"

In 1937 Gordon married his eternal companion, Marjorie Pay. He wrote in retrospect that he couldn't believe they had the courage to get married on a shoestring.[14] His salary from the Church was $65 a month, and he earned an additional $35 a month as a seminary teacher. A hundred dollars then would do more than it does now, but with the crunch of raising a family, it was not enough.

In an effort to improve his situation, he took a part-time job with the Denver and Rio Grande Western Railroad, one of the two major railroads that went through Salt Lake City. Their motto was "Through the Rockies, not around them," and their main headquarters were in Denver. Brother Hinckley correlated the train movements and schedules of the freight trains as they passed through Salt Lake City. He was adept at his job and was eventually offered a full-time position that would require him to move to Denver. It was wartime, and he wanted to assist the war effort, which included keeping the lines of transportation moving. He moved with his family to

Denver for a year; then, when the war was over, they returned to Salt Lake City and Church employment.

President Hinckley has always been a devoted husband and father; he was married to his beloved wife for nearly seventy years. He wrote a letter to his wife that was published in her unique biography, *Glimpses into the Life and Heart of Marjorie Pay Hinckley.* The editors of the book have said in my hearing, "If we had only one letter from President Hinckley to describe his love for his family and his sensitive perception and admiration for his wife and children, that one letter tells it all." And so it does. It is a classic. The letter begins "My darling," and he goes on to say, "It is now more than sixty years since we entered the Salt Lake Temple, there to be married for eternity. . . . I knew what I was getting into, and it has all turned out as I had hoped it would."[15]

Before Sister Hinckley's death, President Hinckley said that he had recently sat near her and looked at her hands—old hands reflecting the results of a long life of hard work, and couldn't imagine what his life would have been like without her.[16]

Underscoring his commitment to family, in the most lucid and pointed words, he issued with his Brethren "The Family: A Proclamation to the World." Significantly, he first announced it in a women's conference, demonstrating his recognition of the crucial roles and influence of women and mothers. If heeded, the proclamation may stem the tide of a collapse of family values that is like an epidemic worldwide.

ASIAN MINISTRY AND THE HONG KONG TEMPLE

There are at least three emphases that President Hinckley seems to have had in his ministry. The first is missionary work.

I once heard him say, "I will do whatever the Brethren ask me to do, but I love missionary work." Another emphasis is that we must retain our converts when we make them. And a third is that we must increase our members' access to temples.

Whenever he speaks about his Asian ministry he uses the word *miracle.* Thirty-five years ago, there was only one LDS meetinghouse in the Philippines. Today there are almost a half million members, plus a temple in Manila. That is a miracle.

Another miracle is the Hong Kong Temple. Many of the converts in Hong Kong were young people who had first put their lives at risk for freedom and only then were prepared to receive the gospel. These young people swam from Red China to the Kowloon peninsula, knowing the patrol boats would try to stop them, knowing the chances of making it were only one in ten, knowing the stories of death and tragedy and perseverance. They took the chance, and thankfully many of them made it. And when they heard the gospel message, it went deeply into their souls.

The question arose: Once Hong Kong grows from a handful of members to a large number of stakes, how can we build a temple in Hong Kong where every square inch is costly?

President Hinckley had a revelation—he himself has so designated it—that the Hong Kong mission home would become the locus of the temple, not on the ground floor, but on the floor above the offices with the baptismal font in the basement. In 1996, President Hinckley dedicated the Hong Kong China Temple.

"I FEEL AT HOME HERE"

Many members who have received baptism and the gift of the Holy Ghost, who are participating fully in Church life and live in the shadow of a temple, often cannot understand what it is like for converts who have to sell a car or a house in order to make one trip to the temple. But President Hinckley understands. When he travels around the world, during his long hours in-flight, he studies maps and globes, longitudes and latitudes, populations and demographics. He is looking for a way that a temple will be only a day's travel from every member of the Church, no matter where a given individual lives. Traveling a full day can still be a severe hardship, but President Hinckley wants an equalization of the privilege of temple worship for all Saints, whether they are lifelong members or recent converts. And he is not thinking only of providing members with one visit to the temple; he is thinking of work for their forebears and the need for many visits.

When he was traveling to Ghana, West Africa (as only one illustration), he stopped at Halifax, Nova Scotia, where the people in the Maritime Provinces have struggled to support a branch and then, eventually, a district. There were some two thousand people in a local hall when President Hinckley arrived. After the closing prayer, President Hinckley stood up and said, "Brothers and sisters, I don't want to leave. I feel at home here. Brothers and sisters, if you will bring into the Church [a certain number] of converts, there will be a temple in Halifax, Nova Scotia."[17] The crowd wept with joy. Those conditions have been fulfilled, and there is a temple in Halifax.

Not only has President Hinckley sought to take temples to many lands, but he has been instrumental in making the temple ceremonies available in many languages. It was under his direction that film was introduced in the temple endowment. The great power of audio translation and the great medium of film has opened the door to people throughout the world to receive the gospel and the temple blessings in their own language.

President Boyd K. Packer has said, "We accept the responsibility to preach the gospel to every person on earth. And if the question is asked, 'You mean you are out to convert the entire world?' the answer is, 'Yes. We will try to reach every living soul.'"[18]

President Howard W. Hunter was asked once, under the lights of reporters, "Why do you build temples?"

He replied, "The purpose of the temple is to reunite the family of man."[19] He was referring to the mission of Elijah and to the power available to seal couples and their children into eternal families. That is the charge President Hinckley carries forward.

In the late 1990s, President Hinckley received inspiration that temples designed to accommodate smaller numbers could be built on land already owned for stake houses or on adjacent property. They could have temple presidents who would have to serve only two or three days a week. They would not have the expense of a laundry or the administrative chores of a cafeteria. President Hinckley realized that it was possible for the highest ordinances of the kingdom to be given to people in remote areas, and his vision is rapidly becoming a reality all over the world. More than half of the temples now in operation were dedicated during the presidency of Gordon B. Hinckley—and many more are planned. And of course, the blessings of his efforts will become exponential.

PERSONALITY AND CHARACTER TRAITS

Some of President Hinckley's qualities have become so well known, they define his personality.

Optimism and humor. President Hinckley, from the days of the Depression, ironically, has been an optimist. His faith enables him to see a way through. He gives sermons in which he says not to be a "pickle sucker."[20] That is a graphic way of describing people who love to speak sour things, and their sour personalities are depressing. President Hinckley is certainly not "a pickle sucker."

With optimism comes humor, and President Hinckley has managed to use humor effectively in the service of the kingdom. Once, in a somewhat hostile setting, surrounded by world-class reporters and journalists and stuffy television personalities, Mike Wallace mentioned that President Hinckley was only eight years older than he was. President Hinckley said, "And here I thought we were the same age, Mike." Everybody in the room laughed and applauded. Mike Wallace, who was equally amused, had thought he had come to hear an old man who wouldn't have any right opinions on any current questions. Instead he was so intrigued, he scheduled an interview on *60 Minutes* with President Hinckley.[21]

His energetic optimism is also often evident in his closing remarks of general conference. The prophet can say whatever he chooses to say, but often President Hinckley closes with the idea that we need to be a little more faithful, we need to be a little more active, we need to be a little more generous, we need to be a little more kind.[22] That is the mentality of a man who has put in effort through long hours and who recognizes that it is important to say to the Saints in the harness and working on all twelve cylinders—a little more, a little more weight on the pedal, a little more dedication. If we are good, we can be better.

Dedication to the kingdom. President Hinckley has an astounding, all-encompassing vision of the mission of the

Church. Early on it was clear to him that the kingdom would roll forth under its divine mandate and that nothing could stop it. While he has frequently warned us that there will continue to be plenty of opposition, he also knows that nothing can stop the Church. He has often quoted the famous lines from Joseph Smith's Wentworth Letter: "No unhallowed hand can stop this work from progressing. . . . Armies may combine, mobs may assemble, . . . but the truth of God will go forth nobly until every ear shall hear, every nation shall be visited, until the Great Jehovah shall say, 'It is done.'"[23] He truly believes those words. We will never find President Hinckley on the side of doom and gloom.

A little-known fact about President Hinckley is that while he was studying English, he wanted to be an architect. What has he done with that propensity? Three hundred fifty chapels have been built each year during most of his mature life. He has been involved personally in the planning, groundbreaking, and dedication (or rededication) of more than one hundred temples and counting. He is responsible for the landscaping and beautification project that transformed the Hotel Utah into the Joseph Smith Memorial Building. Another achievement is the huge Conference Center north of Temple Square. President Hinckley has become virtually an architect, an engineer, and a builder.

Punctuality. Another personality trait is President Hinckley's effective use of time and his punctuality. His father arose at five o'clock every morning and insisted that the children arise, too, for their chores. They would work around the house and on the farm until noon; then the rest of the day was theirs. He does not waste time. For example, when he visited the Holy Land, in or out of meetings he did not dally. He often carried a small tape recorder with him and would record his impressions even as he walked through a holy site or through a museum or to a vantage point.

Financial acumen. He also has solid financial skills from long training. On his desk is a little replica of the "Widow's Mite," which he says reminds him that every penny that comes into this Church's coffers is sacred and may have been earned by mothers on hands and knees scrubbing floors; and therefore, he cannot tolerate waste and unnecessary duplication and extravagance.[24]

Years ago, he told a story to the BYU faculty of a woman who had lived in a small house on the west side of Salt Lake City. She managed to raise a family alone by doing housework. When all her children were married and moved away, she discovered that she had saved enough money over the previous fifty years to either upgrade or move into a new house. Instead, she went to President Hinckley, who was then head of the Church's missionary committee, and committed all her funds to the missionary work of the Church.

He said, "But Sister, you deserve what you have so well earned, you deserve a better home."

She said, "Oh, I'm used to my house, I'm comfortable enough. I want to serve the Lord."

President Hinckley shook his finger at the employees and faculty at BYU and said, "Don't you waste that widow's savings."[25] That story touched many hearts.

During President Hinckley's administration the Church has given a staggering $138 million in humanitarian care around the world. He personally traveled to Honduras and other disaster areas when the people there were in need. He arranged for the Church to make shipments of every kind to help the suffering abroad.

Our relatively small Church, with our limited resources

and only one real source of income—the law of tithing and fast offerings—has added the category "Humanitarian Aid" to the tithing receipt. What happens to the donations? Every penny goes to the people it is most intended to help. Virtually every other charity, benevolent organization, or foundation has overhead costs, and sometimes when money is raised for a certain cause, sticky fingers along the way prevent its delivery to the little, starving children or those for whom it is intended. But President Hinckley has seen to it that the humanitarian aid reaches those in real need. Not only are we carrying our own load and taking care of our own, but we are also taking care of those who are not our own, because the world seems to have shrunk and our neighbor can be as close as next door or as far away as South Africa.

Problem solver. President Hinckley is a problem solver. Elder Russell M. Nelson said, "We sit with him each Thursday. We throw curve balls and hard balls to him, difficult problems. And he fields them all and makes wise decisions. He is brilliant at decision-making."

His colleagues and Brethren say that decision-making for President Hinckley is a two-step process. He will gather the facts, ask the questions, probe and analyze the situation. Only then will he place the decision before the Lord. "Sometimes," one of the Brethren said to me, "he gathers so much data that the decision becomes inevitable."[26]

For example, President Hinckley and Elder Jeffrey R. Holland traveled to Ghana, West Africa, to discuss a possible temple. The faithful converts in Ghana had to travel days and sacrifice much to attend the nearest temple. They wanted a temple in Ghana. Three men met with President Hinckley and for thirty minutes he grilled them with questions: "Where will the water come from? What are the road accesses? How far away are the people? What will be the longest distance traveled?" He raised endless objections and questions to the project until the Saints must have felt like he was their adversary.

Finally President Hinckley turned to Elder Holland and said, "Brother Jeffrey, what do you think?"

And Elder Holland, who had been listening to the discussion, put his head down a minute and then said, "President Hinckley, I think the Lord wants it here."

President Hinckley said, "We will do it."[27]

The Ghanaians were no doubt surprised at how quickly he could go from relentless questioning to a decision.

On the other hand, President Hinckley has tried to guard against being too preoccupied with generalized statistics and with reports. He once stood at a pulpit with a large stack of paperwork on it and said, "That's what's got to change in the Church."[28] He will gather facts and reports as necessary, but he also has a matching concern for individuals, which has grown out of his love for Christ. He has said repeatedly in his teachings, "All of this is important, but more important still is the spiritual life of the individual. That's what I'm concerned most about. That's what the Lord is most concerned about."[29]

I had a personal experience with President Hinckley's wisdom and trust in appointed leaders. When I was a mission president, I once had a case I thought was beyond my ability to solve. I laid out the problem to then-Elder Hinckley, expecting him to say, "You put that person on an airplane an hour from now."

Instead he said in his quiet, patient voice, "Well, President Madsen, we notice you don't solve many problems by changing geography."

I said, "Elder Hinckley, are you saying you want me to solve this here at this level?"

"That's what I'm saying," he replied. "The Lord bless you."

Loyalty. He demonstrated loyalty to the prophets, to those who have preceded him, by often serving in a "no-man's land." When he became a counselor to President Kimball, he was careful not to overstep his bounds even though both President Kimball and President Romney were infirm, bedridden, and unable to fully function under the tremendous pressure of their callings. Such a situation has happened before in the Church, but never on such a scale. So President Hinckley acted as a copilot. He said that if the pilot is not able to fly the plane, then there is another system in place—a copilot and a backup.[30] The Lord has so organized his kingdom.

His discourses on the roles of bishops and of counselors are classics. But it has been said that "hell" could be defined as having responsibility without authority.[31] In a way that was the dilemma President Hinckley found himself in. He either had to table or postpone some decisions until a new president was called, or he had to make decisions without the full involvement of the presidency. Sometimes he had to preside in general conference alone. It was a lonely and difficult assignment, and he was sometimes the object of attacks and criticism.

And yet President Hinckley was supported and protected. I know of a dear sister in the Church who had long sustained the Brethren but who was deeply troubled about the situation President Hinckley was in. She had a dream one night and the conclusion of the dream was this: "Even though you think he cannot go for one more day, I will be with him, and he can."

Compassion and humility. He has also shown a gift of Christlike compassion. When mission presidents were called during his time on the missionary committee, he offered three, one-sentence bits of counsel: "Follow your impressions," "Read the Book of Mormon," and "When making decisions of judgment, err, if you must err, on the side of mercy."[32]

He has repeatedly warned the brethren of the Church in priesthood meetings that they must be filled with persuasion, longsuffering, gentleness, and meekness (see D&C 121:41) or their role as patriarchs and leaders in the Church will be diminished, if not taken away.[33] A gentle man himself, he has pled with brethren not to shout and lose their tempers, with sisters to control their own feelings, and above all, he has pled for peace—peace in the home, peace in the heart, and peace through our relationship with Jesus Christ.

President Hinckley's sermons warn against pride, arrogance, and intellectual egotism.[34] President Grant said of flattery, "It's devil talk, devil talk. Don't listen."[35] President Hinckley says, "Adulation is poison."[36] He once told a story of a man who had given a great talk and was impressed with himself. When he was called another time to speak, he marched up to the pulpit full of confidence, but without the Spirit. He stumbled, fumbled, and finally left the stand confused and upset. President Hinckley said to him, "Brother, if you had gone up the way you came down, you would have gone down the way you came up."

"GOD BLESS YOU FOREVER"

President Hinckley, as one example among many, was involved in the conversion of a man from California who had been a member of the state supreme court. He came to feel that his life was empty, without any real thread or direction. He began to investigate alternative religions. Eventually he decided to work on a graduate degree at the Divinity School at Yale. While at Yale he saw a copy of the Book of Mormon and received permission from his faculty to attend Brigham Young University for a summer session.

He studied and became interested in the Church, but had never attended a single Mormon meeting. His wife, who was a member, one day asked him to attend. After the meeting, he was noticeably silent. She finally asked him about his impressions of the meeting. He said, "They were all like little children . . ." She gasped and thought he was disappointed. He was silent for about five minutes, but then, as they were turning off the freeway, he finished his sentence: " . . . just as Christ would want them to be."

He humbled himself, joined the Church, and later took his wife to the temple. President Hinckley performed the sealing. What a privilege and blessing to dress in pure white and to be in that glorious room appointed for the highest ordinance in the kingdom of God. I will never forget the sweet expression on President Hinckley's face after he spoke the words so loaded with promise and love. When he took their hands and said, "God bless you forever," the couple knew precisely what that meant.

"THE CHURCH WILL CONTINUE TO GROW"

At nine o'clock one morning, the word went out that President Hunter had passed away. President Hinckley's son tried to call home. He tried the house—the line was busy. He tried the office—the line was busy. He tried the family's private line—the line was busy. He tried again. After several minutes, his father answered and his son said, "Dad? Is there anything I can do?"

"Yes," replied President Hinckley, "pray for me. God bless you."[37]

At the press conference, the reporters asked barbed, pressing questions. He handled them with grace and dignity.

"What do you think is the next direction of the Church?"

"The Church will continue to grow."

"What are you doing about the problems that are arising around the world?"

"The Church will go where it is invited. The Church will go through the front door."[38]

In his efforts to open doors he has likewise managed to teach the gospel in a graceful way, in a way that did not arouse antipathy. But always without compromise. The Church is in 160 countries and counting, and President Hinckley has reportedly said that he will be satisfied only if we double our convert rate.[39]

Once again the Lord has raised up a man—a son, a brother, a father—to serve as our exemplar and as our prophet.

As of this writing, Gordon B. Hinckley is not yet our oldest prophet (David O. McKay lived to the age of ninety-six), and he is not the one who served the longest as President of the Church (several served longer). But his influence in the Church and the world has been immeasurable, and, like ripples in a pond, his influence will continue to widen and deepen.

NOTES

CHAPTER ONE: JOSEPH SMITH

1. Joseph Smith, *History of The Church of Jesus Christ of Latter-day Saints,* ed. B. H. Roberts, 2d ed. rev., 7 vols. (Salt Lake City: The Church of Jesus Christ of Latter-day Saints, 1932–51), 6:346.

2. Lucy Mack Smith, *History of Joseph Smith by His Mother,* ed. Preston Nibley (Salt Lake City: Bookcraft, 1979), 82.

3. Smith, *History of Joseph Smith,* 89.

4. Francis M. Gibbons, *Wilford Woodruff: Wondrous Worker, Prophet of God* (Salt Lake City: Deseret Book, 1988), 91.

5. Joseph Smith, *Personal Writings of Joseph Smith,* ed. Dean C. Jessee (Salt Lake City: Deseret Book, 1984), 476; *History of the Church,* 4:603.

6. See Lyman O. Littlefield, "The Prophet Joseph Smith in Zion's Camp," *Juvenile Instructor* 27 (15 January 1892): 57.

7. *History of the Church*, 2:338.

8. *History of the Church,* 6:346.

9. See John Riggs, *Autobiography, 1812–1880*, LDS Church Archives, Salt Lake City, Utah.

10. Wandle Mace, "Autobiography of Wandle Mace," BYU Special Collections, Harold B. Lee Library, Provo, Utah, 207.

11. Brigham Young, in *Journal of Discourses,* 26 vols. (Liverpool: Latter-day Saints' Book Depot, 1854–86), 7:289.

12. Joseph Young, "Enoch and His City," in *History of the Organization of the Seventies* (Salt Lake City: Deseret News Steam Printing Establishment, 1878), 9, quoted in Robert L. Millet and Kent P. Jackson, eds., *Studies in*

Scripture, vol. 2: The Pearl of Great Price (Salt Lake City: Randall Book Co., 1985), 132.

13. See this report of President Snow under the entry 1–1–1892, in *Diary of Abraham H. Cannon,* 16:30. See also Dennis B. Horne, ed., *An Apostle's Record: The Journals of Abraham H. Cannon* (Clearfield, Utah: Gnolaum Books, 2004), 229.

14. *History of the Church,* 1:467.

15. Andrew F. Ehat and Lyndon W. Cook, eds., *The Words of Joseph Smith* (Provo, Utah: BYU Religious Studies Center, 1980), 418.

16. Brigham Young said the same thing of the Kirtland Temple; see *Journal of Discourses,* 2:31.

17. *History of the Church,* 3:415.

18. Ibid., 6:478.

19. B. H. Roberts, *The Gospel and Man's Relationship to Deity,* 11th ed. (Salt Lake City: Deseret Book, 1966), 279.

20. Portions published in *Our Lineage . . . : Courses for first year genealogical classes* (Salt Lake City: Genealogical Society of Utah, 1938).

21. *History of the Church,* 6:594.

22. "An Interesting Journal," *Juvenile Instructor* 21 (15 April 1886): 122.

23. George Q. Cannon, *Life of Joseph Smith, the Prophet* (Salt Lake City: Deseret Book, 1958), 447–50.

24. Horace Cummings, "Conspiracy of Nauvoo," *Contributor* 5 (April 1884): 254–55.

25. *History of the Church,* 6:278.

26. "George Laub Autobiography," BYU Special Collections, Harold B. Lee Library, Provo, Utah, 19.

27. *History of the Church,* 6:88–95.

28. Ibid., 6:508.

29. Ibid., 6:545–46.

30. Truman G. Madsen, *Joseph Smith the Prophet* (Salt Lake City: Bookcraft, 1989), 117, 179.

31. Joseph Smith, *Teachings of the Prophet Joseph Smith,* comp. Joseph Fielding Smith (Salt Lake City: Deseret Book, 1976), 268.

32. Cyrus Wheelock to B. H. Roberts. See "Papers of B. H. Roberts," LDS Church Archives, Salt Lake City, Utah.

33. Ibid.

34. *History of the Church,* 6:550.

35. Ibid., 6:597–98.

36. Ibid., 6:598.

37. See *History of the Church,* 6:520; *Teachings of the Prophet Joseph Smith,* 376–77; B. H. Roberts, *The Rise and Fall of Nauvoo* (Salt Lake City: Bookcraft, 1965), 291.

38. "Autobiography of John Lowe Butler," BYU Special Collections, Harold B. Lee Library, Provo, Utah, 28.

39. *Hymns of The Church of Jesus Christ of Latter-day Saints* (Salt Lake City: The Church of Jesus Christ of Latter-day Saints, 1985), no. 29.

40. *History of the Church,* 7:110.

41. Ibid., 6:626.

42. Brigham Young speech, July 14, 1861, LDS Church Archives, Salt Lake City, Utah.

43. Edward H. Stiles, *Recollections and Sketches of Notable Lawyers and Public Men of Early Iowa* (Des Moines, Iowa: Homestead Publishing, 1916), 26.

44. *History of the Church,* 6:608.

45. Ibid., 7:102.

46. Ibid., 7:103.

47. Willard Richards, "Two Minutes in Jail," in Roberts, *Rise and Fall,* 317.

48. Cannon, *Life of Joseph Smith, the Prophet,* 525.

49. *History of the Church,* 6:621.

50. Recollection of J. Winter Smith (grandson of Samuel Smith) to the author.

51. Ibid.

52. Dix W. Price, "I Met Joseph Smith," *Brigham Young University Speeches of the Year*, April 18, 1962, 8.

53. See *History of the Church,* 6:554–55.

54. Ibid., 6:555.

55. Journal History of The Church of Jesus Christ of Latter-day Saints, June 24, 1844; cited in Madsen, *Joseph Smith the Prophet,* 126.

56. B. H. Roberts, *A Comprehensive History of the Church of Jesus Christ of Latter-day Saints,* 6 vols. (Salt Lake City: The Church of Jesus Christ of Latter-day Saints, 1965), 2:287; *History of the Church,* 6:616.

57. Quoted by Don L. Searle, "Latter-day Saints in Canada," in "News of the Church," *Ensign*, July 1987, 79.

58. Joseph Smith, "Church History," *Times and Seasons* 3 (1 March 1842): 709.

59. Ibid.

60. See John Henry Evans, *Joseph Smith: An American Prophet* (New York: Macmillan, 1933), 9.

CHAPTER TWO: BRIGHAM YOUNG

1. Brigham Young, *Journal of Discourses,* 26 vols. (Liverpool: Latter-day Saints' Book Depot, 1854–86), 10:298.

2. See Heber J. Grant, in Conference Report, June 1919, 7.

3. Brigham Young, "History of Brigham Young," *Millennial Star* 25 (11 July 1863): 439; B. H. Roberts, *A Comprehensive History of the Church of Jesus Christ of Latter-day Saints,* 6 vols. (Salt Lake City: The Church of Jesus Christ of Latter-day Saints, 1965), 1:289.

4. See Orson F. Whitney, *Life of Heber C. Kimball* (Salt Lake City: Bookcraft, 1967), 15–17.

5. Quoted by Brigham Young, in *Journal of Discourses,* 1:313.

6. Quoted by Wilford Woodruff, in Conference Report, April 1898, 57.

7. Leonard J. Arrington, *Brigham Young: American Moses* (New York: Alfred A. Knopf, 1985), 45–46.

8. Joseph Smith, *History of The Church of Jesus Christ of Latter-day Saints,* ed. B. H. Roberts, 2d ed. rev., 7 vols. (Salt Lake City: The Church of Jesus Christ of Latter-day Saints, 1932–51), 7:472.

9. Ibid., 2:107.

10. See Zora Smith Jarvis, *Ancestry, Biography and Family of George A. Smith* (Provo: Brigham Young University Press, 1962), 48–51.

11. *Journal of Discourses,* 2:10; B. H. Roberts, "Brigham Young: A Character Sketch," *Improvement Era* 6 (June 1903), 567.

12. *History of the Church,* 2:182.

13. See Leon R. Hartshorn, Dennis A. Wright, and Craig J. Ostler, eds., *The Doctrine and Covenants, a Book of Answers: The 25th Annual Sidney B. Sperry Symposium* (Salt Lake City: Deseret Book, 1996), 18.

14. *History of the Church,* 2:181; Preston Nibley, *Brigham Young: The Man and His Work,* 4th ed. (Salt Lake City: Deseret Book, 1960), 15–16.

15. *Journal of Discourses,* 9:89.

16. *History of the Church,* 5:412.

17. Ibid., 7:233.

18. Heber C. Kimball, *Journal of Heber C. Kimball,* comp. R. B. Thompson (Nauvoo, Ill.: Robinson and Smith, 1840), 66.

19. Stanley B. Kimball, *Heber C. Kimball: Mormon Patriarch and Pioneer* (Urbana: University of Illinois, 1981), 59, 61.

20. *History of the Church,* 7:394.

21. Quoted by Brigham Young, in *Journal of Discourses,* 18:241.

22. *Journal of Discourses,* 3:266.

23. Ibid., 12:102–3.

24. See S. Dilworth Young, *"Here Is Brigham . . . ": Brigham Young, the Years to 1844* (Salt Lake City: Bookcraft, 1964), 299–300. See also Brigham Young, in *Journal of Discourses,* 18:241.

25. Diary of L. John Nuttall, BYU Special Collections, Harold B. Lee Library, Provo, Utah, 1:18–19.

26. "There are thousands of good people in England. . . . They will flock to Zion." "Journal of Edward Stevenson," LDS Church Archives, Salt Lake City, Utah, 22.

27. Whitney, *Life of Heber C. Kimball,* 188.

28. James B. Allen, Ronald Esplin, and David Whittaker, *Men with a Mission* (Salt Lake City: Deseret Book, 1992), 49–51.

29. A comment made by the Director of the Massachusetts Historical Society, in *Proceedings of the Massachusetts Historical Society* 68 (October 1944–May 1947): 286 n.

30. "I have known legal men all my life. Joseph Smith was the best lawyer that I have ever known in all my life." Cited in *Journal of Jesse N. Smith* (Salt Lake City: Deseret News Press, 1953), 456.

31. *Journal of Discourses,* 1:40; 8:16.

32. Daniel H. Wells, in *Journal of Discourses,* 12:72–74.

33. Daniel H. Wells, as quoted by Lewis Anderson, in Conference Report, April 1918, 136.

34. *History of the Church,* 6:545–46.

35. Reported in Lella Marler, "Elizabeth and Vilate Young," *Young Woman's Journal* 15 (January 1904): 21.

36. Brigham Young, "History of Brigham Young," *Millennial Star* 26 (4 June 1864): 359.

37. *History of the Church,* 7:233, 235.

38. Benjamin F. Johnson, "An Interesting Letter," unpublished letter from Johnson to Patriarch George S. Gibbs, April to July 1903, LDS Church Archives, Salt Lake City, Utah, 53–54.

39. *History of the Church,* 7:240.

40. "A Family Meeting in Nauvoo," *Utah Genealogical and Historical Magazine* 11 (July 1920): 107.

41. George A. Smith, quoted by George Albert Smith, in Conference Report, October 1950, 155.

42. William Clayton, *An Intimate Chronicle: The Journals of William Clayton,* ed. George D. Smith (Salt Lake City: Signature Books, 1995), 244, 247, 250–51, 254, 256.

43. *Journal of Discourses,* 1:120.

44. Truman G. Madsen, *Four Essays on Love* (Salt Lake City: Bookcraft, 1971), 28.

45. *Journal of Discourses,* 1:313.

46. Quoted in John Brown, "Testimony of the Divinity of 'Mormonism,'" *Young Woman's Journal* 6 (December 1894): 114. His vision included a return to Nauvoo. Brigham Young, speaking in the Nauvoo Temple, January 2, 1846: "We can't stay in this house [temple] but a little while. We've got to build another house, it will be a larger house than this, and a more glorious one. We shall build a great many houses, we shall come back here and we shall . . . build houses all over the continent of North America." Kimball, *Journal of Heber C. Kimball,* 312.

47. See *History of the Church,* 6:222.

48. Roberts, *Comprehensive History of the Church,* 3:386; see also B. H. Roberts, in Conference Report, April 1914, 104; B. H. Roberts, in Conference Report, April 1915, 130; E. Cecil McGavin, *The Nauvoo Temple* (Salt Lake City: Deseret Book, 1962), 25.

49. See James B. Allen, ed., "The Historian's Corner," *BYU Studies* 14, no. 1 (1973): 111.

50. Truman G. Madsen, "Power from Abrahamic Tests," *BYU Speeches of the Year,* October 12, 1971 (Provo, Utah: Brigham Young University Press, 1971), 4; see also Truman G. Madsen, *The Highest in Us* (Salt Lake City: Bookcraft, 1978), 55.

51. "Power from Abrahamic Tests," 4.

52. See George A. Smith, in *Journal of Discourses,* 6:87; see also B. H. Roberts, in "General Conference," *Millennial Star* 52 (1 September 1850): 260.

53. Brigham Young to Orson Hyde, October 1, 1865, Brigham Young Papers, LDS Church Archives, Salt Lake City, Utah; see also *Journal of Discourses,* 10:231.

54. Brigham Young lived as he taught. B. H. Roberts recorded that "Senator Chase of Ohio said of Brigham Young—'that no governor had ever done so well by the Indians since William Penn, as Governor Young.'" *Comprehensive History of the Church,* 4:52.

55. Nibley, *Brigham Young: The Man and His Work,* 285.

56. Richard D. Poll, "The Move South," *BYU Studies* 29, no. 4 (1989): 66.

57. James B. Allen and Glen M. Leonard, *The Story of the Latter-day Saints,* 2d ed. (Salt Lake City: Deseret Book, 1992), 327.

58. Arrington, *Brigham Young: American Moses,* 402–9.

59. "Funeral of President Brigham Young," *Millennial Star* 39 (1 October 1877): 642.

60. "John Pulsipher Autobiography," BYU Special Collections, Harold B. Lee Library, Provo, Utah, 9.

61. *Journal of Discourses,* 4:113.

62. LeRoy R. Hafen and Ann W. Hafen, *Handcarts to Zion, the Story of a Unique Western Migration, 1856–1860* (Glendale, Calif.: A. H. Clark Co., 1960), 133.

63. Brigham Young, *The Discourses of Brigham Young,* sel. and arr. John A. Widtsoe (Salt Lake City: Deseret Book, 1954), 2–11.

64. *Journal of Discourses,* 12:70; 16:161.

65. *History of the Church,* 5:517.

66. In a related statement, Brigham Young declared in 1856, "To accomplish this work there will have to be not only one temple but thousands of them." *Journal of Discourses,* 3:372.

67. Susa Young Gates, "Brigham Young's Testimony," *Improvement Era* 32 (June 1929): 637.

68. Journal History of The Church of Jesus Christ of Latter-day Saints, February 23, 1847, LDS Church Archives.

69. *Journal of Discourses,* 11:233.

70. See Brigham Young, in *Journal of Discourses,* 2:256.

71. See Brigham Young, in *Journal of Discourses,* 2:248; 3:208; 7:138. For a contrasting view, see H. Curtis Wright, "Brigham Young and the Natural Man," in *Things of Redeeming Worth: Scriptural Messages and World Judgments,* vol. 16 in Religious Studies Center Specialized Monograph Series (Provo, Utah, and Salt Lake City, Utah: BYU Religious Studies Center and Deseret Book, 2002), 85–124.

72. Brigham Young, in *Journal of Discourses,* 3:157.

73. Jedediah M. Grant, *Three Letters to the New York Herald* (New Haven, Conn.: Research Publications, 1967), 27.

74. Gates, "Brigham Young's Testimony," 638.

CHAPTER THREE: JOHN TAYLOR

1. B. H. Roberts, *The Life of John Taylor* (Salt Lake City: Deseret Book, 2002), 25–27.

2. Ibid., 27–28.

3. Ibid., 28.

4. Ibid., 28–29.

5. Ibid., 35.

6. *Journal of Discourses,* 26 vols. (Liverpool: Latter-day Saints' Book Depot, 1854–86), 5:239.

7. Roberts, *Life of John Taylor,* 36.

8. *Journal of Discourses,* 5:239.

9. Roberts, *Life of John Taylor,* 39–40.

10. Ibid., 47–48.

11. Ibid., 213–14.

12. Roberts, *Life of John Taylor,* 424.

13. "The 113th Anniversary of President John Taylor," *Improvement Era* 25 (November 1921): 79–80.

14. Andrew Jenson, *LDS Biographical Encyclopedia,* 4 vols. (Salt Lake City: Deseret News, 1901), 1:19.

15. Roberts, *Life of John Taylor,* 426.

16. Ibid., 427.

17. David O. McKay, in Conference Report, October 1953, 8.

18. Roberts, *Life of John Taylor,* 65–66.

19. *Journal of Discourses,* 20:259; 24:197, 264; see *Journal of Discourses,* 5:190.

20. *Journal of Discourses,* 24:264.

21. Roberts, *Life of John Taylor,* 100.

22. Journal of John Mills Whitaker, November 1, 1890, University of Utah Library, Salt Lake City, Utah.

23. Moses W. Taylor, "Stories and Counsel of Prest. Taylor," *Young Woman's Journal* 16 (May 1905): 219.

24. See Matthias F. Cowley, in Conference Report, October 1902, 61–62.

25. Taylor, "Stories and Counsel of Prest. Taylor," 218.

26. Ibid.

27. *Journal of Discourses,* 10:149.

28. "Address to the Saints in Great Britain," *Millennial Star* 8 (1 November 1846): 97–98.

29. Joseph Smith, *Teachings of the Prophet Joseph Smith,* comp. Joseph Fielding Smith (Salt Lake City: Deseret Book, 1976), 231–32.

30. John Taylor, *Gospel Kingdom,* ed. G. Homer Durham (Salt Lake City: Bookcraft, 1987), 356.

31. *Journal of Discourses,* 21:163.

32. Joseph Smith, quoted in Oliver B. Huntington, "Words and Incidents of the Prophet Joseph's Life," *Young Woman's Journal* 2 (July 1891): 466.

33. Joseph Smith, *History of The Church of Jesus Christ of Latter-day Saints,* ed. B. H. Roberts, 2d ed. rev., 7 vols. (Salt Lake City: The Church of Jesus Christ of Latter-day Saints, 1932–51), 6:100.

34. Taylor, *Gospel Kingdom,* 359–60.

35. *History of the Church,* 7:101.

36. Ibid., 6:574.

37. Ibid., 7:103.

38. Edward H. Stiles, *Recollections and Sketches of Notable Lawyers and Public Men of Early Iowa* (Des Moines, Iowa: Homestead Publishing, 1916), 6.

39. *History of the Church,* 7:108.

40. See Willard Richards, in *History of the Church,* 6:626; 7:110; William Clayton, "An Interesting Journal," in *Juvenile Instructor* 21 (15 January 1886): 16.

41. *Journal of Discourses,* 11:54.

42. Taylor, *Gospel Kingdom,* 78.

43. Recounted to the author by Elder Hugh B. Brown, whose wife, Zina, was a granddaughter of Brigham Young.

44. In a related incident, Brigham Young is said to have brought his hickory cane down on the pulpit in the assembly room of the St. George Temple, saying, "I shall never be satisfied until Satan is conquered and driven from the face of the earth" (Matthias F. Cowley, *Wilford Woodruff, His Life and Labors* [Salt Lake City: Deseret News, 1916], 494). It is possible that this event occurred only once and that in the process of time the details have become confused.

45. See *Brigham Young University: The First One Hundred Years,* ed. Ernest L. Wilkinson, 4 vols. (Provo, Utah: Brigham Young University Press, 1975–76), 4:410.

46. *Journal of Discourses,* 21:100.

47. *Journal of Discourses,* 10:147.

48. Taylor, *Gospel Kingdom,* 107–8.

49. *Journal of Discourses,* 23:179.

50. John Taylor and Baron Rothschild had earlier met in 1876.

51. *Journal of Discourses,* 25:265.

52. *Temples of the Most High,* comp. N. B. Lundwall (Salt Lake City: Bookcraft, 1966), 87.

53. Ibid., 89.

54. Ibid., 90.

55. Ibid.

56. Brigham Young, *The Discourses of Brigham Young,* sel. and arr. John A. Widtsoe (Salt Lake City: Deseret Book, 1954), 469.

57. Ibid., 91.

58. Ibid., 92.

59. Ibid., 93.

60. Ibid., 94.

61. Taylor, *Gospel Kingdom,* 390.

CHAPTER FOUR: WILFORD WOODRUFF

1. Matthias F. Cowley, *Wilford Woodruff: His Life and Labors* (Salt Lake City: Bookcraft, 1986), 27–30.

2. Cowley, *Wilford Woodruff,* 29–30.

3. Ibid., 32–33.

4. Hoyt W. Brewster Jr., *Doctrine and Covenants Encyclopedia* (Salt Lake City: Bookcraft, 1988), 645.

5. *Journal of Discourses,* 26 vols. (Liverpool: Latter-day Saints' Book Depot, 1854–86), 4:99–100; see also Joseph Smith, *History of The Church of Jesus Christ of Latter-day Saints,* ed. B. H. Roberts, 2d ed. rev., 7 vols. (Salt Lake City: The Church of Jesus Christ of Latter-day Saints, 1932–51), 3:337.

6. Cowley, *Wilford Woodruff,* 16–18.

7. Archibald F. Bennett, *Saviors on Mount Zion* (Salt Lake City: Deseret Sunday School Union Board, 1954), 15, 17.

8. Joseph Smith, *Teachings of the Prophet Joseph Smith,* comp. Joseph Fielding Smith (Salt Lake City: Deseret Book, 1976), 148.

9. Cowley, *Wilford Woodruff,* 5–12.

10. Wilford Woodruff, in Scott G. Kenney, ed., *Wilford Woodruff's Journal* (Midvale, Utah: Signature Books, 1983), March 25, 1842, 2:164.

11. *Temples of the Most High,* comp. N. B. Lundwall (Salt Lake City: Bookcraft, 1966), 119.

12. Cowley, *Wilford Woodruff,* 476–77.

13. Brigham Young, quoted in Bertha Irvine, "A Tribute to a True Latter-day Saint," *Young Woman's Journal* 33 (November 1922): 601.

14. Wilford Woodruff, "Discourse by President Woodruff," *Millennial Star* 53 (12 October 1891): 642.

15. Orson Hyde, quoted in *Wilford Woodruff's Journal,* August 24, 1851, 4:53.

16. *Wilford Woodruff's Journal,* April 27, 1834, 1:9.

17. *Collected Discourses,* comp. and ed. Brian H. Stuy, 5 vols. (Burbank, Calif.: B.H.S. Publishing, 1987–92), 2:207.

18. See Cowley, *Wilford Woodruff,* 291–92.

19. John Taylor, in *Journal of Discourses,* 24:202.

20. William W. Phelps, "The Spirit of God Like a Fire Is Burning," in Hoyt W. Brewster Jr., *Doctrine and Covenants Encyclopedia* (Salt Lake City: Bookcraft, 1988), 405.

21. See Cowley, *Wilford Woodruff,* 69, 92, 93.

22. *Wilford Woodruff's Journal,* April 15, 1837, 1:142–43.

23. *Wilford Woodruff's Journal,* July 2, 1840, 1:475–77.

24. See Cowley, *Wilford Woodruff,* 632.

25. *Journal of Discourses,* 13:164; 19:227.

26. *Journal of Discourses,* 1:364.

27. Cowley, *Wilford Woodruff,* 204–5.

28. Preston Nibley, *The Presidents of the Church* (Salt Lake City: Deseret Book, 1977), 115; Cowley, *Wilford Woodruff,* 204, 208.

29. Nibley, *Presidents of the Church,* 115.

30. Susan Easton Black and Larry C. Porter, *Lion of the Lord: Essays on the Life and Service of Brigham Young* (Salt Lake City: Deseret Book, 1995), 107; *Messages of the First Presidency of the Church of Jesus Christ of Latter-day Saints, 1833–1964,* ed. James R. Clark, 6 vols. (Salt Lake City: Bookcraft, 1965–75), 1:233.

31. Dix W. Price, "I Met Joseph Smith," *Brigham Young University Speeches of the Year*, April 18, 1962, 8.

32. Cowley, *Wilford Woodruff,* 209.

33. *Journal of Discourses,* 9:244; Leah D. Widtsoe, "Brigham Young and the 'Youth Movement,'" *Improvement Era* 38 (June 1935): 382; Cowley, *Wilford Woodruff,* 354.

34. Thomas G. Alexander, *Things in Heaven and Earth: The Life and Times of Wilford Woodruff, a Mormon Prophet* (Salt Lake City: Signature Books, 1991), 136–37.

35. Cowley, *Wilford Woodruff,* 292.

36. *Wilford Woodruff's Journal*, May 13, 1847, 3:175.

37. Wilford Woodruff, in *Journal of Discourses,* 21:299–300; see also Matthew B. Brown, *Symbols in Stone: Symbolism on the Early Temples of the Restoration* (American Fork, Utah: Covenant Communications, 1997), 158 n. 8.

38. *Journal of Discourses,* 2:360; Conference Report, April 1906, 79.

39. *Journal of Discourses,* 19:229; see also Dennis B. Horne, ed., *An Apostle's Record: The Journals of Abraham H. Cannon* (Clearfield, Utah: Gnolaum Books, 2004), 69.

40. Conference Report, April 1898, 89.

41. Cowley, *Wilford Woodruff,* 496.

42. See L. John Nuttall Papers, October 7, 1891, LDS Church Archives, Salt Lake City, Utah; Loren C. Dunn, "The Temple is the 'heart of sacred work,'" *LDS Church News,* February 6, 1993, 3; Richard Neitzel Holzapfel, *Every Stone a Sermon* (Salt Lake City: Bookcraft, 1992), 71.

43. Cowley, *Wilford Woodruff,* 582; *Messages of the First Presidency,* 3:242–44.

44. See Truman G. Madsen, *Joseph Smith the Prophet* (Salt Lake City: Bookcraft, 1989), 48–49.

45. Minutes of Salt Lake Temple dedication, third session, April 7, 1893, LDS Church Archives, Salt Lake City, Utah.

46. Ibid. See minutes for April 10, 1893.

47. *History of the Church,* 2:182.

48. Remarks of Junius Romney, Salt Lake City, Utah, July 31, 1966, unpublished.

49. *Gospel Truth: Discourses and Writings of President George Q. Cannon,* ed. Jerreld L. Newquist, 2 vols. (Salt Lake City: Deseret Book, 1974), 1:293.

50. See Donald Q. Cannon, *Latter-day Prophets and the United States Constitution* (Provo, Utah: Religious Studies Center, Brigham Young University, 1991), 1–15.

51. *Collected Discourses,* 1:221; see also 1:341; 3:60–61.

52. Hoyt W. Brewster Jr., *Behold, I Come Quickly: The Last Days and Beyond* (Salt Lake City: Deseret Book, 1994), 207–9.

53. *Collected Discourses,* 4:67.

54. See *Journal of Discourses,* 24:50–51; *The Discourses of Wilford Woodruff,* ed. G. Homer Durham (Salt Lake City: Bookcraft, 1946), 276.

55. *Collected Discourses,* 5:257–58.

56. Minutes of Salt Lake Temple dedication, April 1893, LDS Church Archives, Salt Lake City, Utah.

57. *Collected Discourses,* 5:258.

58. Ibid.

59. Part of the transcript is in "Record Transcription," *New Era,* January 1972, 66.

60. Cowley, *Wilford Woodruff,* 622.

61. "Joseph Smith put down the fashion of wearing black for the dead, but it had crept amongst us again." Eliza R. Snow, December 3, 1874, 13th Ward Relief Society Notes, LDS Church Archives, Salt Lake City, Utah, 207.

62. Cowley, *Wilford Woodruff,* 622.

CHAPTER FIVE: LORENZO SNOW

1. Blessing given December 15, 1836, in the Kirtland Temple. See also "A Church Leader's Testimony," *Deseret News,* April 15, 1939, 2–3.

2. Brigham Young Jr., *Diary of Brigham Young, Jr,. 1900–1902, New York* (Provo, Utah: Brigham Young University, 1962), 84.

3. On his acute mind, see James E. Talmage, "President Lorenzo Snow," *Young Woman's Journal* 12 (November 1901): 483–84. See also Orson F. Whitney, in *Utah Genealogical and Historical Magazine* 2 (October 1911): 149.

4. Quoted in LeRoi C. Snow, "Devotion to a Divine Inspiration," *Improvement Era* 22 (June 1919): 655.

5. Eliza R. Snow, *Biography and Family Record of Lorenzo Snow* (Salt Lake City: Deseret News Company, 1884), 9.

6. LeRoi C. Snow, "How Lorenzo Snow Found God," *Improvement Era* 40 (February 1937), 84.

7. Snow, *Biography and Family Record of Lorenzo Snow,* 10.

8. Lorenzo Snow, "How I Gained My Testimony of the Truth," *Young Woman's Journal* 4 (February 1893): 217.

9. *Deseret Evening News,* December 30, 1899. See also Office Journal of Lorenzo Snow, LDS Church Archives, Salt Lake City, Utah, 172.

10. See Lorenzo Snow, "A Promise Fulfilled," *Millennial Star* 49 (28 February 1887): 131.

11. Snow, *Biography and Family Record of Lorenzo Snow,* 19.

12. Ibid., 65–66.

13. See Susa Young Gates, *History of the Young Ladies' Mutual Improvement Association* (Salt Lake City: Deseret News, 1911), 18–19.

14. Snow, *Biography and Family Record of Lorenzo Snow,* 65–69.

15. Ibid., 68–70.

16. Conference Report, October 1926, 127.

17. Snow, *Biography and Family Record of Lorenzo Snow,* 70.

18. Ibid.

19. Maureen Ursenbach Beecher, ed., "The Iowa Journal of Lorenzo Snow," *BYU Studies* 24, no. 3 (1984): 268–69.

20. Thomas C. Romney, *The Life of Lorenzo Snow, Fifth President of the Church of Jesus Christ of Latter-day Saints* (Salt Lake City: S.U.P. Memorial Foundation, 1955), 78–79.

21. Franklin D. Richards, in Conference Report, April 1880, 50; Erastus Snow, in Conference Report, April 1880, 52–54; John Taylor, in Conference Report, April 1880, 61–63.

22. Brigham Young, quoted in Leslie Woodruff Snow, "President Lorenzo Snow," *Young Woman's Journal* 14 (September 1903): 388.

23. See Snow, "President Lorenzo Snow," 389.

24. Conference Report, October 6, 1849, quoted in Romney, *Life of Lorenzo Snow,* 79.

25. Conference Report, April 1898, 64.

26. *Journal of Discourses,* 26 vols. (Liverpool: Latter-day Saints' Book Depot, 1854–86), 18:376.

27. Snow, *Biography and Family Record of Lorenzo Snow,* 130–31. See also Lorenzo Snow, "Organization of the Church in Italy," *Millennial Star* 12 (15 December 1850): 373.

28. Snow, *Biography and Family Record of Lorenzo Snow,* 128–29.

29. Ibid., 122, 126; see also 121–36.

30. Lorenzo Snow, *Italian Mission* (London: W. Aubrey, 1851), 20.

31. *Journal of Discourses,* 5:168. See also Gustive O. Larson, "Mormon Reformation," *Utah Historical Quarterly* 26 (January 1958): 44–62.

32. See Gene A. Sessions, *Mormon Thunder: A Documentary History of Jedediah Morgan Grant* (Urbana, Ill.: University of Illinois Press, 1982).

33. "Funeral of Franklin D. Richards," *Latter-day Saints Southern Star* 2 (30 December 1899): 39.

34. Snow, *Biography and Family Record of Lorenzo Snow,* 496; Edward W. Tullidge, *Women of Mormondom* (New York: Tullidge & Crandall, 1877), 482.

35. David B. Galbraith, D. Kelly Ogden, and Andrew E. Skinner, *Jerusalem, the Eternal City* (Salt Lake City: Deseret Book, 1996), 341.

36. See George A. Smith, et al., *Correspondence of Palestine Tourists* (New York: Arno Press, 1977).

37. George A. Smith Journal, March 2, 1873, Special Collections, Marriott Library, University of Utah, Salt Lake City, Utah.

38. Galbraith, Odgen, and Skinner, *Jerusalem,* 342.

39. George A. Smith Journal, vol. 15, Special Collections, Marriott Library, University of Utah, Salt Lake City, Utah.

40. Galbraith, Odgen, and Skinner, *Jerusalem,* 342.

41. Lorenzo Snow Journal, LDS Church Archives, Salt Lake City, Utah, 233, 237.

42. Conference Report, October 1897, 29, 31.

43. George Q. Cannon, *Life of Joseph Smith, the Prophet* (Salt Lake City: Deseret Book, 1958), 385; Joseph Smith, *Teachings of the Prophet Joseph Smith,* comp. Joseph Fielding Smith (Salt Lake City: Deseret Book, 1976), 376; Joseph Smith, *History of The Church of Jesus Christ of Latter-day Saints,* ed. B. H. Roberts, 2d ed. rev., 7 vols. (Salt Lake City: The Church of Jesus Christ of Latter-day Saints, 1932–51), 5:517.

44. Cannon, *Life of Joseph Smith,* 10.

45. See Rudger Clawson, in Conference Report, October 1901, 95.

46. Ibid.

47. *Collected Discourses,* comp. and ed. Brian H. Stuy, 5 vols. (Burbank, Calif.: B.H.S. Publishing, 1987–92), 2:34. See also Lorenzo Snow, "Gems of Truth," *Millennial Star* 50 (10 December 1888): 806.

48. *Collected Discourses,* 2:34.

49. See Truman G. Madsen, *Defender of the Faith: The B. H. Roberts Story* (Salt Lake City: Bookcraft, 1980), 185.

50. Romney, *Life of Lorenzo Snow,* 381–82.

51. Ibid.

52. Snow, *Biography and Family Record of Lorenzo Snow,* 453–87.

53. LeRoi C. Snow, "Raised from the Dead," *Improvement Era* 32 (September 1929): 885–86.

54. Joseph Fielding Smith, *Life of Joseph F. Smith* (Salt Lake City: Deseret Book, 1938), 214–16.

55. Matthias F. Cowley, *Wilford Woodruff: His Life and Labors* (Salt Lake City: Bookcraft, 1986), 467.

56. Snow, *Biography and Family Record of Lorenzo Snow,* 46. See also Lorenzo Snow, "The Grand Destiny of Man," *Deseret Evening News*, July 20, 1901, 22.

57. LeRoi C. Snow, "An Experience of My Father's," *Improvement Era* 36 (September 1933): 677.

58. Ibid., 677, 679.

59. See LeRoi C. Snow, in *Temples of the Most High,* comp. N. B. Lundwall (Salt Lake City: Bookcraft, 1966), 139–42.

60. Journal of Heber J. Grant, September 1898, LDS Church Archives, Salt Lake City, Utah.

61. Conference Report, April 1901, 3.

62. Meeting of First Presidency and Twelve, BYU Special Collections, Harold B. Lee Library, Provo, Utah. For the whole quotation, see Truman G. Madsen, *Highest in Us* (Salt Lake City: Bookcraft, 1978), 11.

63. Ibid.

64. "Characteristic Sayings of President Lorenzo Snow," *Improvement Era* 22 (June 1919): 651

65. Ibid. See also Lorenzo Snow's teachings in Rudger Clawson, *A Ministry of Meetings: The Apostolic Diaries of Rudger Clawson,* ed. Stan Larson (Salt Lake City: Signature Books with Smith Research Associates, 1993); *An Apostle's Record: The Journals of Abraham H. Cannon,* ed. Dennis B. Horne (Clearfield, Utah: Gnolaum Books, 2004); *Supporting Saints: Life Stories of Nineteenth Century Mormons,* ed. Donald Q. Cannon and David J. Whittaker (Provo, Utah: Brigham Young University Religious Studies Center; and Salt Lake City: Bookcraft, 1985); *The Teachings of Lorenzo Snow,* ed. Clyde Williams (Salt Lake City: Bookcraft, 1984).

66. "Characteristic Sayings," 651.

67. Ibid.

68. Ibid.

69. "February Sunday Evening Joint Meeting," *Improvement Era* 33 (December 1929): 143.

70. "Characteristic Sayings," 651.

71. "Joint Meeting," 143.

72. "Characteristic Sayings," 651.

73. Ibid.

74. Nephi Anderson, "Life and Character Sketch of Lorenzo Snow," *Improvement Era* 2 (June 1899): 570.

75. Romney, *Life of Lorenzo Snow,* 14–16.

CHAPTER SIX: JOSEPH F. SMITH

1. The blessing as quoted by Elder M. Russell Ballard: "If it please thee and thou desirest, thou shalt have the power voluntarily to lay down thy life to glorify God." "'Hearts subdued' during Carthage telecast," *LDS Church News,* July 2, 1994, 10.

2. Joseph Smith, *History of The Church of Jesus Christ of Latter-day Saints,* ed. B. H. Roberts, 2d ed. rev., 7 vols. (Salt Lake City: The Church of Jesus Christ of Latter-day Saints, 1932–51), 1:465–71. See also Joseph F. Smith, *Succession in the Presidency of The Church of Jesus Christ of Latter-day Saints* (Salt Lake City, Utah: The Church of Jesus Christ of Latter-day Saints, 1975). Blessing given December 18, 1833.

3. Wandle Mace, "Autobiography of Wandle Mace," BYU Special Collections, Harold B. Lee Library, Provo, Utah, 144.

4. Cyrus Wheelock to B. H. Roberts, LDS Church Archives, Salt Lake City, Utah.

5. Ibid.

6. *History of the Church,* 6:546; Pearson H. Corbett, *Hyrum Smith, Patriarch* (Salt Lake City: Deseret Book, 1963), 46–58; Edward W. Tullidge, *Life of Joseph Smith* (New York: Tullidge & Crandall, 1878), 74–91.

7. Don Cecil Corbett, *Mary Fielding Smith: Daughter of Britain, Portrait of Courage* (Salt Lake City: Deseret Book, 1966), 161–70.

8. Francis M. Gibbons, *Joseph F. Smith: Patriarch and Preacher, Prophet of God* (Salt Lake City: Deseret Book, 1984), 9.

9. Hyrum M. Smith III and Scott G. Kenney, *From Prophet to Son: Advice of Joseph F. Smith to His Missionary Sons* (Salt Lake City: Deseret Book, 1981).

10. See Bruce Van Orden, "Joseph F. Smith," in *Encyclopedia of Mormonism,* ed. Daniel H. Ludlow, 4 vols. (New York: Macmillan, 1992), 3:1350.

11. Ibid.

12. Joseph Fielding Smith, *Life of Joseph F. Smith* (Salt Lake City: Deseret Book, 1938), 216.

13. Ibid.

14. Ibid., 170.

15. Conference Report, April 1952, 103.

16. Smith, *Life of Joseph F. Smith,* 185–86; Charles W. Nibley, "Reminiscences of President Joseph F. Smith," *Improvement Era* 22 (January 1919): 193–94.

17. Smith, *Life of Joseph F. Smith,* 179–80.

18. Ibid., 184–85.

19. Andrew Jenson, *LDS Biographical Encyclopedia,* 4 vols. (Salt Lake City: Deseret News, 1901), 1:66.

20. Smith, *Life of Joseph F. Smith*, 197.

21. Joseph F. Smith, mission journal entry, January 13, 1862, Chesterfield, England, LDS Church Archives, Salt Lake City, Utah.

22. Smith, *Life of Joseph F. Smith,* 456.

23. Ibid., 455–57.

24. Recollection of Buddy Youngreen to the author, after interview with Willard R. Smith.

25. Wilford Woodruff Journal, July 1, 1886; cited in Matthias F. Cowley, *Wilford Woodruff, His Life and Labors* (Salt Lake City: Bookcraft, 1986), 445–46.

26. The monument, which is technically in South Royalton, stands between the town centers of Sharon and South Royalton.

27. *Proceedings at the Dedication of the Joseph Smith Memorial Monument* (Salt Lake City: Deseret News Press, 1905), 25.

28. See Heber J. Grant, in Conference Report, October 1934, 16.

29. Quoted in Truman G. Madsen, *Defender of the Faith: The B. H. Roberts Story* (Salt Lake City: Bookcraft, 1980), 223–25.

30. Ibid., 226.

31. Ibid., 307–8.

32. Orson F. Whitney, *Saturday Night Thoughts* (Salt Lake City: Deseret News, 1921), 294–95.

33. Joseph F. Smith, *Gospel Doctrine* (Salt Lake City: Deseret Book, 1946), 13–14.

34. Lynn A. McKinlay, "Giving Thanks," *BYU Speeches of the Year,* November 22, 1955, 4. Also in *The Divine Journey Home: A Lynn A. McKinlay Odyssey: An Assembly of Discourses,* comp. Daniel B. McKinlay (n.p., 2002), 4.

35. Conference Report, April 1916, 3–4.

36. Smith, *Gospel Doctrine*, 432; Conference Report, April 1916, 4.

37. *Journal of Discourses,* 26 vols. (Liverpool: Latter-day Saints' Book Depot, 1854–86), 22:350–53; Smith, *Gospel Doctrine,* 429–32; Conference Report, April 1916, 2–4.

38. *Hymns of The Church of Jesus Christ of Latter-day Saints* (Salt Lake City: The Church of Jesus Christ of Latter-day Saints, 1985), no. 292.

39. Smith, *Life of Joseph F. Smith,* 452.

40. Conference Report, April 1898, 69.

41. B. H. Roberts, *A Comprehensive History of the Church of Jesus Christ of Latter-day Saints,* 6 vols. (Salt Lake City: The Church of Jesus Christ of Latter-day Saints, 1965), 6:184, 482.

42. Conference Report, April 1898, 65–66.

43. Reminscence, in files of Buddy Youngreen, unpublished.

44. Conference Report, June 1919, 11.

45. Reminscence of Lynn A. McKinlay to author.

CHAPTER SEVEN: HEBER J. GRANT

1. Heber J. Grant, *Gospel Standards,* ed. G. Homer Durham (Salt Lake City: Improvement Era, 1941), 341; Rachel Ridgeway Grant, in "Joseph Smith, the Prophet," *Young Woman's Journal* 16 (December 1905): 550–51.

2. Mary G. Judd, *Jedediah M. Grant: Pioneer–Statesman* (Salt Lake City: Deseret News Press, 1959), 58.

3. Joseph Smith, *History of The Church of Jesus Christ of Latter-day Saints,* ed. B. H. Roberts, 2d ed. rev., 7 vols. (Salt Lake City: The Church of Jesus Christ of Latter-day Saints, 1932–51), 6:554.

4. *Journal of Discourses,* 26 vols. (Liverpool: Latter-day Saints' Book Depot, 1854–86), 5:168.

5. *LDS Church News,* September 3, 1938, 7; see also Conference Report, October 1919, 32.

6. *LDS Church News,* September 3, 1938, 7.

7. Heber J. Grant, in "Work, and Keep Your Promises," *Improvement Era* 3 (January 1900): 196–97.

8. Heber J. Grant Journal, April 13, 1901, LDS Church Archives, Salt Lake City, Utah.

9. See Ronald W. Walker, "Qualities That Count," *BYU Studies* 43, no. 1 (2004): 55.

10. Ibid., 50–57.

11. Conference Report, October 1934, 124–25.

12. Conference Report, October 1934, 125–26.

13. Heber J. Grant, in letter to his daughters, December 28, 1943, LDS Church Archives, Salt Lake City, Utah. See also Conference Report, October 1934, 125–26.

14. Grant, *Gospel Standards,* 192.

15. Heber J. Grant, "Some Things for Our Young People to Remember," *Improvement Era* 42 (July 1939): 393.

16. Heber J. Grant, in letter of November 2, 1914, LDS Church Archives, Salt Lake City, Utah.

17. See Heber J. Grant, "Riches," *Contributor* 12 (September 1891): 467–71.

18. Remarks made at Heber J. Grant's 68th birthday celebration, November 1924, at home of George Q. Cannon.

19. "Some Things for Our Young People to Remember," *Improvement Era* 42 (July 1939): 437.

20. See Heber J. Grant, "Conference Address of President Heber J. Grant," *Liahona: The Elder's Journal* 32 (23 April 1935): 510.

21. "The 'Still Small Voice,'" *Improvement Era* 41 (December 1938): 712.

22. Conference Report, October 1922, 2–3.

23. *Messages of the First Presidency of the Church of Jesus Christ of Latter-day Saints, 1833–1964,* ed. James R. Clark, 6 vols. (Salt Lake City: Bookcraft, 1965–75), 2:348.

24. Conference Report, October 1922, 2–3.

25. Grant, *Gospel Standards,* 100.

26. Memoirs of Axel A. Madsen, unpublished manuscript in author's possession.

27. Grant, *Gospel Standards,* 296.

28. Heber J. Grant, in Conference Report, April 1941, 5; "President Grant's Opening Conference Message," *Improvement Era* 44 (May 1941): 267, 315

29. These are the words of Joseph Smith to the Twelve in Nauvoo; recorded by Wilford Woodruff on September 21, 1883; see "Letters, 1844," Envelope #104, LDS Church Archives, Salt Lake City, Utah.

30. "Opening Conference Message," *Improvement Era* 44 (May 1941): 267, 315.

31. Letter to Brigham Young Jr., September 8, 1892, LDS Church Archives, Salt Lake City, Utah.

32. Wilford Woodruff, quoted by Heber J. Grant, in Conference Report, June 1919, 8–9.

33. See Ronald W. Walker, "Crisis in Zion," *Arizona and the West* 21 (Autumn 1979): 257–78.

34. Heber J. Grant kept a copy of almost every letter he wrote, and 52,000 of them are on file in the LDS Church Archives. Sometimes he dictated, so some of his letters lack his model penmanship.

35. Heber J. Grant, in a letter to his wife Emily Grant, 1893, LDS Church Archives, Salt Lake City, Utah.

36. For background on the Kirtland Safety Society, see Scott H. Partridge, "Failure of the Kirtland Safety Society," *BYU Studies* 12, no. 4 (1972): 437–54.

37. For examples of Heber J. Grant's remarks on this subject, see Grant, *Gospel Standards,* 110–13.

38. Remarks made at Heber J. Grant's 68th birthday celebration, November 1924, at home of George Q. Cannon.

39. Conference Report, October 1933, 7.

40. Gordon A. Madsen, "Heber J. Grant in Japan: A Personal Account," unpublished manuscript, 2003. See also Gordon A. Madsen "A Japanese Journal," private family printing, 5.

41. Heber J. Grant Journal, 16 May 1901, LDS Church Archives, Salt Lake City, Utah.

42. Ibid.

43. Grant, *Gospel Standards,* 331–37.

44. Ralph Waldo Emerson, quoted by Heber J. Grant, in Conference Report, April 1901, 63.

45. Quoted by Heber J. Grant, in Conference Report, April 1900, 62.

46. "Learning to Sing," *Improvement Era* 3 (October 1900): 889.

47. Heber J. Grant, in a letter to his daughter Jessie, December 2, 1901, in author's possession.

48. "On the Cover," *Improvement Era* 73 (March 1970): 1. See also Lorenzo Snow's prediction, in B. H. Roberts, *A Comprehensive History of the Church of Jesus Christ of Latter-day Saints,* 6 vols. (Salt Lake City: The Church of Jesus Christ of Latter-day Saints, 1965), 6:117, 377.

49. "Greetings across the Sea," *Improvement Era* 40 (July 1937): 405.

50. Heber J. Grant, quoted by President Hugh B. Brown to missionaries in New England, December 1963, unpublished.

51. Heber J. Grant, in a letter to Lucy Grant Cannon, December 17, 1902, LDS Church Archives, Salt Lake City, Utah.

52. See *Improvement Era* 15 (June 1912): 726–27.

53. Notes on temple meeting, May 20, 1890, LDS Church Archives, Salt Lake City, Utah, 382.

54. "In the Hour of Parting," *Improvement Era* 43 (June 1940): 330, 383.

55. Heber J. Grant, Patriarchal Blessing Book, blessing given 11 June 1917, LDS Church Archives, Salt Lake City, Utah.

56. Heber J. Grant, in a letter to Grace Grant Evans, in author's possession.

57. "The Spirit and the Letter," *Improvement Era* 42 (April 1939): 201.

58. Heber J. Grant, in a letter to Grace Grant Evans, in author's possession.

59. Conference Report, October 1939, 8.

60. Recollection of a friend who was in New York City at the time of this event to the author.

61. "Answering Tobacco's Challenge," *Improvement Era* 34 (June 1931): 450.

62. Reminiscences of Jessie Grant Boyle, unpublished manuscript, in author's possession.

63. Heber J. Grant, in Conference Report, April 1941, 6.

64. Recollections of Lucy Grant Cannon, unpublished manuscript, in author's pssession.

65. Joseph Anderson, *Prophets I Have Known* (Salt Lake City: Deseret Book, 1973), 33.

66. See "Work, and Keep Your Promises," *Improvement Era* 3 (January 1900): 197.

67. Roberts, *Comprehensive History of the Church,* 6:469.

68. *Collected Discourses*, comp. and ed. Brian H. Stuy, 5 vols. (Burbank, Calif.: B.H.S. Publishing, 1987–92), 2:137.

69. *Collected Discourses,* 1:81.

70. *Collected Discourses,* 3:188.

71. *Collected Discourses*, 5:71.

72. *Collected Discourses,* 2:21.

73. Ibid.

74. See Heber J. Grant, in a letter to his family from Tokyo, May 1903, LDS Church Archives, Salt Lake City, Utah.

75. See Conference Report, October 1907, 26; and Heber J. Grant, "Honoring Karl G. Maeser," *Improvement Era* 38 (June 1935): 339.

76. "A Marvelous Growth," *Juvenile Instructor* 64 (December 1929): 697.

77. Conference Report, October 1919, 28.

78. Inscription in James Allen, *As a Man Thinketh* (New York: Barse & Hopkins, 1910).

79. *Collected Discourses,* 4:34.

80. "Settlement," *Improvement Era* 44 (January 1941): 9.

81. Heber J. Grant, in Conference Report, April 1908, 57.

82. "'Mormon' View of Evolution," *Improvement Era* 28 (September 1925): 1090.

83. Wilford Woodruff, "Discourse by Wilford Woodruff," *Millennial Star* 56 (15 October 1894): 657.

84. Truman G. Madsen, ed., "Heber J. Grant Speaks to Our Time," unpublished manuscript, 287. See also Heber J. Grant, Conference Report, October 1911, 23.

85. *My Kingdom Shall Roll Forth* (Salt Lake City: The Church of Jesus Christ of Latter-day Saints, 1979), 87.

86. Madsen, "Heber J. Grant Speaks to Our Time," 366.

87. Eliza R. Snow, "Anniversary Tribute to the Memory of Pres. Joseph Smith," *Woman's Exponent* 2 (1 January 1874): 117. See also Eliza R. Snow, "Sketch of My Life," *Relief Society Magazine* 31 (March 1944): 136.

CHAPTER EIGHT: GEORGE ALBERT SMITH

1. Conversation at the New England Mission office, Cambridge, Massachusettes, as recounted to the author, 1963.

2. Recollection of Murray Stewart, as recounted to the author. The blessing was given January 16, 1884.

3. Bryant S. Hinckley, "Greatness in Men: Superintendent George Albert Smith," *Improvement Era* 35 (March 1932): 269.

4. John D. Giles, "President George Albert Smith," *Improvement Era* 48 (July 1945): 430.

5. Statement of D. Arthur Haycock to the author.

6. Recollection of Heber J. Grant to the author.

7. See "Pres. Smith's Leadership Address," *LDS Church News,* February 16, 1946, 1.

8. See Moses Thatcher, in *Collected Discourses,* comp. and ed. Brian H. Stuy, 5 vols. (Burbank, Calif.: B.H.S. Publishing, 1987–92), 4:317; see Rulon S. Wells, in Conference Report, April 1910, 23.

9. "Pres. Smith's Leadership Address," 1.

10. Francis M. Gibbons, *George Albert Smith: Kind and Caring Christian, Prophet of God* (Salt Lake City: Deseret Book, 1990), 21.

11. Ibid.

12. See Willis E. Robison, "An Unpublished Letter on the Tennessee Massacre," *Improvement Era* 2 (November 1898): 1–14; see also Joseph Fielding Smith, *Essentials in Church History* (Salt Lake City: Deseret Book, 1950), 486–87.

13. Hinckley, "Greatness in Men," 295.

14. See Susan Arrington Madsen, *The Lord Needed a Prophet* (Salt Lake City: Deseret Book, 1996), 128–29.

15. See Madsen, *The Lord Needed a Prophet,* 129.

16. Gibbons, *George Albert Smith,* 38–39. Gibbons notes that the friend who ran instead of George Albert Smith was Reed Smoot, who was not only a member of the Twelve along with George Albert but was also a United

States Senator for thirty years. He points out that had George Albert decided to run, it is likely that he, and not Reed Smoot, would have been the United States Senator.

17. George Albert Smith, "Scouting Saves the Church," *Improvement Era* 51 (September 1948): 558.

18. Gibbons, *George Albert Smith,* 82–83.

19. See ibid., 43–44.

20. See Heber J. Grant, in Conference Report, April 1937, 123.

21. See Gibbons, *George Albert Smith,* 68–69.

22. See Peggy A. Guetter, "New Honor Accorded Elder George Albert Smith," *Improvement Era* 45 (July 1942): 442.

23. Gibbons, *George Albert Smith,* 102–3.

24. Hinckley, "Greatness in Men," 295.

25. The depth of George Albert's forbearance is exemplified in the fact that the chief opponent to Emily's reinstatement was David O. McKay (Gibbons, *George Albert Smith,* 151–52). George Albert Smith called David O. McKay as one of his counselors in the First Presidency.

26. Gibbons, *George Albert Smith,* 203–4; "The Church Moves On," *Improvement Era* 39 (May 1936): 299.

27. Irene Jones, "A Tribute to George Albert Smith," *Improvement Era* 43 (July 1940): 423. The family was so touched by this poetic tribute that Sister Jones's poem was read at George Albert's funeral. See Irene Jones, in Conference Report, April 1951, 174.

28. See Spencer W. Kimball, *The Miracle of Forgiveness* (Salt Lake City: Bookcraft, 1969), 284.

29. See Thomas S. Monson, *Inspiring Experiences That Build Faith: From the Life and Ministry of Thomas S. Monson* (Salt Lake City: Deseret Book, 1994), 214–15.

30. See George Albert Smith, in Conference Report, October 1947, 5–6.

31. Gibbons, *George Albert Smith,* 310–12.

32. Henry A. Smith, *Matthew Cowley, Man of Faith* (Salt Lake City: Deseret Book, 1954), 152.

33. Recollection of Lowell Bennion of the University of Utah Institute to the author.

34. Matthew Cowley, "Miracles," in *Matthew Cowley Speaks* (Salt Lake City: Deseret Book, 1954), 237.

35. William Congreve, *The Mourning Bride* (1697), act 1, scene 1.

36. Bryant S. Hinckley, "Service through Industry . . . George Albert Smith as a Businessman," *Improvement Era* 53 (April 1950): 282.

37. Recollection of George Albert Smith III to the author.

38. Statement made by David O. McKay at George Albert Smith's funeral. See Preston Nibley, *The Presidents of the Church,* 13th ed. rev. (Salt Lake City: Deseret Book, 1974), 303.

39. Doyle L. Green, "Tributes Paid President George Albert Smith," *Improvement Era* 54 (June 1951): 405.

40. Conference Report, October 1932, 27; see Conference Report, April 1942, 14; Conference Report, April 1948, 185.

41. Conference Report, April 1946, 124.

42. Ibid.

43. Conference Report, April 1946, 125.

44. Conference Report, April 1946, 126.

45. Conference Report, October 1917, 43.

46. Conference Report, October 1941, 101.

47. Ibid.

48. See Conference Report, April 1937, 33.

49. Conference Report, April 1939, 124.

50. George Albert Smith, "Give the Lord a Chance," *Improvement Era* 49 (July 1946): 427; see Conference Report, October 1948, 163.

51. This degree, the honorary doctor of humanities degree, was conferred on President Smith in February 1950 at the University of Utah.

52. Conference Report, October 1931, 120.

53. Conference Report, April 1951, 157.

54. Recollection of George Albert Smith III to the author.

55. Conference Report, April 1951, 166, 168.

56. Conference Report, April 1951, 158.

57. Recollection of J. Reuben Clark Jr. to the author.

58. George Albert Smith, "Value of Testimony," *Improvement Era* 49 (May 1946): 332.

CHAPTER NINE: DAVID O. McKAY

1. Preston Nibley, "Tributes to President David O. McKay," *Improvement Era* 66 (September 1963): 782.

2. David O. McKay, "Motherhood," *Improvement Era* 39 (May 1936): 269.

3. See Conference Report, October 1952, 40.

4. Conference Report, April 1952, 25.

5. Conference Report, October 1968, 85–86.

6. See Conference Report, October 1968, 86.

7. Conference Report, October 1968, 86.

8. Quoted by Gordon B. Hinckley, in Conference Report, October 1958, 13–14.

9. See Llewelyn R. McKay, *Home Memories of President David O. McKay* (Salt Lake City: Deseret Book, 1956), 222–24.

10. Recollection of N. Eldon Tanner to the author.

11. Conference Report, October 1967, 149.

12. McKay, *Home Memories,* 269.

13. Ibid., 269–70; see also David O. McKay, in Conference Report, October 1922, 78–80.

14. See David O. McKay, *Cherished Experiences from the Writings of President David O. McKay,* rev. and enl., comp. Clare Middlemiss (Salt Lake City: Deseret Book, 1955), 148.

15. Hugh J. Cannon, "The Chinese Realm Dedicated for the Preaching of the Gospel," *Improvement Era* 24 (March 1921): 443.

16. Cannon, "Chinese Realm Dedicated," 445.

17. Ibid.

18. McKay, *Cherished Experiences,* 101–2.

19. For examples of President McKay's teachings on being "partakers of the divine nature," see David O. McKay, *Stepping Stones to an Abundant Life,* comp. Llewelyn R. McKay (Salt Lake City: Deseret Book, 1971), 6–31; David O. McKay, *Man May Know for Himself: Teachings of David O. McKay,* comp. Clare Middlemiss (Salt Lake City: Deseret Book, 1967), 12–16, 101–7.

20. See McKay, *Cherished Experiences,* 130–31.

21. See McKay, *Cherished Experiences,* 51–52, see also Lavina Fielding Anderson, "Prayer under a Pepper Tree: Sixteen Accounts of a Spiritual Manifestation," *BYU Studies* 33, no. 1 (1993): 55–78.

22. Harold B. Lee, "'May the Kingdom of God Go Forth,'" *Ensign,* January 1973, 24.

23. Harold B. Lee, *Stand Ye in Holy Places* (Salt Lake City: Deseret Book, 1974), 204.

24. Hugh J. Cannon in 1936 report to Ensign Stake, unpublished, in author's possession.

25. See Conference Report, October 1945, 111.

26. Quoted by Clare Middlemiss, in "Tributes to President David O. McKay," 778.

27. Lee, *Stand Ye in Holy Places,* 189.

28. David O. McKay, "The Purpose of the Temples," *Improvement Era* 67 (May 1964): 353.

29. Quoted by Joseph Anderson, in "Tributes to President David O. McKay," 784.

30. Conference Report, April 1950, 34.

31. Spencer W. Kimball, in "Tributes to President David O. McKay," 749.

32. Quoted by Marion D. Hanks, in "Tributes to President David O. McKay," 762.

33. Quoted in "Tributes to President David O. McKay," 786.

34. See John Longden, in "Tributes to President David O. McKay," 762.

35. Reminiscence of S. Dilworth Young to author; see also Benson Young Parkinson, *S. Dilworth Young: General Authority, Scouter, Poet* (American Fork, Utah: Covenant Communications, 1994), chapter 10.

36. Quoted by Florence S. Jacobson, in "Tributes to President David O. McKay," 780–81.

37. Reminiscence of Robert McKay to the author.

38. See David O. McKay, in Conference Report, April 1915, 105. See also "'Choose You This Day Whom Ye Will Serve,'" *Improvement Era* 52 (May 1949): 271; "Something Higher Than Self," *Improvement Era* 61 (June 1958): 406–9; "A Word in Parting," *Improvement Era* 62 (December 1959): 962; Ezra Taft Benson, "The Greatest Work in the World," *Improvement Era* 70 (January 1967): 24–25.

39. David O. McKay, quoted in Terry W. Call, "Ninth President evoked image of a prophet," *LDS Church News,* September 25, 1993, 12.

40. See Friedrich Nietzche, *The Antichrist,* translated by H. L. Mencken (New York: Alfred Knopf, 1920).

41. David O. McKay, "Dedicatory Addresses Delivered at Swiss Temple Dedication," *Improvement Era* 58 (November 1955): 795. See also Richard L. Evans, in Conference Report, October 1955, 9.

42. See David O. McKay, "Closing Address," *Improvement Era* 62 (June 1959): 479.

43. Joseph Anderson, *Prophets I Have Known* (Salt Lake City: Deseret Book, 1973), 122; see also N. Eldon Tanner, "'Choose You This Day Whom Ye Will Serve,'" *BYU Speeches of the Year,* March 27, 1963, 11; Delbert L. Stapley, in "Tributes to President David O. McKay," 749.

44. See Conference Report, April 1963, 90.

45. See Jeanette McKay Morrell, *Highlights in the Life of President David O. McKay* (Salt Lake City: Deseret Book, 1966), 271–79.

46. Remarks at a Missionary Conference in Cambridge, Massachusetts, December 1963.

47. David O. McKay, in Conference Report, October 1907, 62.

48. Quoted by Ted Cannon, in "Tributes to President David O. McKay," 785–86.

49. See Conference Report, October 1933, 11; David O. McKay, "Man . . . the Jewel of God," *Improvement Era* 72 (December 1969): 39.

50. Conference Report, April 1940, 115.

51. See Conference Report, April 1946, 111–17.

52. Conversation of author with caretaker at Palmyra visitors' center, Palmyra, New York, 1954.

53. See Conference Report, October 1969, 9.

54. David O. McKay, in Conference Report, October 1911, 58–59; see also David O. McKay, in Conference Report, October 1958, 87.

55. Personal recollection.

56. Quoted in Truman G. Madsen, *The Radiant Life* (Salt Lake City: Bookcraft, 1994), 125.

CHAPTER TEN: JOSEPH FIELDING SMITH

1. Joseph Smith, *Teachings of the Prophet Joseph Smith,* comp. Joseph Fielding Smith (Salt Lake City: Deseret Book, 1976), 40.

2. Matthias F. Cowley, *Wilford Woodruff, His Life and Labors* (Salt Lake City: Deseret News, 1916), 535. The prediction was given at Nephi, Utah.

3. See Joseph Fielding Smith, *Doctrines of Salvation,* ed. Bruce R. McConkie, 3 vols. (Salt Lake City: Bookcraft, 1954–56), 3:199.

4. Jessie Evans Smith, in conversation with the author.

5. Smith, *Doctrines of Salvation,* 1:56.

6. Herbert Maw, a former governor of Utah who was twenty years younger than Joseph Fielding, once challenged him to a game of handball. "He gave me the trouncing of my life!" Maw said later. See Joseph Fielding Smith Jr. and John J. Stewart, *The Life of Joseph Fielding Smith* (Salt Lake City: Deseret Book, 1972), 15.

7. Richard O. Cowan, "Advice from a Prophet: Take Time Out," *BYU Studies* 16, no. 3 (1976): 417; Smith and Stewart, *Life of Joseph Fielding Smith,* 1–2.

8. B. H. Roberts, "Physical Development," *Improvement Era* 15 (August 1912): 919.

9. Recollection of Lucy Grant Cannon to the author.

10. See Joseph Fielding Smith, "Sealing Power and Salvation," in *BYU Speeches of the Year,* January 12, 1971, 1–3. See also Conference Report, April 1941, 38; Joseph Fielding Smith, *Answers to Gospel Questions: The Classic Collection in One Volume* (Salt Lake City: Deseret Book, 1998), 3:143–44; 4:197.

11. Smith, *Doctrines of Salvation*, 3:178.

12. Conference Report, April 1970, 59.

13. See D. Arthur Haycock, "Exemplary Manhood Award," in *BYU Speeches of the Year,* April 18, 1972, 3; see also Ruth Christensen, "Let's 'Duet,'" *Ensign,* August 1972, 44.

14. Smith and Stewart, *Life of Joseph Fielding Smith,* 3–4.

15. David O. McKay and Joseph Fielding Smith went with Alvin R. Dyer to Missouri in June 1966. See Alvin R. Dyer, *The Refiner's Fire* (Salt Lake City: Deseret Book, 1968), 10–16.

16. Joseph Fielding Smith, *Church History and Modern Revelation,* 4 vols. (Salt Lake City: The Church of Jesus Christ of Latter-day Saints, 1946–49), 1:96.

17. Recollection of Oscar W. McConkie Jr. to the author.

18. Recollection of Assistant Church Historian Preston Nibley to the author.

19. Recollection of Oscar W. McConkie Jr. to the author.

20. Ibid.

21. At guide meeting on Temple Square, June 1963.

22. Joseph Fielding Smith letter on D&C 132:26, LDS Church Archives, Salt Lake City, Utah.

23. Conference Report, October 1941, 93.

24. Account of Karen Elaine Brown, mimeographed, unpublished.

25. Harold B. Lee at a district conference in Portland, Maine, about 1950. See also Spencer W. Kimball, in Bruce R. McConkie, "Joseph Fielding Smith: Apostle, Prophet, Father in Israel," *Ensign,* August 1972, 28.

26. Recollection of Lynn A. McKinlay, Ensign Stake Genealogical Committee, to the author.

27. Joseph Fielding Smith, "'I Know That My Redeemer Liveth,'" *Ensign,* December 1971, 27.

28. Recollection of Jay M. Todd, assistant managing editor of *Improvement Era,* to the author.

29. See Truman G. Madsen, *Joseph Smith, the Prophet* (Salt Lake City: Bookcraft, 1989), 104; Zina D. H. Young, *Woman's Exponent* 16 (1 July 1887): 23.

30. Recollection of Historian A. William Lund to the author.

31. See Smith, *Doctrines of Salvation,* 1:305–6; Smith, *Answers to Gospel Questions,* 2:146.

32. Joseph Anderson, *Prophets I Have Known* (Salt Lake City: Deseret Book, 1973), 169–81; Smith, *Church History and Modern Revelation,* 3:76–77; Joseph Fielding Smith, in Conference Report, April 1925, 73–74; October 1928, 101–2.

33. See Joseph Fielding Smith, "Faith Leads to a Fulness of Truth and Righteousness," *Utah Genealogical and Historical Magazine* 21 (October 1930): 145–58.

34. See Joseph Fielding Smith, *Take Heed to Yourselves* (Salt Lake City: Deseret Book, 1966,) 145; John A. Widtsoe, *Joseph Smith As Scientist* (Salt Lake City: Bookcraft, 1964), 137–38.

35. B. H. Roberts, *The Truth, the Way, the Life* (Provo, Utah: BYU Studies, 1994), 317–18.

36. L. Jackson Newell, *Matters of Conscience: Conversations with Sterling McMurrin* (Salt Lake City: Signature Books, 1996), 191–94.

37. Ibid., 194–95.

38. Recollection of Robert Howells to the author.

39. Recollection of Gustive O. Larson to the author.

40. Recollection of David A. Smith to general board of the Mutual Improvement Association.

41. "The Reins of Responsibility and Leadership," *Improvement Era* 73 (June 1970): 27.

42. Joseph Fielding Smith, *Restoration of All Things* (Salt Lake City: Deseret Book, 1973), 41 n.

43. Conference Report, April 1970, 4.

44. Conference Report, October 1966, 84.

45. Smith, *Doctrines of Salvation,* 3:131–32; Conference Report, October 1970, 91, 92.

46. Joseph Fielding Smith, *Elijah the Prophet and His Mission* (Salt Lake City: Deseret Book, 1957), 24, 31.

47. Conference Report, October 1959, 20.

48. Smith, *Doctrines of Salvation,* 2:347.

49. Conference Report, April 1966, 102.

CHAPTER ELEVEN: HAROLD B. LEE

1. See Brent L. Goates, *Harold B. Lee: Prophet and Seer* (Salt Lake City: Bookcraft, 1985), 614; Neal A. Maxwell, *One More Strain of Praise* (Salt Lake City: Bookcraft, 1999), 103.

2. Personal recollection.

3. Conference Report, April 1941, 121.

4. Ibid.

5. Conference Report, April 1952, 126–27.

6. Quoted by B. H. Roberts, in Truman G. Madsen, *Defender of the Faith: The B. H. Roberts Story* (Salt Lake City: Bookcraft, 1980), 108.

7. See Conference Report, April 1963, 82.

8. Conference Report, April 1966, 68.

9. Harold B. Lee, *Stand Ye in Holy Places* (Salt Lake City: Deseret Book, 1974), 346.

10. Ibid., 265.

11. Ibid.

12. Harold B. Lee, *The Teachings of Harold B. Lee,* ed. Clyde J. Williams (Salt Lake City: Bookcraft, 1996), 317.

13. Lee, *Stand Ye in Holy Places,* 280–81.

14. Ibid., 265.

15. Francis M. Gibbons, *Harold B. Lee: Man of Vision, Prophet of God* (Salt Lake City: Deseret Book, 1993), 139.

16. Recollection of C. Terry Warner to the author.

17. Harold B. Lee, "'Successful' Sinners," *Ensign,* July 1971, 2–3; Lee, *Stand Ye in Holy Places,* 218.

18. Recollection of Daniel H. Ludlow to the author.

19. J. Thomas Fyans, "The Fullness of the Gospel in Each Man's Language," *Ensign,* July 1972, 92.

20. See Conference Report, April 1906, 3.

21. See Marion G. Romney, *Look to God and Live: Discourses of Marion G. Romney,* comp. George J. Romney (Salt Lake City: Deseret Book, 1971), xi–xiii.

22. See Harold B. Lee, in Conference Report, April 1973, 179.

23. Recollection of Spencer W. Kimball to the author.

24. Ibid.

25. Russell M. Nelson, *From Heart to Heart* (Salt Lake City: Nelson, 1979), 127, 155, 162–65.

26. Russell M. Nelson, quoted in Gerry Avant, "Pres. Kimball was a 'man who knew Lord,'" *LDS Church News,* November 17, 1985, 14.

27. See Lee, *Stand Ye in Holy Places,* 139; Goates, *Harold B. Lee,* 414.

28. Recollection of S. Dilworth Young to the author.

29. See Goates, *Harold B. Lee,* 414.

30. Recollection of Brent L. Goates to the author.

31. Recollection of B. West Belnap to the author.

32. Goates, *Harold B. Lee,* 507.

33. See Lee, *Teachings of Harold B. Lee,* v.

34. See Conference Report, October 1955, 55; see also Conference Report, October 1964, 86.

35. See Harold B. Lee, in Conference Report, April 1973, 6–7.

36. See Harold B. Lee, in Conference Report, October 1942, 73.

37. Harold B. Lee, in Conference Report, October 1973, 169.

38. See Joseph F. Smith, in Conference Report, April 1916, 2–4; Harold B. Lee, "Divine Revelation," *BYU Speeches of the Year,* October 15, 1952, 8.

39. See Conference Report, April 1969, 130–31.

40. *Strengthening the Home,* pamphlet (Salt Lake City: The Church of Jesus Christ of Latter-day Saints, 1973), 7.

41. Harold B. Lee, "The Viewpoint of a Giant," Summer School Devotional Address, Department of Seminaries and Institutes of Religion, July 18, 1968, 6.

42. See Harold B. Lee, in Conference Report, April 1951, 31.

43. See Lee, *Stand Ye in Holy Places,* 115–16.

44. Lee, *Teachings of Harold B. Lee,* 101.

45. Personal advice given to teachers at a BYU faculty meeting, 1972.

46. Paraphrased by Harold B. Lee, in Conference Report, April 1950, 102; see Harold B. Lee, in Conference Report, October 1973, 166–67.

47. Lee, *Teachings of Harold B. Lee,* 393.

48. Ibid., 155.

49. Conference Report, October 1961, 81; see Lee, *Stand Ye in Holy Places,* 152–53.

50. Lee, *Stand Ye in Holy Places,* 153.

51. Lee, *Teachings of Harold B. Lee,* 124.

52. Conference Report, April 1964, 25.

53. James L. Barker and Roy A. Welker, *The Divine Church: Down through Change, Apostasy Therefrom, and Restoration,* 5 vols. (Salt Lake City: Council of the Twelve Apostles of The Church of Jesus Christ of Latter-day Saints, 1951–56), 1:76, quoted in Lee, *Stand Ye in Holy Places,* 322.

54. Ibid.

55. Nelson, *From Heart to Heart,* 188; see Richard O. Cowan, *Temples to Dot the Earth* (Salt Lake City: Bookcraft, 1989), 177–78.

56. Lowell Berry to the author.

57. Ibid.

58. Lucy Grant Cannon to the author.

CHAPTER TWELVE: SPENCER W. KIMBALL

1. Recollection of Hong Kong District President.

2. *A Noble Son, Spencer W. Kimball: A Curious Combination of Cousins* (Salt Lake City: Institute of Family Research, 1979).

3. Andrew Jenson, *LDS Biographical Encyclopedia,* 4 vols. (Salt Lake City: Deseret News, 1901), 1:632.

4. Edward L. Kimball and Andrew E. Kimball Jr., *Spencer W. Kimball, Twelfth President of The Church of Jesus Christ of Latter-day Saints* (Salt Lake City: Bookcraft, 1977), 23.

5. Kimball and Kimball, *Spencer W. Kimball*, 19.

6. Recollection of Calvin Cook to the author.

7. Recollection of Andrew E. Kimball Jr. to the author.

8. See Spencer W. Kimball, "The False Gods We Worship," *Ensign,* June 1976, 3–6.

9. See Kimball and Kimball, *Spencer W. Kimball,* 130.

10. See *Encyclopedia of Mormonism,* ed. Daniel H. Ludlow, 4 vols. (New York: Macmillan, 1992), 4: 1597; David Croft, "Idaho Members Fight Flood," *LDS Church News,* June 12, 1976, 3, 7, 13.

11. Spencer W. Kimball, in Conference Report, October 1943, 15–16.

12. See Kimball and Kimball, *Spencer W. Kimball,* 197–98.

13. See ibid., 195.

14. See ibid., 198.

15. Letter to the author, 1963.

16. Conference Report, October 1943, 18.

17. Recollection of Quinn Gardner to the author.

18. Conference Report, April 1954, 103.

19. Spencer W. Kimball, in Conference Report, April 1954, 107–8.

20. Kimball and Kimball, *Spencer W. Kimball*, 245–46.

21. Recollection of Brent W. Hardy to the author.

22. Recollection of Ned Winder to the author.

23. See Spencer W. Kimball, *Miracle of Forgiveness* (Salt Lake City: Bookcraft, 1969), 342–43.

24. Recollection of Edward L. Kimball to the author.

25. Spencer W. Kimball, *The Teachings of Spencer W. Kimball,* ed. Edward L. Kimball (Salt Lake City: Bookcraft, 1982), 351.

26. See Kimball and Kimball, *Spencer W. Kimball,* 312.

27. Letter to the author, February 24, 1970.

28. Russell M. Nelson, remarks to Sunday School General Board, about 1973.

29. See Spencer W. Kimball, "A Giant of a Man," *Ensign,* February 1974, 86.

30. Russell M. Nelson, *From Heart to Heart* (Salt Lake City: Nelson, 1979), 185.

31. Recollection of Louise Lake to the author.

32. Spencer W. Kimball, *An Apostle Speaks about Marriage to John and Mary* (Salt Lake City: The Church of Jesus Christ of Latter-day Saints, 1974).

33. Address to Young Adults of the Central Utah Stakes, Manti, Utah, July 10, 1974, cassette recording (Salt Lake City: Covenant Recordings, 1988).

34. See Spencer W. Kimball, "Marriage and Divorce," *BYU Speeches of the Year,* September 7, 1976, 146.

35. Recollection of Stephen R. Covey to the author.

36. Conversation at Lion House, about 1960.

37. Spencer W. Kimball, *A Style of Our Own: Modesty in Dress and Its Relationship to the Church* (Provo, Utah: Brigham Young University, 1951).

38. Conference Report, October 1962, 57.

39. Notes of Fred Schwendeman, unpublished.

40. See Spencer W. Kimball, "Peter, My Brother," *BYU Speeches of the Year,* July 13, 1971, 1–8.

41. See Spencer W. Kimball, "Welfare Services: The Gospel in Action," *Ensign,* November 1977, 76–79.

42. Marion G. Romney, in Conference Report, October 1980, 137.

43. See *Journal of Discourses,* 26 vols. (Liverpool: Latter-day Saints' Book Depot, 1854–86), 1:114–15.

44. See Spencer W. Kimball, in Conference Report, October 1964, 26.

45. Kimball, *Teachings of Spencer W. Kimball,* 68.

46. Spencer W. Kimball, "Be Ye Therefore Perfect," *BYU Speeches of the Year,* September 17, 1974, 237.

47. See Spencer W. Kimball, "Privileges and Responsibilities of Sisters," *Ensign,* November 1978, 103.

48. Spencer W. Kimball, in Conference Report, April 1974, 172.

49. See Spencer W. Kimball, "Education for Eternity," *BYU Speeches of the Year, 1967–1968,* September 12, 1967, 2.

50. Kimball, *Teachings of Spencer W. Kimball,* 509.

51. Ibid., 119.

52. See Spencer W. Kimball, in Conference Report, April 1951, 104.

53. Recollection of Patriarch Elwood Peterson to the author.

54. See Marvin J. Ashton, in Conference Report, April 1980, 49–54.

55. Nelson, *From Heart to Heart,* 180.

56. Kimball, *Teachings of Spencer W. Kimball,* 141.

57. Ibid., 140.

58. Spencer W. Kimball, *Faith Precedes the Miracle* (Salt Lake City: Deseret Book, 1972), 3–12.

59. Recounted by Spencer W. Kimball at a wedding reception, 1965.

60. Recollection of Andrew E. Kimball Jr. to the author.

61. As told to the author by a student who was present.

CHAPTER THIRTEEN: EZRA TAFT BENSON

1. See Conference Report, October 1963, 15.

2. Ezra Taft Benson, *The Teachings of Ezra Taft Benson* (Salt Lake City: Bookcraft, 1988), 528.

3. *Reader's Digest,* November 1954, 97.

4. See Sheri L. Dew, *Ezra Taft Benson: A Biography* (Salt Lake City: Deseret Book, 1987), 46–47.

5. Ezra Taft Benson, "Godly Characteristics of the Master," *Ensign,* November 1986, 46–48.

6. See Hugh B. Brown, "Father, Are You There?" Brigham Young University Fireside (Provo, Utah: Brigham Young University Press, 1967), 12–13.

7. See Ezra Taft Benson, "Preparing Yourselves for Missionary Service," *Ensign,* May 1985, 36–37; see Dew, *Ezra Taft Benson,* 62–63.

8. See Benson, *Teachings of Ezra Taft Benson,* 489.

9. See Ezra Taft Benson, *God, Family, Country: Our Three Great Loyalties* (Salt Lake City: Deseret Book, 1974), 80.

10. *Outstanding Stories by General Authorities,* comp. Leon R. Hartshorn, 2 vols. (Salt Lake City: Deseret Book, 1971), 2:27–28.

11. Conference Report, October 1943, 19; see Dew, *Ezra Taft Benson,* 174.

12. Dew, *Ezra Taft Benson,* 219.

13. Frederick Babbel, *On Wings of Faith* (Salt Lake City: Bookcraft, 1972).

14. David O. McKay, in Conference Report, October 1954, 118.

15. Dew, *Ezra Taft Benson,* 255.

16. See ibid., 253–56.

17. Recollection of Mark W. Cannon to the author.

18. Dew, *Ezra Taft Benson,* 291.

19. See Dew, *Ezra Taft Benson,* 310–16.

20. Quoted in Benson, *God, Family, Country,* 360.

21. Recollection of Ralph Meacham to the author.

22. Dew, *Ezra Taft Benson,* 280–81.

23. See ibid., 302.

24. Ezra Taft Benson, *So Shall Ye Reap,* comp. Reed A. Benson (Salt Lake City: Deseret Book, 1960), 87–88.

25. See Ezra Taft Benson, "To the Humble Followers of Christ," *Improvement Era* 72 (June 1969): 43–44.

26. Ezra Taft Benson touched many lives. See "Leaders recall life of service," *Deseret News*, May 31,1994, 1, 2.

27. "A Church Service in Soviet Russia," *U.S. News & World Report,* October 26, 1959, 76.

28. See Dew, *Ezra Taft Benson,* 344.

29. See ibid., 405–6.

30. Harold B. Lee, *Stand Ye in Holy Places* (Salt Lake City: Deseret Book, 1974), 149–50.

31. Joseph Smith, *Teachings of the Prophet Joseph Smith,* comp. Joseph Fielding Smith (Salt Lake City: Deseret Book, 1976), 24.

32. *Journal of Discourses,* 26 vols. (Liverpool: Latter-day Saints' Book Depot, 1854–86), 2:207; quoted in Ezra Taft Benson, "Prepare for the Days of Tribulation," *Ensign,* November 1980, 33.

33. Ezra Taft Benson, "To the Fathers in Israel," *Ensign,* November 1987, 49.

34. Dew, *Ezra Taft Benson,* 446–47, 490.

35. See Conference Report, October 1969, 60–64.

36. Personal conversation with Robert N. Bellah, 1978.

37. Recollection of Charles Bradford to the author.

38. Benson, *Teachings of Ezra Taft Benson,* 174–75.

39. See Ezra Taft Benson, "The Lord's Base of Operations," *Improvement Era* 65 (June 1962): 456; Ezra Taft Benson, "America—A Man and an Event," *Improvement Era* 68 (December 1965): 1150; Ezra Taft Benson, "Our Divine Constitution," *Ensign,* November 1987, 4.

40. See Benson, *Teachings of Ezra Taft Benson,* 14.

41. See, for example, Ezra Taft Benson, *A Witness and a Warning: A Modern-day Prophet Testifies of the Book of Mormon* (Salt Lake City: Deseret Book, 1988), ix, 56, 76.

42. Benson, *Teachings of Ezra Taft Benson,* 64.

43. Churchwide Parents Fireside, February 22, 1987 (Salt Lake City: The Church of Jesus Christ of Latter-day Saints, 1987).

44. See Ezra Taft Benson, in Conference Report, October 1952, 120; Benson, *Teachings of Ezra Taft Benson,* 215.

45. Ezra Taft Benson, "Jesus Christ: Our Savior and Redeemer," *Ensign,* November 1983, 6.

46. Bruce R. McConkie, "The New Revelation on Priesthood," in *Priesthood* (Salt Lake City: Deseret Book, 1981), 128.

47. See Conference Report, April 1965, 121.

48. See Ezra Taft Benson, "Cleansing the Inner Vessel," *Ensign,* May 1986, 6–7. See also Ezra Taft Benson, "Beware of Pride," *Ensign,* May 1989, 4–7.

49. Benson, *Teachings of Ezra Taft Benson,* 133.

50. Benson, "Beware of Pride," *Ensign,* May 1989, 4–6.

51. See Ezra Taft Benson, in Conference Report, October 1955, 108.

52. See Ezra Taft Benson, "Prepare Yourselves for the Great Day of the Lord," in *Brigham Young University 1981 Fireside and Devotional Speeches,* April 14, 1981 (Provo, Utah: University Publications, 1981), 68.

53. See Ezra Taft Benson, "A Vision and a Hope for the Youth of Zion," in *1977 Devotional Speeches of the Year,* April 12, 1977 (Provo, Utah: Brigham Young University Press, 1978), 74.

54. "Presentation of Scouting Award to President Benson," *Ensign,* May 1989, 34.

55. Sumner G. Whittier, in Conference Report, April 1960, 39.

56. Dew, *Ezra Taft Benson,* 175, 179.

57. Ezra Taft Benson, "Do Not Despair," in *Peace* (Salt Lake City: Deseret Book, 1998), 135–42.

CHAPTER FOURTEEN: HOWARD W. HUNTER

1. See Eleanor Knowles, *Howard W. Hunter* (Salt Lake City: Deseret Book, 1994), 284, 343.

2. Nancy F. Nowell, *Testimony of Nancy Nowell* (Salt Lake City: George Q. Cannon and Sons, 1892), 299.

3. Knowles, *Howard W. Hunter,* 62.

4. Ibid., 22–23.

5. See ibid., 25.

6. This concept is reflected in an unsigned article in *Improvement Era* 38 (March 1935): 171.

7. Knowles, *Howard W. Hunter,* 71.

8. Ibid., 72.

9. Ibid., 77.

10. Ibid., 79.

11. See ibid., 80–81.

12. Ibid., 92.

13. Ibid., 93.

14. Ibid., 121.

15. Ibid., 122.

16. Ibid., 143.

17. Ibid., 144.

18. Ibid.

19. Ibid., 144–45.

20. Matthew Cowley, *Matthew Cowley Speaks* (Salt Lake City: Deseret Book, 1954), 342.

21. Knowles, *Howard W. Hunter,* 145.
22. Ibid., 147.
23. Ibid., 156.
24. Ibid., 181.
25. Ibid., 185–86.
26. Ibid., 304–5, 343–44 n. 3.
27. As remembered by the Israel District Presidency, 1992.
28. Knowles, *Howard W. Hunter,* 205.
29. Ibid., 177–78.
30. See Howard W. Hunter, "All Are Alike unto God," *BYU Devotional Speeches of the Year* (Provo, Utah: Brigham Young University Press, 1979), 35–36. See also Truman G. Madsen, in Steven W. Baldridge, *Grafting In: A History of the Latter-day Saints in the Holy Land* (Israel: Jerusalem Branch, The Church of Jesus Christ of Latter-day Saints, 1989), i–iv.
31. See James P. Bell, *In the Strength of the Lord: The Life and Teachings of James E. Faust* (Salt Lake City: Deseret Book, 1999), 209–10.
32. Recollection of James E. Faust to the author.
33. In a meeting with Howard W. Hunter in Jersualem, 1989.
34. Isaac Watts, "When I Survey the Wondrous Cross," *The New English Hymnal* (Norwich, England: Canterbury Press, 1986).
35. Frederick F. Weatherly, "The Holy City," sheet music (London: Boosey and Hawkes, 1961).
36. See James E. Faust, "'The Way of an Eagle,'" *Ensign,* August 1994, 10; see also "President Howard W. Hunter: The Lord's 'Good and Faithful Servant,'" *Ensign,* April 1995, 16.
37. Knowles, *Howard W. Hunter,* 272.
38. Howard W. Hunter, "The Opening and Closing of Doors," *Ensign,* November 1987, 54.
39. Knowles, *Howard W. Hunter,* 272–73.
40. Howard W. Hunter, quoted in Faust, "'The Way of an Eagle,'" 2.
41. Unpublished discourse given to religious educators in the Assembly Hall, Salt Lake City, Utah.
42. Howard W. Hunter, "The Dauntless Spirit of Resolution," *BYU 1991–92 Devotional and Fireside Speeches* (Provo, Utah: University Publications, 1992), 40.
43. Ibid., 41.
44. Ibid.
45. Howard W. Hunter, "Commitment to God," *Ensign,* November 1982, 57.

46. Howard W. Hunter, "Reading the Scriptures," *Ensign,* November 1979, 65.

47. Howard W. Hunter, in Conference Report, April 1969, 138.

48. Howard W. Hunter, in Conference Report, April 1961, 18.

49. "'Fear Not, Little Flock,'" *BYU 1988–89 Devotional and Fireside Speeches* (Provo, Utah: University Publications, 1989), 115.

50. See Howard W. Hunter, *The Teachings of Howard W. Hunter,* ed. Clyde J. Williams (Salt Lake City: Bookcraft, 1997), 34.

51. Howard W. Hunter, "'Jesus, the Very Thought of Thee,'" *Ensign,* May 1993, 64–65.

52. See Dell Van Orden, "President Hunter Reflects on 30 Years of Service," *LDS Church News,* June 25, 1988, 6.

CHAPTER FIFTEEN: GORDON B. HINCKLEY

1. See Sheri L. Dew, *Go Forward with Faith: The Biography of Gordon B. Hinckley* (Salt Lake City: Deseret Book, 1996), 14.

2. Bryant S. Hinckley to Young Men's Mutual Improvement Association General Board, about 1935. Recalled in unpublished memoirs of Axel A. Madsen.

3. Ibid.

4. Dew, *Go Forward with Faith,* 35.

5. Gordon B. Hinckley, "Some Lessons I Learned as a Boy," *Ensign,* May 1993, 53.

6. See Gordon B. Hinckley, *The Teachings of Gordon B. Hinckley* (Salt Lake City: Deseret Book, 1997), 209, 422.

7. Dew, *Go Forward with Faith,* 60.

8. Hugh B. Brown, in Truman Madsen interview, in *Deseret News,* November 1989, 3.

9. Gordon B. Hinckley, in Conference Report, April 1962, 73.

10. "Missionary Theme Was Pervasive During Visit of President Hinckley," *LDS Church News,* September 9, 1995, 4.

11. Dew, *Go Forward with Faith,* 64.

12. Recollection of Rowland H. Merrill to the author.

13. Dew, *Go Forward with Faith,* 84–85.

14. Ibid., 106–7.

15. Virginia H. Pearce, *Glimpses into the Life and Heart of Marjorie Pay Hinckley* (Salt Lake City: Deseret Book, 1999), 193.

16. See Dew, *Go Forward with Faith,* 526–27.

17. As described by Aubry Fielden in personal correspondence with the author.

18. Conference Report, October 1975, 145.

19. Recollection of George I. Cannon to the author.

20. See Gordon B. Hinckley, "Let Not Your Heart Be Troubled," *Speeches of the Year: Brigham Young University Devotional and Ten-Stake Fireside Addresses 1974* (Provo, Utah: Brigham Young University Press, 1975), 266.

21. Dew, *Go Forward with Faith,* 538.

22. See Gordon B. Hinckley, "Each a Better Person," *Ensign,* November 2002, 99.

23. Joseph Smith, *History of The Church of Jesus Christ of Latter-day Saints,* ed. B. H. Roberts, 2d ed. rev., 7 vols. (Salt Lake City: The Church of Jesus Christ of Latter-day Saints, 1932–51), 4:540.

24. See Gordon B. Hinckley, in Conference Report, October 1996, 69.

25. See also Gordon B. Hinckley, "The Widow's Mite," *BYU 1985–86 Devotional and Fireside Speeches* (Provo, Utah: Brigham Young University, 1986), 10.

26. Comment of Elder M. Russell Ballard at a recent fireside.

27. Recollection of Elder Jeffrey R. Holland.

28. Recollection of B. West Belnap.

29. See Gordon B. Hinckley, "This Work Is Concerned with People," *Ensign,* May 1995, 52–53; "Messages of Inspiration from President Hinckley," *LDS Church News,* May 5, 2001, 2.

30. See Gordon B. Hinckley, "The Church Is on Course," *Ensign,* November 1992, 53, 59.

31. J. Reuben Clark Jr., quoted in Gordon B. Hinckley, "'In . . . Counsellors There Is Safety,'" *Ensign,* November 1990, 50.

32. See Dew, *Go Forward with Faith,* 390.

33. See "'Mighty Priesthood' Gathers to Fireside," *LDS Church News,* May 9, 2002, 6.

34. "Messages of Inspiration from President Hinckley," *LDS Church News,* October 3, 1998, 2; July 1, 2000, 2.

35. See Heber J. Grant, in a letter to his family from Tokyo, May 1903, LDS Church Archives, Salt Lake City, Utah.

36. Dew, *Go Forward with Faith,* 512.

37. Recollection of Richard Hinckley to the author.

38. See "President Hinckley Ordained Prophet," *LDS Church News,* March 18, 1995, 10.

39. For additional information, see John L. Hart, "'Totally unneccessary to lose any of those who are baptized,'" *Church News,* July 4, 1998, 4, 11.

ADDITIONAL READING

Those who desire more detail on the lives and teachings of our Latter-day prophets may consider the following works.

JOSEPH SMITH

Bushman, Richard L. *Joseph Smith and the Beginnings of Mormonism*. Urbana, Ill.: University of Illinois Press, 1984.

Madsen, Truman G. *Joseph Smith the Prophet*. Salt Lake City: Bookcraft, 1989.

Remembering Joseph: Personal Recollections of Those Who Knew the Prophet Joseph Smith. Compiled by Mark L. McConkie. Salt Lake City: Deseret Book, 2003.

Smith, Joseph. *Encyclopedia of Joseph Smith's Teachings*. Edited by Larry E. Dahl and Donald Q. Cannon. Salt Lake City: Deseret Book, 2000.

———. *The Personal Writings of Joseph Smith*. Edited Dean C. Jessee, rev. ed. Salt Lake City: Deseret Book; Provo, Utah: Brigham Young University Press, 2002.

———. *Teachings of the Prophet Joseph Smith*. Compiled by Joseph Fielding Smith. Salt Lake City: Deseret Book, 1976.

———. *The Words of Joseph Smith*. Edited by Andrew F. Ehat and Lyndon W. Cook. Provo, Utah: Religious Studies Center, Brigham Young University; Salt Lake City: Bookcraft, 1980.

Smith, Lucy Mack. *The Revised and Enhanced History of Joseph Smith by His Mother*. Edited by Scott Facer Proctor and Maurine Jensen Proctor. Salt Lake City: Bookcraft, 1996.

BRIGHAM YOUNG

Arrington, Leonard J. *Brigham Young: American Moses.* New York: Knopf, 1985.

Young, Brigham. *Discourses of Brigham Young.* Compiled by John A. Widtsoe. Salt Lake City: Bookcraft, 1998.

JOHN TAYLOR

Roberts, B. H. *The Life of John Taylor.* Salt Lake City: Bookcraft, 1963.

Taylor, John. *The Gospel Kingdom.* Edited by G. Homer Durham. Salt Lake City: Bookcraft, 1943.

WILFORD WOODRUFF

Cowley, Matthias F. *Wilford Woodruff: History of His Life and Labors.* Salt Lake City: Bookcraft, 1964.

Woodruff, Wilford. *The Discourses of Wilford Woodruff.* Edited by G. Homer Durham. Salt Lake City: Bookcraft, 1969.

LORENZO SNOW

Gibbons, Francis M. *Lorenzo Snow: Spiritual Giant, Prophet of God.* Salt Lake City: Deseret Book, 1982.

Snow, Eliza R. *Biography and Family Record of Lorenzo Snow.* Salt Lake City: Deseret News, 1884.

Snow, Lorenzo. *The Teachings of Lorenzo Snow.* Edited by Clyde J. Williams. Salt Lake City: Bookcraft, 1984.

JOSEPH F. SMITH

Smith, Joseph F. *Gospel Doctrine.* Salt Lake City: Deseret Book, 1946.

Smith, Joseph Fielding. *Life of Joseph F. Smith.* 2d ed. Salt Lake City: Deseret Book, 1969.

HEBER J. GRANT

Gibbons, Francis M. *Heber J. Grant: Man of Steel, Prophet of God.* Salt Lake City: Deseret Book, 1979.

Grant, Heber J. *Gospel Standards.* Edited by G. Homer Durham. Salt Lake City: Bookcraft, 1998.

Walker, Ronald W. *Qualities That Count: Heber J. Grant as Businessman, Missionary, and Apostle.* Provo, Utah: Brigham Young University Press, 2004.

Additional Reading

GEORGE ALBERT SMITH

Gibbons, Francis M. *George Albert Smith: Kind and Caring Christian, Prophet of God.* Salt Lake City: Deseret Book, 1990.

Smith, George Albert. *Sharing the Gospel with Others.* Compiled by Preston Nibley. Salt Lake City: Deseret Book, 1948.

———. *The Teachings of George Albert Smith.* Edited by Robert K. McIntosh and Susan McIntosh. Salt Lake City: Bookcraft, 1996.

DAVID O. McKAY

Gibbons, Francis M. *David O. McKay: Apostle to the World, Prophet of God.* Salt Lake City: Deseret Book, 1986.

McKay, David Lawrence. *My Father, David O. McKay.* Edited by Lavina Fielding Anderson. Salt Lake City: Deseret Book, 1989.

McKay, David O. *Cherished Experiences from the Writings of President David O. McKay.* Revised and enlarged. Compiled by Clare Middlemiss. Salt Lake City: Deseret Book, 1976.

———. *Gospel Ideals.* Salt Lake City: Bookcraft, 1998.

———. *The Teachings of David O. McKay.* Compiled by Mary Jane Woodger. Salt Lake City: Deseret Book, 2004.

McKay, Llewelyn R. *Home Memories of President David O. McKay.* Salt Lake City: Deseret Book, 1956.

JOSEPH FIELDING SMITH

Smith, Joseph Fielding. *Doctrines of Salvation.* 3 vols. Edited by Bruce R. McConkie. Salt Lake City: Bookcraft, 1998.

Smith, Joseph Fielding, Jr., and John J. Stewart. *Life of Joseph Fielding Smith.* Salt Lake City, Deseret Book Co., 1972.

HAROLD B. LEE

Goates, L. Brent. *Harold B. Lee: Prophet and Seer.* Salt Lake City: Bookcraft, 1985.

Lee, Harold B. *The Teachings of Harold B. Lee.* Edited by Clyde J. Williams. Salt Lake City: Bookcraft, 1996.

SPENCER W. KIMBALL

Kimball, Edward L. and Andrew E. Kimball Jr. *Spencer W. Kimball.* Salt Lake City: Bookcraft, 1977.

Kimball, Spencer W. *The Teachings of Spencer W. Kimball.* Edited by Edward L. Kimball. Salt Lake City: Bookcraft, 1982.

Additional Reading

EZRA TAFT BENSON

Benson, Ezra Taft. *The Teachings of Ezra Taft Benson.* Salt Lake City: Bookcraft, 1988.

Dew, Sheri L. *Ezra Taft Benson: A Biography.* Salt Lake City: Deseret Book, 1987.

HOWARD W. HUNTER

Hunter, Howard W. *The Teachings of Howard W. Hunter.* Edited by Clyde J. Williams. Salt Lake City: Bookcraft, 1997.

Knowles, Eleanor. *Howard W. Hunter.* Salt Lake City: Deseret Book, 1994.

GORDON B. HINCKLEY

Dew, Sheri L. *Go Forward with Faith: The Biography of Gordon B. Hinckley.* Salt Lake City: Deseret Book, 1996.

Hinckley, Gordon B. *The Teachings of Gordon B. Hinckley.* Salt Lake City: Deseret Book, 1997.

OTHER READING

Anderson, Joseph. *Prophets I Have Known: Joseph Anderson Shares Life's Experiences.* Salt Lake City: Deseret Book, 1973.

Gibbons, Francis M. *Dynamic Disciples, Prophets of God: Life Stories of the Presidents of The Church of Jesus Christ of Latter-day Saints.* Salt Lake City: Deseret Book, 1996.

Holzapfel, Richard Neitzel, and William W. Slaughter. *Prophets of the Latter Days.* Salt Lake City: Deseret Book, 2003.

Madsen, Susan Arrington. *The Lord Needed a Prophet.* 2d ed. Salt Lake City: Deseret Book, 1996.

The Presidents of the Church: Biographical Essays. Edited by Leonard J. Arrington. Salt Lake City: Deseret Book, 1986.

West, Emerson R. *Profiles of the Presidents.* Revised edition. Salt Lake City: Deseret Book, 1980.

INDEX

Index

Index

Index

Index

Index

Index